CRIMINALIZING WOMEN

CRIMINALIZING WOMEN
GENDER AND (IN)JUSTICE
IN NEO-LIBERAL TIMES

EDITED BY
GILLIAN BALFOUR AND ELIZABETH COMACK

FERNWOOD PUBLISHING • HALIFAX

Editing: Robert Clarke
Cover Art: Jackie Traverse
Printed and bound in Canada

Published in Canada by Fernwood Publishing
Site 2A, Box 5, 32 Oceanvista Lane
Black Point, Nova Scotia, B0J 1B0
and 324 Clare Avenue, Winnipeg, Manitoba, R3L 1S3
www.fernwoodbooks.ca

Fernwood Publishing Company Limited gratefully acknowledges
the financial support of the Department of Canadian Heritage,
the Nova Scotia Department of Tourism and Culture and
the Canada Council for the Arts for our publishing program.

Library and Archives Canada Cataloguing in Publication

Balfour, Gillian, 1965-
Criminalizing women: gender and (in)justice in neoliberal
times / Gillian Balfour, Elizabeth Comack.

ISBN 1-55266-187-3

1. Female offenders--Canada. 2. Women prisoners--Canada.
3. Sex discrimination in criminal justice administration--Canada.
4. Criminal justice, Administration of--Canada. 5. Women's rights--Canada.
I. Comack, Elizabeth, 1952- II. Title.

HV6046.B345 2006   364.3'74'0971   C2006-900217-7

CONTENTS

PART III
REGULATING WOMEN AND GIRLS / 153

PART IV
MAKING CHANGE / 287

This book is dedicated to
All the criminalized women
Whose lives shine with resilience and strength
And remind us that the struggle continues

CONTRIBUTORS

GILLIAN BALFOUR is an Assistant Professor in the Department of Sociology at Trent University, where she teaches in the areas of socio-legal theory and criminology. She has co-authored *The Power to Criminalize* (2004) with Elizabeth Comack. Her current research focuses on the implications of sentencing law reforms for Aboriginal peoples.

STEVEN BITTLE is a Ph.D. student in the Department of Sociology at Queen's University. His research interests include the sociology of law and control, youth involvement in prostitution, and corporate criminal liability.

SUSAN C. BOYD is a Senior Research Fellow at the Centre for Addictions Research–BC and Associate Professor in Studies in Policy and Practice, University of Victoria. She is also a community activist working with drug-user and anti-drug-war groups.

CHRIS BRUCKERT is an Assistant Professor in the Department of Criminology at the University of Ottawa. She has undertaken research in a number of sectors of the sex industry, including erotic dance, street sex work, in-call sex work, and escort work.

ELIZABETH COMACK is a Professor of Sociology at the University of Manitoba, where she teaches courses in the sociology of law and feminist criminology. Her publications include *Women in Trouble* (1996), *Locating Law* (as editor, 1999), and *The Power to Criminalize* (co-authored with Gillian Balfour, 2004).

DOROTHY E. CHUNN is a Professor of Sociology at Simon Fraser University. Her main areas of interest are feminism, law and social change; politics of family; sociology of crime, madness, and welfare; and media depictions of social "problems." Recent publications include *Women, Madness and the Law* (with Wendy Chan and Robert Menzies, 2005).

NAHANNI FONTAINE is the Director of Justice for the Southern Chiefs' Organization, an indigenous political organization representing thirty-six Southern First Nations in Manitoba. She is also an Interdisciplinary Ph.D. student at the University of Manitoba, specializing in Native studies, anthropology, and sociology.

SHELLEY A. M. GAVIGAN is a member of the Faculty of Osgoode Hall Law School of York University, where she teaches courses on criminal law, family law, and children and the law. She has published numerous articles in the areas of legal form, legal history, and socio-legal regulation of familial relations, welfare law, lesbian parenting, and abortion law reform and is co-author (with Jane Jenson and Janine Brodie) of *The Politics of Abortion* (1992).

KELLY HANNAH-MOFFAT is an Associate Professor in the Department of Sociology and acting Chair, University of Toronto, cross-appointed to the Centre of Criminology. She worked as a researcher and policy advisor for Madam Justice Arbour on the *Commission of Inquiry into Certain Events at the Prison for Women in Kingston* and is a past president of the Toronto Elizabeth Fry Society. In addition to numerous journal articles, her publications include *Punishment in Disguise* (2000) and *An Ideal Prison?* (co-edited with Margaret Shaw, 2000).

In 1995 GAYLE HORII joined with other formerly incarcerated women and women advocates in social justice arenas to incorporate the Strength in Sisterhood (SIS) Society, a national equality-seeking organization that states as one of its purposes "the promotion of the abolition of the imprisonment of women through the consultation and development of alternatives to prisons for women with other women's organizations in participation with and in response to the needs articulated by the women affected." She is completing her tenth year on full parole while serving her life sentence in the community.

YVONNE JOHNSON is a Cree artist and writer. She is the co-author (with Rudy Wiebe) of *Stolen Life: The Journey of a Cree Woman*. She has served sixteen years of a life sentence for first-degree murder and became eligible for full parole in the fall of 2005.

MADONNA MAIDMENT is an Assistant Professor in the Department of Sociology and Anthropology at the University of Guelph. Her teaching, research, and activist interests focus on the lives of criminalized women and the wrongfully convicted.

ROBERT MENZIES is Professor and J.S. Woodsworth Scholar in the Department of Humanities and Institute for the Humanities at Simon Fraser University. His interests include the history of madness; the sociology of citizenship; and the gender, race, and class dimensions of psychiatric regulation. His most recent book is *Women, Madness and the Law* (co-edited with Wendy Chan and Dorothy E. Chunn, 2005).

JOANNE C. MINAKER is a faculty member of the Department of Psychology and Sociology at Grant MacEwan College in Edmonton, Alberta. Her research interests are in the areas of violence against girls and women, prostitution, and youth crime.

COLETTE PARENT is an Associate Professor in the Department of Criminology, University of Ottawa. She has worked on women's issues in the areas of violence against women, sex work, and feminist theories in criminology for more than twenty years.

DEBRA PARKES teaches in the Faculty of Law at the University of Manitoba. Her research addresses, in a variety of contexts, the possibilities and challenges of rights litigation by equality-seeking groups. She sits on the board of the Canadian Association of Elizabeth Fry Societies (CAEFS), where she is involved in advocating for systemic change to respect the human rights of criminalized women and girls.

KIM PATE is Executive Director of the Canadian Association of Elizabeth Fry Societies. A teacher and lawyer by training, she has worked with marginalized, criminalized, and imprisoned youth, men, and women for about twenty-five years.

SHOSHANA POLLACK is an Associate Professor in the Faculty of Social Work at Wilfrid Laurier University. She has worked in the area of the marginalization and criminalization of women for the past fifteen years.

LAUREEN SNIDER is a Professor of Sociology at Queen's University in Kingston, Ontario. Her interests and publications centre on critical theory, feminism and punishment, and corporate crime.

JACKIE TRAVERSE is an Ojibway artist who is completing her Fine Arts degree at the University of Manitoba.

ACKNOWLEDGEMENTS

We started this journey over a year ago. Living in different provinces and immersed in various volunteer projects as well as raising families and doing teaching and research, we quickly realized that the process of producing an edited book depends on a great many resources and friendships.

We thank each of the contributors, whose scholarship and activism on behalf of criminalized women and girls inspired us to imagine the possibility of this book. We truly appreciate their willingness to manage tight deadlines and frenetic emails amidst their own busy schedules of work and family life. Their respectful and insightful reviews of each other's work also helped to ensure that we all got the story straight.

We also thank Jackie Traverse, whose artistic talent is featured on the front cover of the book. She has ably captured the images of women's experiences of social exclusion and imprisonment, as well as the possibilities for change. Jackie was also generous in allowing us to reproduce her piece on scars (p. 152). We are grateful as well to Yvonne Johnson for allowing us to share her writing, and to Gayle Horii for allowing us to feature her artwork on the dedication page.

As always, we owe a special thanks to the folks at Fernwood Publishing for working so tirelessly to support critical Canadian scholarship. We are especially indebted to our publisher, Wayne Antony, for his commitment to this project and for putting his trust in our ability to deliver the final product. Special thanks (once again) to Robert Clarke for putting his fine copy-editing skills to work and Beverley Rach for her work on the design and layout and her creativity in designing the book's cover. We are also thankful for the assistance of Arthur Antony for checking the references in the individual chapters, Marianne Rogowy for her attention to detail in helping with the tables and bibliography, Debbie Mathers for inputting the copyedit changes, and Brenda Conroy for proofing the final copy. Books don't sell themselves, so we acknowledge the labour of Errol Sharpe, Lindsay Sharpe, Eileen Young, Kim Goodliffe, Ellen Johnson, Cynthia Martin, and Nancy Malek in making that happen.

Of course, our families have persevered alongside of us as we completed this project. Too many evenings and weekends were spent in front of the computer or on the phone rather than sitting down to dinner or helping out with homework. To Quinn and Ana, whose childhoods seem to be marked by manuscript deadlines as well as birthday parties, thank you for giving me the time to do this work. To Wayne, Jess, and Arth, thanks for keeping me sane with your laughter.

In keeping with the collective and political nature of this project, the royalties from this book will be donated to groups working in support of criminalized women and girls.

Gillian Balfour and Elizabeth Comack

INTRODUCTION

Gillian Balfour and Elizabeth Comack

Criminalizing women has become an increasing and widespread phenomenon, as women are the fastest growing segment of the prison populations in Western industrialized countries such as Canada, the United States, Britain, and Australia (Sudbury 2005b; CAEFS 2003; Bloom, Owen, and Covington 2003). For those of us seeking answers as to why this is the case, turning to the media might seem an obvious move. Over the last decade, media accounts have proclaimed that "sugar and spice is not so nice," and that women are now men's equals in violence and are "getting away with murder" (Laframboise 1997 and 1999; Pearson 1993, 1995, 1998). Adding fuel to such pronouncements were the tragic deaths of three young women in Canada in the 1990s. The convictions of Karla Homolka for her part in the deaths of Kristen French and Lesley Mahaffy in Ontario and Kelly Ellard for hers in the beating death of Reena Virk in British Columbia were the bread and butter of media tabloids. Even Hollywood got in on the action, releasing the blockbuster film *Monster* — the story of Aileen Wuornos, a woman executed in the United States after robbing and killing seven men, earning her the label of America's first female serial killer.[1]

But feminists working as advocates for criminalized women inside courtrooms, jails, and university classrooms knew there was another story to be told — one of social exclusion brought on by poverty, racism, and the trauma of sexual violence. Many of these pathways into crime and criminalization were not new to feminist criminologists, who since the 1980s had been documenting how social conditions framed women's choices. However, by 2005 something was different. It seemed that despite two decades of dogged activism, research, and policy-making, other details about criminalized women's lives were not being heard, including:

- In 1990 a survey of federally sentenced women[2] exposed how little was known about women in conflict with the law in Canada. Some two-thirds of the women surveyed reported being physically abused as children; over half of them said they had been sexually abused. The numbers were even more startling for Aboriginal women: 90 percent said they had been physically abused — usually regularly over long periods — and 61 percent said they were sexually abused (Shaw et al. 1991). Many women reported chronic cross-addictions to prescription and street drugs, as well as alcohol. Incarcerated women were also more likely to be diagnosed with a mental illness. A majority of women prisoners were single mothers and likely to have only a grade 8 level of formal education and little work experience.

- In 1993 the first national Violence Against Women Survey revealed the degree and frequency of violence in many women's lives across Canada. The survey found that 51 percent of Canadian women had experienced at least one incident of physical or sexual assault since the age of 16; 10 percent had been victims of violence in the twelve months preceding the survey. Some 39 percent of the women reported experiences of sexual assault, and 29 percent of ever-married women had been assaulted by a spouse (including common-law relationships) (Johnson 1996).

- A study of provincially incarcerated women in Manitoba (Comack 1993b, 1996) found that 565 of 727 (78 percent) women prisoners admitted to prison between 1988 and 1993 reported being sexually and/or physically abused in their lifetimes. Some 33 percent of the women told of three or more abusive relationships. Women's accounts of their lives revealed profound neglect and isolation. Some women talked about imprisonment as another form of abuse, but some, sadly, spoke of prison as a safe place.

- On April 26, 1994, at the federal Prison for Women in Kingston, Ontario, an all-male Institutional Emergency Response Team was called in to forcefully remove eight women prisoners from their segregation cells and conduct a strip search, including body cavity searches. A Commission of Inquiry headed by Madam Justice Louise Arbour was appointed to review the events that took place at the Prison for Women. After an extensive and thorough examination, Justice Arbour released a report of her findings that widely condemned the Correctional Service of Canada (CSC) for its disregard for the human rights of prisoners. The Commissioner of Corrections was forced to resign.

- On August 9, 2001, in Sudbury, Ontario, Kimberly Rogers, a single mother who was eight months pregnant, died in her apartment. She had been confined there under house arrest during a stifling heat wave after having been convicted of welfare fraud for collecting social assistance as a full-time university student. A coroner's inquest recommended that the zero tolerance lifetime ineligibility for social assistance as a result of the commission of welfare fraud, as set out in the neo-conservative Ontario Works legislation, should be eliminated. The government was not found responsible for Kimberly's death.[3]

• In May 2005, Sandy Paquachon, an Aboriginal woman who had spent most of her life as a prisoner of the residential school and prison systems, was involuntarily transferred from a women's prison in Edmonton to a psychiatric centre in Saskatoon. During the transfer she was physically and chemically restrained and, while left in an unconscious state, she aspirated into her lungs, causing pneumonia. Unconscious and in need of intensive care, Sandy was transported to hospital, where she was placed on a respirator. Throughout this ordeal she was kept in handcuffs and shackles. Although the restraints were later removed, the CSC continues to treat Sandy as a maximum-security prisoner, regardless of the seriousness of her injuries.[4]

What do these events and circumstances reveal about the conditions of criminalized women's lives in Canada? Clearly, they reveal the systemic nature of violence, racism, and poverty in Canadian women's lives — and the consequences to women who resist these conditions, as well as the political silence that surrounds their treatment. Still, while women inside and outside the criminal justice system share a proximity to violence as well as poverty and the failure of the state to remedy conditions of inequality, criminalized women have oftentimes been considered by politicians, policy-makers, and criminologists as "too few to count" (Adelberg and Currie 1987a) or "more mad than bad" (Allen 1987).

Part I of the book begins (chapter 1) with an intellectual history of feminist criminology that highlights the various ways in which criminalized women have been represented and understood. Feminist criminology has assumed different epistemological positions over the decades and has provided several analytical tools that reveal who criminalized women are and how they come to be criminalized. The chapter opens with an outline of the invisibility of women in the research and theory-building of criminologists such as Robert Merton (1938), Edwin Sutherland (1949), Travis Hirschi (1969), and Howard Becker (1963) (see also Leonard 1982; Naffine 1987). Even radical criminologists who roundly criticized the criminological canon overlooked women entirely (Taylor, Walton, and Young 1973).

Disenchanted with conventional approaches of criminology, feminists began to transgress the boundaries of the discipline through the use of standpoint methodologies that revealed the prevalence of male violence against women and poverty in the lives of criminalized women, and a postmodern epistemology that drew attention to questions of how women and girls were constituted or defined by professional discourses and how particular techniques of governance (in a number of different sites) work to contain, control, or exclude those who are marginalized in society. The chapter also discusses how the knowledge produced about criminalized women is always framed by the socio-political context. In these terms, the shift from a social welfare to neo-liberal and neo-conservative rationalities of governance have had a profound impact on how several events that occurred in the 1990s — the Karla Homolka case, the killing of Reena Virk, and the use of the male Institutional Emergency Response Team at the Prison for Women in April 1994 — came to be framed in the public discourse. This shifting socio-political context created a powerful back-lash against feminist knowledge claims, especially the efforts by feminist criminologists to draw connections between women's experiences of marginalization and victimization and their involvement in crime.

In Part II the discussion moves into an investigation of the nature and extent of women's involvement in crime and explores the issues of women and poverty and the overrepresentation of Aboriginal women and women of colour in the criminal justice system so that we can better understand how class, race, and gender intersect in the lives of criminalized women. Each of the chapters in Part II takes up an issue that enables us to question the common-sense understandings and representations that prevail about criminalized women and girls. In their discussions of the "erring female" of an earlier era, women who work in the sex trade, Aboriginal women and girls' participation in "gangs," and women's involvement in the drug trade, the authors also allow us to reconnect the choices that women make to the conditions of their lives.

Part III focuses on the various techniques of regulation — including psychiatric, welfare, and penal regimes — that have been used against women and girls from the early twentieth century until now. In particular, we see how certain representations of women as incorrigible, dangerous, dependent, and risky frame the changing modes of regulation. Throughout the chapters we are reminded of the implications of engaging with the state, such as the emergence of gender-responsive programs in prisons and secure-care regimes for young women on the street. It would seem that neo-liberal governments are likely to appropriate feminist knowledge claims to construct women as damaged and in need of therapy rather than providing affordable housing and meaningful employment to end the cycle of violence and poverty. Feminists are caught in the paradox of relying on the legitimacy and resources of the criminal justice system to provide safety and assistance to women, while important public resources such as income assistance, shelters, food banks, and day-care centres are collapsing under the ruinous economic policies of neo-liberal provincial governments. Fuelled by an anxious middle class fixated on their own economic uncertainty, governments have successfully launched new crime-control strategies, such as welfare-fraud snitch lines that disproportionately place women at greater risk of being criminalized. Further economic savings have been achieved by off-loading greater responsibility for the care and control of women in their communities through strategies of transcarceration.

Finally, in Part IV, we are left to determine what possibilities exist for making change in these neo-liberal times. Much has happened in the nearly forty years since the first feminist scholarship emerged in Canadian criminology. Feminist criminology has gained importance in the specific contexts of university teaching and research. However, feminists remain on the margins of important political discussions about what to do about the issue of "law and order." Laureen Snider (2003) points out that feminist academics and activists have yet to become "authorized knowers." Snider maintains that feminists are on the defensive as they face the brunt of powerful neo-conservative claims-making. The task now is to re-imagine a feminist criminology that can capture the necessary institutional resources — and the moral and social capital — required to draw attention to the perilous impact of neo-liberal policies on women. Exciting possibilities lie in the forging of international connections with other social justice organizations, as well as the implications of bringing international law to bear on the Canadian government to hold it accountable for its mistreatment of criminalized women.

In sum, this book is about trying to make sense of the impact on women and girls of neo-liberal economics and concomitant neo-conservative crime-control agendas. It seeks to provide a space for "subversive tales" (Ewing and Silbey 1995) about criminalized women to be told as a way of countering the hegemony of women as "misfits" or "monsters." In the process, the chapters in this collection provide a thoughtful yet rigorous accounting of the gendered conditions of poverty, violence, racism, and the regulation of women in Canada.

NOTES

1. As one illustration of this attention, an Internet search of Canadian web pages showed 55,500 hits on Karla Homolka, 1,430 on Kelly Ellard, and 840 for Aileen Wuornos.

2. In Canada, offenders sentenced to two years or more are sent to federal prisons, while those sentenced to two years less a day serve their sentences in provincial institutions.

3. For more details on the Kimberly Rogers case see <http://dawn.thot.net/Kimberly_Rogers/>. (Accessed October 17, 2005.)

4. For further information on the treatment of Sandy Paquachon, see <http://dawn.thot.net/sandyp.html>. (Accessed October 17, 2005.)

Part 1
WOMEN, CRIMINOLOGY, AND FEMINISM

1. THE FEMINIST ENGAGEMENT WITH CRIMINOLOGY

Elizabeth Comack

The feminist engagement with criminology began almost forty years ago, when pioneers in the discipline such as Marie-Andrée Bertrand (1967) and Frances Heidensohn (1968) first called attention to criminology's amnesia when it came to women. Heidensohn (1968: 171), for instance, described the analysis of women and crime as "lonely uncharted seas" and suggested that what was needed was a "crash programme of research which telescopes decades of comparable studies of males." Since that time, feminist work in this area has developed at a fast pace, to the point where it has become increasingly difficult to keep abreast of the research and publications on women and crime.

There is little doubt about the validity of Heidensohn's claim that women traditionally have been neglected as an object of knowledge production in criminology. Like other academic disciplines, criminology has been a decidedly male-centred enterprise. Despite the use of generic terms — such as "criminals," "defendants," or "delinquents" — criminology has historically been about what men do, so much so that women have been invisible in mainstream criminological theory and research. This is not to say, however, that women have been completely ignored. From criminology's inception, there have been some (rather dubious) efforts to make sense of women and girls who come under the purview of the criminal justice system. Variously referred to as monsters, misfits, and manipulators, women — and especially women who engaged in criminal activity — were relegated by early criminologists to the status of "Other."

My main interest in this chapter is to map out the feminist engagement with criminology, to provide a sense of how women as an object of knowledge production have been understood (or ignored) by the criminological discipline over time, and how feminists have not only challenged these understandings but also promoted alternative claims about women and their involvement in crime. Offering this kind of intellectual history can be a wide-ranging endeavour. Much has happened over the past four decades — both within academia and the wider society — that has played a role in instigating and contouring the kinds of work that feminists have undertaken in this area. Like all knowledge production, therefore, the rendering of an intellectual history in this chapter will at best be partial.

THE INVISIBLE WOMEN OF MAINSTREAM CRIMINOLOGY

To a certain extent the male-centredness of criminology makes sense when you examine the official statistics on crime. In 2003 women comprised only 19 percent of adults charged with Criminal Code offences in Canada, while men made up the lion's share — 81 percent — of those charges (Wallace 2004: 25). Data from Australia indicate that females made up 21 percent of individuals charged in three states (Victoria, Queensland, and South Australia) in 2001–02 (Australian Institute of Criminology 2003: 47). A similar percentage exists for the United States, where females made up 22 percent of those arrested in 1998 (Belknap 2001: 82). Yet, even though this sex/crime ratio has long been recognized in the discipline, most mainstream criminologists have never really stopped to question it. Instead, they proceeded to develop theories of crime causation that took men — or, more accurately, poor inner-city Black men — as their subject, even when the theorist was intent on framing a general theory of crime ostensibly applicable to the whole population.

This invisibility of women can be easily demonstrated by examining some of the mainstream theories that make up the criminological canon. Robert Merton's (1938) anomie theory, for example, was offered as a general theory explaining crime in relation to the strain that results from the disjunction between culture goals (like monetary success) and institutionalized means (education, jobs). While Merton's theory reflected a sensitivity to the class inequalities that exist in society, the same could not be said with regard to an awareness of gender inequalities. If lower-class individuals were more likely to engage in crime because of a lack of access to the institutionalized means for achieving monetary success, then it follows that women — who as a group experience a similar lack of access — should also be found to commit their share of crime as a consequence of this strain. But the statistics tell us that this is not the case.

Like anomie theory, Edwin Sutherland's (1949) differential association theory was presented as a general theory of crime. Sutherland focused on the processes by which individuals learn definitions of the legal code as either favourable or unfavourable, and posited the existence of a "cultural heterogeneity" in society with regard to pro- and anti- criminal associations. Yet, this "general" theory only applied to half the population. Sutherland suggested that while men were individualistic and competitive, women were more altruistic and compliant. So, while cultural homogeneity could account for men's involvement in crime, it did not seem to apply to women, leading Sutherland to surmise that women were an exception or anomaly in his theory because they displayed a "cultural homogeneity."

Travis Hirschi's (1969) control theory was also characterized by a neglect of the female. While other criminologists focused their attention on explaining deviance, Hirschi turned the tables and set out to explain conformity. Since women appear to be more conformist than men (given, for example, their underrepresentation in crime statistics), it would have made sense for Hirschi to treat women as central to his analysis. Nevertheless, despite having collected data on females, he simply set these data aside and — like his colleagues — concentrated on males.

With the advent of labelling and conflict theories in the 1960s and 1970s, the potential for a more gender-inclusive approach to crime increased. Nonetheless, while Howard Becker's (1963) labelling theory raised the question of "Whose side are we on?" and advocated an approach to deviance that gave voice to those who were subjected to the labelling process, it was never fully realized in the case of women. Similarly, Ian Taylor, Paul Walton, and Jock Young's The New Criminology (1973), which offered up a devastating critique of traditional criminological theories, failed to give even a mention to women.

WOMEN AS OTHER: MONSTERS, MISFITS, AND MANIPULATORS

Women were not completely ignored in criminological thought. A small body of work, dating back to the nineteenth century, attempted to account for women's involvement in crime. What could be classified as the early approaches to explaining women's crime began with Cesare Lombroso and William Ferrero's The Female Offender in 1895, followed by W.I. Thomas's The Unadjusted Girl in 1923, Sheldon Glueck and Eleanor Glueck's 500 Delinquent Women in 1934, and Otto Pollak's The Criminality of Women in 1950. While differences exist between these approaches, they all share in common the view of women as "other" than men, and women who engage in criminal activity as even more so. For these theorists, it is women's "inherent nature" that accounts for both the nature and extent of their criminality. In particular, women are cast as sexual beings, and women's sexuality is at the root of their involvement in crime.

Lombroso and Ferrero based their theorizing on an examination of the physical characteristics of a group of 119 "criminal" women, which they compared with a control group of fourteen "non-criminal" women. In applying the concepts of atavism (the idea that some individuals were born criminals) and social Darwinism (the idea that those who get ahead in society are the most fit to survive), they suggested that women as a group possessed limited intelligence. Women were also less sensitive to pain than men, full of revenge and jealousy, and naturally passive and conservative. These traits had a physiological basis. For instance, Lombroso and Ferrero (1895: 109) assert that women's passivity was demonstrated by the "immobility of the ovule compared to the zoosperm." Atavistically, women offenders were considered to display fewer signs of degeneration than men. The reason, according to Lombroso and Ferrero, was that women (and non-white males) had not advanced as far along the evolutionary continuum as (white) males, and so could not degenerate as far. Given that women were relatively "primitive," the criminals among them would not be highly visible. However, those women who were criminal were cast as excessively vile and cruel in their crimes. They ostensibly combined the qualities of the criminal male with the worst characteristics of the female: cunning, spite, and deceitfulness. Lacking "maternal instinct" and "ladylike qualities," criminal women were deemed to be "monsters":

> The born female criminal is, so to speak, doubly exceptional as a woman and as a criminal. For criminals are an exception among civilized people, and women are an exception among criminals.... As a double exception, the criminal woman is consequently a *monster*. Her normal sister is kept in the paths of virtue by many causes, such as maternity, piety, weakness, and when these counter influences fail, and a woman commits a crime, we may conclude that her wickedness must have been so enormous before it could triumph over so many obstacles. (Lombroso and Ferrero 1895: 151–52; emphasis added)

Like Lombroso and Ferrero, W.I. Thomas (1923/1967) framed his theorizing about women on presumed "natural" or biological differences between men and women. Thomas suggested that human behaviour is based on four wishes: desires for adventure, security, response, and recognition. These wishes corresponded to features in the nervous system that were expressed as biological instincts of anger, fear, love, and the will to gain status and power. However, Thomas asserted that men's and women's instincts differed both in quantity and quality. Since women had more varieties of love in their nervous systems, their desire for response was greater than men's. According to Thomas, it was the need to feel loved that accounted for women's criminality, and especially for their involvement in prostitution.

Sheldon Glueck and Eleanor Glueck (1934) continued in this same tradition with their book *500 Delinquent Women*. The Gluecks described the women in their study as a "sorry lot. Burdened with feeblemindedness, psychopathic personality, and marked emotional instability, a large proportion of them found it difficult to survive by legitimate means." The view of criminal women as Other is clearly evident: "This swarm of defective, diseased, antisocial misfits... comprises the human material which a reformatory and a parole system are required by society to transform into wholesome, decent, law-abiding citizens! Is it not a miracle that a proportion of them were actually rehabilitated?" (Glueck and Glueck 1934: 299, 303).

Two decades later, Otto Pollak attempted to account for what he described as the masked nature of women's crime. Sceptical of the official data on sex differences in crime, Pollak (1950) suggested that women's crime was vastly undercounted. He put forward the view that female criminality was more likely to be hidden and undetected. According to Pollak, women were more often the instigators than the perpetrators of crime. Like Eve in the Garden of Eden, they manipulated men into committing offences. Women, he claimed, were also inherently deceptive and vengeful. They engaged in prostitution and blackmailed their lovers. As domestics they stole from their employers, and as homemakers they carried out horrendous acts on their families (like poisoning the sick and abusing children). According to Pollak, woman's devious nature was rooted in her physiology. While a man must achieve erection in order to perform the sex act (and hence will not be able to conceal orgasm), a woman can fake orgasm (Pollak 1961: 10). This ability to conceal orgasm supposedly gave women practice at deception.

Pollak also argued that the vengefulness, irritability, and depression that women encountered as a result of their generative phases caused female crime. For example, menstruation drove women to acts of revenge by reminding them of their inferior status (and their ultimate failure to become men). The concealed nature of their crimes, the vulnerability of their victims, and their chivalrous treatment by men who cannot bear to prosecute or punish them combined to mask women's offences. When these factors are taken into account, according to Pollak, women's crimes are equal in severity and number to those of men.

For these early criminologists, then, the women involved in crime were monsters, misfits, or manipulators. While we can look back on these constructions of women with some amusement, it bears noting that these kinds of knowledge claims about women and the reasons for their involvement in crime have not disappeared. Throughout the 1960s, researchers continued to rely on the assumptions and premises of the earlier approaches. John Cowie, Valerie Cowie, and Eliot Slater (1968), for example, in the tradition of Lombroso and Ferrero, looked for "constitutional predisposing factors" to explain female delinquency. In a similarly disparaging manner the same authors (1968: 167) characterized delinquent girls as "oversized, lumpish, uncouth and graceless." Gisella Konopka (1966), in extending Thomas's analysis, equated sexual delinquency in girls with a desperate need for love. Following on the footsteps of Otto Pollak, a more contemporary version of these theories links hormonal changes associated with women's menstrual cycles to their involvement in crime.

Premenstrual syndrome (PMS) has been described as a condition of "irritability, indescribable tension" and a "desire to find relief by foolish and ill-considered actions," something that is thought to occur during the week or two prior to the onset of menstruation (Frank cited in Osborne 1989: 168). With no biomedical tests for determining its existence, PMS is the only "disease" not dependent on a specific type of symptom for its diagnosis. Nevertheless, PMS has been argued to be a cause of violent behaviour in women who suffer from it. Premenstrual syndrome gained popularity as an explanation for women's criminality in the 1980s, when it was introduced in two British court cases as a mitigating factor in homicide (Luckhaus 1985). Research linking PMS to women's criminality has been criticized for its methodological deficiencies (Morris 1987; Kendall 1991, 1992). As an explanation for women's involvement in crime, however, PMS clearly locates the source of the problem in women's "unruly" bodies. Because of their "nature," women are supposedly prone to madness once a month.

ENTER FEMINISM...

In its initial stages, feminist criminology took the form of a critique of the existing approaches to explaining crime. Writers such as Dorie Klein (1973), Carol Smart (1976, 1977), Eileen Leonard (1982), Allison Morris (1987), and Ngaire Naffine (1987) took issue with the sexism of criminological theories — socially undesirable characteristics were attributed to women and assumed to be intrinsic characteristics of their sex.

With regard to the early approaches to explaining crime (offered by Lombroso and Ferrero, Thomas, the Gluecks, and Pollak), Heidensohn (1985: 122) noted how they lent an aura of intellectual respectability to many of the old folk tales about women and their behaviours. Their constructions of the "female offender" reflected the widely held assumptions about "women's nature," including the good girl/bad girl duality and a double standard that viewed sexual promiscuity as a sign of amorality in women but normality in men. Relying on common sense, anecdotal evidence, and circular reasoning — that is, "things are as they are because they are natural, and they are natural because that is the way things are" (Smart 1976: 36) — the early theorists failed to call into question the structural features of their society and the gendered nature of the roles of men and women. For these early criminologists, sex (a biological difference) and gender (a cultural prescription) were equated as one and the same, with the "ladylike" qualities of the middle-class and upper-class white woman used as the measuring rod for what is inherently female. In the process, feminists castigated these early theories for being not only sexist, but also racist and classist.

Mainstream theories of crime (such an anomie, differential association, social control, labelling, and conflict theories) came under a similar scrutiny. The invisibility of women and the failure to adequately explain or account for women's involvement in crime led feminist criminologists to label such theories as not just mainstream but "malestream." As Lorraine Gelsthorpe and Allison Morris asserted:

> Theories are weak if they do not apply to half of the potential criminal population; women, after all, experience the same deprivations, family structures and so on that men do. Theories of crime should be able to take account of *both* men's and women's behaviour and to highlight those factors which operate differently on men and women. Whether or not a particular theory helps us to understand women's crime is of *fundamental*, not marginal importance for criminology. (Gelsthorpe and Morris 1988: 103; emphasis added)

Kathleen Daly and Meda Chesney-Lind (1988) refer to one issue raised by the feminist critique of the mainstream theories as the generalizability problem: can theories generated to explain males' involvement in crime be modified to apply to women? Several feminist criminologists responded to this problem by attempting to make the mainstream theories of crime "fit" women.

Eileen Leonard (1982), for example, in a reformulation of Merton's strain theory, suggested that females are socialized to aspire to different culture goals than are males, in particular relational goals concerning marriage and having children. Following this line of reasoning, women's low rate of criminal involvement compared to men could be explained by the relatively easy manner in which females can realize their goals. Nevertheless, as Allison Morris (1987) notes, such a formulation relies on an idealized and romanticized version of women's lives. Not only does it display an insensitivity to the strains and frustrations associated with women's familial role (raising children and maintaining a household), it fails to acknowledge the very real and pressing economic concerns that women confront in the process (making ends meet and paying the bills).

Such efforts to revise mainstream theories of crime to include women have been referred to as the "add women and stir" approach (Chesney-Lind 1988b). Part of the difficulty with this project is that women are presented merely as afterthoughts, not as integral to the arguments being developed (Gelsthorpe and Morris 1988). Naffine (1997: 32) captures a more significant problem with this effort: "The point of these exercises has been to adapt to the female case, theories of crime which purported to be gender-neutral but were in fact always highly gender specific. Not surprisingly, the results have been varied and generally inconclusive."

A second issue raised by the feminist critique of mainstream criminology is one that Daly and Chesney-Lind (1988: 119) refer to as the gender-ratio problem. Why are women less likely than men to be involved in crime? What explains the sex difference in rates of arrest and in the variable types of criminal activity between men and women? Attention to the gender-ratio problem sparked a multitude of studies in the 1970s and 1980s on the criminal justice system's processing of men and women (see, for example, Scutt 1979; Kruttschnitt 1980–81, 1982; Steffensmeier and Kramer 1982; Zingraff and Thomson 1984; Daly 1987, 1989). The main question that guided much of this research stemmed from Pollak's assertion of the chivalry on the part of criminal justice officials. Are women treated more leniently than men? As in the generalizability problem, the results were mixed. For instance, research that supported this chivalry hypothesis indicated that when it does exist, chivalry benefits some women more than others — in particular, the few white, middle-class or upper-class women who come into conflict with the law. It also appears to apply only to those female suspects who behave according to a stereotypical female script, that is, "crying, pleading for release for the sake of their children, claiming men have led them astray" (Rafter and Natalizia 1981: 92). In this regard, Nicole Rafter and Elena Natalizia argue that chivalrous behaviour should be seen as a means of preserving women's subordinate position in society, not as a benign effort to treat women with some special kindness. Naffine (1997: 36), however, points to a larger problem with this research. By turning on the question of whether women were treated in the same way as men, or differently, the chivalry thesis (and its rebuttal) took men to be the norm: "Men were thus granted the status of universal subjects, the population of people with whom the rest of the world (women) were compared."

At the same time that research on the chivalry thesis was drawing the attention of criminologists in the 1970s and 1980s, another thesis was attracting considerable attention. The women's liberation thesis posited that women's involvement in crime would come to resemble men's more closely as differences between men and women were diminished by women's greater participation and equality in society. As reflected in the work of Rita Simon (1975) and Freda Adler (1975), the thesis suggested that changes in women's gender roles would be reflected in their rates of criminal involvement. Simon argued that the increased employment opportunities that accompanied the women's movement would also bring an increase in opportunities to commit crime (such as embezzlement from employers). Adler linked the apparent increase in women's crime statistics to the influence of the women's movement and suggested that a "new female criminal" was emerging: women were becoming more violent and aggressive, just like their male counterparts.

The women's liberation thesis "captured the imagination of the media and practitioners" (Morris and Gelsthorpe 1981: 53 cited in Gavigan 1993: 221). While law enforcement officials were quick to affirm its tenets, charging that the women's movement was responsible for triggering a massive crime wave, the media had a heyday with its claims, featuring headlines such as "Lib takes the lid off the gun moll" (*Toronto Star* 15 May 1975; cited in Gagivan 1993: 222). Nevertheless, representations of emancipated women running amok in the streets and workplaces did not hold up under closer scrutiny (see, for example, Chesney-Lind 1978; Weiss 1976; Steffensmeier 1980; Naffine 1987; Gavigan 1987). Smart (1976), for one, noted that the women's liberation thesis was premised on a "statistical illusion" in that the supposed increases in women's crime were being reported as percentages. Given the small base number of women charged with criminal offences, it did not take much of a change to show a large percentage increase. Holly Johnson and Karen Rodgers

(1993: 104) provided an example of this problem using Canadian data. Between 1970 and 1991, charges against women for homicide increased by 45 percent, but that figure reflected a real increase of only fifteen women charged with that offence. As well, while the women's movement was primarily geared toward privileged white women, poor women and women of colour were most likely to appear in police and prison data. These women were not inclined to think of themselves as "liberated" and — far from considering themselves as feminists — were quite conventional in their ideas and beliefs about women's role in society. For many feminist criminologists, the main difficulty with the women's liberation thesis — similar to the chivalry thesis — was that it posed a question that took males to be the norm: were women becoming more liberated and thus more like men, even in their involvement in crime? In Naffine's (1997: 32) judgment, the thesis that women's liberation causes crime by women has been "perhaps the most time-consuming and fruitless exercise" in criminology.

Another effort to attend to the gender-ratio problem was put forward by John Hagan and his colleagues (Hagan, Simpson, and Gillis 1979, 1987; Hagan, Gillis, and Simpson 1985), who combined elements of feminist theory with Hirschi's control theory to fashion a power-control theory of sex and delinquency. Focusing attention on the gender roles and differential socialization of males and females, power-control theory was designed to explain the sex differences in delinquency by drawing linkages between the variations in parental control and the delinquent behaviour of boys and girls. More specifically, Hagan and his colleagues suggested that parental control and adolescents' subsequent attitudes toward risk-taking behaviour as influenced by family class relations. They distinguished two ideal types of family: the patriarchal family, in which the husband is employed in an authority position in the workforce and the wife is not employed outside the home; and the egalitarian family, in which both husband and wife are employed in authority positions outside the home. Hagan and his colleagues suggested that in the former a traditional gender division exists, whereby fathers and especially mothers are expected to control their daughters more than their sons. Given the presence of a "cult of domesticity," girls will be socialized to focus their futures on domestic labour and consumption activities, while boys will be prepared for their participation in production activities. In the egalitarian family, parents will redistribute their control efforts such that girls are subject to controls that are more like the ones imposed on boys. "In other words, in egalitarian families, as mothers gain power relative to husbands, daughters gain freedom relative to sons" (Hagan, Simpson, and Gillis 1987: 792). As such, the authors predicted that these different family forms will produce differing levels of delinquency in girls: "Patriarchal families will be characterized by large gender differences in common delinquent behaviours, while egalitarian families will be characterized by smaller gender differences in delinquency" (Hagan, Simpson, and Gillis 1987: 793).

While Hagan and his colleagues endeavoured to place delinquency by girls in a broader structural context (by attending to the labour force participation of parents), they made an important assumption: if a woman is working for wages, there will be "equality" within the household. Their formulation does not pay enough attention to the nature of women's paid work and to other variables that might be in operation (such as how power and control may be exercised between males and females within the household). As well, Chesney-Lind regards power-control theory as a variation on the women's liberation thesis because it links the emergence of the egalitarian family with increasing delinquency among girls. In effect, "mother's liberation causes daughter's crime" (Chesney-Lind 1989: 20 cited in Boritch 1997: 71).

FEMINIST EMPIRICISM: COUNTERING BAD SCIENCE

In their engagement with criminology during the 1970s and 1980s, feminists tended to work within the confines of positivist social science. In other words, they subscribed to the belief that the methods of the natural sciences (measurement and prediction) could be applied to the study of social life. Their critiques of mainstream work in the discipline amounted to the claim that what was being produced was "bad science." In her elaboration of different feminist epistemologies, philosopher Sandra Harding (1990) named this approach feminist empiricism. Feminist empiricists in criminology held that bringing women into the mix and attending more rigorously to the methodological norms of scientific inquiry could rectify women's omission from the criminological canon. Feminist empiricism is very much reflected in the attempts to reformulate the mainstream theories of crime to include women. It is also reflected in the empirical research conducted to test the chivalry hypothesis and women's liberation thesis.

Yet, given the difficulties encountered in the efforts to respond to the generalizability and gender-ratio problems — in particular, the tendency to take men as the standard or measuring rod — many feminist criminologists saw the need to "bracket" these issues for the time being in order to understand better the social worlds of women and girls (Daly and Chesney-Lind 1988: 121). Maureen Cain (1990) took this suggestion further. She noted that while feminist criminologists needed to understand women's experiences, existing criminological theory offered no tools for doing this. Therefore, feminists needed to transgress the traditional boundaries of criminology, to start from outside the confines of criminological discourse. In carrying out this project, feminist criminologists drew inspiration from the violence against women movement.

TRANSGRESSING CRIMINOLOGY: THE ISSUE OF MALE VIOLENCE AGAINST WOMEN

At the same time as feminists were fashioning their critiques of criminology, the women's movement in Canada and other Western countries was breaking the silence around the issue of male violence against women. This violence was understood as a manifestation of patriarchy — the systemic and individual power that men exercise over women (Brownmiller 1975; Kelly 1988).

As a political movement united around improving the condition and quality of women's lives, feminism in the 1970s took as one of its key issues the provision of support to women who had been victimized by violence. One of the first books ever published on the subject of domestic violence was Erin Pizzey's (1974) *Scream Quietly or the Neighbours Will Hear You*. Pizzey is also credited for opening, in England in 1971, one of the first refuges for battered women and their children. Rape crisis centres and shelters for abused women also began to appear on the Canadian landscape in the 1970s. With their establishment came the recognition that male violence against women was a widespread and pervasive phenomenon.

In the early 1980s the Canadian Advisory Council on the Status of Women (CACSW) estimated that one in every five Canadian women will be sexually assaulted at some point in her life, and one in every seventeen will be a victim of forced sexual intercourse. In 1981 CACSW released a report, *Wife Battering in Canada: The Vicious Circle*. Linda MacLeod, author of the report, noted, "Women are kicked, punched, beaten, burned, threatened, knifed and shot, not by strangers who break into their houses or who accost them on dark streets, but by husbands and lovers they've spent many years with — years with good times as well as bad" (MacLeod 1980: 6). She estimated that, every year, one in ten Canadian women who is married or in a relationship with a live-in partner is battered.

More recently, in 1993 Statistics Canada released the findings of the

Violence Against Women (VAW) Survey. The first national survey of its kind anywhere in the world, the VAW Survey included responses from 12,300 women (see Johnson 1996). Using definitions of physical and sexual assault consistent with the Canadian Criminal Code, the survey found that one-half (51 percent) of Canadian women had experienced at least one incident of physical or sexual violence since the age of sixteen. The survey also confirmed the results of other research in finding that women face the greatest risk of violence from men they know. "Almost half (45%) of all women experienced violence by men known to them (dates, boyfriends, marital partners, friends, family, neighbours, etc.), while 23% of women experienced violence by a stranger (17% reported violence by both strangers and known men)" (Statistics Canada 1993: 2). The VAW Survey also found that 29 percent of ever-married women had been assaulted by a spouse.

A pivotal moment in the violence against women movement occurred on December 6, 1989, when a man entered a classroom at the École Polytechnique in Montreal, separated the men from the women students, proclaimed, "You're all a bunch of feminists," and proceeded to gun them down. He killed fourteen women and wounded thirteen others that day. The gunman's suicide letter explicitly identified his action as politically motivated: he blamed "feminists" for the major disappointments in his life. Police also found a hit list containing the names of prominent women. The Montreal Massacre served in a most profound way to reinforce what women's groups across the country had been arguing for two decades: that violence against women is a serious social problem that takes many forms, including sexual harassment in the workplace, date rape, violent sexual assaults, and wife abuse.

The violence against women movement had a number of implications for the work of feminist criminologists. First, the movement allowed feminists to break away from the confines of mainstream criminology, which had been complicit in the social silencing around the issue of male violence against women. Official statistics suggested that crimes like rape were relatively infrequent in their occurrence. Victim surveys — which asked respondents whether they had been victimized by crime — indicated that the group most at risk of victimization was young males, not women. Most mainstream criminologists took these data sources at face value. They seldom questioned whether (and why) acts like rape might be underreported, undercharged, or underprosecuted, or the extent to which victim surveys had been constructed in ways that excluded the behaviours that women feared most. When criminologists did turn their attention to crimes like rape, the focus was on the small group of men who had been convicted and incarcerated for the offence, and these men were typically understood as an abnormal and pathological group. Much of traditional criminology also tended to mirror widely held cultural myths and misconceptions about male violence against women (such as women "ask for it" by their dress or their behaviour; see Morris 1987; Busby 1999). In his "classic" study of rape, for example, Menachem Amir (1971) introduced the notion of "victim precipitation," suggesting that some women are "rape prone" or invite rape. Amir's work essentially blamed the victim for the violence she encounters. In these terms, the issue of male violence against women pointed to significant knowledge gaps in mainstream criminology and encouraged a host of studies by feminist criminologists intent on rectifying this omission (see Dobash and Dobash 1979; Klein 1982; Stanko 1985; Gunn and Minch 1988).

Second, the violence against women movement brought to the fore the issue of engaging with the state to address the issue — especially in light of law's role historically in condoning the violence, for example, by granting husbands the right to consortium (which meant that wives had a legal obligation to provide sexual services to their husbands such that rape in marriage was not a crime) and the right to chastise their wives (which meant that husbands had the authority to use force in order to ensure that wives fulfilled their marital obligations) (Dobash and Dobash 1979; Edwards 1985; Backhouse 2002). While some feminist criminologists joined with other women's advocates and academics in lobbying the state to reform laws relating to sexual assault and domestic violence, others engaged in critical treatises on the wisdom of engaging the criminal justice system to promote feminist concerns (see Smart 1989; Snider 1985, 1991, 1994; Los 1990; Faith and Currie 1993; Comack 1993a).

Finally, in pointing to the widespread and pervasive nature of male violence against women, the movement raised the issue of the impact that experiences of violence have had on women who come into conflict with the law. Several quantitative studies in the 1990s began to expose the extent of abuse experienced by women caught up in the criminal justice system. In interviewing women serving federal sentences, Margaret Shaw and her colleagues (1991) found that 68 percent had been physically abused as children or as adults, and 53 percent were sexually abused at some point in their lives. Among Aboriginal women, the figures were considerably higher: 90 percent said that they had been physically abused, and 61 percent reported sexual abuse (Shaw et al. 1991: vii, 31). Another study of women in a provincial jail (Comack 1993b) found that 78 percent of the women admitted over a six-year period reported histories of physical and sexual abuse. To address this issue of the relation between victimization and criminalization, several feminist criminologists adopted the position known as standpoint feminism (Harding 1990).

STANDPOINT FEMINISM: WOMEN IN TROUBLE

Influenced by Cain's call to transgress the boundaries of criminology and discover more about the lives of the women who were coming into conflict with the law, standpoint feminists began to engage in qualitative research, interviewing women about their lives to better understand the factors and conditions that brought them into conflict with the law. As Naffine (1997: 46) notes, while standpoint feminism assumed a number of forms — ranging from the assertion that women are the "experts" of their own lives to the proposal that an adequate social science must be capable of grasping the forms of oppression that women experience — the overall intention was "to place women as knowers at the centre of inquiry in order to produce better understandings of women and the world." Central to much of this research were links between women's victimization and their criminal involvement.

In the United States, Mary Gilfus (1992) conducted life history interviews with twenty incarcerated women to understand their entry into street crime. Most of these women had grown up with violence; thirteen of them reported childhood sexual abuse, and fifteen had experienced "severe childhood abuse" (Gilfus 1992: 70). Among the women Gilfus interviewed were eight African-Americans. While there were no race-based differences in reported abuse, the African-American women were more likely than their white counterparts to grow up in economically marginalized families. Violence, loss, and neglect were prevalent themes in their narratives about their childhoods. Violence was also a common feature of their relationships with men: sixteen of the twenty women had lived with violent men. Repeated victimization experiences, drug addiction, involvement in the sex trade, relationships with men involved in street crime, and the demands of mothering: these themes marked the women's transitions from childhood to adulthood.

Beth Richie's (1996) study focused on African-American battered women in prison. Richie (1996: 4) developed a theory of "gender entrapment" to explain the "contradictions and complications of the lives of the African-American battered women who commit crimes." According to her, gender entrapment involves understanding the connections between violence against women in their intimate relationships, culturally constructed gender-identity development, and women's participation in illegal activities. In these terms, battered Black women were "trapped" in criminal activity in the same way that they were trapped in abusive relationships.

Working in Canada, Ellen Adelberg and Claudia Currie (1987a, 1993) reported on the lives of seven women convicted of indictable offences and sentenced to federal terms of imprisonment. Regularly occurring themes in these women's lives included "poverty, child and wife battering, sexual assault, and women's conditioning to accept positions of submissiveness and dependency upon men," which led Adelberg and Currie to conclude: "The problems suffered by women offenders are similar to the problems suffered by many women in our society, only perhaps more acutely" (Adelberg and Currie 1987b: 68, 98).

My own work, *Women in Trouble* (Comack 1996), was built around the stories of twenty-four incarcerated women. The women's stories revealed complex connections between a woman's law violations and her history of abuse. Sometimes the connections are direct, as in the case of women sent to prison for resisting their abusers. Janice, for instance, was serving a sentence for manslaughter. She talked about how the offence occurred at a party:

> *I was at a party, and this guy, older guy, came, came on to me. He tried telling me, "Why don't you go to bed with me. I'm getting some money, you know." And I said, "No." And then he started hitting me. And then he raped me. And then [pause] I lost it. Like, I just, I went, I got very angry and I snapped. And I started hitting him. I threw a coffee table on top of his head and then I stabbed him.* (Cited in Comack 1996: 96)

Sometimes the connections only become discernible after a woman's law violations are located in the context of her struggle to cope with the abuse and its effects. Merideth, for example, had a long history of abuse that began with her father sexually assaulting her as a young child, and the abuse extended to several violent relationships with the men in her life. She was imprisoned for bouncing cheques — she said she was writing the cheques to purchase "new things to keep her mind off the abuse."

> *I've never had any kind of conflict with the law. [long pause] When I started dealing with all these different things, then I started having problems. And then I took it out in the form of fraud.* (Cited in Comack 1996: 86)

Sometimes the connections are even more entangled, as in the case of women who end up on the street, where abuse and law violation become enmeshed in their ongoing, everyday struggle to survive. Another woman in prison, Brenda, described her life on the street:

> *Street life is a, it's a power game, you know? Street life? You have to show you're tough. You have to beat up this broad or you have to shank this person, or, you know, you're always carrying guns, you always have blow on you, you always have drugs on you, and you're always working the streets with the pimps and the bikers, you know? That, that alone, you know, it has so much fucking abuse, it has more abuse than what you were brought up with!... I find living on the street I went through more abuse than I did at home.* (Cited in Comack 1996: 105–106)

This kind of work subsequently became known as pathways research — a term that has been applied to a variety of different studies, all of them sharing the effort to better understand the lives of women and girls and the particular features that helped lead to their criminal activity (see, for example, Chesney-Lind and Rodriguez 1983; Miller 1986; Arnold 1995; Heimer 1995; and Chesney-Lind and Shelden 1998). In considering this research, Kathleen Daly (1992, 1998) suggests that there is a feminist composite or "leading scenario" of women's lawbreaking:

> Whether they were pushed out or ran away from abusive homes, or became part of a deviant milieu, young women began to engage in petty hustles or prostitution. Life on the streets leads to drug use and addiction, which in turn leads to more frequent lawbreaking to support their drug habit. Meanwhile, young women drop out of school because of pregnancy, boredom or disinterest in school, or both. Their paid employment record is negligible because they lack interest to work in low-paid or unskilled jobs. Having a child may facilitate entry into adult women's networks and allow a woman to support herself in part by state aid. A woman may continue lawbreaking as a result of relationships with men who may also be involved in crime. Women are on a revolving criminal justice door, moving between incarceration and time on the streets. (Daly 1998: 136)

Daly maintains that although this leading scenario draws attention to the gendered contexts that bring girls to the streets, and to the gendered conditions of their survival once they get there, questions continue to linger. In particular, "What lies in the 'black box' between one's experiences of victimization as a child and criminal activities as an adult? Is there something more than economic survival which propels or maintains women in a criminalized status?" (Daly 1998: 136–37). Drawing on pre-sentence investigation reports dealing with the cases of forty women convicted in a New Haven felony court between 1981 and 1986, Daly maps out five different categories: street women, harmed and harming women, battered women, drug-connected women, and a final category that she labels "other women." Arguing for a more multidimensional approach to why women get caught up in crime, she proposes three other routes — in addition to the leading scenario of the street woman — that lead women to felony court: 1) abuse or neglect suffered as a child, an "out of control" or violent nature; 2) being (or having been) in a relationship with a violent man; and 3) being around boyfriends, mates, or family members who use or sell drugs, or wanting more money for a more economically secure and conventional life (p.148).

Overall, these efforts to draw out the connections between women's victimization experiences and their lawbreaking activities had the benefit of locating law violations by women in a broader social context characterized by inequalities of class, race, and gender.

In contrast to the women's liberation thesis, feminist criminologists suggest that increases in women's involvement in crime are more directly connected to the feminization of poverty than to women's emancipation. In recent decades, poverty has increasingly taken on a "female face" — especially in terms of the number of single-parent families headed by women (Gavigan 1999; Little 2003; chapter 8 here). As more and more women are confronted with the task of making ends meet under dire circumstances, the link between poverty and women's lawbreaking becomes more obvious.

Locating women's involvement in crime in its broader social context also means attending to racial inequalities. For instance, Aboriginal people in Canada are disproportionately represented in crime statistics, but the overrepresentation of Aboriginal women in Canadian prisons is even greater than that of Aboriginal men. Aboriginal women are incarcerated for more violent crimes than are non-Aboriginal women; and alcohol has played a role in the offences of twice as many Aboriginal women in prison as it has for Aboriginal men (La Prairie 1993; Royal Commission on Aboriginal Peoples 1996; Statistics Canada 2001b). The historical forces that have shaped Aboriginal experience — colonization, economic

and political marginalization, and forced dependency on the state — have
culminated in a situation in which violence and drugging and drinking
have reached epidemic proportions in many Aboriginal communities.
As Patricia Monture Angus (1999: 27) notes, "Aboriginal people do not
belong to communities that are functional and healthy (and colonialism
is significantly responsible for this fact)."

Attention to gender inequality — and its interconnections with race
and class — has assisted, for example, in explaining some forms of prostitution or sex trade work (Brock 1998; Phoenix 1999). According to Holly
Johnson and Karen Rodgers (1993: 101), women's involvement in prostitution is a reflection of their subordinate social and economic position
in society: "Prostitution thrives in a society which values women more
for their sexuality than for their skilled labour, and which puts women
in a class of commodity to be bought and sold. Research has shown one
of the major causes of prostitution to be the economic plight of women,
particularly young, poorly educated women who have limited *legitimate*
employment records."

In learning more about the lives of women and the "miles of problems" (Comack 1996: 134) that brought them into conflict with the law
— problems with drugs and alcohol use, histories of violence and abuse,
lack of education and job skills, and struggles to provide and care for their
children — feminist criminologists took pains to distance their work from
formulations that located the source of women's problems in individual
pathologies or personality disturbances. Instead, the structured inequalities in society that contour and constrain the lives of women provided the
backdrop for understanding women's involvement in crime. As British
criminologist Pat Carlen (1988: 14) noted, "Women set about making
their lives within conditions that have certainly not been of their own
choosing."

BLURRED BOUNDARIES: CHALLENGING THE VICTIM/OFFENDER DUALISM

Efforts to draw connections between law violations and women's histories
of abuse led to a blurring of the boundaries between "offender" and "victim" and raised questions about the legal logic of individual culpability
and law's strict adherence to the victim/offender dualism in the processing
of cases (for not only women, but also poor, racialized men). Blurring
the boundaries between offender and victim also had a decided influence
on advocacy work conducted on behalf of imprisoned women. For instance, *Creating Choices*, the 1990 report of the Canadian Task Force on
Federally Sentenced Women, proposed a new prison regime for women

that would incorporate feminist principles and attend to women's needs (see Shaw 1993; Hannah-Moffat and Shaw 2000a). The near-complete absence of counselling services and other resources designed to assist women in overcoming victimization experiences (see Kendall 1993) figured prominently in the Task Force's recommendations.

As Laureen Snider (2003: 364) notes, feminist criminologists at that time succeeded in reconstituting the female prisoner as the "woman in trouble." Less violent and less dangerous than her male counterpart, she was more deserving of help than of punishment. When women did engage in violence, it was understood as a self-defensive reaction typically committed in a domestic context (Browne 1987; Jones 1994; Dobash and Dobash 1992; Johnson and Rodgers 1993). Heidensohn (1994) considers this feminist work to be a positive contribution. In comparing her research in the 1960s and 1990s, she argues that the later female prisoners were better equipped to share their standpoints. In the past, not only did women "not easily find voices, there were only limited discourses in which they could express themselves and few places where such expressions could be made" (p.31). According to Heidensohn, feminist research provided these women "with a particular language, a way of expressing themselves" (p.32).

Nevertheless, while the concept of blurred boundaries and the construct of the woman in trouble were important feminist contributions to criminology, they were to later have particular ramifications for the ability of feminist criminologists to counter competing knowledge claims — ones founded on representations of women not as victims but as violent and dangerous.

POSTMODERN FEMINISM: CRIMINALIZED WOMEN

In addition to feminist empiricism and standpoint feminism, a third position has informed the work of feminist criminologists over the last decade or so. Postmodern feminism emerged largely as a critique of the other two positions. In particular, postmodern feminists reject the claims to "truth" proposed by scientific objectivity. "Reality," they say, is not self-evident, something that can simply be revealed through the application of the scientific method. While the postmodern critique of empiricism does not negate the possibility of doing empirical research — that is, of engaging with women, interviewing them, documenting their oral histories (Smart 1990: 78–79) — postmodernists are sceptical of attempts to challenge male-centred approaches by counterposing them with a more accurate or correct version of women's lives. Given the differences of female perspectives and identities, they question whether such diversity can be formulated or expressed in a single account or standpoint of women.

Feminist empiricism and standpoint feminism are still very much firmly grounded on a modernist terrain. Postmodern feminism, however, "starts in a different place and proceeds in other directions" (Smart 1995: 45). While modernist approaches are characterized by the search for truth, the certainty of progress, and the effort to frame grand narratives about the social world, postmodernism draws attention to the importance of discourse — "historically specific systems of meaning which form the identities of subjects and objects" (Howarth 2000: 9). Discourses are contingent and historical constructions. As David Howarth describes it, their construction involves "the exercise of power and a consequent structuring of the relations between different social agents" (p.9). Through the method of deconstruction — which involves taking apart discourses to show how they achieve their effects — postmodernists endeavour to reveal how certain discourses (and their corresponding discursive practices or ways of acting) come to dominate in society at particular points in history.

Adopting a postmodern epistemology has led feminist criminologists to interrogate the language used to understand women's involvement in crime. Writers such as Carol Smart (1989, 1995), Danielle Laberge (1991), and Karlene Faith (1993) point out that crime categories (such as "crimes against the person," "crimes against property," or "public order offences") are legal constructions that represent one way of ordering or making sense of social life. In these terms, the offences for which women are deemed to be criminal are the end result of a lengthy process of detection, apprehension, accusation, judgment, and conviction; they constitute the official version of women's actions and behaviours. As well, crime categories are premised on a dualism between the criminal and the law-abiding, which reinforces the view of women involved in crime as Other and thereby misses the similarities that exist between women. In this respect, women who come into conflict with the law are in very many ways no different from the rest of us. They are mothers, daughters, sisters, girlfriends, and wives, and they share many of the experiences of women collectively in society. Given that crime is the outcome of interactions between individuals and the criminal justice system, Laberge (1991) proposed that we think not in terms of criminal women but of criminalized women.

Throughout the 1990s, in addition to the increasing influence of a postmodern epistemology, feminist criminologists also began to draw heavily on the ideas of the French poststructuralist theorist Michel Foucault. Much of Foucault's (1977, 1979) writing was concerned with the relation between power and knowledge. Rejecting the notion that power was a "thing" or commodity that can be owned, Foucault concentrated on the mechanisms of power that came with the development of what he called the "disciplinary society," characterized by the growth of new knowledges or discourses (such as criminology, psychiatry, and psychology) that led to new modes of surveillance of the population. For Foucault, knowledge is not objective but political; the production of knowledge has to do with power. A reciprocal relation exists between the two: power is productive of knowledge, and knowledge is productive of power. In his later work, Foucault (1978a) replaced his notion of power/ knowledge with the concept of governmentality to address the specific "mentality" of governance — the links between forms of power and domination and the ways in which individuals conduct themselves.

Australian criminologist Kerry Carrington (1993) employed Foucault's notion of power/knowledge to explore how certain girls come to be officially defined as delinquents. Critical of feminist work depicting male power over women as direct, monolithic, coercive, and repressive, Carrington emphasized the fragmented, fluid, and dispersed nature of disciplinary power. In a similar fashion, British criminologist Anne Worrall (1990) adopted a Foucaultian approach to explore the conditions under which legal agents (judicial, welfare, and medical) claim to possess knowledge about the "offending woman" and the processes whereby such claims are translated into practices that classify, define, and so domesticate her behaviour. Taking a critical view of feminist studies of women's punishment because of their failure (among other things) to take gender seriously as an explanatory variable, Adrian Howe (1994) argued for the need to consider the gendered characteristics — for both women and men — of disciplinary procedures in advancing the project of a postmodern penal politics.

Feminist postmodernism has had a decided impact on the trajectory of feminist criminology. Not interested so much in the task of explaining *why* women come into conflict with the law, those who work in this area raise important *how* questions, such as how women and girls are constituted or defined by professional discourses, and how particular techniques of governance (in a number of different sites) work to contain, control, or exclude those who are marginalized in society. The postmodern attention to discourse has also opened the way to a questioning of the kinds of language used by criminologists and criminal justice officials. Under the tutelage of postmodernists, terms such as offenders, inmates, clients, and correctional institutions — although still widely disseminated — are no longer uncontested.

Nevertheless, at the same time as feminist criminologists were being influenced by the epistemological and theoretical shifts occurring within academia during the 1990s, shifts in the socio-political context and a series of notable events relating to the issue of women and crime were having a significant impact on the work of feminist criminologists. More specifically, as the century drew to a close, neo-liberal and neo-conservative political rationalities had begun to take hold and were readily put to work in the construction of women and girls as violent, dangerous — and downright "nasty."

THE SHIFTING SOCIO-POLITICAL CONTEXT: NEO-LIBERALISM AND NEO-CONSERVATISM

In the initial phases, the efforts of the women's movement to address women's inequality in society were fed by a sense of optimism. Given the expressed commitment by the Canadian state to the ideals of social citizenship — that all citizens had a right to a basic standard of living, with the state accepting responsibility for the provision of social welfare for its citizenry — the prospects of realizing substantive change on issues like violence against women and women's treatment by the criminal justice system seemed bright. This change was made all the more possible with the entrenchment of the Canadian Charter of Rights and Freedoms in 1982, and especially the invoking of section 15 (the equality section) in 1985, which prohibited discrimination on the basis of sex. In a climate that appeared to be favourable to hearing women's issues, feminists and women's advocates organized and lobbied throughout the 1980s to bring about a number of changes (including reforms to rape legislation and the provision of resources for women in abusive relationships) and launched human rights and Charter challenges to address the unfair treatment of imprisoned women. With regard to women in prison, many observers took the government's acceptance of the *Creating Choices* report in 1990 as a sign that a sea change was underway, that substantive reform was possible.

Yet also transpiring in the 1980s was a distinct shift in the socio-political terrain. Under the sway of globalization, the state's expressed commitment to social welfare was being eroded. In its place, neo-liberalism became the new wisdom of governing. Neo-liberalism is a political rationality founded on the values of individualism, freedom of choice, market dominance, and minimal state involvement in the economy. Under neo-liberalism, the ideals of social citizenship are replaced by the market-based, self-reliant, and privatizing ideals of the new order. As political scientist Janine Brodie (1995: 57) explains it:

> The rights and securities guaranteed to all citizens of the Keynesian welfare state are no longer rights, universal, or secure. The new ideal of the common good rests on market-oriented values such as self-reliance, efficiency, and competition. The new good citizen is one that recognizes the limits and liabilities of state provision and embraces her or his obligation to work longer and harder in order to become more self-reliant.

In this era of restructuring, government talk of the need for deficit reduction translated into cutbacks to social programs (McQuaig 1993), and gains that the women's movement had realized in the previous decade were now under serious attack (Brodie 1995; Bashevkin 1998; Rebick 2005).

In the criminal justice arena, these economic and political developments ushered in an extraordinary expansion in the scope and scale of penalization. Rising crime rates and a growing economic recession in the 1980s gave way to a crime-control strategy that rejected rehabilitation and correction as the goals of the criminal justice system and replaced them with a concern for risk management: the policing and minimization of risk that offenders pose to the wider community. Under this neo-liberal responsibilization model of crime control (Hannah-Moffat 2002), criminals are to be made responsible for the choices they make: "Rather than clients in need of support, they are seen as risks that must be managed" (Garland 2001: 175).

But neo-liberalism was not the only ideology to inform criminal justice practices. Subjecting the economy to market forces and cutting back on social welfare meant that increasing numbers of people were left to fend for themselves, without the benefit of a social safety net. As well, the precariousness of middle-income families engendered a social anxiety that easily translated into fear of crime — especially of those groups and individuals left less fortunate by virtue of the economic transformations. Calls for more law and order became louder. In tandem with neo-liberalism, therefore, a neo-conservative rationality premised on a concern for tradition, order, hierarchy, and authority fostered crime-control policies aimed at "getting tough" on crime. Zero tolerance for domestic violence, "super max" prisons, parole-release restrictions, community notification laws, and boot camps for young offenders increasingly became the order of the day (Comack and Balfour 2004: 42–43).

This broader neo-liberal and neo-conservative socio-political context proved to be significant in framing how a number of events that occurred in the 1990s came to be understood. These events — and the ways in which they were being framed in the public discourse — were instrumental in assertions about women and girls that had much in common with constructions that had prevailed in earlier times.

VIOLENT WOMEN AND NASTY GIRLS

One decisive event was the Karla Homolka case. In July 1993 Karla Homolka was sentenced to twelve years in prison for her part in the deaths of two teenaged girls, Kristen French and Leslie Mahaffy. Homolka's sentence was part of a plea bargain reached with the Crown in exchange for her testimony against her husband, Paul Bernardo. The Crown had entered into this plea bargain prior to the discovery of six homemade videotapes that documented the sexual abuse and torture of the pair's victims — including Homolka's younger sister, Tammy. Bernardo was subsequently convicted of first-degree murder, kidnapping, aggravated sexual assault, forcible confinement, and offering an indignity to a dead body. He was sentenced to life imprisonment in September 1995 (McGillivray 1998: 257).

During Bernardo's trial the real challenge came in trying to explain the role of Homolka, the prosecution's key witness. As Helen Boritch (1997: 2) notes, "Among the various professionals who commented on the case, there was a general agreement that, as far as serial murderers go, there was little that was unusual or mysterious about Bernardo. We have grown used to hearing about male serial murderers." Homolka, however, was the central enigma of the drama that unfolded, transforming the trial into an international, high-profile media event.

The legal documents and media accounts of the case offered two primary readings of Homolka. The first reading constructed her as a battered wife, one of Bernardo's many victims (he had also been exposed as "the Scarborough rapist"). A girlish seventeen-year-old when she first met the twenty-three-year-old Bernardo, Homolka had entered into a relationship that progressed to a fairytale wedding (complete with horse-drawn carriage) and ended with a severe battering (complete with darkened and bruised raccoon eyes).

According to this first reading, Homolka was under the control of her husband, having no agency of her own. Like other women who find themselves in abusive relationships, she was cast as a victim and diagnosed as suffering from the Battered Woman Syndrome, a psychological condition of "learned helplessness" that ostensibly prevents abused women from leaving the relationship (see Walker 1979, 1987). The representation of Homolka as a battered wife and compliant victim of her sexually sadistic husband (see Hazelwood, Warren, and Dietz 1993) was meant to bolster her credibility as a prosecution witness and validate her plea bargain.

This first reading was met with strong resistance in the media and public discourse, leading to the second reading. Journalist Patricia Pearson (1995), for one, vigorously countered the picture of "Homolka as victim" and instead demonized her as a "competitive narcissist" willing to offer up innocent victims (including her own sister) to appease the sexual desires of her sociopathic husband. In a similar fashion, other writers offered diagnoses like "malignant narcissism": "This personality cannot tolerate humiliation. It is capable of destroying others in the service of meeting its ego needs" (Skrapec, cited in Wood 2001: 60).

Despite their divergent viewpoints, both of these readings relied on the discourse of the "psy-professions" (psychology, psychotherapy, and psychiatry) to make sense of Homolka. Feminist criminologists offered competing knowledge claims, for instance, by pointing out that women are seldom charged with the offence of murder and, when they do kill, women are most likely to kill their male partners — or that while Homolka's middle-class background and lifestyle set her apart from the vast majority of women charged with criminal offences, her efforts to conform to the standard feminine script (dyed blond hair, fairytale wedding) put her in company with a host of other women. But these claims were seldom heard. Instead, the cry that "Women are violent, too!" grew louder, even to the point of arguing that women's violence was quantitatively and qualitatively equal to that of men's.

In a widely publicized book, *When She Was Bad: Violent Women and the Myth of Innocence*, Pearson (1997; see also Dutton 1994, Laframboise 1996) argued not only that "women are violent, too," but also that their violence can be just as nasty as men's. Following on the footsteps of the 1950s criminologist Otto Pollak, Pearson (1997: 20–21) suggested that women's violence was more masked and underhanded than men's: women kill their babies, arrange for their husbands' murders, beat up on their lovers, and commit serial murders in hospitals and boarding houses. Nevertheless, argued Pearson (1997: 61), when their crimes are discovered, women are more likely to receive lenient treatment from a chivalrous criminal justice system. In a fashion that hearkened back to other early criminologists, Pearson (1997: 210) also stated: "Female prisoners are not peace activists or nuns who were kidnapped off the street and stuck in jail. They are miscreants, intemperate, willful and rough."

Pearson drew support for her position from studies that utilize the Conflict Tactics Scale (CTS) to measure abuse in intimate relationships. Most criminologists who use this scale have found equivalent rates of violence by women and men (Straus 1979; Straus and Gelles 1986; Straus, Gelles, and Steinmetz 1980; Steinmetz 1981; Brinkerhoff and Lupri 1988; Kennedy and Dutton 1989). Despite the scale's popularity, however, it has been subject to extensive critiques (DeKeseredy and MacLean 1998; DeKeseredy and Hinch 1991; Dobash et al. 1992; Johnson 1996). Nevertheless, Pearson argued that such critiques amounted to unwarranted attacks by feminists and their supporters, who were invested in a gender dichotomy of men as evil/women as good. In this regard, unlike earlier conservative-minded criminologists, Pearson asserted that women were no different than men. While feminists were intent on gendering violence by drawing its connections to patriarchy, Pearson (1997: 232) was adamant that violence be de-gendered: violence was simply a "human, rather than gendered, phenomena." Framing the issue in neo-liberal terms, violence was a conscious choice, a means of solving problems or releasing frustration by a "responsible actor imposing her will upon the world" (p.23).

While the Homolka case generated extensive media attention on the issue of women's violence, the spectre of the "nasty girl" was added into the mix with the killing of fourteen-year-old Reena Virk by a group of mostly teenaged girls in November 1997. Early on, in 1998, six girls were convicted of assault for their part in Virk's death. In 1999 Warren Glowaski was convicted of second-degree murder. In April 2005, after three trials, Kelly Ellard was convicted of second-degree murder.

According to the court documents, Virk was confronted by a group of girls under a bridge in Victoria, B.C., and accused of stealing one of their boyfriends. When she tried to leave she was punched and kicked, and one of the girls stubbed out a cigarette on her forehead. Glowaski testified at his trial that he and Ellard had followed Virk across the bridge and confronted her a second time. The pair kicked and stomped her until she was unconscious and then dragged her body to the water's edge, where she subsequently drowned. While Ellard admitted to being an active participant in the initial attack on Virk, she denied any involvement in the second attack. Asked in court whether the thought of seeing Reena left crumpled in the mud made her upset, Ellard replied, "*Obviously — I am not a monster*" (Armstrong 2004: A7).

Ellard's statement notwithstanding, events like the beating and murder of Reena Virk generated a series of media exposés on the "problem" of girl violence. As one CBC documentary, *Nasty Girls* (airing on March 5, 1997), put it: "In the late 1990s almost everything your mother taught you about polite society has disappeared from popular culture, and nowhere is this more apparent than in what is happening to our teenage girls. Welcome to the age of the nasty girls!" (cited in Barron 2000: 81). Girls, so we were told, were not "sugar and spice" after all — but "often violent and ruthless monsters" (McGovern 1998: 24).

These depictions of women and girls as violent, dangerous, and downright nasty were also playing out in relation to what was then the only federal prison for women in Canada — the P4W.

LOMBROSO REVISITED? FRAMING THE P4W INCIDENT

In February 1995 CBC-TV's *Fifth Estate* aired a video of an all-male Institutional Emergency Response Team (IERT) entering the solitary confinement unit at the Prison for Women (P4W) in Kingston, Ontario, and proceeding to extract women from their cells, one by one. The video showed the women's clothing being removed (in some cases the men forcibly cut it off) and the women being shackled and taken to the shower room, where they were subjected to body cavity searches. The program reported that after the segregation cells were completely emptied (including beds and mattresses), the women were placed back in the cells with only security blankets for clothing.

Some of the women were kept in segregation for up to eight months afterward. They were given no hygiene products, no daily exercise, no writing materials, and no contact with family. Their blankets were not cleaned for at least a month. As part of the program, reporter Ann Rauhala also interviewed several of the women, who recounted their feelings of violation and degradation and drew similarities to their past experiences of being raped and sexually victimized.

When the report of Justice Louise Arbour (1996) into the events of April 1994 was released two years later, the CBC's news program *The National* re-televised segments of the program, including the IERT video. Emails posted on *The National's* discussion site in response to the segments revealed pieces of the public discourse that prevailed around women prisoners:

> While I can see how some of the pictures shown could be disturbing to some viewers, I am more disturbed at your handling of the

story…. These women were not ordinary citizens…. They are in a correctional facility because they are CONVICTED FELONS, not Sunday School Teachers.

Myself, I would see nothing wrong with a guard beating these inmates every once in a while! After all they lost their rights when they committed their crimes in the first place.

Don't give me the bleeding heart crap. This is what has screwed up society. These women created their own situation — let them deal with the fallout.

The women involved in this incident were the creators of their own misfortune — both in the short term and the long term…. In recent years, it seems that the courts and government have become too lenient with the likes of these women, and men for that matter. The special interest groups and the "politically correct" that are constantly fighting for the rights of prisoners only undermine the rights of law-abiding citizens.

Clearly, the neo-conservative calls to "get tough on crime" — especially in relation to women — were finding supporters in the public at large. Much like the early criminological constructions of women involved in crime, these CBC viewers rejected the depiction of the women as victims and instead saw them as Other, roundly deserving of the brutal treatment they received.

Such law and order populism was no doubt instrumental in bolstering a neo-liberal realignment by the Correctional Service of Canada (CSC) when it came to implementing the *Creating Choices* (1990) recommendations. *Creating Choices* had been silent around the issue of women's violence. According to Shaw (2000: 62), "Overall, the report portrayed women as victims of violence and abuse, more likely to injure themselves than others as a result of those experiences." The April 1994 event, however, was held out as evidence to the contrary. The CSC maintained that calling the male IERT to the women's prison had become necessary to contain "unruly women" after a fight had broken out between six of the prisoners and their guards. In 1996, in a move that marked an about-turn from the Task Force's women-centred approach and the attendant focus on addressing women's needs, CSC adopted a new scheme for managing women prisoners, the Offender Intake Assessment Scheme, designed for male prisoners. Now, women's needs — including the need to recover from experiences of victimization — were to be redefined (in neo-liberal terms) as risk factors in predicting a woman's likelihood of reoffending. That same year the CSC announced that all women classified as maximum security would not be allowed at the new regional centres (including the Aboriginal healing lodge) that had been constructed on the basis of the *Creating Choices* recommendations. Instead, the women were to be housed in maximum-security facilities located inside men's prisons. As well, CSC implemented a new mental health policy for women thought to be experiencing psychological and behavioural problems. In contrast to its initial endorsement of the *Creating Choices* report, therefore, the government was clearly moving in a different direction.

FEMINIST CRIMINOLOGISTS RESPOND TO THE BACKLASH

The apparent ease with which the neo-conservative and neo-liberal readings of events like the Homolka case, the Virk killing, and the P4W incident took hold in the public discourse was emblematic of the dramatic shifts in the socio-political context that were occurring in the 1990s. For the most part, these readings can be interpreted as part of a powerful backlash against feminist knowledge claims, especially the efforts by feminist criminologists to blur the boundaries between offender and victim. In what Snider (2004: 240) refers to as the "smaller meaner gaze of neo-liberalism," the sightlines were closely fixed. "'Victims' were those who suffered from crime, not those who committed it — and the higher their social class, the more traditional their sexual habits and lifestyles, and the lighter their color, the more legitimate their victim status became." Feminist criminologists would respond to this backlash on a number of fronts.

Committed to the view of criminalized women as victims in need of help rather than punishment, feminist criminologists were initially caught off guard by the Homolka case. To be sure, the woman in trouble envisioned by feminist criminologists was not a privileged young woman who engaged in sadistic sex crimes. But repeating the refrain "Homolka is an anomaly, Homolka is an anomaly" did little to prevent her from becoming the public icon for women caught up in the criminal justice system — women who are likely to be racialized, poor, and convicted of property crimes rather than of violent sex offences (see the articles in Part II here).

With Pearson's assertions about women and violence continuing to hold sway in the popular press, feminist criminologists countered by offering up pointed critiques of her work. In her review of *When She Was*

Bad, for instance, Meda Chesney-Lind (1999) took Pearson to task for her routine conflation of aggression and violence. "This is either very sloppy or very smart, since anyone familiar with the literature on aggression ... knows that when one includes verbal and indirect forms of aggression (like gossip), the gender difference largely disappears" (p.114). Similar to those who claim merit in the women's liberation thesis, Pearson also based her argument on percentage increases in women's arrests for violence, "without any mention of the relatively small and stable proportion of violent crime accounted for by women or the fact that small base numbers make huge increases easy to achieve" (p.115). Pearson's misuse of research findings, which Chesney-Lind saw as rampant throughout the book, included citing a study that found women's prison infractions to be higher than men's to support her claim that women in prison are "miscreants, intemperate, willful and rough" (Pearson 1997: 210). What Pearson neglected to mention was that these women were being charged with extremely trivial forms of misconduct, such as having "excessive artwork" on the walls of their cells (that is, too many family photos on display). Chesney-Lind concluded her review by acknowledging that feminist criminologists must theorize women's aggression and women's violence, but that "we need a nuanced, sophisticated, and data driven treatment — and most importantly — one that begins by placing women's aggression and violence in its social context of patriarchy" (p.118).

Feminist criminologists also undertook research of their own to evaluate the claim that women are "men's equals" in violence. To explore qualitative differences in men's and women's violence, for example, Vanessa Chopyk, Linda Wood, and I drew a random sample of 1,002 cases from police incident reports involving men and women charged with violent crime in the city of Winnipeg over a five-year period at the beginning of the 1990s. While studies that utilize the Conflict Tactics Scale have concluded that a sexual symmetry exists in intimate violence (men are as likely as women to be victims of abuse, and women are as likely as men to be perpetrators of both minor and serious acts of violence), we found that a different picture emerged in the police incident reports (Comack, Chopyk, and Wood 2000, 2002). First, the violence tactics used by men and women differed in their seriousness. Men were more likely to use their physical strength or force against their female partners, while women were more likely to resort to throwing objects (such as TV remote controls) during the course of a violent event. Second, female partners of men accused of violence used violence themselves in only 23 percent of the cases, while male partners of women accused of violence used violence in 65 percent of the cases. This finding suggests that the violence that occurs between intimate partners is not "mutual combat." Third, almost one-half (48 percent) of the women accused — as opposed to only 7 percent of the men accused — in partner events were injured during the course of the event, adding weight to the argument that violent events between men and women are not symmetrical.

Finally, in incidents involving partners, it was the accused woman who called the police in 35 percent of the cases involving a female accused (compared with only 7 percent in those involving a male accused). If we interpret calls to the police as a form of "help-seeking behaviour" on the part of someone in trouble, this finding suggests that in more than one-third of the cases involving a woman accused, she was the one who perceived the need for help. Nevertheless, the woman ended up being charged with a criminal offence.

These findings are supported by data from the General Social Survey conducted by Statistics Canada (2005a), which show the nature and consequences of spousal violence to be more severe for women than for men. Female victims of spousal violence were more than twice as likely to be injured as were male victims. Women were also three times more likely to fear for their lives, and twice as likely to be the targets of more than ten violent episodes. In countering the arguments made by writers like Pearson, then, the feminist agenda placed the issue of women's violence and aggression in a prominent position (see also Kelly 1996; Chan 2001; Mann 2003; Morrisey 2003; Comack and Balfour 2004).

In the wake of the moral panic generated by media reports of a violent crime wave by girls (Schissel 1997, 2001), feminists also set out to counter the claim that girls were becoming "gun-toting robbers" (Pate 1999b: 42; see also Artz 1998; Barron 2000; Chesney-Lind 2001; Bell 2002; Burman, Batcheler, and Brown 2003; Alder and Worrall 2003). In her analysis of official statistics on youth crime, Heather Schramm (1998) warned that any arguments about a dramatic increase in the rate of girls' offending should be interpreted with caution. The theme here was similar to the critique of the women's liberation thesis: because only a small number of girls are charged with violent offences, changes in the rates of girls' violent crime inflate drastically when expressed as a percentage. Marge Reitsma-Street (1999) pointed out that the majority of the increase in the rate of girls' violent crime could be accounted for by an increase in the charges of common or level-one assault (for example, for pushing, slapping, and threatening). Anthony Doob and Jane Sprott (1998: 185) concluded that the rising rate of girls (and youths in general) being charged with violent crimes did not indicate an increase in the nastiness of girls; rather, the change "relates more to the response of adult criminal justice officials to crime than it does to the behaviour of young offenders."

As well, feminist criminologists drew on postmodern insights to counter the legal and media representations of the Virk killing. Specifically, by framing the murder in terms of the "empty concept" of "girl violence" (Kadi, cited in Batacharya 2004: 77), dominant approaches rarely addressed the issues of "racism, sexism, pressures of assimilation, and the social construction of Reena Virk as an outcast," and "when they were addressed, it was always in the language of appearance" (Jiwani 2002: 441). In Yasmin Jiwani's view, the erasure of race/racism in judicial decision-making and the media coverage of the case was "symbolic of the denial of racism as a systemic phenomenon in Canada" (p.42; see also Batacharya 2004).

Feminist criminologists also engaged in extensive critiques of the use of male-centred risk scales for managing women prisoners (Stanko 1997; Hannah-Moffat and Shaw 2001; Chan and Rigakos 2002). They provided critical commentaries on the apparent transformation of the original feminist vision of *Creating Choices* to fit neo-liberal and neo-conservative correctional agendas (Hannah-Moffat and Shaw 2000a), and they reflected on the lessons to be learned from efforts to refashion prison regimes (Hannah-Moffat 2002). Countering the tendency of the legal establishment and media to revert to individualized and pathologized renderings of women prisoners — an approach placing the spotlight on the personal failings of these women while keeping the political and economic factors that drive prison expansion in the shadows — some feminist criminologists began the work of connecting "the individual and personal with macroeconomic and geopolitical analyses" in the context of the global expansion of women's imprisonment (Sudbury 2005b: xvi).

THE POWER AND THE CHALLENGE

From invisibility and the Othering of women to the emergence of feminist criminology in the 1970s and the particular pathways that feminist criminologists have followed as they put women at the centre of their knowledge production: over the past forty years we have slowly moved from Heidensohn's "lonely uncharted seas" to reach the point where it has become increasingly difficult to keep abreast of the research and publications on women and crime. In their own ways, the different epistemological positions of feminist empiricism, standpoint feminism, and postmodern feminism have enabled an incredible growth in knowledge about women and crime. Because of this work, we now know so much more about the lives of criminalized women — who they are, the social contexts in which they move, and the processes by which they are regulated and controlled — far more than we would have thought possible some four short decades ago. Still, as we have seen, feminist criminology has not developed in a vacuum. In the past forty years feminist criminologists have drawn energy and insights from work in other arenas — particularly the violence against women movement — as well as responding to events and developments occurring within the ever-changing socio-political climate.

As Snider (2003; see also chapter 14 here) notes, it is one thing for feminists to produce particular discourses about women and crime, and it is quite another to have those discourses heard.

> Knowledge claims and expertise always work to the advantage of some and the detriment of others, strengthening some parties and interests while weakening others. Those with power to set institutional agendas, with superior economic, political, social and moral capital, are therefore able to reinforce and promote certain sets of knowledges while ignoring, ridiculing or attacking others. (Snider 2003: 355)

But the feminist engagement with criminology is by no means complete. As the chapters in this book demonstrate, it is very much a vibrant, continuing process. And in these neo-liberal times, meeting the challenge of containing — and especially countering — dominant understandings about women and crime is all the more necessary.

NOTE

This chapter has benefited from the input of a number of individuals, specifically Wayne Antony, Gillian Balfour, Dorothy Chunn, Laureen Snider, and Tracey Peter. As usual, any errors or omissions are my own doing.

Part II
MAKING CONNECTIONS:
CLASS/RACE/GENDER INTERSECTIONS

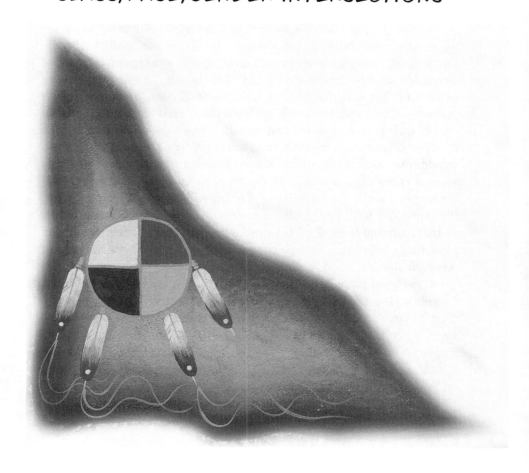

INTRODUCTION

Elizabeth Comack

In the days leading up to July 5, 2005, the Canadian media's attention was squarely fixed on the doors of the Joliette Institution in Quebec, awaiting the release of "Canada's most notorious female offender."[1] Karla Homolka had reached the end of the twelve-year sentence that she had received for her part in the deaths of Kristen French and Leslie Mahaffy, two young women who had been abducted, sexually assaulted, and killed by Homolka and her partner, Paul Bernardo.

Although Homolka may be the most notorious, she is by no means the most representative of the women who come into conflict with the law. Indeed, Homolka is very much an anomaly or exception in terms of women most likely to be criminalized. This claim holds true for a number of reasons. For one thing, women are most likely to be charged with property offences such as theft and fraud rather than with serious violent crimes such as murder and sexual assault. When women are charged with a violent offence, it is most likely to be for level one or common assault. In addition, what distinguishes Karla Homolka from most criminalized women is her class position. Homolka grew up in a suburban middle-class home, while the majority of women who come into conflict with the law come from marginalized economic situations. Race is another factor separating Homolka from most of the women who are criminalized. Homolka's "whiteness" can be contrasted with the overrepresentation of Aboriginal women and women of colour in Canada's prisons.

Clearly, to place all the media attention that has been focused on Canada's "most notorious female offender" into its proper context, we need a better appreciation of the nature and extent of women's involvement in crime and the ways in which class/race/gender intersect in the lives of criminalized women.

Table 1: Women as a Proportion of Persons Accused of *Criminal Code* Offences, 2003

	Adults (18 and over)	
	Male	Female
	%	%
Homicide	90	10
Attempted Murder	85	15
Assaults	82	18
Sexual Assaults	98	2
Other Sexual Offences	97	3
Abduction	42	58
Robbery	91	9
Violent Crime – Total	84	16
Break and Enter	93	7
Motor Vehicle Theft	91	9
Fraud	71	29
Theft over $5,000	82	18
Theft $5,000 and under	70	30
Property crime – Total	78	22
Mischief	87	13
Arson	83	17
Prostitution	51	49
Offensive Weapons	82	18
Criminal Code – Total (excluding traffic)	81	19
Impaired Driving[1]	87	13
Cannabis Offences	88	12
Cocaine Offences	82	18
Other Drug Offences	84	16

1. Includes impaired operation of a vehicle causing death, causing bodily harm, alcohol rate over 80 mg., failure/refusal to provide a breath/blood sample.

Source: Wallace 2004.

THE NATURE AND EXTENT OF WOMEN'S INVOLVEMENT IN CRIME

A Female Crime Wave?

Women have historically comprised a relatively small percentage of adults charged with Criminal Code offences in Canada. In 2003, for example, 19 percent of adults charged with Criminal Code offences were women (see Table 1). This figure, however, is larger than it was in previous decades. The total number of Criminal Code charges against women increased from just under 24,000 in 1970 to just over 95,000 in 1991, representing 8 percent and 16 percent, respectively, of adults charged with Criminal Code offences in those years (see Table 2). Stated differently, there was an overall increase of 297 percent in women charged with Criminal Code offences between 1970 and 1991.

Statistics like these could be taken as evidence that a female crime wave has occurred, fuelling media and public concerns that women are becoming more violent and dangerous, more like their male counterparts. Holly Johnson and Karen Rodgers (1993), however, note that media reports of a so-called female crime wave typically rely on comparing percentage increases in Criminal Code charges laid against women and men, but "because of the much lower base number of charges against women for any given offence, percentage increases consistently give the false impression of much greater increases in the number of women offenders relative to men" (Johnson and Rodgers 1993: 104). For instance, Johnson and Rodgers point out that the total overall increase of 297 percent of women charged between 1970 and 1991 represents a difference in actual numbers of about 71,000. The corresponding change for men was 90 percent, representing an additional 244,700 men charged over the same period (see Table 3). In more recent years, the figure for women as a percentage of all adults charged with Criminal Code offences has increased from 16.5 percent in 1993 to 19 percent in 2003. Nevertheless, the number of women charged actually declined over this period — from 110,083 in 1993 to 84,104 in 2003 (a 23 percent decrease). The percentage of women charged went up because the number of charges against men declined by an even greater margin; there were 556,623 men charged in 1993 and 400,595 in 2003 (a 28 percent decrease) (Hartnagel 2000: 105; Statistics Canada 2004).

Examining crime statistics on the basis of rates provides a better sense of what is happening, because crime rates account for changes in population (see Table 4).[2] The overall charge rate for women has increased since 1968 (as it did for men). However, the rate of women charged per 100,000 women in the population increased from 152 in 1968 to 479.2

Table 2: Women Charged with Criminal Code Offences, 1970–2003

	1970		1991		2003	
	Number	Percent	Number	Percent	Number	Percent
Violent Offences[1]						
Murder/Manslaughter	33	0.1	48	0.1	49	0.1
Attempted Murder/Wounding/Assault	1,667	7.0	11,989	12.6	18,113	21.5
Sexual Assault/Other Sexual	31	0.1	222	0.2	138	0.2
Robbery	206	0.9	647	0.7	682	0.8
Total Violent	1,937	8.1	12,906	13.6	18,982	22.6
Property Offences						
Break and Enter	545	2.3	1,759	1.9	1,540	1.8
Theft over[2]	1,509	6.3	1,956	2.1	1,340	1.6
Theft under	8,414	35.1	30,077	31.6	16,483	19.6
Possession of Stolen Goods	497	2.1	1,991	2.1	3,602	4.3
Fraud	2,197	9.2	11,890	12.5	6,071	7.2
Total Property	13,162	54.9	47,673	50.2	29,036	34.5
Other Offences						
Prostitution-Related	1,427	6.0	5,601	5.9	1,808	2.1
Impaired Driving	1,916	8.0	9,812	10.3	8,979	10.7
Other CC Traffic[3]	624	2.6	1,170	1.2	1,488	1.8
Other Criminal Code[4]	4,899	20.4	17,895	18.8	23,811	28.3
Total Criminal Code	23,965	100.0	95,057	100.0	84,104	100.0
Liquor Offences	N/A		15,211		N/A	
Drug Offences	1,519		5,455		6,298	

1. For all offences, double counting occurs if an individual is charged in more than one incident.
2. Legislative amendments in late 1985 increased the theft categories (over and under) from $200 to $1,000; in 2003 the category used is (over and under) $5,000 and includes Motor Vehicle Theft.
3. Includes dangerous operation, failure to stop at the scene of an accident, driving while disqualified.
4. Includes gaming and betting, offensive weapons, arson, kidnapping and abduction, wilful damage and other Criminal Code offences.

Sources: Johnson and Rodgers 1993: 99; Statistics Canada 2004.

Table 3: Men Charged with Criminal Code Offences, 1970–2003

	1970		1991		2003	
	Number	Percent	Number	Percent	Number	Percent
Violent Offences[1]						
Murder/Manslaughter	298	0.1	486	0.1	372	0.1
Attempted Murder/ Wounding/Assault	24,822	9.1	90,299	17.4	85,189	21.3
Sexual Assault/Other Sexual	3,768	1.4	11,449	2.2	7,442	1.8
Robbery	3,399	1.2	7,950	1.5	6,322	1.6
Total Violent	**32,287**	**11.8**	**110,184**	**21.2**	**99,325**	**24.8**
Property Offences						
Break and Enter	19,872	7.3	37,654	7.3	18,248	4.6
Theft over[2]	19,879	7.3	16,395	3.2	9,208	2.3
Theft under	24,273	8.9	60,613	11.7	40,010	10.0
Possession of Stolen Goods	6,755	2.5	14,612	2.8	15,760	3.9
Fraud	13,952	5.1	29,072	5.6	14,660	3.6
Total Property	**84,731**	**31.0**	**158,355**	**30.6**	**97,886**	**24.4**
Other Offences						
Prostitution-Related	452	0.2	5,162	1.0	1,633	0.4
Impaired Driving	76,178	27.9	101,372	19.6	55,919	14.0
Other CC Traffic[3]	21,436	7.8	16,711	3.2	13,224	3.3
Other Criminal Code[4]	58,079	21.3	126,140	24.4	132,608	33.1
Total Criminal Code	**273,163**	**100.0**	**517,924**	**100.0**	**400,595**	**100.0**
Liquor Offences	N/A		128,713		N/A	
Drug Offences	10,873		34,764		35,624	

1. For all offences, double counting occurs if an individual is charged in more than one incident.
2. Legislative amendments in late 1985 increased the theft categories (over and under) from $200 to $1,000; in 2003 the category used is (over and under) $5,000 and includes Motor Vehicle Theft.
3. Includes dangerous operation, failure to stop at the scene of an accident, driving while disqualified.
4. Includes gaming and betting, offensive weapons, arson, kidnapping and abduction, wilful damage and other Criminal Code offences.

Sources: Johnson and Rodgers 1993: 103; Statistics Canada 2004.

Table 4: Rates of Adults Charged by Sex per 100,000 Population for Selected Criminal Code Offences, Canada, 1968, 1996, 2000

	1968		1996		2000	
	Men	Women	Men	Women	Men	Women
Violent Offences	270.5	15.0	699.3	97.1	652.7	112.7
Property Crimes	639.7	79.2	870.3	245.3	636.1	176.7
Criminal Code	1443.4	152.0	2334.6	479.2	2059.7	432.4

Source: Adapted from Hartnagel 2000: 104; 2004: 130.

in 1996, but then declined to 432.4 in 2000. (A similar pattern occurred for men as well, with the rate of men charged increasing from 1,443.4 in 1968 to 2,334.6 in 1996 and then declining to 2,059.7 in 2000.) The bulk of the increase from 1968 to 1996 for women is accounted for by property-related offences. Women's charge rate for property-related offences then declined from 245.3 in 1996 to 176.7 in 2000, while the charge rate for violent offences increased from 97.1 to 112.7 during the same period. Men's charge rate for both property offences and violent offences decreased from 1996 to 2000.

Johnson and Rodgers (1993) make the point that official crime statistics are subject to a number of influences, including changing police enforcement practices, technological developments, increased societal intolerance for specific forms of behaviour (such as drinking and driving), political pressures, and legislative changes. Indeed, one factor that may be related to increases in women's charges for violent offences in the 1990s is police practices in the area of domestic violence. In 1993, for instance, the Winnipeg Police Department implemented a change in protocol for responding to domestic violence, taking up an approach that came to be known as the "zero tolerance policy." Under this policy, police officers were mandated to lay charges anytime a complaint was made, regardless of the presence (or absence) of corroborating evidence. The zero tolerance policy led to more women being charged with violent offences. Data collected from the Winnipeg Police Department over a five-year period (1991 to 1995) showed that in 1991, 23 percent of women's charges for violent crime involved partner violence. By 1995, with the implementation of the new policy, 58 percent of women's charges involved partner violence (and 80 percent of these charges were subsequently stayed by the Crown) (Comack, Chopyk, and Wood 2000).

What Types of Offences are Women Most Likely to be Charged With?
Official statistics indicate that women are most likely to be charged with
property-related crimes. In 1970, for example, 55 percent of all charges
against women were for property offences (see Table 2). This proportion
remained relatively stable — at 50 percent — in 1991. Some 46 percent
of all women charged with Criminal Code offences in 1991 were fingered
for theft or fraud. In 2003 women made up 22 percent of adults charged
with property crimes (Table 1). As in previous years, the most common
charge for women was theft and fraud. In the same year, 35 percent of all
Criminal Code charges against women involved crimes against property;
28 percent of all women charged were charged with theft or fraud. While
crimes against property made up a smaller proportion of women's charges
in 2003 than in previous years, they constitute a greater share of wom-
en's charges than men's. Some 24 percent of all Criminal Code charges
against men in 2003 involved crimes against property; 16 percent of all
men charged were charged with theft or fraud (see Table 3).

Women accounted for 16 percent of adults charged with violent crimes
in 2003; 10 percent of adults charged with homicide were women, and
only 2 percent of those charged with sexual assault were women (Table 1).
Crimes against the person accounted for 23 percent of women's charges
in 2003 (see Table 2). Of these charges, 62 percent (11,834) involved the
least serious form, level one or common assaults.

Karla Homolka and Paul Bernardo were charged in the deaths of
two young women who were strangers to the couple. It bears noting that
stranger homicide is a relatively rare occurrence in Canada, as homicide
data consistently indicate that victims are far more likely to be killed
by someone they know than by a stranger. For instance, among the 407
solved homicides in 2003, 86 percent of the victims knew their assailant;
half (51 percent) of the victims were killed by an acquaintance (that is,
non-family), and another one-third (34 percent) were killed by a family
member. In only 14 percent of homicides in 2003 was the victim killed
by a stranger (Dauvergne 2004: 8).

Prostitution-related offences (bawdy house, procuring, living off the
avails, and communicating) comprise the only category of Criminal Code
offences in which the actual number of women's charges is consistently
greater than men's (see Shaver 1993). In 2003, 3,441 adults were charged
with prostitution-related offences; 1,808 (53 percent) of those charged were
women. As in previous years, the vast majority (88 percent) of charges
involved communicating for the purpose of prostitution, and 52 percent of
those charged for communicating were women (Statistics Canada 2004).

Nevertheless, as Frances Shaver (1993: 155) points out, women actually represent a small proportion of those involved in the sex trade:

> Conservative estimates based on the ratio of female to male street prostitutes in Montreal in 1991 (4:1), and the average number of male clients they service each week (20 and 10 respectively) indicate that only 4 percent of those involved (or at least potentially involved) in communicating for the purpose of prostitution are women. The remainder — a full 96 percent — are men, and of those, the vast majority (99 percent) are clients.

In 2003 women accounted for 13 percent of adults charged with impaired driving, 12 percent of adults charged with cannabis offences, 18 percent of adults charged with cocaine offences, and 16 percent of adults charged with offences involving other drugs (Table 1). As Johnson and Rodgers (1993: 102) suggest, these figures "most certainly underestimate the number of women who find escape through alcohol or drugs, and who suffer severe health and social consequences as a result." As well, the Task Force on Federally Sentenced Women (Shaw et al. 1991: vi) found that 71 percent (120) of the women surveyed indicated that substance abuse played a part in their law violations. Some 73 percent (88) of these women said that they were under the influence of drugs and/or alcohol at the time, and one-third (40) said that they had committed an offence to support a habit.

While these data provide us with information about the extent and nature of women's involvement in crime, we need to inquire further into how class/race/gender inequalities have a bearing on which women are most likely to be criminalized.

WOMEN AND POVERTY

Gender inequality in Canada comes in a number of forms, but the most apparent manifestation is economic. Although more and more women are working for wages, and more and more women are obtaining university degrees and full-time employment, disparities between women and men in the labour market continue to prevail. The federal government report *Women in Canada* (Statistics Canada 2001a) provides data on this issue:

- Most employed women work in occupations in which women have traditionally been concentrated. In 1999, 70 percent of all employed women (compared with 29 percent of employed men) were working in teaching, nursing and related health occupations, clerical or other administrative positions, and sales and service occupations.

- Since the 1970s women have consistently accounted for about seven in ten part-time employees (whose job benefits are minimal and working conditions precarious).
- Young women are considerably more likely than other women to be unemployed. In 1999, 13 percent of female labour participants aged 15–24 were unemployed, compared with just 7 percent of those aged 25–44 and 5 percent of those aged 45–64.
- Women's average earnings are still substantially lower than men's. In 1998 women had average earnings of just over $22,000, which was only 63 percent of the average earnings of all men with jobs. Even when women were employed on a full-time basis, their earnings remained below that of their male counterparts. In 1998 women working full-time had average earnings that were just 72 percent of those of men working full-time.
- In 1998, 2.8 million women — 18 percent of the total female population — were living in low-income situations.

The *Women in Canada* report also notes that much of the economic disparity between women and men is related to how women constitute the overwhelming majority of single parents.

- There has been a dramatic growth in the number of women who are lone parents over the past several decades. In 1996 there were 945,000 female-headed lone-parent families in Canada, representing 19 percent of all families with children. In contrast, female lone parents headed 10 percent of families with children in 1971.
- In 1996 women headed 83 percent of all one-parent families.
- Female lone parents are considerably less likely to be employed than are parents in two-parent families. In 1999, 61 percent of female lone parents with children under the age of sixteen living at home were employed, compared with 70 percent of their counterparts in two-parent families.
- In 1998, 53 percent of all families headed by lone-parent mothers had incomes that fell below the low-income cutoffs.

These data provide an important context for understanding the issue of women's involvement in crime, especially in terms of the links between crime and poverty. Similar to their male counterparts, "Women who come into conflict with the criminal justice system tend to be young, poor, under-educated, and unskilled" (Johnson and Rodgers 1993: 98). One study (Comack 1993b) of 727 women admitted to a provincial jail over a six-year period found that over half (53 percent) of the women were under the age of twenty-nine, 69 percent had grade 10 or less education, and the vast majority (85 percent) were unemployed at the time of their arrest. Similarly, a one-day snapshot survey of all inmates who were on-register in adult correctional facilities on October 5, 1996 (Finn et al. 1999) found that:

- over 40 percent of female prisoners were between the ages of twenty-five and thirty-four years;
- 35 percent of females in provincial/territorial institutions and 48 percent of females in federal facilities had grade 9 or less education (compared with a national figure of 19 percent);
- 64 percent of female inmates in provincial/territorial institutions and 80 percent of those in federal institutions were unemployed at the time of admission (compared with 43 percent and 54 percent, respectively, for males). In comparison, 10 percent of adults in Canada in 1996 were unemployed.

As Margaret Jackson (1999: 201) observes, "Over 80% of all incarcerated women in Canada are in prison for poverty related offences." In a similar fashion, Johnson and Rogers (1993: 98) locate women's participation in property offences in terms of "their traditional roles as consumers and, increasingly, as low-income, semi-skilled sole-support providers for their families. In keeping with the rapid increase in female-headed households and the stresses associated with poverty, increasing numbers of women are being charged with shoplifting, cheque forgery, and welfare fraud."

Nevertheless, class is not the only factor to consider in locating women's law violations. Aboriginal women and women of colour are overrepresented in crime statistics relative to their numbers in the general Canadian population.

RACIALIZED WOMEN

The overrepresentation of Aboriginal peoples in the Canadian criminal justice system is a problem of historic proportions that is now widely recognized (Jackson 1988–89; Hamilton and Sinclair 1991; Royal Commission on Aboriginal Peoples 1996; La Prairie 1996). The statistics are telling.

- While Aboriginal people comprised 3 percent of the total Canadian adult population in 2001, they made up 21 percent of admissions to provincial/territorial institutions, 18 percent of federal custody admissions, 14 percent of probation intakes, and 17 percent of conditional sentence admissions (Johnson 2004).
- The overrepresentation of Aboriginal women is even more acute than it is for Aboriginal men. In the one-day snapshot of all inmates who were on-register in adult correctional facilities on October 5, 1996 (Finn et al. 1999), Aboriginal women accounted for almost one-quarter (23 percent) of the female inmate population in provincial/territorial institutions, whereas Aboriginal men accounted for 18 percent of the male inmate population. In federal facilities, Aboriginal women accounted for 20 percent of the female inmate population, whereas Aboriginal men accounted for 14 percent of the male inmate population. More recent data (Canadian Human Rights Commission 2003) indicate that Aboriginal women now comprise 29 percent of women in federal prisons.
- Within the Prairie region, the figures are even more concerning. In its one-day snapshot of persons held in provincial custody in Manitoba on September 6, 2000, the Aboriginal Justice Implementation Commission (2001) found that while 63 percent (731 of 1153) of men held in custody were Aboriginal, 73 percent (41 of 56) of the women were Aboriginal.

The intersections of race/class/gender are clearly evident in the lives of many Aboriginal women in Canada. As Carol La Prairie (1987: 122, cited in Jackson 1999: 201) notes, Aboriginal women are "among the most severely disadvantaged of all groups in Canadian society." Statistics Canada's (2001b) report, *Aboriginal Peoples in Canada*, provides data to confirm this assessment:

- Unemployment: According to the 1996 census, Aboriginal people are much less likely than their non-Aboriginal counterparts to be part of the paid workforce; 48 percent of Aboriginal men aged fifteen and over (compared with 66 percent of their non-Aboriginal counterparts) and 41 percent of Aboriginal women (versus 53 percent of non-Aboriginal women) were part of the paid labour force in 1996. Almost one in four (24 percent) Aboriginal labour force participants were unemployed, more than double the rate for non-Aboriginal people (10 percent).

- Single-parent families: Aboriginal children are significantly more likely to be members of a lone-parent family than are non-Aboriginal children. In Western cities such as Regina, Saskatoon, and Winnipeg, close to half of all Aboriginal children lived with a single parent in 1996. Women head 86 percent of all Aboriginal lone-parent families.
- Education: 54 percent of Aboriginal people had not completed high school (compared with 34 percent of the non-Aboriginal population).
- Income: In 1995 Aboriginal people had an average income from all sources of $15,700, just 62 percent of the figure for the non-Aboriginal population ($25,400); 46 percent had incomes of less than $10,000, compared with 27 percent of the non-Aboriginal population.

There is an inescapable connection between the criminalization and overincarceration of Aboriginal peoples and the historical forces that have shaped contemporary Aboriginal communities. The processes of colonization — including colonial state policies such as the Indian Act, the intergenerational effects of residential schools, and the removal of Aboriginal children from their homes through child welfare practices — have led to the economic, social, and political marginalization of Aboriginal peoples (Royal Commission on Aboriginal Peoples 1996; Hamilton and Sinclair 1991). As the Supreme Court of Canada acknowledged, "Many aboriginal people are victims of systemic and direct discrimination, many suffer the legacy of dislocation, and many are substantially affected by poor social and economic conditions" (*Gladue* 1999: 20).

One of the legacies that colonialism has wrought on Aboriginal communities is inordinately high levels of violence. While many Canadian women and children encounter violence in their lives (Johnson 1996; Statistics Canada 2005a), violence against Aboriginal women and children is an even more pressing social issue. La Prairie's (1994) research involving interviews with 621 Aboriginal people living in the inner city of four Canadian urban centres found that 70 percent of the males and 75 percent of the females reported family violence in childhood. A study by the Ontario Native Women's Association (1989) found that eight out of ten Aboriginal women had experienced violence, many of them as young children. The 1999 General Social Survey conducted by Statistics Canada found that 25 percent of Aboriginal women (compared with 8 percent of non-Aboriginal women) were assaulted by their partners in the five years preceding the interview (Brownridge 2003; see also Canadian Panel on Violence Against Women 1993; Moyer 1992).

While studies that report on the incidence of particular types of abuse are useful in documenting the nature and extent of the violence encountered by women and children, several writers have noted that separating out and focusing on specific forms of abuse is highly problematic. Sharon McIvor and Teressa Nahanee (1998: 63) maintain that "compartmentalizing 'types' of violence within Aboriginal communities into distinct categories of investigation is counter-productive. Sexual, physical, and emotional attacks are inter-related and inter-generational in our communities. Treating these acts as discrete events serves only to obscure our everyday lives." Similarly, Patricia Monture-Angus (1995: 171) tells us that "focusing on a moment in time or incidents of violence, abuse or racism, counting them — disguises the utter totality of the experience of violence in Aboriginal women's lives." Indeed, one factor that comes across clearly in the literature is that the violence experienced by Aboriginal peoples is systemic; it "has invaded whole communities and cannot be considered a problem of a particular couple or an individual household" (Royal Commission on Aboriginal Peoples 1996).

One explanation often offered to account for the high levels of violence in Aboriginal communities is the use of alcohol. The correlation between alcohol use by Aboriginal peoples and violence has been often noted. Sharon Moyer (1992), for instance, found that 70 percent of the homicide incidents involving Aboriginal people between 1962 and 1984 involved the use of alcohol.[3] Accordingly, alcohol use is taken as a sign of "cultural difference" that marks Aboriginal peoples off from the rest of Canadian society. In this view, excessive drinking has become commonplace in Aboriginal communities, to the point where it is now an accepted cultural practice that leads to "drinking parties" in which violence is likely to break out.

However, resting an explanation for violence in Aboriginal communities on the use of alcohol and, more generally, on the notion of "cultural difference," contains a number of problems. For one, the issue is confined to being a problem of Aboriginal people, thereby neglecting the role of alcohol as a socially sanctioned resource in our society. Many of the Aboriginal women interviewed for the book *Women in Trouble* (Comack 1996) indicated that they turned to alcohol (and other drugs) as a way of escaping their difficult pasts (see also McEvoy and Daniluk 1995). In this regard these women are no different than many other Canadians who regularly turn to alcohol as a means of coping with deep distress in their lives.

Indeed, to say that violence in Aboriginal communities is the result of cultural differences leads to the question: Different from what? More often than not, the standards of the dominant culture are being used as the measuring rod by which Aboriginal people are transformed into the delinquent Other. Such an approach only works to reproduce the racism that prevails in the mainstream society. In this regard, centring explanations for violence in Aboriginal communities on the use of alcohol can slip too easily into the perpetuation of racist stereotypes. Two of the most invidious of these stereotypes are the "squaw" and the "drunken Indian" (see Sangster 2001; LaRocque 2000; Comack and Balfour 2004). Such representations merely function to objectify and devalue Aboriginal women and men and, in the process, cast them as being responsible for their own victimization.

Explanations that rest on the idea of cultural difference to account for the prevalence of violence in Aboriginal communities are highly suspect and have been subject to vigorous challenge. The Royal Commission on Aboriginal Peoples, for example, stated, "The distorted view held by some non-Aboriginal people, including judges ruling on cases of violence, that family violence has a cultural explanation or justification, must be vigorously denounced" (Royal Commission on Aboriginal Peoples 1996).

Aboriginal women and men are not the only marginalized group to experience overrepresentation in the criminal justice system. According to the 2001 census, Black people comprise 2 percent of the Canadian population — 6.5 percent in the Toronto area. Black women comprised 2.3 percent of the total population of Canadian females in 2001 (cited in *Hamilton* 2003). Yet, as the *Report of the Royal Commission on Systemic Racism in the Ontario Justice System* (Ontario 1995) noted, Black women are disproportionately represented in Ontario prisons, being sentenced to prison at "almost seven times that of white women" (cited in Pollack 2000a: 75). Additionally, the Correctional Service of Canada reported in February 2001 that while Black women represented 1 percent of the federal women offender population in 1981, this figure rose to 9 percent by 1998 (cited in *Hamilton* 2003).

Shoshana Pollack's (2000a) interviews with Black women serving federal sentences in Ontario revealed that the women's main motivation for breaking the law was economic. Some of the women in Pollack's study had previously been in paid employment in low-level jobs in financial institutions, corporations, and medical care facilities.

A few participants were working at these jobs at the time of their arrest. They were also either sole providers for their children or supporting themselves through part-time work while continuing their education at college or university. However, most of the women found that the wage they received was not sufficient for providing for their families, even with subsidized child care, and sometimes turned to illegal means to supplement their income. (Pollack 2000a: 77)

Pollack suggests that Black women's conflicts with the law emanated from their concern to assert their independence and resist marginalization and state-enforced dependency (such as welfare): "Shoplifting, fraud and drug importation were a means of releasing Black women from poverty and racist practices that reinforced their marginalization. Relying upon or supplementing their income through illegal jobs, women were able to adequately support themselves and their family" (Pollack 2000a: 78).

These patterns are not unique to Canada. As Laureen Snider (2004: 213) notes, "Everywhere those most likely to be imprisoned are racial and ethnic minorities, especially people of colour." In fifteen U.S. states, Black women are imprisoned at rates of between ten and thirty-five times greater than white women (CCPA Monitor 2004: 3). In the United Kingdom, as of June 1999, women from minority ethnic groups comprise 6 percent of the British population but 25 percent of the female prison population (British Home Office 1999: 5, cited in Snider 2004: 231). In Australia, Aboriginal peoples make up less than 2 percent of the population overall, but represent 19 percent of the Australian prison populations (Carcach and Grant, 2000, cited in Snider 2004: 231).

While the media may be content to devote considerable attention to sensational crimes committed by the likes of Karla Homolka, the vast majority of offences committed by women are "poverty crimes" that reflect the systemic inequality, discrimination, and marginalization emanating from their class/race/gender locations.

REPRESENTATIONS OF CRIMINALIZED WOMEN

If we were looking to typecast the so-called typical criminalized woman, we might be better advised to turn our attention away from Homolka and consider the story of Lisa Neve.

In November 1994, Lisa Neve, a twenty-one-year-old Aboriginal woman, became the second woman ever in Canada to be labelled a dangerous offender and sentenced to an indeterminate sentence.[4] Lisa's life story is one that resonates for too many young Aboriginal women in Canada. She was adopted out to a white family at three months of age.

At the age of twelve she was expelled from school for drinking with a group of friends. The police were called, and she was apprehended and put into secure custody. Lisa says that she learned early on that

> *acting out meant people didn't try to shrink me, I just got attention. So I would freak out and get restrained and sent to segregation. I was always in segregation for something or other, because I was so bitter and angry. I felt robbed of my childhood, so I misbehaved. I think I was ill back then, I remember having so many issues in my mind, voices, but I didn't want to tell anybody because I thought they would send me over to the hospital. They had sex offenders there and I didn't want to go, so I just acted out, cut myself, banged my head, and scratched myself. I don't know what I was doing.* (Neve and Pate 2005: 20)

Like many young women in her situation, Lisa's response was to run away to the streets, where she was introduced to prostitution, drug use (cocaine, marijuana, heroin, and Ritalin), and violence. In addition to her own experiences of victimization, Lisa too engaged in violence. She soon developed a reputation on the street as an "enforcer" because she was not afraid to protect other women involved in the sex trade from their pimps. By the age of eighteen, Lisa had some twenty-two charges against her, many of them imposed while she was in custody. As Kim Pate (2002: 466) notes:

> It did not take long for the adults in authority to label Lisa as a "problem" in need of "correction." Once the labels were applied, they not only stuck, but they also attracted other labels that built upon and expanded those prior. Consequently, although Lisa had started out as "mischievous," or "a brat," she was later labelled an instigator, negative, and eventually, aggressive, sociopathic and finally, a dangerous offender.

As an adult Lisa was convicted of aggravated assault, robbery, uttering threats, and assault with a weapon. The assaults and robbery arose from disputes with other women engaged in the sex trade. In 1991, in retaliation for a previous beating that put one of her friends in hospital, Lisa forced another woman to strip, then cut up her clothes and left her on a busy highway. In 1992 she stabbed a woman with the unopened end of an exacto knife. The conviction for uttering threats came about after Lisa checked herself into a psychiatric facility in 1993 and told a psychiatrist that she wanted to kill a lawyer and his family. The lawyer in question had subjected Lisa to a brutal cross-examination during the trial of her boyfriend, who was eventually jailed for beating her. (The lawyer challenged her credibility with questions such as "Aren't you in fact a prostitute?") When the robbery charge (taking the woman's clothes) went to court in November 1994, Lisa was declared a dangerous offender and sentenced to an indeterminate sentence.

At the dangerous offender hearing, Lisa was repeatedly questioned about her sexual orientation. This issue was ostensibly relevant as a result of psychiatric evidence that she was a "sadistic homosexual." The leading Crown psychiatrist characterized her as "the equivalent of a male lust murderer." These assessments were based largely on statements that Lisa had made to psychiatrists and police officers, which she testified were fictitious and made up to shock persons in authority. Although the designation as a dangerous offender was ultimately overturned on appeal in June 1999, as a result of that designation Lisa Neve was classified as a maximum-security prisoner and spent six years in prison (including pre-trial detention), most of it in segregated, maximum-security units in two different men's prisons (Pate 2002: 466).

In overturning the dangerous offender designation, the Court of Appeal noted the typical nature of this young woman's "violent" offences, in that "every offence which Neve committed was entangled in some way with her life as a prostitute" (cited in Pate 2002: 467). The court took into account the nature of life on the street, particularly for young sex trade workers. According to Neve and Pate (2005: 26):

> For instance, they highlighted the fact that many young prostitutes are assaulted and murdered and that the majority of those murdered were female. They went on to assert that "No one should be surprised, therefore, to learn that many prostitutes arm themselves for defensive purposes.... It is not possible to evaluate moral blameworthiness without having an understanding of the context in which the criminal act occurred."

Since her release, Lisa has continued to work hard at overcoming the impact of her imprisonment and struggles to manage her mental health issues. But as Pate (2002: 467) notes, "The biggest danger for Lisa remains, however, the reaction of others to her infamous dangerous offender label."

As Lisa Neve's story illustrates, women and girls are routinely sanctioned not only for violating legal codes, but also for violating codes of conduct that regulate and patrol the boundaries of "appropriate" female behaviour. In chapter 2, Joanne Minaker provides a historical perspective on this issue by focusing on the work of a group of affluent, white, upper-middle-class women called the Founders, who ran the Toronto Magdalen Asylum, a refuge for women and girls that operated between 1853 and 1939. Minaker shows us how the representation of the "erring female" — the term used by the Founders to refer to the women and girls they sought to help — worked as a censure or category of denunciation in a particular historical, political, and structural context. In the early twentieth century, the idea of the "erring female" reproduced and reinforced the dualism between "good girls" (those who are chaste, virtuous, and pious) and "bad girls" (those who are sexually deviant and wayward). In the process, it operated to keep female sexuality in check.

Minaker makes the point, however, that the claims that justified the institutionalization of "erring females" were not just related to their sexuality — how it is perceived and who controls it — but their very life chances. As well, that females incarcerated under the Female Refuges Act did not have to engage in criminal activity suggests, according to Minaker, that something else was at stake — namely, reproducing a gendered, classist, and racialized social order. While the "erring female" of earlier times was constituted by her immorality, degradation, mental defect, and/or intemperance, later on female transgression became defined by inadequate parenting, Fetal Alcohol Spectrum Disorder (FASD), promiscuity, and/or drug abuse. In both eras, the "erring female" is one who is censured for deviating from the dominant (class-based and racialized) standards of "appropriate" femininity.

Prostitution has historically been considered a status conferred on women who sell sexual services in exchange for monetary or other rewards. Traditionally within criminology, the focus has been on the woman involved in prostitution, with very little attention devoted to the men who sought her services. The purpose of prostitution was seen to be the servicing of men's needs, which was premised on a particular understanding of male sexuality. Specifically, men had insatiable sex drives and desires that women must somehow satisfy (cf. Davis 1937). In this traditional, male-centred view, the prostitute was positioned as the quintessential bad girl, the Other, and the focus of investigation was on trying to account for the sources of her difference. Why did women enter this profession? What is it about these women that accounts for their deviance and disrepute? Answers to these questions typically singled out factors such as family dysfunction, poor socialization, bad upbringing, and individual pathology. Little effort was made to consult with the women themselves or to attend to the ways in which broader social inequalities conditioned and limited women's choices and opportunities.

To counter this male-centred view, as well as the legal and conceptual baggage associated with the term prostitution, women involved in this activity began to emphasize it as "work." As Chris Bruckert and Colette Parent note in chapter 3, "sex work" is a contentious term for both the women who work in this area and feminists alike. Some women in the trade (notably erotic dancers) reject the term as being inappropriate to the work they do. Some feminists argue that prostitution is a manifestation of patriarchy, a symbol of the sexual, social, and economic domination of men by women. Bruckert and Parent, however, situate their analysis within a body of literature that understands sex work as a job that shares much in common with other work that women carry out in a neo-liberal, post-industrial labour market increasingly characterized by "McJobs" (Ritzer 2004).

Focusing on in-call sex workers — women who provide sexual services to clients in establishments such as massage parlours, brothels, and dungeons — Bruckert and Parent draw on narratives of women involved in this sector of the sex industry to explore the labour structure and process of their work and how it is subjectively experienced by the women. Doing so enables the authors to draw parallels to the work of working-class women in other consumer services, all the while being attentive to how the social, moral, and criminal justice regulation of sex work creates particular challenges and problems for the women. By analyzing in-call sex work from a perspective that straddles labour theory and criminology, Bruckert and Parent offer an important corrective to traditional male-centred constructions of the prostitute as Other. When placed in the context of the data presented earlier on women's inequality and labour force participation, as well as the nature of women's "McJobs" under neo-liberal market conditions, their argument for retaining the term sex work becomes all the more compelling.

Yet, while Bruckert and Parent are attentive to the ways in which racialization and race/ethnic stratification intersect with class and gender to condition women's choices and opportunities, their research was unable to shed light on the impact of racialization on the women in this sector of the industry. In these terms, Nahanni Fontaine's chapter provides us with a different vantage point from which to explore women and girls' involvement in the sex trade — the racialized spaces of the inner city.

Drawing on narratives of Aboriginal women and girls — Anishinaabe

Ikwe — Fontaine explores their participation in the "gang." As she notes, most media and law enforcement representations fail to locate the phenomena of the "Aboriginal gang" in the context of colonization. By doing that very thing Fontaine is able to show us the profound impact that colonization is wreaking on Aboriginal youth who live in inner-city spaces. According to Fontaine, colonization has not only conditioned the life chances of Aboriginal peoples, but has also led to the internalization of dominant Eurocentric, patriarchal beliefs. As revealed by the women and girls that she interviewed, relations to men in the gang are defined by a hierarchy of roles comprising "old ladies," "bitches," and "hos." Given their subordinated position both in relation to the gang and in the wider society, Anishinaabe Ikwe are left to "take it like a woman" and "be solid" in their efforts to negotiate place and space. Nevertheless, a paradox emerges in the women's accounts: despite the violence encountered in their relations with the men in the gang, the women in Fontaine's study were provided — through that gang — with a space in which they could find solidarity and pride in their Aboriginal identities.

In chapter 5, Susan Boyd explores the historical and contemporary representations of women as traffickers, importers, and users of illicit drugs — representations that shape public imagination and policy. Contemporary accounts of drug traffickers and users have not strayed far from earlier racialized and class-based constructions of women as either "uncivilized and drunken squaws" or white "fragile ladies." A succession of contemporary drug scares (around heroin, marijuana, cocaine, ecstasy, and the like) share in the common narrow representations of drug traffickers, importers, and producers as racialized, foreign Others who pose a threat to Christian nation-states. Despite government commitments to arresting top-level drug traffickers, many of those who end up incarcerated for drug offences are racialized, poor, undereducated, single-parent women. Boyd argues that to understand the criminalization of women for drug offences, we need to attend to the broader economic, social, and political structures that shape women's lives — at both the national and global levels. The feminization of poverty exacerbated by neo-liberal globalization, neo-conservative tough-on-crime agendas, the transnational war on drugs, and the global prison-industrial complex are key factors, according to Boyd, in explaining stepped-up levels of state coercion and rising incarceration rates.

Similar to Bruckert and Parent's analysis of in-call sex workers, Boyd locates women's involvement in the drug trade in their exploited position as workers in the neo-liberal capitalist labour market. With limited access to meaningful, legitimate employment, the drug trade offers women the possibility of providing for themselves and their families. Nevertheless, while drug trafficking and importing are by no means limited to the poor or people of colour, dominant representations that rely on gender and racial profiling mean that poor women and women of colour are the people most vulnerable to arrest and conviction.

The artwork of Jackie Traverse brings this part of the book to a close. As Cathy Fillmore and Colleen Dell (2001) found in their interviews with criminalized women, self-harm in the form of slashing is one way of coping with and surviving deep emotional pain and distress. Traverse's work reveals what while the resulting scars may be a source of pointed questioning from others, they are also markers of a past that is to be honoured.

NOTES

I want to thank Wayne Antony, Gillian Balfour, and Kim Pate for their feedback on earlier drafts of this Introduction. I also want to thank Marianne Rogowy for her assistance in compiling the tables of criminal justice data.

1. A search of the Internet using these keywords (on July 12, 2005) produced 38 hits of news articles, all of them in reference to Homolka.
2. It is difficult to get access to crime rates that are differentiated on the basis of sex. The rates presented here were calculated by Hartnagel 2000, 2004.
3. Note, however, that the percentage changed over the period of study, as 78 percent of incidents involved alcohol in 1962–65 whereas 59 percent did in 1981–84 (Moyer 1992).
4. The dangerous offender legislation was passed in 1977. Between 1977 and 1999, a total of 271 people (99.3 percent of whom were male) were given that designation. Marlene Moore was the only other woman to be declared a dangerous offender (in 1985). Moore committed suicide in the Kingston Prison for Women in 1988 at the age of thirty-one (see Kershaw and Lasovich 1991 and Balfour's introduction to Part II here). Including Lisa Neve, only ten individuals have had the dangerous offender designation overturned by the courts (Mahoney 1999: A3).

2.   SLUTS AND SLAGS: THE CENSURING OF THE ERRING FEMALE

Joanne C. Minaker

> *On learning I had run off with a Chinese man my father came to Toronto. There was a loud banging at the door when my boyfriend and I were having breakfast. Two policemen came in followed by my father. I was ordered to get dressed and taken to a place where I was put in a barred cage. Shortly, I was taken into a room and interviewed by a woman. She asked if I had ever slept with anyone else. I felt I would have to damage my character to save my boyfriend from any blame. I said, "Yes." She asked, "How many?" I said, "Two." She asked me their names and I gave them. Although I wasn't sure, I told her I was pregnant, hoping that would help. I have never told anyone I was pregnant before. Almost immediately I was taken to a courtroom. I stood with my back towards the judge who sat about 10 feet away.... A policeman spoke.... He related the address where he found me, my boyfriend's name and that he was wearing pajamas. The judged asked me, "Are you pregnant?" I said, "Yes." He asked, "How far along?" I said, "Three months — I'll get married if you'll just let me out of here long enough." The judge said, "Remanded one week for sentence." I was taken in a black van to a jailhouse. I sat and slept on a bench in a barred enclosure and ate greasy stew at a long table with male prisoners. When I returned to court, the judge said, "You are charged with being incorrigible and I sentence you to one year in the Belmont Home [Toronto Industrial Refuge]." (Demerson 2001: 1)[1]*

It was May 30, 1939, and Velma's crime of being "incorrigible" — a code word for errant female sexuality, illegitimate motherhood, and miscegenation — essentially that she was eighteen, pregnant, unmarried, and in love with the baby's Chinese father. Deemed out of control by her father, police officers, and a magistrate, Velma was to be placed under control and punished. Paternalistically, such male authorized knowers argued that she needed punishment, not out of vengeance, but for her own good. When the Toronto Industrial Refuge closed its doors in June

1939, Velma was transferred to the Mercer Reformatory, where she stayed until March 1940.

In her eighties Velma recently put her experiences into a book, aptly titled *Incorrigible* (Demerson 2004). Little, however, is known about the institution she referred to in her writing as "Belmont Home." Nor do we know much about the legislation — the Female Refuges Act (FRA) — that sanctioned her incarceration, or the ways in which females like Velma were represented. My purpose here is not to tell Velma's story or re-create the lives of other women. Instead, this chapter is about the censuring practices that the women Founders of the Refuge deployed, their responses to "girls in trouble," or "erring females," and the discourses and representations upon which their efforts were conceived and justified.

In effect, the censuring practices of the Founders of the Toronto Industrial Refuge facilitated the criminalization of thousands of girls and women between 1853 and 1939. Although Velma was not involved in the sex trade, that she — a single, white female (of English and Greek heritage) — had slept with a Chinese man and was carrying his "illegitimate" child made her deserving of the title of prostitute. The Founders were (re)producing a discourse that had tremendous social consequences for young women like Velma.[2]

Central to this process was the construction of what Carol Smart (1995: 227) refers to as a "perpetually problematic" body: "The woman who sells what should be given away for free in the name of love (as with prostitution) merits punishment.... There is a powerful double bind here which we are still far from resolving but which constructs women's bodies as perpetually problematic."

With its uneasy combination of protection and punishment and women as its focus, the Refuge offers a unique venue for examining the criminalization of working-class girls and women deemed "erring." Despite immense social change and increasing tensions, the Refuge endured for eighty-six years. Looking at the records they left behind we can learn a great deal about how the governors viewed their charges and the discourses upon which their representations were based. A posh retirement centre in midtown Toronto called Belmont House — a legacy of the Toronto Industrial Refuge — houses largely forgotten annual reports, meeting minutes, and other documents from its previous incarnation. A small storeroom became my own personal archive, and I spent countless hours there trying to disentangle the threads of the institution's past. This chapter is based on my analysis of those records, focusing specifically on representations of, and claims made about, the inmates institutionalized at the Refuge.

A vast literature examines the moral and social regulation of women and girls (cf. Sangster 1999; Valverde 1991; Strange 1995). Such studies pay attention to the contradictory punitive and benevolent nature of institutional practices, but leave open much room for examining the claims that justified the institutionalization of large numbers of girls and women. I argue that the struggles of those like Velma are not just over their sexuality — how it is perceived and who controls it — but over their very life chances, which in turn are inexorably linked to race, class, and gender inequalities. While its context is historical, this all too familiar theme — the gendered, classist, and racialized punishment of female sexuality — resonates today. Legislation such as Alberta's Act for the Protection of Children Involved in Prostitution (PCHIP) and British Columbia's Secure Care Act punishes females in the name of protection (see Bittle 2002 and chapter 7 here).

THEORETICAL UNDERPINNINGS: THE ERRING FEMALE AS CENSURE

The Founders of the Refuge referred to those they sought to help as "erring females."[3] Specific historical discourses produce particular representations — like the erring female — both explicitly and tacitly. I understand the term "the erring female" as a censure. Colin Sumner (1990: 28–29) defines censures as "categories of denunciation or abuse lodged within very complex, historically loaded practical conflicts and moral debates." As Sumner's work suggests, ideological formations, social relations, and human fears of the day support and constitute censures. Pivotal in the articulation and proliferation of knowledge claims are what Laureen Snider (2002, 2003) calls "authorized knowers," those individuals and/or groups with the capacity and authority to have their claims heard and acted upon. Those occupying dominant gender, class, race, and ethnic positions have greater capacity to assert their censures in the legal and moral discourses of the day. The Founders were people who had managed to attain the status of authorized knowers.

This brings us to the phenomena that censures interpret or signify. In Foucaultian terms, discourses are normalizing in that they create, fuel, and sustain norms for behaviour, by dividing people into categories like good (normal) and bad (abnormal) (Foucault 1983). The concept of "erring female" as a censure was a means of keeping female sexuality in check, delineating social deviance and legitimate responses to those so classified. Rather than being used to explain behaviour (for example, socially deviant conduct) or people (criminalized girls), the censure "erring female" became a way of making knowledge claims. As a social censure, the sign "erring" signifies a problematic female, in body, mind, or character. That the inmates of the Refuge supposedly shared certain characteristics and actions — like intemperance, prostitution, or immorality — was something set completely apart from their common social-structural disadvantage and marginalization, which tended to be obscured in the process.

As Joan Sangster (1999: 34) argues, "This 'censuring process' of distinguishing the immoral from the moral woman... constituted and reproduced relations of power based on gender, race, and economic marginality." Thus, the sense of an Other is always at the heart of both the censures and the identity of authorized knowers: the term "erring female" evokes both the image of immorality, sexual deviance, and waywardness (that is, on the part of the inmates) as well as its complement — chaste, pious, and virtuous femininity (on the part of the Founders). Here we see the double bind that Smart refers to — a double standard of sexual morality that places females into either the good girl or bad girl category. In Pat Carlen's (1995: 220) terms, the erring female is "outwith" gender norms, family norms, and other social norms, and thereby deemed a failure as wife/partner, mother, daughter, and worker.

Censures are also historically situated and tied to particular calls for action. As long as social relations are conditioned and contoured by ethnicity, race, class, and gender, these axes of power imbue their application. The concept of erring female operated as a powerful censure that facilitated the criminalization of those marginalized by gender, class, and race. Actual girls and women were targeted for reform because they were mistaken for this erring female.[4] Indeed, to some extent challenging dominant ideologies of female sexuality and gender, the Founders viewed prostitutes, drunkards, and homeless and otherwise destitute women as objects of denigration and pity, not objects for harsh punishment. The Founders advocated various strategies in the name of protection that would bring erring females back "within" feminine restraint. They claimed that "the erring female is at once crushed by public sentiment," yet saw prostitution and sexual immorality not as causes but as consequences of their poor social position.[5] This view certainly does belie how they bought into the prevailing assumption that female prostitutes were sexually loose and in need of character reformation. They emphasized that without good moral influences, erring women would find loose company, take stimulants, and thereby slide or be induced into prostitution. Underlying their (re)production of the erring female censure was not only the desire to control or govern, but also the desire to help or protect. That they believed their work was benevolent and that they defended it in the name of protection, are significant, but should not overshadow their class and race privileges. They acknowledged that social structures ("abounding inequity") and poverty ("great waywardness") propelled some women onto the streets, but nevertheless stressed the women's lack of feminine virtue over their lack of economic or social opportunities. They also tied to ethnicity their notions of female (dis)respectability and assumptions about working-class women's failure to conform to romanticized standards of ideal femininity. By stigmatizing and targeting Irish and Italian immigrants in the early years, and by casting other racial/ethnic groups (for example, Aboriginals, Eastern Europeans) as entirely beyond the pale of their interventions, the Founders (re)produced an outcast class.

THE SOCIO-POLITICAL CONTEXT OF CENSURE

The Toronto Industrial Refuge emerged during an intense period of state formation and nation-building and amidst widening class and ethnic divisions, new fears of social degeneration (fed by declining birth rates among Anglo-Saxon versus non-British immigrants) and Victorian expectations of femininity, domesticity, and restrained sexuality. The Founders' claims were mediated by middle-class fears of working-class vice, and tensions between middle-class sensibilities and working-class realities. They were also informed by Christian beliefs and maternalism.

During the mid-nineteenth century, immigration, urbanization, and industrialization were changing the economic, political, and cultural terrain of a sparsely populated agrarian society (Jarvis 1979). Nearly 100,000 immigrants, primarily Irish and Catholic, had fled to Canadian shores during the Irish potato famine of the 1840s (Duncan 1965). Difficulty finding paid work and the meagre wage offered to women forced many Irish Catholic women, impoverished and socially dislocated, onto the streets. During the 1850s and 1860s Irish women made up almost 90 percent of females imprisoned for crimes of vagrancy, drunkenness, and prostitution (Phillips 1986).

In Toronto an influx of immigrants, growing poverty, emigration from rural areas, rising crime rates, and the increased visibility of prostitution all contributed to a perceived need to deal with the excesses of vast social change. Toronto's reform-minded citizens were quick to find a scapegoat. As capitalism expanded and the working class grew, so too among the political, business, religious, and social elite did the perception of a "working-class problem." In response Toronto's police force was expanded, and by 1886 it included a morality branch with sweeping powers of arrest. Although reformers mainly directed their claims of moral decay at the urban problem of crime, female sexual immorality was a key reform target. While out-of-control working-class male youth also captured the elite's ire, the "boy problem" was primarily couched in languages of aggression and masculinity, and was widely understood as a class issue.[6] For women and girls, the temptations of the city took on a distinctly gendered character. That houses of ill fame increasingly cropped up and more women solicited on city streets (making prostitution more visible) did not help. Members of the clergy, politicians, and social reformers constructed prostitution as a female problem, deflecting attention away from men. In short, prostitution symbolized the growing problems of nineteenth century urban Canada (Strange 1995). As a group prostitutes were outside the bounds of acceptability and largely perceived of as being disposable.[7]

The regulation of prostitution is a classic example of how criminalization is gendered. In the nineteenth century, prostitution was not a rigidly defined indictable crime, but a status offence having to do with lifestyle. Legislators passed statutes authorizing arrest and detention of prostitutes as early as 1759 in Nova Scotia, 1839 in Lower Canada, and 1858 in Upper Canada. An early Quebec ordinance read: "All common prostitutes or night walkers wandering in the fields, public streets or highways, not giving satisfactory account of themselves" may be arrested.[8] In 1867 Parliament passed An Act Respecting Vagrancy, which singled out "all common prostitutes, or night walkers," and added that all "keepers of bawdy houses and houses of ill-fame, or houses for the resort of prostitutes, and persons in the habit of frequenting such houses, not giving a satisfactory account of themselves" warranted punishment.[9] Hence, practices across the country, which continue to this day, of incarcerating women involved in the sex trade were codified in law. Police, magistrates, and judges presumed that prostitution was a female vice that signalled sexual immorality, undermined the morality of a growing nation, and therefore required a punitive response.

A woman found in a public space without an "acceptable" reason for her presence could find herself under suspicion of prostitution; or it could happen simply as a result of dress, demeanour, or presumed flawed character. Police exercised considerable discretion in deciding when and against whom to apply laws. Without sufficient grounds for being in public places, working-class and impoverished women were, in Smart's terms, "perpetually problematic." Mariana Valverde (1991) argues that with sexuality constructed as belonging to the exclusively familial sphere, the notoriously public quality of prostitution makes it inherently problematic. Of course, given a woman's presumed place in the private sphere, the woman who sells sex in the marketplace is beyond the confines of heterosexual, upper-middle-class femininity. Ravaged by poverty, disease, and alcohol, and subject to unrelenting police attention, scores of nineteenth-century women found themselves detained in local jails and housed together with habitual male offenders (Backhouse 1991). By the early 1850s, some females were supervised by female officials in makeshift wings of mixed prisons.[10] Between 1867 and 1917 criminal laws delineating prostitution grew from a few regulations directed against prostitution as vagrancy, to a more complex set of provisions with wide police powers of arrest and detention (McLaren 1986). In other words, the net of social control over "perpetually problematic" females was strengthened and cast wider.[11] It is in this punitive context of women's penalty that the efforts of the Refuge's Founders must be understood.

"OUR HOME IS FOR FALLEN WOMEN":
THE EMERGENCE OF THE TORONTO INDUSTRIAL REFUGE

At a time when women were excluded from public affairs, the Friends of the Magdalen Society, comprising a small group of Protestant, upper-middle-class British and Scottish women, proposed an alternative to the prevailing conditions. English and Scottish clergy, businessmen, and local state representatives had established separate, non-statutory institutions called "Magdalene homes," intended to divert young women away from prisons and poorhouses. [12] Linda Mahood (1990) argues that male reformers used their roles as professionals (doctors, lawyers, and ministers) to legitimate their participation in prostitution control. In Canada the Founders of the Toronto Industrial Refuge – many of whom had themselves grown up in England and Scotland – were influenced by the Magdalene homes and refuges in Europe, and by 1853 had developed their own rescue and reform strategy on Canadian soil. To begin a small group of Protestant, upper-middle class British and Scottish women (married to prominent men from Toronto's legal, medical, and business elite) established the Toronto Magdalen Asylum, later called the Industrial House of Refuge for Females, or Belmont House. The institution's humble beginnings can be largely attributed to the work of Elizabeth Dunlop, who organized a group of like-situated women to construct a "Home for Fallen Women" for the purpose of providing institutional care and rehabilitation to would-be prostitutes and those likened to them (Minaker 2003). The institution opened in one of the Founder's homes, and in its first year admitted nineteen inmates. In contrast to their European counterparts, the Refuge was entirely volunteer-based, women-run, and, until the 1920s, located at a distance from the penal system.[13]

Prostitution and the Erring Female

The dominant mid-Victorian discourse defined the female prostitute and other intemperate, homeless, or otherwise destitute women as "fallen women." The metaphor permeated art, literature, and upper-middle-class consciousness (Winnifrith 1994). The female prostitute, as the dominant culture constructed her, had fallen more deeply and required more punishment than male customers or male prostitutes. Indeed, the legal and state authorities, prison officials, and religious male elite constituted female offenders as beyond penitence and rescue. The Founders were critical of this dominant male penal approach that criminalized women and were troubled by the plight of the women caught up in it. In their view, incarcerating women in prison was an ineffective strategy to thwart prostitution. More importantly, the Founders believed that such women deserved Christian sympathy and maternal compassion, not scorn or ridicule. Put simply, erring females required protection, not punishment. In this ethos, the Founders directed their efforts toward the moral reformation of prostitutes and other working-class women whom they saw (because of intemperance, promiscuity, or abandonment) in danger of becoming prostitutes.

The Founders were both constrained and privileged by gender. To the dominant male business, political, and social elite (many of whom were their husbands), they were subordinate. Nevertheless, they exerted considerable power in their ability to both contest and (re)produce an erring female as being someone in need of rescue and reform. In keeping with the view that the female prostitute was a prime target for intervention, the Founders advocated a different form of detention. They argued, "Vice pollutes the moral atmosphere, then, is the call for an antidote."[14] Their institution, they proposed, was a "home for fallen women," a place of safety that offered moral, religious, and domestic training.[15] Like U.S. reformatories, as Estelle Freedman (1981) and Nicole Rafter (1985a) have argued, the Refuge sought to fulfil the mutually reinforcing functions of sexual and vocational control.

The Founders did not contest the social structural conditions and ideological relations that segregated working-class women as different, as Other. Rather, they reinforced the divide between propertied and non-propertied, elite and poor, men and women, white and non-white, good girls and bad girls. The lives of the working-class women who became inmates were constrained not just by their gender, but also by their marginalized class and (for many) ethnic or race position. As Freedman (1981: 20) explains, "The line that separated the pure woman from the fallen woman demarcated privilege on one side and degradation on the other."

Christian Stewardship and Maternalism

A Christian stewardship approach underlined the Founders' view that (prospective) inmates were more sinned against than sinning. Their model was Mary Magdalene, whom, according to the New Testament, Jesus Christ befriended and saved, curing her of evil spirits, "from whom seven demons had come out."[16] To convince a Bible-reading, churchgoing Protestant community of the worthiness of their mission, the Founders' choice of Mary Magdalene was a clever one. Insofar as they required public support and held their Christian beliefs sacred, the Founders constructed the erring female as their "fallen daughter," one warranting public sympathy, Christian compassion, and, just as significantly, pecuniary assistance.

Underlying their campaign was not only their sense of Christian duty to solve moral problems, but also their belief that being female provided them with a special expertise for intervening in such matters.[17] They relied on this "innate woman's knowledge" to justify their self-assigned status as moral reformers. In (re)producing the erring female they simultaneously constituted themselves as Christians and as respectable women, as "best suited to reform the fallen and degraded of [their] sex."[18] The image that the Founders had of themselves was dependent, then, on the women they sought to help — and so too were their careers, given that they found purpose in organizing and managing the Refuge.

SHIFTING REPRESENTATIONS AND THEIR IMPLICATIONS

The category of erring female was not stable; it was a shifting representation held together by the theme of "wayward" sexuality. Between 1853 and 1939, different representations of the erring female proliferated and rendered her governable. The women who found themselves inside the Refuge were marked with a variety of problematic identities, including the "fallen woman" and the "incorrigible girl."

Fallen Woman/Voluntary Prisoner: The Erring Female as Rescuable

The Founders preferred to view inmates as "voluntary prisoners" and declared their door open to any woman who "earnestly desire[d] reform."[19] Jane W.'s case exemplifies this representation at work. Making good on her promise to visitors at a local gaol, Jane entered the Refuge on December 14, 1859. Erring females like her, a twenty-nine-year-old prostitute, were prime candidates. The Admission Committee asked Jane her motive, country of origin, and requested information about her parents and friends. Jane, it turned out, was an Irish immigrant whose life in Canada was marked by economic and social deprivation. More importantly (to them), the Committee members asked Jane how long she had been leading "an abandoned or dissipated life."[20] She explained that she had arrived in Canada in 1856 and became involved in prostitution soon after that. Next, Jane listened to the rules of the institution and the conditions under which her entry would be granted. Like all prospective inmates, Jane had to promise to remain in the institution for twelve months (a required probation period to test the inmate's sincerity for reform), to "be obedient, industrious, clean and tidy," and to refrain from "all bad language, and improper conduct." Jane expressed her desire to reform and pledged that she would stay for one year. With a signed order from the Committee, Jane met the matron, who found her a room in an open dormitory.

Jane began a regimented routine of moral and industrial training (learning domesticity through work in the laundry) in order to "bring about a healthy state of mind and body," and she was given religious instruction and guidance (learning piety through church services).[21] This routine was augmented by a maternal discipline because, as the Founders put it, "the selfish and the violent [require] control, and our only power over them is the firm hand and tender heart."[22] The Founders argued that the routine, habits, and skills developed in the Refuge would prepare the inmates both physically and mentally for usefulness as domestic servants after they left the home. They argued: "We aim at making them good servants, and would deprecate teaching them any habit in the home that might seriously interfere with their usefulness as domestics."[23]

The Founders distanced the institution from the punitive taint of a reformatory or penitentiary, emphasizing that the Refuge was a benevolent, Christian home. They adamantly argued that "the Refuge is in no sense a prison... it is voluntary and reformatory."[24] As the Founders put it, "Recollect they are voluntary prisoners, we cannot keep them against their wills."[25] For decades, the Founders' discourse of voluntariness legitimated the institutionalization of females for their own protection.

Another inmate, Alice B., was recorded as "voluntarily" committing herself to the Refuge on March 2, 1879, at age sixteen — and did not leave until June 13, 1935. Was Alice a "voluntary prisoner?" The voluntariness of the institution was more rhetoric than practice, as Alice's case suggests.

Sarah H. entered the Refuge in the late nineteenth century of "her own free will," at age thirty-four. An English, single domestic living in Toronto, Sarah had one child. Viewed as immoral, she is typical of how the Founders saw their charges in the early years. The Founders believed that women like Sarah could be rescued if they voluntarily submitted themselves to the kindness and restraints of the Refuge. This "choice," most likely made in dire circumstances, signalled for the Founders that an inmate was an erring female in need of reformation, but also signified her consent to submit to the strategies employed to regulate, control, and otherwise govern her. Only a voluntary prisoner could be "invited, encouraged and protected" to a place of safety. Only a female in need of protection could require a probation period of twelve months to test her sincerity. Only in a Christian home could she be rescued, reformed, and restored.

By the turn of the twentieth century the Refuge had become an accepted non-penal, volunteer-run site for the governance of female sexuality. The Founders carved a niche for their institution and themselves among the Christian community, philanthropic elite, and general public of Toronto not by challenging views of the prostitute and those likened to her as Other, but by reproducing widely accepted censures. Looking beyond what the Founders claimed to what they did not say reveals that they took up the call to respond to this problematic female without disrupting, but rather by upholding, traditional race, class, and gender hierarchies. Insofar as they remained silent on several significant issues, the Founders (re)produced the erring female censure.

First, they remained silent about the role of men in prostitution. While the Founders displayed more sympathy than did male lawmakers to the plight of working-class women, they echoed the law's reading of prostitution by identifying prostitution with the women who sold their services, and they ignored male clients.

Second, they remained silent about social structures. In so doing, the Founders directed their energies only on one manifestation of poverty — namely, the presence of working-class women on the streets, in houses of prostitution, and in gaols. While women like the "good hearted, but immoral,"[26] Lizzie G. may have been responding to the stresses and strains of marginalization (rather than intentionally bumping up against middle-class sensibilities of gender and sexuality), they surely offended the standards of respectability held dear to the Founders. Whereas the

Founders admitted that exposure to evil environments was the chief factor that contributed to a woman's downfall, they believed this exposure was a moral problem that could be solved by reforming individual characters. Such reformation, rather than dealing with the constraints of social structures, relied on women making "better choices," a view indicative of the responsibilization that accompanied the moral censuring of profligate young women during this era. The Founders argued, "We must never forget that many girls when 'out of place' have no homes to go to, and are driven, from want of funds to pay for respectable board, into wretched hovels, which are in most cases the haunts of vice."[27] The Founders acknowledged that social structures such as poverty compelled some women onto the streets, but refused to question the women's lack of economic and social opportunities.

Third, while the Founders inferred manifestations of poverty, crime, and destitution from women's appearance, dress, behaviour, and attitude, these conditions mattered insofar as they signified the moral character, not structural location, of each female. The Founders took such attributes as signs of individual failing rather than signals of structural circumstances. At least rhetorically, an inmate's past was deemed irrelevant once inside, as evidenced in the phrases "not a veil but a thick curtain" and "no allusion to past character" that guided the rules of management.[28] The rhetorical erasure of a woman's past history notwithstanding, censuring practices inside the Refuge were more likely rife with references to these women's "immoral" backgrounds.[29]

Finally, although the Founders emphasized that the door was open to "all fallen and degraded women," they did turn potential inmates away. In other words, there was a limited range of acceptability for potential inmates; some were found unreformable or beyond the pale of rescue. Reformability was equated with (among other criteria) degrees of whiteness, as the reformable, socially tolerable erring female was Irish or Scottish, while the unreformable Other was non-white or non-Anglo Celtic. Admission records show no Black or Aboriginal women (until the 1920s, when the state took over admission). The Founders did not question, but reproduced the gender, class, and racial order of the day.

Incorrigible Girl: The Erring Female as Punishable

Eugenics discourse in the early 1910s reshaped the representation of the erring female, as someone errant not only in soul and body, but also now in mind (cf. Galton 1907; McLaren 1990; Dowbiggin 1997). Eugenicists argued that female sexuality was the source of race degeneracy. Indeed, eugenics discourse reinforced race, class, and gender anxieties about female sexuality, influencing the creation of the medical category "feeble-mindedness" (not medically insane or an idiot, but simple). It also led to a proliferation of techniques for diagnosing and treating venereal disease, and brought about an increased attention to sexual promiscuity among females.[30] During this period of heightened social tensions, a little-used act of 1897 amended in the Revised Statues of the Female Refuges Act (1917) would come to have an impact on the Refuge.

In 1919 the lieutenant-governor of Ontario designated the Refuge as "an institution for the care of females" under the Female Refuges Act. Consequently, admission policies changed such that the Board no longer controlled who entered and how long they stayed. Clause 13 of the FRA stipulated: "No person shall be admitted to an Industrial Refuge except on warrant, signed by a Judge; or a transfer Warrant signed by the Inspector." The Refuge could no longer claim that the inmates were "voluntary prisoners." Legally committed to the institution, inmates were required by law to stay indefinitely to a maximum of two years.

To be criminalized under the FRA, girls and women did not have to commit infractions against the Criminal Code. Rather, their conduct, dress, disposition, character, and habits got them incarcerated insofar as they transgressed gender-appropriate cultural scripts. The concerns raised by child-savers, juvenile justice officials, and parents over working-class girls' wayward characters diverged from the anxieties that these same actors attached to delinquent boys. Then again, the subjection of girls to a sexual double standard was nothing new. Before the FRA, as feminist historians have observed, girls — unlike their male counterparts — were arrested and institutionalized for violations of virtuous feminine conduct and errant sexuality (Odem 1995; Myers 1999; Sangster 2000). With the FRA, girls needed only to betray their gender to warrant incarceration.

The Female Refuges Act was unique in the kinds of regulatory offences that it controlled — discursive constructions of errant sexuality such as "incorrigible," "unmanageable," "idle and dissolute" — and in its scope. The FRA constructed the erring female's sexuality by equating categories of idleness and dissoluteness with promiscuity and lax working-class morals (Sangster 1996). Not coincidentally, females of childbearing years were the main subjects of the Act's provisions. Under the FRA, any female between the ages of fifteen and thirty-five could be imprisoned for behaviours such as public drunkenness, promiscuity, and pregnancy out of wedlock. As Smart (1995: 55) poignantly puts it: "Women and girls who have sex outside of marriage are still regarded as promiscuous, or more colloquially as slags and sluts; unmarried women are still unable to legitimize their children without getting married." Anyone, such as a husband or parent, could swear before a magistrate as to the inappropriate behaviour of a wife or daughter. The burden rested upon the female, whose only recourse was to prove that she was not "unmanageable" or "incorrigible" — and few were successful in doing so.

The FRA appeared to invest non-state agencies and actors, such as the Refuge and the Founders, with the power to criminalize in the context of regulatory offences (Comack and Balfour 2004). Through the lens of censure, we can begin to see the expansive forms of the moral regulation of women and girls beyond the criminal justice system. Ontario's FRA, in place between 1897 and 1956, demonstrates that the power to criminalize is not restricted to criminal law. The legitimacy of the FRA, in effect, gave non-criminal offences the meaning and penal consequences of crimes, thereby criminalizing those under its purview. The authority of the FRA was not questioned until the Elizabeth Fry Society called for its repeal fifty years later.

That females incarcerated under the FRA did not have to have engaged in criminal activity suggests that something else was at stake — namely, reproducing a gendered, classist, and racialized social order. Like the Refuge, the FRA not merely upheld upper-middle-class standards of femininity, but was also a key part of state formation and the building of a white, male-dominated Canada. The FRA did not radically restructure the practices at the Refuge, which suggests that the legislation merely replicated widespread racist, class, and gendered biases that were already at work there.

FROM FRA TO PCHIP, OLD WHINE IN A NEW BOTTLE?

The censure of "erring female" found its shape, tone, and effect in the rhetoric and practices of the Refuge, but did not originate there. Today, the erring female has not disappeared but rather has emerged in different forms. For example, under Alberta's PCHIP Act (which came into force on February 1, 1999), police and child welfare officials are empowered to incarcerate children (read young females) "whose safety is at risk, but who will not voluntarily end their involvement in prostitution" (Alberta Government 1999). Although PCHIP emerged in the context of neo-liberalism and neo-conservatism decades after the FRA, both are provincial pieces of regulatory legislation that had and have the power to criminalize. In effect, both were and are justified through a discourse of protection. Under the guise of protection, today young women are being detained against their will, held on non-criminal charges, and otherwise punished for conditions that are not of their own choosing, as they were in the Refuge, before and after FRA. Their struggles (the experiences that led to their involvement with reformers or child welfare workers) are not just over their sexuality but also over their life chances, and are inexorably connected to race, class, and gender. In other words, the real problem is not incorrigibility or errant sexuality, but rather their marginalization.

Before the Refuge came under the FRA, race, class, and gender determined whether one was to be "kept" or a "keeper" inside the Refuge. These censures are still class-compounded and racialized today. Errant sexuality has been reinvented as sexual exploitation, but a similar response continues. Why? For what it sustains and replicates. The erring female incarnate represents girls and women who — by immorality, degradation, mental defect, intemperance (historically), or inadequate parenting, Fetal Alcohol Spectrum Disorder (FASD), promiscuity, drug abuse (today) or otherwise — deviate from the dominant standards of appropriate femininity. More importantly, the erring female censure works to reinforce and reproduce dominant power relations.

Despite shifting representations, the sexual double standard remains irrefutably transfixed at the centre of the good girl/bad girl dichotomy. Historically, the underlying social structural constraints (race, class, and gender inequalities) in the lives of criminalized girls and women were obscured from view under the FRA and within the Refuge. They go unchecked today because they are the very conditions that, in the great majority of cases, distinguish "good girls" from "bad girls" and work to sustain the ideological and social order.

NOTES

I want to thank Gillian Balfour, Elizabeth Comack, Bryan Hogeveen, and Bob Menzies for sharing their ideas, insights, and inquiries with me and for the enormous assistance such provided.

1. For more on Velma's case, see Daply 2002; Landsberg 2001; and Wong 2002.
2. For a similar point about the concentration of liminal "moral deviant" females in the anti-vice campaigns in Vancouver during the early 1940s, see Freund 2002.
3. *Annual Report*, Toronto Industrial Refuge, 1860, p.1.
4. Carol Smart (1995: 231) makes a similar point: "I think we do need to address this Woman of legal discourse... because actual women are affected by being mistaken for her, or for failing to conform to her and so on."
5. *Annual Report*, Toronto Industrial Refuge, 1860, p.1.
6. For a discussion of the boy problem see Hogeveen 2003. For a discussion of the girl problem see Strange 1995 and Alexander 1995.
7. For a contemporary example we need look no further than the recent deaths of numerous women in the sex trade in Western Canada and the police treatment of those deaths.

8. An Ordinance for Establishing a System of Police for the Cities of Quebec and Montreal, 2 Vict. (1) (1839), c. 2 (Lower Canada).
9. 32 and 33 Vict. (1869) c. 28, s.1 (Dominion of Canada).
10. Following England's Elizabeth Fry, the idea of providing separate reformatory institutions for such women first materialized on North American soil in the U.S. reformatory movement, which began in 1840 and peaked between 1870 and 1920. See Freedman 1981 and Rafter 1985a.
11. In addition to harsh criminal law, nineteenth-century legislators made other types of legislation to govern female sexuality. The Contagious Diseases Act, enacted in 1865, permitted detaining women with venereal disease. Though repealed in 1870 and not fully enforced, it was the beginning of a proliferation of responses to errant female sexuality.
12. See Peter Mullan's 2002 film, *The Magdalene Sisters*.
13. While the U.S. reformatory movement influenced the role that women came to play in the development of the Refuge, the Toronto Magdalen Asylum predated the Canadian government's establishment of the Andrew Mercer Reformatory for Females by twenty-one years. See Minaker 2003.
14. *Annual Report*, Toronto Industrial Refuge, 1870, p.8.
15. *Annual Report*, Toronto Industrial Refuge, 1880, p.7.
16. The Holy (Christian) Bible, New Testament, Luke 8:2.
17. Notably, they did not extend this ability to those they sought to help.
18. *Annual Report*, Toronto Industrial Refuge, 1872, p.7.
19. *Annual Report*, Toronto Industrial Refuge, 1868, p.7.
20. *Annual Report*, Toronto Industrial Refuge, 1868, pp.7, 14.
21. *Annual Report*, Toronto Industrial Refuge, 1870, p.9.
22. *Annual Report*, Toronto Industrial Refuge, 1893, p.8.
23. *Annual Report*, Toronto Industrial Refuge, 1860.
24. *Annual Report*, Toronto Industrial Refuge, 1862, p.7.
25. *Annual Report*, Toronto Industrial Refuge, 1877.
26. Case Records, Toronto Industrial Refuge, no date.
27. *Annual Report*, Toronto Industrial Refuge, 1864, p.8.
28. Rules for Management, Toronto Industrial Refuge, 1876.
29. Special thanks to Bob Menzies for helping me to clarify this point.
30. *Annual Report*, Toronto Industrial Refuge, 1909.

3. THE IN-CALL SEX INDUSTRY: CLASSED AND GENDERED LABOUR ON THE MARGINS

Chris Bruckert and Colette Parent

Prostitution has long (albeit inaccurately) been referred to as the world's oldest profession. It is striking, therefore, that the women employed in the sex industry have rarely been defined as workers — much less professionals — in either popular discourse or academic analysis. For the most part, until the 1960s, when symbolic interactionists shifted the focus (cf. Bryan 1965; Laner, 1974; Velarde 1975; Heyl 1977, 1979), positivist accounts of prostitution dominated the debate (cf. Lombroso 1890; Flexner 1920; Rolph 1955; Greenwald 1958; Glover 1969). In the 1970s new voices emerged. While radical feminists developed a gender-based analysis on the issue, sex workers in a number of countries — including Canada, the United States, England, and the Netherlands — started to organize, to speak about their work, and to defend their interests in groups such as CORP, COYOTE, PROS, and the Red Thread. In opposition to the work of radical feminists, who perceived prostitution as victimization, the discourses that emerged from women within the industry emphasized the activity as work, thereby denouncing the legally defined classifications and the conceptual baggage encapsulated in the term "prostitution."

The term "sex work," famously coined by Scarlet Harlot (Koyama 2002: 5), represents much more than a linguistic subtlety. It is a powerful concept that undermines normative assumptions as it compels reconsideration not only of the industry, but also of the relegation of sexuality to the private realm. It is a reframing that continues to be challenged from a number of different quarters. Radical feminists maintain that the trades are not work but sexual exploitation (Jeffreys 2005), while the conservative right moralizes the issue and asserts that the mechanics of sexual stimulation are so simple and natural that they require no specialized knowledge (Chapkis 1997: 71). At the same time a measure of resistance comes from particular sectors of the industry itself. Some workers — most explicitly erotic dancers — rather than embracing an alliance, reject the term. These workers reproduce hierarchical stratifications and actively oppose being categorized along with prostitutes (cf. Cario 1968; Cooke,

1987; McDonald, Moore, and Timoshking 2000; Smyth 2003).

In this chapter we draw on qualitative research to explore the implications, limits, and potential for conceptualizing prostitution as sex work — specifically by integrating labour theory into criminology to examine the often overlooked but long-established commercial in-call sex industry.[1] The term "in-call sex work" emerged from the research and speaks to the subjective importance of specific labour structures. In contrast to out-call workers (such as escorts), in-call workers provide sexual services to clients in establishments such as massage parlours, brothels, and dungeons.

A number of theoretical and political implications emerge when we think about women's work in the sex industry as classed, raced, and gendered labour. The labour structure, labour process, and experience of women workers in this sector are all key to this discussion, and so too are links to the work of working-class women labouring in other consumer services. Indeed, numerous points of convergence speak not only to the validity of framing sex work as "work," but also to the importance of rethinking women's labour in the new economy and destabilizing the private/public and sexuality/work dichotomies.

THEORIZING SEX WORK AS "WORK"

While feminist engagement with the question of prostitution dates back to the progressive era of the early twentieth century, it was in the 1970s, in the context of a broader rethinking of gender and patriarchy, that prostitution emerged as the symbol of the social, sexual, and economic domination of women by men.[2] Within this framework developed by radical feminists, prostitutes — and by extension pornography workers and erotic dancers — emerged as victims: of social structures, including discriminatory laws and their enforcement; of the socio-economic system, sex-role stereotypes, and patriarchy; of individual men as pimps and customers; of collective men who objectify women, express hatred for women, and experience a sense of power over all women through the "purchase" of one representative member; and of childhood sexual abuse, incest, and rape as well as more generally the circumstances of their lives (cf. Millet 1971; James 1977; Barry 1979; Wilson 1983; Jeffreys 1985; O'Hara 1985; Wynter 1987).

This perspective continues to resonate in recent writings that evoke powerful and disturbing images by likening sex work to slavery (Barry 1995; Carter 2004; Jeffreys 2004) and suicide (Lee 2004), and by asserting that sex work must be coerced and cannot be a matter of choice because "no one wants to rent out her vagina as a garbage can for hoards of anonymous men" (Hoigard and Finstad 1992: 180). Other scholars and activists, as part of a broader revisiting of second wave feminisms' white, middle-class and First World bias, seek to insert race, racialization, and racism into the analysis of sex work. For example, Sherene Razack (1998: 357) supports the understanding of prostitution as violence, but argues that such a monocausal analysis obscures how "prostitution reaffirms not only the hierarchies of gender but also of class, race and sexual orientation." Razack draws attention to the racialized spaces and bodies that are "marked for the purposes of prostitution" so that "prostitution is the zone of violence that keeps in place the respectability of others" (pp.374, 375).

Sex workers also draw into question racist industry practices (Stella 2003; Miller-Young 2005). However, unlike radical feminists, they maintain that even though some of them are operating outside of questions of choice and are compelled to engage in "desperation sex,"[3] the victim status is, in the main, inappropriate. These women speak of their identity as workers and, in some cases, as sex radicals.[4] In the 1990s some feminists started to reassess sex work (*Feminist Review* 2001), listen to industry workers, and integrate the workers' discourse into their analysis. The result is stimulating research that includes an examination of the labour challenges of sex workers (Chapkis 1997); anti-sex-industry moral panics (Brock 1998); myths and misconceptions about sex work (Shaver 1996; Benoit and Millar 2001); sex workers' identity management (Phoenix 2000); the history of erotic dance (Ross 2000); emotional labour and power relations in strip clubs (Price 2000; Wood 2000); dancers' narrative resistance strategies (Ronai and Cross 1998); the question of agency in sex work (Kesler 2002); the relation between sex work and sexual identity (Parent 2001); negotiations around intimacy (Frank 1998); the regulation of the escort trade (Lewis and Maticka-Tyndale 2000); and strip-club regulation (Lewis 2000; Bruckert and Dufresne 2002).

Our work here, which straddles labour theory and criminology, is situated within this emerging body of literature. Labour theory not only reflects the subject position of workers in the industry, but also allows us to step outside of the traditional criminological analysis of deviance to examine these jobs as jobs. A recognition of sex work as gendered and classed labour immediately places the industry and its workers within a dynamic socio-economic context transformed by the emergence of the global economy, the new technological revolution, and the shift of manufacturing to the Third World (Phillips 1997). In Canada not only do working-class women continue to be ghettoized in sales, service, and clerical occupations (Statistics Canada 2001a), but the post-industrial labour market is also increasingly characterized by "McJobs" (Ritzer 2004: 148): low-paid, deskilled, monotonous, and highly monitored service-sector work that offers workers neither satisfaction nor stability — nor, for that matter, a living wage (Ritzer 2004: 108–15). Moreover, at the same time another parallel trend is obvious. Women are increasingly in a precarious labour-market location — 41 percent of Canadian women are involved in non-standard labour arrangements[5] (Townson 2003: 1). The practice exacerbates marginality: women workers in this sector not only experience greater gender income disparity than do their counterparts in the traditional labour market, but are also still clustered in sales and service; and 75 percent of them work part-time (Hughes 1999: 2). It is within the context of these constraints and alternatives that women are "choosing" to work at McDonald's, in the retail sector — or in the sex industry.

The labour lens also allows us to shift our focus from structure to practices — or what workers *do* (Phillips 1997) — and positions us to consider the nature of the labour. It allows us to render skills and competencies visible, examine social and work relations, and reflect on how workers experience the physical, emotional, and sexual dimensions of their labour. This attention to grounded experience also speaks to specificity within the broadly defined sex industry, thereby providing an antidote to the tendency to unquestionably conflate the divergent labour practices of cam-girls,[6] peep-show attendants, phone-sex operators, street-sex workers, erotic dancers, and massage parlour/brothel employees under the rubric of "moral transgression."

While invaluable, labour theory in and of itself is incomplete — sex work may be work, but it is work that is marginal, stigmatized, and criminalized. It is imperative that we integrate into the analysis the unique configuration of challenges, problems, and difficulties confronted by women working in sectors of the labour market characterized by social, moral, and criminal justice regulation. By bringing criminology into labour theory, we can attend to the ways in which social and legal discourses and practices influence the organization of labour and the labour process, increase the danger and stress negotiated by workers, and shape the relations of workers to their social and personal worlds.

Before continuing, we also need to note that sex work, its organization, and how it is subjectively experienced are conditioned by the intersection of class, gender, and race. Race/ethnic stratifications have "always been one of the bedrock institutions of Canadian society embedded in the very fabric of our thinking, our personality" (Shadd 1991: 1). As numerous authors have demonstrated, Canadian society is characterized by discriminatory immigration policies, systemic racism, stereotypical media portrayals, and racist discourses that have resulted in a distribution of economic, social, and discursive resources that put visible minority Canadians generally and women in particular at a disadvantage (Henry et al. 2000; Dhruvarajan 2002). Put another way, race intersects with class and gender to condition women's choices and opportunities. It is certainly no coincidence that Aboriginal women are overrepresented in the street-sex trade and are therefore among the sex workers most vulnerable to criminalization and sexual and physical violence (Lowman 2000).

A recognition of racialization raises a number of important questions. How do racializing discourses and racialized spaces structure the in-call sex industry? How do racializing practices and discourses condition the experience of women of colour labouring in the sex industry? At a more theoretical level we can ask, how can we analytically separate race and class and produce an analysis that attends to intersectionality while avoiding the pitfalls of cumulative or essentialist approaches (Joseph 2006)? Or avoids reducing class exploitation to "a bit player" (Razack 1998: 355)? Unfortunately, since the issue of race did not emerge in our interviews this research sheds little light on these important questions.[7]

IN-CALL SEX WORK AS (CRIMINALIZED) WOMEN'S WORK

In-call work can be broadly defined as women providing sexual services in establishments. But the variety of these services — ranging from marginal to illegal — makes classification problematic. Some of the establishments we focused on in our project were massage parlours that offered non-contact erotic entertainment and visual titillation only (such as vibrator and hot-tub shows); others offered erotic massage and manual (and in some cases oral) stimulation; others were brothels in which massage was rare but complete sexual services were available. Still other businesses were dungeons, devoted to domination and submission and allowing clients to self-stimulate only. In short, we found considerable variety in work that falls under the rubric of in-call sex work.

That diversity is echoed in the women's perspectives. Some of the respondents had jobs that did not require them to have sex, and that aspect was a precipitating factor in their decisions to work in that sector of the industry. Jacqueline, a Toronto-area dungeon worker specializing in domination, explained: "*Escort work I never really considered. I, I don't know, I'm just, uh, not entirely comfortable with, with the idea of actually having sex.*" Other workers actively engaged with sexuality, and many took pleasure in the exploration of this element of the labour. As Crystal, a massage-parlour worker, told us: "*I love sex. I can really let myself go at work. I like to experience new things and try out new things.*"

The Regulatory Context

In Canada, although prostitution per se is not (and has never been) illegal, the industry and the workers are criminalized and sex workers are vulnerable to charges of communicating for the purposes of prostitution (section 213), procuring/living off the avails of prostitution (section 212), or falling under the common bawdy house provisions (section 210). Women working in massage parlours, brothels, or dungeons are most frequently criminalized under the bawdy house provisions, which stipulate that being an inmate (a resident or regular occupant) of a common bawdy house is an offence punishable by summary conviction. The Criminal Code defines a common bawdy house as "a place that is a) kept or occupied or b) resorted to by one or more persons, for the purposes of prostitution or the practice of acts of indecency" (section 197).[8]

In addition to the criminalization of their labour (or more specifically, of their labour site), some workers in the in-call sex industry (unlike their colleagues in the street trade, for example, but like erotic dancers) are also regulated in a number of municipalities through municipal by-laws pertaining to the body-rub industry. A body-rub is defined as the "kneading, manipulating, rubbing, massaging, touching, or stimulating by any means, of a person's body or part thereof, but does not include medical or therapeutic treatment" (City of Toronto 2000) — activities that could well be defined as prostitution under Canadian jurisprudence. In effect, we see a layering of regulation over criminalization, and while in principle these by-laws could create a safe and controlled space for workers, in practice they extend the regulation, impose additional levels of control, and offer few benefits.

Labour Structure

Despite the diversity of the in-call sex industry, we can identify broad organizational similarities. In general, workers are scheduled for relatively long shifts of ten to twelve hours, although some places have eight-hour shifts and others allow women to select either long or short shifts. In most establishments, workers are expected to do receptionist duties — which can include answering the phone, booking appointments, explaining (using more or less explicit code) the services offered, describing the workers, identifying and declining undesirable clients, and laundry duties. In addition to these tasks, the women are required to remain on the premises for the duration of their shifts, although they are free to fill their time according to their personal inclinations — sleeping, cooking, reading, studying, socializing.[9] The establishment sets rates, which in our sample varied from $40 for thirty minutes to $200 an hour. The workers receive 40 or 50 percent of these rates, an amount that supplements the income they generate through tips and/or the provision of "extras." The workers appreciated the potential revenues — they spoke of their ability to adequately support themselves (and in some cases their children) through sex work.

These women, whose highly variable incomes ranged from $40 to $800 per day, can be understood as own-account, self-employed workers operating within a fee for service structure without benefit of a guaranteed income. While independent vis-à-vis income, they are nonetheless dependent contractors to the extent that they are reliant on, and required to meet the expectations of, a single operator for the physical space, equipment, supplies, advertisement, and sometimes the services of support staff. These labour sites appear, then, to be consistent with the trend toward non-standard labour arrangements. While not all non-standard workers are vulnerable[10] (Saunders 2003), for working-class women this labour-market position is, generally speaking, precarious. In many cases the jobs operate as "no more than disguised forms of casualized wage-labour, often marked by dependency on capitalist employers through some sort of sub-contracting system" (Bradley 1996: 49).

The disadvantages of the labour structure notwithstanding, workers see some positive elements in addition to the income potential. Most of the women interviewed appreciated the flexibility that allowed them to integrate and manage the many components of their lives (school, children, art, for example). Of course, the desirability of non-standard labour arrangements must be understood within the context of the dismantling of the welfare state throughout the 1980s and 1990s, which has expanded poor women's burdens. Women are increasingly required not only to assume extra labour but also to organize their employment in a manner that allows them to meet their myriad obligations. Non-standard labour arrangements, including contract and self-account work, may therefore be embraced by women workers who need to satisfy increasing family and financial obligations as the state decreases its levels of support.

As independent workers, the women are in a paradoxical position. On the one hand, in-call sex workers in commercial establishments, including erotic dancers, aestheticians, massage therapists, and hair stylists, are managed as employees — even though they are not wage labourers in the traditional sense but are exchanging free labour and/or a percentage of their earnings for legal protection and access to the necessary legitimizing context, physical space, equipment, and technical support. In short, these workers are exploited in a Marxian sense of having "free" labour extracted and receiving less remuneration than the value that their labour adds to the product/service (Marx 1974/1859). On the other hand, as "disguised" employees, in-call sex workers are denied the security and access to statutory protection and legal recourse traditionally associated with employment. The precarious labour-market situation of in-call sex workers, like that of many other workers employed in non-standard labour arrangements, is at least in part a function of their exclusion from social security protection (such as Employment Insurance, Canadian Pension Plan), non-statutory benefits (health and dental plans, disability benefits, paid sick leave), and statutory rights (minimum wage, holiday and overtime pay, job protection, notice of termination) (Saunders 2003: 6).

The issue is even more complicated when their labour-market position intersects and interacts with stigma, marginality, and criminal law. Not only are workers vulnerable to criminalization, but the illicit status of their labour site (bawdy house) also de facto excludes them from gaining access not only to their rights as workers (for instance, health and safety, labour regulations/agreements) and professionals (to form provincially authorized associations, as do realtors or massage therapists), but also as citizens (to have police protection, for instance). Their position is simultaneously hyper-regulated and unregulated, with many implications for their well-being.

Labour Practices
Paying closer attention to labour practices and skills in commercial in-call sex work does a couple of things: first, it makes the invisible visible; and second, by exploring the intersections of class and gender we can highlight the role of criminalization and stigmatization in conditioning the work of women in this sector of the sex industry.

Like much service-sector employment, in-call sex work is physically demanding labour that requires stamina, physical strength, and endurance. In stark contrast to the discourse suggesting that sex work is somehow "natural" and therefore not really work (and certainly not skilled work), our research found that success in this area is contingent on a particular and not uncomplicated set of skills. One worker, Crystal, explained that in her job at a massage parlour, "*You learn every day and learn new things every day.*" Like waitresses, hair stylists, and other women employed in the service sector, successful in-call sex workers have to be sociable, patient, courteous, and polite, and they have to be capable of dealing with a variety of people. They must present a pleasant and professional demeanour to clients.

Success also calls for a number of more specialized prerequisites, including creativity, an open attitude toward sexuality, and a positive as-sessment of men. In addition, workers must have basic anatomic/sexual knowledge, be able to master massage and sexual techniques, create and maintain an erotic and pleasing presentation of self, discern and respond to clients' (often non-verbalized) needs or wishes, and promote or sell their service. Crystal and Maud, another massage parlour worker, explained that their work necessitated performance skills not only to "*become the whore at work*" but also to put "*on a mask and play a certain character.*" They need to be able to improvise a role play based on their reading of the expectations of clients or on the (sometimes detailed) "scripts" of clients.

Women who work in domination require additional knowledge. They must be trained to use the equipment in a safe and effective manner as well as know how to clean and care for it. They must also learn where to strike without leaving marks or doing damage. They need to know anal training techniques, recognize code words (such as yellow for caution, red for stop), and know how to instruct clients. As one of them, Anaïs, noted, providing domination services in a dungeon is a job that requires both openness and insight: "*It's more than just being aggressive and angry. It's about understanding where the bottom's [the client receiving domination services] coming from.*" According to Charlotte, another dun-geon worker, this specialization also requires finely tuned sensitivity so that the worker is "*able to gauge, you know, how light or heavy they [the clients] are, 'cause for a lot of them it's just visual.... They think they're very heavy into it, but they're not really.*" Charlotte also spoke about the need to "*contact your anger*" when necessary. Her strategy was to recall her experience, many years earlier, of being raped by three men: "*That's how I get into the roles sometimes if I'm having trouble with it.*" Some workers, like Anaïs, can, despite being bound and "submissive," retain control and "*top the scene from the bottom.*"

In-call sex work is not only physically demanding skilled labour, but can also be dangerous. This is, of course, characteristic of many work-ing-class jobs that — computerization and automation notwithstanding

— extract a physical toll from workers (Shostak 1980; Houtman and Kompier 1995: 221). Here, however, we see a particular cluster of risks. Workers in the in-call sex industry risk exposure to infectious diseases (including, but not restricted to, sexually transmitted diseases). Additionally, a number of respondents spoke of the ever present potential for clients to be sexually and/or physically aggressive. Workers develop strategies to minimize these risks. In the case of the health risks, their tactics include the use of condoms, gloves, and lubricants, the visual inspections of clients' sexual organs, washing hands with antiseptic soap, and disinfecting equipment. They can mediate the potential for physical/sexual aggression through measures such as identity checks, security cameras, in-house alarm systems, the proximity of other workers or sympathetic neighbours, and their own labour practices (including the refusal to participate in submission, abstaining from alcohol or drugs at work, carrying pepper spray, and creating a "virtual" bouncer).[11]

A number of respondents evoked the language of gendered sensibility when they spoke of refusing men whom they "intuitively" perceived to be threatening — an ability based on the knowledge of experience, which allows the workers to perceive and interpret numerous minute signs of potential danger. Karen, reflecting on her own experience as a massage parlour employee, noted that workers are *"thinking all the time; you gotta be quick in case any of [the clients] try to pull something on you."* Women who offer submission services are in a particularly vulnerable position. The implications of a client's incompetence, ignorance, or maliciousness range from bruises to welts to permanent organ damage.

Sex work can be emotionally demanding on a number of different levels. Like other direct-service employees — including waitresses (Paules 1991) and domestics (Salzinger 1991) — sex workers must retain a positive self-concept in the face of clients who, according to Jacqueline, a dungeon employee, *"don't seem to realize that you're, you're another person."* Moreover, Angelica explained that sometimes her clients at the massage parlour *"assume I'm really stupid... like, I'm pretty much an object or a service."* The women must also cope with the valorization of youth and socially constructed beauty that permeates society and is played out in the rejection of some workers. Moreover, like women workers in other service sectors of the labour market (including bartenders and hair stylists), in-call sex workers also sometimes have to deal with manipulative clients who, to procure extra services, pout, nag, flatter, or threaten to take their business elsewhere. In the sex industry, however, the stakes are high and the process is complicated by the ever-present spectre of criminalization. Not only are some clients seeking sexual services that the woman is not prepared to offer and that may endanger her (sex without a condom, for instance), but she is operating in a non-institutionally structured space in which the rules and expectations are, for the most part, either not clearly defined or difficult to enforce.

At other times workers are required to engage in emotional labour (Hochschild 1983). Some clients seek more than sexual services; they seek personal intimacy. Crystal explained that as a worker in a massage parlour, "*You got to be sweet and all that. You gotta really play the role.*" Occasionally clients are seeking companionship. Jade, who works in a brothel, recalled her experience: "*There was a guy, seventy-six years old, who took two hours at a time. I took off my top but kept my bra on and we played cards... we drank wine. The guy was all alone and his kids didn't see him.... Some I've seen for five years and we did nothing.*"[12] This aspect of the work requires workers to engage in "deep acting," re-creating personal experiences to "induce or suppress feeling in order to sustain the outward countenance that produces the proper state of mind in others" (Hochschild 1983: 7) in a commercial setting. This demanding expectation is hardly unique to sex workers; arguably, it is increasingly a job requirement of women working in numerous other areas of the service sector, including beauticians (Sharma and Black 2001), flight attendants (Hochschild 1983), and erotic dancers (Wood 2002).

Unlike some of those other sectors, however, in-call sex workers are positioned to negotiate the nature and extent of their emotional labour. In a brothel, a dungeon, or, for that matter, a beauty salon, clients receive a technical service (intercourse, domination, a pedicure) and may anticipate additional intimacy and interpersonal interaction. This condition is not, however, an inherent one within the institutional confines of the service encounter. It follows that the workers at these kinds of sites are left with the choice of whether or not they will engage in emotional labour to improve the service encounter — and they might choose to do so either out of a personal inclination or to secure a regular clientele.[13]

In-call sex work thus requires workers to vigilantly guard against physical and/or sexual danger, to maintain their personal boundaries at the same time as they create an environment of intimacy, and to strive to realize the sexual (and sometimes interpersonal) fantasy of their clients. Not surprisingly, as Wendy Chapkis (1997: 79) points out, an ability to distinguish between the work domain and the personal realm is imperative for maintaining emotional equilibrium. Catherine explained that as a worker in an erotic establishment: "*You really have to be mentally strong.... You have to dissociate from your private life. You have to see it as a job."* Many sex workers are able to draw on their professionalism (Chapkis 1997: 77) to mediate the emotional expectations of clients. Angelica described her work in a massage parlour: *"You can actually, like, give someone what they need emotionally but still be disconnected. It's a pretty amazing thing.... But it's not taking a lot out of me. Like, it's my work."*

The stresses of the demands of the job are further exacerbated by the illegal nature and stigmatic assumptions of outsiders. The illegality means that workers are susceptible to charges under section 210 of the Canadian Criminal Code, which necessitates continual vigilance, assessment of clients, and self-monitoring because, as Angelica pointed out, *"One day you could say the wrong thing to the wrong person."* One of the more disconcerting findings of our study was the lack of accurate legal knowledge on the part of most of the workers. As a result of misconceptions, women took ineffectual precautionary measures (such as not touching the money prior to engaging in the sex act and refraining from intercourse).

Ultimately the women's vulnerability to arrest denies workers potential resources in their negotiations with clients. Among other things, the fear of denunciation by disgruntled customers complicates workers' maintenance of their personal boundaries. Moreover, women are hesitant to turn to the police for protection or to report violent clients. Karen, a massage parlour worker, noted: *"It would feel a lot safer [with decriminalization] because you'd know that if anything happened, people would listen to you and there'd be a place to go. You wouldn't have to worry about going to jail or telling a cop. Maybe people wouldn't try stuff as much as they do."* Criminalization also denies workers the ability to negotiate labour conditions with their employers through professional organizations or organized labour action, or by evoking their statutory labour rights.

Moreover, although numerous workers — including morticians, custodians, and some sectors of the sales force — labour in stigmatized occupations, when they leave the labour site women in the in-call sex industry must cope with the condemnation that accompanies the stigma of "whore" (Pheterson 1989). Annabelle, a massage parlour worker, recognized: *"It is not easy to fight against a whole population and against ideas so deeply entrenched in people's heads."* According to Karen, who also works in a massage parlour, this stigma necessitates that a woman *"not let it get you down and take your work home with you.... Don't view yourself the way society views you.*" Consequently, some workers seek to isolate themselves from public censure by closeting their occupational location, creating fictitious jobs, and separating their work and private lives (including not associating with other sex workers).

Unfortunately, these tactics also mean a lack of insider support. Angelica, who had been working in a massage parlour for five months, found that her counterculture friends were carefully non-judgmental. Nonetheless, she bemoaned her lack of a network:

> *It's hard to get a certain type of support. Like, people who don't do it are always like well "just stop doing it," "why are you doing it if it's hard?" It's like, well everything is hard! You know? Like, if you're working, you're making six dollars an hour at a coffee shop, you're gonna have to deal with people you hate, but that's part of your job.*

In practice, it appears that workers must negotiate and maintain a balance between what emerges as competing objectives of anonymity and support. While workers are, for the most part, able to find a personally suitable space on the spectrum of anonymity/no support at one end to strong social support/vulnerability to public and private condemnation at the other, the conditions nonetheless increase the day-to-day stress, and, regardless of any compromise position adopted, the women are left in a precarious situation. Moreover, the experience of stress is intensified when the worker lacks social support in the home (Levi, Frankenhauser, and Gardell 1986: 55). As Meg Luxton and June Corman (2001) point out, a lack of support has particular relevance for women whose role and labour force challenges may not be fully acknowledged within social and familial areas — which is certainly the case for sex workers, whose job is frequently not even acknowledged to be work.

Still, despite the myriad challenges and stressors confronted by these women workers, all of our respondents identified positive aspects of their jobs. While the financial benefits that allowed them to participate in the social sphere were foremost among these, they also identified a number of other benefits, including flexibility, free time, and a pleasant, relaxed work environment.[14] Moreover, they also noted a wide range of intrinsic rewards. Anaïs saw her job in a dungeon as being *"entertaining, it's fun sometimes and it's very mundane, but you know usually you don't know what to expect so it's kind of fun. It's exciting."* Some women appreciated the skills they develop. For Maud, a massage parlour worker, this included learning *"how to take control and assert limits."* Others highlighted pleasurable social and/or sexual interactions with clients. For Anaïs it was also "*a legit way of expressing resistance against society.*" Similarly, for Angelica, who has experienced sexual harassment throughout her life, the work allows her to "*manipulate this [sexism] for my own benefit.... I feel like I'm beating the man, you know? I literally get to beat the man!*" Perhaps these features are all the more striking in contrast to the monotonous, repetitive, and unsatisfying alternatives readily available to young working-class women — the "McJobs" (Ritzer 2004).

THE COMPLEXITIES OF SEXUALIZED COMMERCE

We are left, then, with the question of the suitability of the term "sex work" — and the critiques from radical feminists as well as from the conservative right that the sex industry does not constitute work, either because it is sexual exploitation or because the prerequisite competencies are natural and therefore do not constitute skills. Is the concept, as Sheila Jefferys (2005) maintains, simply an attempt to make the industry more palatable through "euphemistic neutral terms"?

Stepping outside of normative assumptions, we can listen to workers such as Lea, who has a job in a massage parlour and asserted: "*It's a service that I offer.*" We can make links to "reputable" jobs by applying a labour analysis. In doing this a number of commonalities emerge. On a structural level these jobs are consistent with the broader trend toward women's increased participation in service-sector employment and nonstandard labour arrangements that positions women workers outside of the stability and protection traditionally associated with employment. When we shift to labour process, we see that like other working-class women's work in the consumer service sector, the job of sex-trade workers requires the application of (rarely acknowledged) skills,[15] is physically demanding, and potentially dangerous and stressful, and requires workers to undertake emotional labour. It is certainly not an easy job. In the course of their workday, workers must confront and negotiate a myriad of challenges and stressors. Moreover, many workers in the commercial in-call sex industry who labour under conditions of third-person control are, in a Marxian sense, exploited workers.

In light of these commonalities, the pivotal question becomes: does the sexual component mark the industry as being outside the framework of labour? Despite the challenges introduced by the sex radical discourse (Califia 1994; Johnson 2002), the private/public and sex/labour dichotomies continue to be so firmly embedded in our consciousness that the term "sex work" is virtually an oxymoron. This approach is reproduced in labour studies in which work-site sexuality is either invisible or an inherently harmful expression of patriarchal power that renders the atmosphere oppressive (Hearn and Parkin 1995; Lobel 1993).

Arguably, this positioning is highly problematic. On the one hand, "Sexuality is a structuring process of gender" (Adkins 1992: 208), and gender and sexuality are central "to *all* workplace power relations" (Pringle 1988: 84). The traditional skills that women are required to bring to the labour market include the ability to assume an attractive "made-up" appearance so that "part of the job for women consists of looking good" (Adkins 1992: 216). However, more than just a good appearance is required. Increasingly, the prerequisite presentation of self is sexualized so that much of the labour that working-class women undertake has a visible sexual subtext and necessitates that workers negotiate a sexualized labour terrain. On the other hand, our sexuality — in our private and professional lives — is subjectively experienced, and we must take care to acknowledge not only that class may condition the approach and meaning ascribed to sexuality (Aronowitz 1992: 62),[16] but also that there are a variety of positions vis-à-vis labour-site sexuality that speak to a spectrum of engagement. For some working-class women, the distinction between sex work and other consumer service work may be one of degree and explicitness. This is a connection that Angelica, a massage parlour worker, made when she reflected on her previous labour experiences:

> *I've been a cocktail waitress and that was sex work too, but it's just over the table sex work that the government supports.... Basically, you're hired 'cuz you're pretty. Start there. Then... the money you make is based on the shifts that you work, the shifts you get. So in order to get the good shifts you have to sell the most drinks. In order to sell the most drinks you have to be flirtatious. So, it's totally sex work.*

In short, the many points of convergence support the conceptualization of women employed in sexualized commerce as working-class women workers in the new economy, and they lend support to the linguistic shift towards the term "sex work." The illegal/illicit status of the labour not only raises the spectre of criminalization, but also facilitates an additional level of exploitation in that it inhibits workers from gaining access to their statutory labour rights as well as their rights as citizens. Moreover, many of the challenges and stressors of the job emerge not from the labour itself, but are a by-product of discourses of immorality, the lack of recognition as workers, limited social and interpersonal support, a lack of police or legal protection, criminalization, and, of course, stigma.

The sex industry's long tradition of adapting both to changing market, social, and moral conditions and technological innovations[17] has resulted in increasingly varied industry practices and structures, which in turn have opened up the industry to new workers (Bruckert 2002). Today a sex worker may be a stay at home mother who responds to erotic telephone calls (Flowers 1998) or a high-school student who types erotic messages on the Internet and exchanges pictures for gifts (Robinson 2004). She may be a secretary subsidizing her wages by working as an erotic dancer two nights a week (DERA forthcoming), a woman on social assistance who makes ends meet through street-sex work (Benoit and Millar 2001), or a full-time worker, either independent or under third-person control, offering sexual services in a brothel or hotel room. All of this diversity not only destabilizes stereotypical assumptions about sex workers, but also highlights the problems of an occupational classification that encompasses such a range of labour structures and processes.

The problem, then, lies not with the term "sex work," but with the imposed limits embedded in its application. On the one hand, the term continues to situate the trades in question outside of women's work, obscuring how the jobs inhabit a particular location on the axis of sexual labour and emotional labour characteristic of much women's work. On the other hand, it fails to capture the complexity of "sex industry" labour practices, in which sexuality is but one component. The solution may not be to abandon the particular vocabulary but to destabilize the dichotomies by inserting the private, the sexual, and the intimate into the language of labour. In this manner, we can develop a more nuanced and inclusive analytic framework of sexualized commerce to make sense of the labour of women workers — both in and outside of the "trades."

NOTES

1. For this discussion we draw on empirical data from a qualitative research project on the in-call sex industry that we undertook in 2002 (Parent and Bruckert 2005). The research was guided by the feminist commitment to methodological approaches that centre the voices and experiences of women. Accordingly, the questions we posed were designed to illicit information regarding labour structure and process, and how that work is subjectively experienced. The research, funded by the Law Commission of Canada, was a collaborative effort of Stella (a sex-worker rights organization in Montreal) and the authors. Using snowball sampling, we conducted a series of fourteen in-depth semi-structured interviews (in French and English) lasting between one and three hours during the summer and fall of 2002. The women were all employed, or at least very recently employed, in the in-call sex industry in Montreal (eight of them) and Toronto (six). Ranging in age from twenty-one to forty, and with between four months to seven years of experience, the respondents

represented a diverse cross-section of industry workers and offered rich insights.

2. The initial analyses that situated the trade within questions of class, gender, and economic vulnerability were quickly displaced by the concern about the white slave trade (Walkowitz 1980; Rosen 1982; DuBois and Gordon 1983). Within this framework, these feminists started to demonize individual men as threatening to "innocent womanhood" and campaigned for greater regulation and laws. The attempts by turn of the century feminists to help prostitutes — all the while condemning prostitution — had disastrous consequences for women in the trade (Rosen 1982: 102). For an overview of later feminist positions on prostitution, see Tong 1984, Järvinen 1993, and Parent 1994.

3. The concept of "survival sex," coined to theorize the experience of youth who exchange sex for shelter, clothes, food, and/or drugs, while interesting, is problematic. Certainly some women are "choosing" to work in the trade in the context of very limited and often unpleasant choices, but that does not mean that sex work is more of a survival tactic than is working at one of the "McJobs" (Ritzer 2004). That said, some women are compelled (or perceive themselves to be compelled) to employ sex by their abusive partners, their substance or drug use, their fear of deportation, or their abject poverty. For these women, prostitution is not sex work — in the sense of a job — but rather one of a number of income-generating activities in which they participate. As we have documented elsewhere (Parent and Bruckert forthcoming), the issue of substance use/abuse is key. While many women workers in the sex industry are not drug consumers and others maintain a professional labour relationship to the industry despite being consumers of illicit substances, there is a small minority of women for whom sex work is intertwined with their drug consumption patterns and who will, unlike the women whose relationship to the industry is one of work, exchange sex for drugs.

4. See Aline 1987; CORP 1987. Reinserting sexuality into the debate, these workers challenge the appropriation of sexuality of women by men and maintain their right to control their bodies, and to define their sexuality outside both traditional moral discourse and the feminist discourse that associates feminine sexuality with love and warmth. In short, these sex workers are part of a broader rethinking of sexuality as a contested terrain, the site and source of subversion (McClintock 1993; Chapkis 1997).

5. Non-standard labour arrangements are relationally understood to standard employment — which is defined as the "employment of individuals for wages and salaries by a single firm, where individuals work full time on the employer's premises, and expect (and are expected) to be employed for an indefinite period of time" (Canada 1999: 2) — and includes part-time, seasonal, short-term contracts, temporary employment, and own-account work.

6. "Cam-girls" exchange revealing photos for "gifts" with individuals they have contacted through the Internet (Robinson 2004).

7. See Bannerji 2005 for a discussion of pitfalls of feminist anti-race theorizing. That our interviews did not raise the issue of race may have been a function of the racial composition of our sample — the majority of women where white (twelve), one woman was Asian, and another Black.

8. Canadian jurisprudence specifies that the definition of "prostitution" does not require actual sexual intercourse, nor need there be physical contact. This very broad definition has led to convictions under section 210 of the Criminal Code of women who worked in strip clubs where dancers gyrated on the laps of fully clothed patrons

(*Caringi* 2002); massage parlours that offered full body massages (including manual masturbation) but no oral, vaginal, or anal sexual intercourse (*Brandes* 1997); and sado-masochism dungeons in which neither intercourse nor masturbation was offered.

9.   The women working in one establishment (a dungeon) were (unless they booked off for a set period) expected to be available to be paged seven days a week, twelve hours a day in addition to working one receptionist shift per week without pay. With the exception of this receptionist shift, they were not required to be on-site.

10. There are also highly skilled and well-compensated workers such as researchers, contract computer programmers, self-employed business people, and marketing consultants who operate non-standard labour arrangements.

11. A number of establishments did employ security personnel; but even when no such individual was on-site the women workers sometimes led clients to believe that this was the case.

12. The interview quotations from Jade, Catherine, and Annabelle have been translated by the authors.

13. By contrast, for dancers in "straight" strip clubs, where physical contact is prohibited, the technical service oftentimes is the interaction so that emotional labour becomes a job requirement (Bruckert 2002; Wood 2002).

14. Whether or not a job meets middle-class standards of "interesting" or "rewarding," there may be non-economic benefits. It may offer women social contacts and friendships (MacDonald and Connelly 1986: 66), and recognition of their labour that is not afforded full-time homemakers (Reiter 1991: 106). Greater economic contribution can also be correlated to power within the family (Feree 1984: 75), independence, status, and a sense of self-worth and self-esteem (Penney 1983: 21).

15. That skills are largely dismissed or rendered invisible is not unique to in-call sex workers, but characterizes many working-class women's jobs. It does, however, affirm once again the relative and subjective nature of what are defined as skills. Class and gender continue to be associated with skills in complex ways (Gaskell 1986).

16. For example, sexual interaction may not necessarily be understood as sexual harassment (Westwood 1984). In fact, ethnographic accounts offer a very different image of such practices as sexually explicit shop-floor banter (Barber 1992: 81). Furthermore, positioned to recognize the costs of capitalism and patriarchy, working class women may deconstruct the advantages afforded by an asexual presentation of self (Feree 1990).

17. For example, the trajectory of strip clubs and the transformation of dancers from performers to service workers speak to the intersection of broader market forces and marginal labour. Between 1973 and 1995, the work of erotic dancers was "de-professionalized"; workers went from being salaried performance artists to service-sector employees labouring for tips (Bruckert 2002). In a similar vein, the sex industry's use of print media, telephones, and the computer speaks to its adaptability. Certainly, Internet technology has had a major impact, transforming both existing practices (many escorts now advertise and interact with clients via the Internet) and facilitating the emergence of new practices (such as cam-girls).

4. SURVIVING COLONIZATION: ANISHINAABE IKWE GANG PARTICIPATION

Nahanni Fontaine

> If you have come here to help me you are wasting your time.
> But if you have come because your liberation is connected to
> mine, then we can work together.
> — Lilla Watson, a Murri woman who has been active in the
> struggle of Aboriginal peoples in Australia.

In June 2003 several body parts were found along the shoreline of the Red River in Winnipeg, They were quickly identified as belonging to Felicia Solomon Osborne, a sixteen-year-old girl from the Norway House Cree Nation. Few media sources bothered to cover this story. Those that did stated that Felicia Solomon had gang ties and had been working the streets.

The murder of Felicia Solomon raises questions about the lived experiences of Aboriginal women — Anishinaabe Ikwe — and their participation in gangs. Ultimately, however, the question becomes what do we need to learn as a community about Aboriginal women and girls and the contemporary context in which they find themselves? To address such a question, we need to hear from them.

At a gathering in the summer of 2003, several organizations — Southern Chiefs' Organization (SCO), Mother of Red Nations Women's Council of Manitoba (MORN), and Ka Ni Kanichihk Inc. — resolved to reach out to Anishinaabe Ikwe in order to grasp and appreciate their standpoint with respect to gangs. It was agreed that the participants in the study ought to be interviewed in a culturally appropriate, safe manner. There was also a consensus that the study should be pursued and presented from within an Aboriginal framework because there is now little indigenously driven research or analysis on the issue. As both the Manitoba Aboriginal Justice Inquiry (Hamilton and Sinclair 1991) and the Royal Commission on Aboriginal Peoples (1996) recommended, all research and program development as it relates to Aboriginal peoples must be pursued by and for Aboriginal peoples so that it is more effective, responsive, and culturally sensitive to the needs of the Aboriginal collective.

My purpose here is to report on some of the findings of this study. To be clear, this chapter is not about "Aboriginal gangs." That is to say, I will not be discussing the creation, structure, hierarchy, and activities of "the gang" as an Aboriginal phenomenon. No. This chapter concerns Aboriginal women's and girls' particular experiences in relation to the gang. That being said, we require a broader context in which we can situate the participants of the study, one that deconstructs the traditional discourse offered to account for the phenomenon of the gang. Simply put, Aboriginal gangs are not what the dominant white society socially constructs them — a malignant and deviant thorn in the side of a so-called upstanding, productive, middle-class, Christian civilization. Rather, Aboriginal gangs are the result of the colonial experience and context in contemporary Canada.

Edward Said's work on post-colonialism offers a theoretical foundation for this analysis. What Said called "Orientalism," as he pointed out, "operates in the service of the West's hegemony over the East primarily by producing the East discursively as the West's inferior 'Other,' a manoeuver which strengthens — indeed, even partially constructs — the West's self-image as a superior civilization" (cited in Moore-Gilbert 1997). Similarly, the work of Gayatri Chakravorty Spivak (1987) contains the important insight that in the struggle to de-colonize, women's voices, contexts, and issues are structurally marginalized and frequently erased both by the colonial mainstream and within the indigenous collective. The colonial mainstream all but negates the views, beliefs, traditions, and experiences of indigenous women. Indigenous male leaders ask or demand that their women put so-called "women's issues" on the back burner in the interests of collective de-colonization. They often seem to believe that a focus on women's issues will have a divide and conquer effect.

Clearly, both Said and Spivak offer valuable insights about the context, space, and experience of Anishinaabe Ikwe gang participation. Contemporary indigenous research efforts that fail to apply a post-colonial theoretical foundation — while touting the supposed benefits of their version of so-called "truth" — simply continue to support the subjugation and oppression of one segment of our society.

THE COLONIAL EXPERIENCE

Since 1991 Manitoba, and particularly the City of Winnipeg, has apparently seen a dramatic rise in the establishment and activity of "Aboriginal gangs."[1] A report released by the Royal Canadian Mounted Police "D" Division, Manitoba, in 2004 stated:

> The last two decades have seen numerous street gangs rise within both urban and rural areas of Manitoba. Although there are not any strictly aboriginal street gangs, aboriginal membership in several gangs is quite dominant. Some of the major aboriginal-based street gangs in effect, per se, are the Manitoba Warriors, the Native Syndicate and the Indian Posse. Alliances and rivalries are sometimes formed between these gangs, other street gangs and even the Outlaw Motorcycle Gangs in order to control the drug trade, prostitution and other illegal activities.
>
> Recruitment of gang members is an on-going process that is done by most gangs in order to build the gang in both numbers and strength. Once focusing on the major urban centres, recruitment has now filtered into the aboriginal communities of Manitoba. A growing scenario consists of a member from the community being arrested and then later incarcerated. Upon incarceration, this person is then recruited into the gang. Some are compelled to join a gang within the correctional centre in order to ensure their protection for fear of being targeted by the gangs within the centre. Others join to belong, because they know someone in the gang or are lured by the thought of quick money and the gang lifestyle. Upon their release, they return to their communities and begin gang activity there, including recruitment of new members. (McLeod 2004)

Similarly, the 2004 *Annual Report on Organized Crime in Canada* of Criminal Intelligence Service Canada asserted:

> Aboriginal-based street gangs are generally involved in opportunistic, spontaneous and disorganized street-level criminal activities, primarily low-level trafficking of marijuana, cocaine and crack cocaine and, to a lesser extent, methamphetamine. The gangs are also involved in prostitution, break-and-enters, robberies, assaults, intimidation, vehicle theft and illicit drug debt collection. Although the gangs' capability to plan and com-

mit sophisticated or large-scale criminal activities is low, their propensity for violence is high, posing a threat to public safety. (Criminal Intelligence Service Canada 2004)

These reports share in common an interpretation of the gang as a deviant subculture centred on criminal activity, a subculture that persists because of the attraction of the gang lifestyle to its members. What many, if not all, such reports fail to recognize is the historical and contemporary context that precipitated the advent of Aboriginal gangs. Gangs did not arise owing to the "gang lifestyle," as some commentators naively argue and try to convince the general public. Aboriginal gangs surfaced, developed, and organized in response to the reality and experience of colonization and its perpetual legacy in our daily lives. Aboriginal gangs are the product of our colonized and oppressed space within Canada — a space fraught with inequity, racism, dislocation, marginalization, and cultural and spiritual alienation (Razack 2002). It is a space of physical and cultural genocide that continues to exist even at this very moment.

From first contact with Europeans, indigenous peoples' cultures, political systems, economies, lands, and traditional social constructions and mores have been systematically and methodically attacked. In this respect, there is nothing "post-colonial" about Aboriginal peoples' experience. They continue to endure dislocation, de-culturalization, ecocide, and forced assimilation. Indeed, the question often posed by outsiders is "why can't you people just leave that in the past?" Without a doubt, colonialism is alive and well in Canada, and remains an insidious force permeating every aspect of the lives of the original inhabitants and rightful owners of this land.

An important illustration of the lingering effects of colonialism is the altered power relations between the sexes within our indigenous societies. Traditionally, Anishinaabe Ikwe's roles and responsibilities encompassed every aspect of community life. As life-givers and primary caregivers, women were respected and had a significant role in the decision-making processes of the community. Social relations were of an equal nature and did not involve notions that one sex was superior to the other (Gunn Allen 1992; Anderson 2000). Unfortunately, as a result of the introduction of Christianity and forced Christian marriages, incorporation into a wage economy, residential schools, and the introduction of alcohol, Aboriginal men's and women's roles changed significantly.

As Carol Devens argues, "The friction between men and women is in fact the bitter fruit of colonization" (Devens 1992: 5). This is not to imply that gendered roles and responsibilities would have remained static and unchanging, but that colonialism directed their development in ways that indigenous peoples would not have chosen. As a consequence of colonial processes, Anishinaabe Ikwe are doubly victimized; they are disempowered and oppressed within both the Euro-Canadian mainstream and the indigenous collective. Anishinaabe Ikwe have become what one prominent Winnipeg community member calls "collaterals of war." Leslie Spillett, the provincial speaker for the Mother of Red Nations Women's Council of Manitoba, suggests, "In most wars women and children are collateral damage, and we can extend this concept in which 'gangs' constitute, within the Canadian colonial context, external/internal warfare whereby women and children are both victimized" (personal communication, Oct. 20, 2005).

Surely, one contributing factor toward gang involvement for Anishinaabe Ikwe is the abject poverty faced by our communities. Darren Lezubski, Jim Silver, and Errol Black (2000: 39) commented on the "astonishingly high" poverty rates for Aboriginal peoples, particularly in inner-city Winnipeg:

> They are so high, in fact that they ought to bring shame not only to the City of Winnipeg but also to Manitoba and Canada. Almost two-thirds of all Aboriginal households in Winnipeg — 64.7 percent — have incomes below the poverty line; more than four-fifths of Aboriginal households in Winnipeg's inner city — 80.3 percent — are below the poverty line.

Anishinaabe Ikwe leaving poor socio-economic conditions in their home communities (First Nation reserves and Métis communities) often come to the city alone or with their families in search of equitable opportunities and a better standard of living, but instead find a dominant Euro-Canadian mainstream society culturally alien and the antithesis to their own experiences. Most, if not all, indigenous newcomers to the urban environment face myriad racist, alienating, and patronizing realities firmly entrenched within mainstream social institutions.

The second contributing factor is the loss or interruption of indigenous cultural identity. The Royal Commission on Aboriginal Peoples (1996) noted that a fundamental component in Aboriginal youth joining gangs is the loss or dislocation of traditional Aboriginal culture. John Berry, who conducted interviews with Aboriginal peoples on the notion of cultural identity for the Royal Commission on Aboriginal Peoples, argued that "behavioural expression" among the Aboriginal population was the most "concrete feature" of their sense of identity (Berry 1994). Looking at the use of an Aboriginal language and the "daily activities related to one's culture (e.g., language, social relations, dress, food, music, arts, and crafts)" as indicators of behavioural expression, Berry (1994) found:

> Of the total adult population (aged 15 years and over), 65.4% of North American Indians on Reserve (NAI), 23.1% of NAI off Reserve, and 17.5% of Métis were able to use their Aboriginal language; 74.6% of Inuit were able to do so. There is a similar results [sic] for children (aged 5 to 14 years), but with even lower levels: 44.3%, 9.0%, 4.9% and 67.0% respectively. For participation in traditional Aboriginal activities, the pattern is repeated. For adults, the participation rates were 65.2%, 44.8%, 39.8% and 74.1%; and for children, they were 57.5%, 39.5%, 28.7% and 70.2%.

Berry interpreted these data to mean that Aboriginal peoples, particularly children, had lost a considerable degree of cultural identity since the advent of colonization.

It is under these circumstances that Anishinaabe Ikwe, some as young as eleven, are recruited by gang members and often targeted for exploitation in the sex and drug trades. According to Karen Busby and her colleagues (2002: 94), of the girls and women working in the sex trade on the streets of Prairie Canada, a higher percentage were of Aboriginal descent (58 percent) than Caucasian (42 percent). However, within the province of Manitoba, particularly in Winnipeg, that figure is likely to be much higher. According to "Urban Survivors, Aboriginal Street Youth: Vancouver, Winnipeg and Montreal," a research paper prepared for the Royal Commission on Aboriginal Peoples (Gilchrist 1995):

> [The] Lord Selkirk Park community is almost 100 per cent Aboriginal and is also a major location for the city's sex trade. The majority of sex trade workers on the low track, as this area is referred to, are mostly Aboriginal children, some as young as eleven years. The majority of the men who come to this area are white and middle class.

THE STUDY PARTICIPANTS

The collaborative, participatory project undertaken with Aboriginal women and girls was designed taking into consideration the expressed needs and concerns of the participants, that is to say, as the principal investigator, my main priority was to ensure that the participants felt safe and secure in sharing their narratives. I conducted a series of individual tape-recorded, life-history interviews (repeated over time) with nineteen Anishinaabe Ikwe at an agreed upon time and location. More often than not, this involved picking up the participant and going out for breakfast or lunch. As part of the exchange, each of the participants got an honorarium and a tobacco tie as recognition of the spiritual connection that occurs when two people discuss ideas, experiences, beliefs, emotions, and the like.

The study participants ranged in age from thirteen to forty-four years and were from a variety of First Nation and Métis communities in Manitoba and Ontario. Geographically they came from both northern and southern regions. One woman was born in the United States but had left early on in her childhood to come back to Manitoba. The First Nations participants had lived both on and off reserve, reflecting the migratory reality of indigenous communities. At the time of the interviews, six of the participants were housed at the Portage Correctional Facility (a women's prison) in Portage La Prairie, and four were living at a Winnipeg inner-city girls' group home. One woman was living in Northern Ontario, and the rest of the women lived in either central Winnipeg (downtown) or the notorious "North End," an area now both physically and socially constructed as poor, decrepit, violent, gang-infested, and degenerated. Of the nineteen participants, all but two had parents who had attended state-regulated and mandated residential schools; seventeen of the participants had grandparents and extended family members who had attended residential schools. All of the participants reported that one or both of their parents had been involved in drugs and alcohol from early childhood. Most of the participants had experienced encounters with Child and Family Services; indeed, one nineteen-year-old participant had over 136 placements — all of them with non-Aboriginal families.

Their oral narratives[2] provided new insights into urban Aboriginal gender relations, power structures, and strategies for coping with cultural dislocation. Overall, the project provided an opportunity for Anishinaabe Ikwe involved in gangs to shed light on their experience and to assert their contemporary identity to the broader community.

ANISHINAABE IKWE IN RELATION TO THE "GANG"

More and more on a daily basis, in Winnipeg at least, we hear stories about Aboriginal women and girls with reference to the "increasing numbers" and "increasing violence" of female gang members or female gangs.

Interestingly, however, only three of the participants in the study (the oldest ones) declared that there were Aboriginal female gang members or Aboriginal female gangs. These participants told me that at one time in Winnipeg (in the early 1980s), there was a semblance of a women's gang deriving from one of the first Aboriginal gangs in Manitoba, the Main Street Rattlers. According to Tamara, the Main Street Rattlers was born out of *"youth just hanging out, trying to survive."* Mary insisted that the formation of gangs in Winnipeg occurred as a result of youth hanging out at Rossbrook House, an inner-city neighbourhood centre for young people that, ironically, is described on its website as being established for the purpose of offering "a constant alternative to the destructive environment of the streets."[3] Tamara explained:

> *From the Rattlers came the Overlords and then from the Overlords they split. They changed themselves to the Manitoba Warriors. And they started feuding, so they went and said, "Well, we are going to make our own little gang called the Indian Posse."*

Lucy maintained that the gang was different back then:

> *At that time, they seemed to have a code of ethics, kind of like, "do no harm" within the gang. They had a sisterhood and a brotherhood, it was a family. It was a fine line that was drawn in terms of the "do no harm" within the gang system. I remember a time when they thought it was honourable to fight with your hands, not with weapons. And that female gang members who were a part of the gang, a lot of them went into prostitution and they could not participate in the heavy use of drugs. It was frowned upon because of the "do no harm" philosophy. It was never worded that but just the way they had a reverence for each other in that way. If you got into heavier drugs, it was frowned upon from higher-ranking members in the gang.*

Lucy was also of the view that relations between the sexes in these gangs were equal: *"But at that time it seemed like it was equal. Base power to both the male and female. Like it was so closely relational. Like, you know, really cared for each other."* By the early 1990s, however, the core of the gang *"quickly turned to something else."* I asked her why she thought this change had occurred. She replied:

> *Because maybe not having the skill to be able to put forth their message. You know, not having the resources. Not having the*

> *support of the community because of where they come from.*
> *Because in our own community they put value on the paper, on*
> *a degree. On some kind of status that puts us in a certain type*
> *of leadership. I started seeing pieces that were starting to go*
> *on because the crime started to become more intense and more*
> *violent, like break-ins and the robberies and what not. Of course,*
> *it was fuelled by addictions.*

In opposition to these stories, however, most participants in the study maintained that there were now no female gang members or female gangs, only "old ladies," "bitches," and "hos," each with very specific defined roles and responsibilities. Participants explained that Anishinaabe Ikwe had their connection to the gang only by virtue of their relationships with male gang members. While many participants had family relations with gang members (a father, brother, uncle, and/or cousin were in the gang), for the most part participants saw their connection to the gang as deriving from their relationship with a male gang member. This relation to male gang members defined and constructed particular aspects of women's and girls' experiences and spaces.

Old Ladies
Throughout the interviews, many participants referred to themselves as "so and so's old lady." Old ladies are the girlfriends of male gang members. That is to say, they are women or girls with whom male gang members have some semblance of a committed and loving relationship. Tamara explained that a women's position in the gang was to further their "old man's" place and space within the gang: "*It depends who your old man is too. What his role is within the gang.*" Many participants noted that some women had decision-making capacities in the gang as well, depending upon how they were perceived by male gang members. Tamara explained:

> *Her knowledge and her experience in the gang — they [male*
> *gang members] just analyze the situation with certain women.*
> *Like they think "Oh you are so fucking stupid, you don't know*
> *what the hell you are talking about" or "Hey, that's something*
> *to really think about." They categorize it like that.*

Another participant, who happened to be the boss's[4] old lady, noted that once a woman is considered and known as an old lady, everyone knows, respects, and ensures that place, particularly if her partner is incarcerated.

All those little men, they watch you. They follow you around or stop you for the old man... even when he was in the Remand Centre. His little friends would come to my mom's and buzz me. I came down and he would be on the cell phone and ask why I am not answering the phone.... I went up North. No one, nobody knew I went up North. Nobody. Just me and my mom. I don't know how they knew I went up North.

While Aboriginal gangs do not necessarily have written codes of ethics or behaviour, there are unspoken, expected, and prescribed protocols, rules, and responsibilities that everyone — including old ladies — must adhere to. Primarily, old ladies were expected to be "good." Candace explained that to be good meant, *"Don't drink or run around with guys or go to the bars. Just stay home, that's what they expect you to do. Why would you make your old lady stay at home and stay indoors? Don't go outside, talk, speak when spoken to, stuff like that."* Candace went on to explicitly note: *"Gang members and their old ladies aren't allowed to do drugs."*

Old ladies were expected to "be solid" — which implies, in the instance of physical assault, that a woman would just take the beating. To be solid means that an old lady does not seek help from social service agencies or the police, or that she does not try to leave her partner for a women's shelter. As Tamara explained:

If you get out of it, the other women just say, "Okay, well then you are not solid enough." They just kind of shun you... for complaining. You don't mention it [abuse shelters] but if you mention something like that then your old man is going to get mad at you, "Why are you fucking talking that shit?"

Tamara also maintained that Anishinaabe Ikwe stay out of the physical assaults of other Anishinaabe Ikwe by their intimate partners as a way of "being solid" with the gang: *"You just stay out of it."* Mary similarly argues that other old ladies had to stay out of each other's business:

We couldn't stop it because we had to take it like a woman. If your man beats you up, take it. That's your norm. That is normal. Like my ex, I got all my teeth knocked out from him and you know I got stabbed so many times. You just take it.

Candace shared one incident (of many) in which she was being physically assaulted. Her story showed that not only women, but also male gang members, do not report or intervene in domestic relationships.

> *He has beaten me up a couple of times around his friends. There is like twenty guys there. I was twenty-six and he must have been like thirty... there would be like twenty of them when they went to drink and he beat me up right in front of them. He just got out of remand and he said I was dogging him — fooling around on him.... They just watch. They stood back and watched. I can't believe it, a bunch of them could have stopped him, pulled him away from me cause he had me up against the wall off my feet. Like he had his hands around my neck and he was just yelling at me.*

The normalization of abuse and the pressures on the women to "be solid" have meant that some old ladies will actually make up stories about being physically abused in order to fit in with the other old ladies. Cathy explained:

> *You have to just accept it. If it is not happening to you, then you are lucky and you just keep quiet about it. I heard one girl saying things that her old man had pushed her head into the mirror while she was putting makeup on but she didn't have any marks to show for it. We'd all be showing our marks, our bruises and she didn't have any marks so we didn't believe her. So when we're alone with our old man we ask him that we heard so and so was beating up on so and so and he'll confirm that it's not like that.*

Nevertheless, many respondents emphasized that a kind of sisterhood cultivates among old ladies because they are going through the same struggles and joys and operate within the same gang context. As Candace explained it, *"We know each other and we know what we are going through and we all know what it is like."* Cathy said:

> *It just seems like if you're with a man that's in a gang — like, all the women that are going out with these gang members — they are automatically friends, even if you don't like someone. You have to be polite to her when you go to their house. And your kids all hang out together too.*

Even if an Anishinaabe Ikwe is no longer with a particular gang member, according to many participants she will always have that connection through her child or children. Tamara described this connection:

If you have a kid from a gang member you will always be involved in that gang even if it was twenty years ago, thirty years ago. You will always be connected, especially the kids, especially the kids. They are second generation. They are like blessed. They get blessed into the gang. It is like they don't have to do anything to be in a gang. It is automatically a gang member.

While an old lady's place in the gang is determined largely by her relation with a male gang member, Cathy maintained that old ladies had some semblance of decision-making capacities and other responsibilities within the gang. For instance, some old ladies were solicited for their advice by male gang members: *"When they were selling rock, they used to ask us, 'Should we go over here tonight?' or 'What area should we do?' or 'Whose place should we go to first?' That is what they would be doing, asking us."* Cathy also explained that some old ladies were designated as "drivers," which involved chauffeuring male gang members to various locations for a variety of activities (picking up drugs, committing break and enters).

Bitches and Hos

Most, if not all, study participants argued that at the lower rung of the hierarchy of Anishinaabe Ikwe involved in gangs were the "bitches" and "hos." These women and girls were not looked upon favourably and were always described in pejorative ways. Sabrina noted that gang members *"always have a girl [old ladies] at home that they like and stay with. But at the same time they are fucking all these other girls. Man, bringing home shit."* Sabrina went on to note that "bitches" and "hos" also get pregnant from gang members:

> *But at the same time these girls run around, "like this is your baby" but meanwhile, they are fucking all these other guys, so nobody really knows what is going on. A "bitch" are the girls that dress all skanky and they run around.*

Lorna maintains that *"Bitches and hos are just the girlfriends that work the streets. They call them bitches and hos. They just feed them drugs."* Candace referred to women and girls that work the streets as *"just money-makers."* The possibility of attracting such negative labels, however, was an ever-present concern for many of the women. Sabrina, for instance, commented that even by simple association, a woman or girl could be considered a "bitch" or "ho":

> *You hang out with a bunch of "hos" then you are going to look like a "ho." I try to stay away from all girls because they make you look bad. They bring you down. They want to go scamming shit.*

In addition to highlighting the nature of women's and girls' participation in the gang, these narratives begin to reveal the pervasive nature of violence in the lives of Anishinaabe Ikwe. The subject of violence permeated the discussions with the women and girls, who spoke of intergenerational violence, residential school physical and sexual abuse, and intrafemale violence. One predominant theme was that of violence between male gang members and women. Violence in interpersonal relationships was not just an experience encountered by the older women in the study. One participant, who was turning fourteen at the time of the interview, recounted how when she was twelve, she was assaulted by a fourteen-year-old gang member:

> *I used to hang out with other gang members. I went to this one house because there was this guy that I liked. He asked me if I wanted to come over. I stayed there for a while. We usually got high, drank sometimes. This one day I said, "I want to go home." And all of a sudden, he turns out the lights. He had this white thing, it was hard. He started hitting me with it, yelling, "You're not fucking going anywhere." He was just hitting me and I was crying... when [her friend] went in [the room], he was like, "Get the fuck out of here!" and he starts hitting her. I tried running out of the room but he just grabbed me and slammed me against the wall. I was all bruised up and beaten up.*

Of all the narratives I heard concerning interpersonal violence between male gang members and women, Candace's account of one particular incident (of the many more she was to encounter) had by far the most profound effect on me. Candace shared how, when she was around seventeen, she was pregnant with her first child and only a week away from her due date when she and her boyfriend got into an argument over another man at a party. The fight escalated to where her boyfriend: *"grabbed a knife out of nowhere."*

> *And he stabbed me in the stomach. It hit the baby through the baby's back and it almost came out the stomach. So after that they rushed me, everybody left that party and they phoned the*

*ambulance. The cops took him and they don't know where the
weapon was. I was in the hospital. I don't remember being in
the hospital but I was there. I had a cesarean, they took it out. It
was stillborn. I was due the next week.*

How can we begin to make sense of these narratives, in terms of what
they tell us not only about the relations between women and men, but
also about those between the women and girls involved in gang activity?
Again we have to keep in mind that relations between indigenous men
and women pre-contact were of an equal, fluid nature, and that the processes of colonization have had a dramatic impact on relations between the
sexes. As the Royal Commission on Aboriginal Peoples (1996) stated:

> The stereotyping and devaluing of Aboriginal women, a combi-
> nation of racism and sexism, are among the most damaging of
> attitudes that find expression in Canadian society. These attitudes
> are not held exclusively by non-Aboriginal people either.…
> Members of powerless groups who are subjected to demeaning
> treatment tend to internalize negative attitudes toward their own
> groups. They then act on these attitudes in ways that confirm the
> original negative judgement.

Métis scholar Emma LaRocque (2000) also discusses this process of
"internalization," whereby, as a result of colonization, Aboriginal peoples have come to judge themselves against the standards of the white
society. According to LaRocque (2000: 149), part of this process entails
"swallowing the standards, judgements, expectations, and portrayals of
the dominant white world."

In these terms, the violence encountered by Anishinaabe Ikwe in
their intimate relationships with men can be interpreted as a reflection of
the patriarchal ideas about women (and how they should be treated) that
prevail in the wider society. To this extent, colonization has now taken
on a new guise. While physical violence historically played a major role
in ensuring colonial rule, violence is now taken up by our men and inflicted on our women within this new, internalized colonial regime. Given
their disenfranchised and subordinate position both within the gang and
the wider society, it should not surprise us that Aboriginal women and
girls would compete amongst themselves in an effort to negotiate their
place and space. "Being solid," "taking it like a woman," and creating
a distance from those women and girls who have less status therefore
become important survival strategies.

SURVIVING COLONIALISM

Throughout each of the interviews, colonization and its impact on our indigenous culture, traditions, and existence permeated the discussions. While the study participants may not have named their lived experience using the language of colonialism, time and time again Anishinaabe Ikwe made references to "*how it was before the 'White Man.'*" It is within this colonial context that the role of the gang as a source of support and resistance must be located.

Euro-Canadian dominant discourse would have us believe that the conditions in which Aboriginal peoples now find themselves derive primarily from the First Nations' own lack of enterprise, poor work ethic ("lazy Indians"), and overall inadequate economic, political (corrupt), social (savage), and cultural (backwards) capacities. On the contrary, Aboriginal peoples' socio-economic, political, social, and cultural conditions fundamentally derive from our collective experience of colonization. Christian missionary conversion mandates, state-regulated and executed residential school systems, the prohibition of voting, the forbidding of participation in traditional cultural and spiritual activities, and the entrenchment of the racist and sexist Indian Act are just a few of the many policies and strategies imposed upon the indigenous collective. Each of these various activities has had — and continues to have — profound effects on generations of Aboriginal peoples in Canada.

In particular, think about the impact of the residential school system: indigenous children as young as three were involuntarily taken away from parents, grandparents, and community and forced to live away for ten months at a time or, in some cases, years at a time. What happens to children, families, communities, and nations when our children, who, as the "Circle of Law" teaches us, are the "Fire" and "Motivation" of the indigenous collective, are taken away and "taught" (enforced, strictly regulated, brainwashed) that everything they knew, experienced, and believed to be true about their world was "savage" and that they were "less than"? Children, families, communities, and nations slowly die physically, socially, culturally, and spiritually. The formation of Aboriginal gangs primarily derives from this ancestral and generational colonial history and experience.

Given this context, many study participants not surprisingly relayed how their association with the gang provided them with a space in which they could be themselves and where they found solidarity and pride in being indigenous. Tamara stated: "*What's the gang to me? Well, obviously, they have been around. They have been a support. They have been the backbone to me being alive and taking care of me."* Cathy told me how the gang allowed her the freedom and strength to counter dominant "white" society and claim her space as one of the original peoples of this land: *"It is very powerful. Like you know they ["white" society] put you really down. I find they get ignorant and racist. Like it is almost like you're dirt. And for me, I would just stand up and say, 'No, I'm not dirt.' You know if they want to play the part, so can I. Reverse psychology because that is how dirty they get."* Louisa asserted that the gang provided her with an environment in which she had a connection and understanding:

> *Strengths. I met a lot of friends. They took care of me and I always had money. It was someone I knew that was there for me and kind of helping me. When I was in that group home there were white, black people. It was okay but I was more happy being around my own people. And there were a couple of people from The Pas. It was nice to know somebody from The Pas. There was more understanding, like I could understand too. I was like their little sister. That was cool.*

In these terms, Aboriginal gangs do not develop solely because of a desire or need for money and power. Aboriginal gangs develop simply because our people are not afforded the same educational, employment, political, and cultural opportunities as the rest of Canadian society. From the moment we take our first breath to the moment we take our last, we are under assault by virtue of the Indian Act. We start school only to learn that we were or are "savages" and are a burden on society. We do not see ourselves reflected positively in schools, work, or government. It is only once we start to acknowledge and recognize this factor that we can begin to move to more worthwhile approaches in dealing with Aboriginal gangs and, in particular, Aboriginal women's place and space.

The dominant discourse surrounding gangs mostly pertains to so-called "exiting" models premised on the notion that gang members just need to either formally (request to leave) or informally (hide out and eventually be forgotten) exit the gang. Unfortunately, this is far too simplistic a solution. Gangs provide members with a sense of family, both literally and symbolically (as in "you're my homie"). Many of the study participants noted the literal family connections that many gang members have. Freda maintained that even though gang members (and their old ladies) may be from different gangs, family connections override any prescribed gang norms or codes of behaviour. She said:

They are all connected through their families. Some will have a cousin that is a Warrior and his cousin will be an Indian Posse and then that one's sister or stepsister will be going out with a guy that is from Native Syndicate. If you are in the same room with all of them, it's a family gathering.

That gang members end up being family members complicates whether or not it is ever truly possible to "leave the gang."

GANGS: STRENGTH AND SURVIVAL

I have been only able to offer here a portion of the various narratives and themes shared by the study participants over the span of almost two years. Nevertheless, what I have endeavoured to show is that Aboriginal gangs — and women's particular context within the gang — did and does not develop divorced from the colonial context in Canada. Contrary to what most may believe, colonialism is not something that occurred in the past. The colonial experiment in Canada has never ended — European settlers did not de-colonize and go "back home." We are still under the rule of the colonizer, with all of its Western Euro-Canadian ethnocentric ideologies and institutions.

Conducting the interviews for this study was by far the most difficult research I have ever done, but I would not have traded one moment. I was so privileged to have time with these women. Far from the media portrayal of violent female equivalents of "thugs," these women represent the strength, perseverance, and beauty of the indigenous peoples in Canada. Remembering a time when our people, our nations, and our cultures were thought to be "vanishing," I can see that these women counter that notion with their very struggle and, most importantly, survival. We were not supposed to be here. Indeed, that was the plan so methodically and strategically executed. But despite every imaginable assault, we are still here and, in some capacity or another, flourishing.

NOTES

I would like to say "meegwetch" to Elizabeth Comack for all the support and help she provided throughout the process of writing this piece, particularly her wonderful editing. Truly, this paper would not have been completed had it not been for her time, energy, and spirit.

1. Writers such as Bernard Schissel (1997) argue that much of the media coverage of the "gang" issue has verged on a moral panic that succeeds in generating considerable (yet unfounded) fears on the part of the public. Schissel (1997: 59–60) also suggests that in Prairie cities such as Winnipeg and Saskatoon, "gang" has become a racist code word in the media to refer to Aboriginal kids.

2. I have not edited and/or grammatically altered the participants' narratives. Specifically, I wanted to ensure respect and appreciation for participants and what they had to say and did not feel I had the right or the authority to change anything that was so freely communicated and shared.
3. See <www.rossbrookhouse.ca/about/index.htm>. (Accessed September 9, 2005.)
4. A "boss" is a president of one of the gangs.

5. REPRESENTATIONS OF WOMEN IN THE DRUG TRADE

Susan C. Boyd

In a popular representation of today's drug trafficker, a man of colour flashes his wealth, gangsta style. He is portrayed in a violent, hyper-masculine form, as a menace to society. Sometimes he is joined by other popular stereotypes: cartel drug traffickers and traffickers with links to organized crime and "terrorist groups."

Strangely, these common depictions of drug traffickers do not reflect Canadian criminal justice drug-arrest statistics. In Canada the majority of drug traffickers arrested are poor, street-level dealers. Since the enactment of our first narcotic legislation, the prime police target for drug offences has been poor people and people of colour. A significant number of women have also been charged, and are serving time, for drug offences. Moreover, today most drug offences in Canada involve cannabis, and the bulk of charges laid are for simple possession rather than trafficking. In Canada it is the cannabis user who is most at risk for arrest (Desjardins and Hotton 2004: 3).

While men involved in the drug trade have been represented in a hyper-masculine form, women have not escaped similarly gendered representations. This chapter explores the historical and contemporary representations of women as traffickers, importers, and users of illegal drugs that shape public imagination and policy — moving through the background of contemporary drug regulation in Canada (including the colonization of First Nations peoples and the representation of Aboriginal women as well as the targeting of other racialized groups and the "protection" of moral white women) and contemporary representations of the drug trafficker — and then provides a feminist analysis of representations of women as drug users, traffickers, and couriers in the context of the economic, social, and political structures that shape women's lives. I also look at the criminal justice response to women in the drug trade, highlighting two recent groundbreaking Canadian drug courier cases that are significant in illustrating the typical situations of women involved in importing drugs.

THE ROOTS OF DRUG REGULATION IN CANADA

Colonization and Representations of Aboriginal Women

The regulation of drugs is not new. During the colonization of what is now Canada, Christian missionaries condemned a wide array of spiritual, healing, and shamanic practices, which the state later criminalized. Although the colonizers brought their drug of choice — alcohol — and introduced it to indigenous people in Canada, they took several measures to ensure that alcohol's legal use was reserved for non-Aboriginal peoples.

One of the provisions of Canada's Indian Act in 1886 prohibited Aboriginal people from consuming alcohol. Those categorized by the state as "status Indians" were prohibited from buying or possessing alcohol — an aspect of the legislation that was not completely repealed until 1985. While a hundred years of prohibition did not stop Aboriginal people from drinking, it did change the way they drank. Thousands of Aboriginal people were arrested and jailed for alcohol-related offences (Maracle 1993).

Aboriginal women arrested for public drunkenness were constructed as being more immoral and deviant than both their male counterparts and white women. They were accused of contributing to "race suicide" by setting up house with non-Aboriginal men and producing "mixed race children." Their adult children were also accused of being the "kingpins" of the illegal alcohol trade (Mawani 2002a; Nelson 2002). For instance, between 1930 and 1960, many Aboriginal women were charged and convicted under the Ontario Female Refuges Act (FRA) for alcohol-related charges and sexual immorality. Originally enacted in 1897, the FRA was broadened in 1919 to enable women to be incarcerated by police, parents, welfare agents, and the Children's Aid Society for being "out of sexual control" (see chapter 2). Most of the women charged under the FRA were white; however, as Joan Sangster (2002a: 47) points out, "The legal and social understandings of 'promiscuity' — so central to the FRA — were racialized." Sangster states that by the end of the nineteenth century, "political and media controversies" served to promote and maintain negative stereotypes of Aboriginal women in the public imagination. Aboriginal women were represented as easily corrupted, lacking morality, sexually promiscuous, and a "threat to public 'morality and health.'" They were also depicted as wild, able to lead others astray, and in need of containment (Sangster 1999: 43, 44). Moral reformers ignored the negative impact of colonization, law, and religion. Legal, psychiatric, and social work discourses fuelled the practice of incarcerating Aboriginal women.

Opium Laws and Racial Profiling

Canada's second drug law — and the country's first legislated control of narcotics — was enacted in 1908 to regulate opium production, even though no pharmacological evidence existed at the time to support the need for this new legislation. There is little debate that this law, enacted to limit the use of opium smoking by Chinese labourers in Western Canada, was fuelled by moralism, racism, gender, and class conflict (King 1908; Solomon and Madison 1976-77; Small 1978; Comack 1986).

Capitalists had brought Chinese labourers to Canada as a cheap labour source to supply the large projects of industrialization (such as the building of the national railway system). Following the Anti-Asiatic Riot in Vancouver in 1907 — an event sparked by the economic fears of white labourers toward their Chinese counterparts — William Lyon Mackenzie King, then Canada's deputy minister of labour, was sent to settle damages for what the federal government had defined as a labour conflict. After discovering that the opium trade was unregulated, and hearing the complaints of several affluent Chinese Canadians about the opium industry, King proclaimed, "We will get some good out of this riot yet" (Boyd 1984; Comack 1986).

King subsequently submitted a report on the smoking of opium to the federal government. In response, Parliament passed Canada's first Opium Act (King 1908: 7, 8). King's report drew heavily from newspaper reports depicting opium as corrupting the morality of white women. In particular, King (1908: 13) represented the smoking of opium as an "evil" that threatened the "principles of morality" that should "govern the conduct of a Christian nation." He provided no evidence to support his claims about the dangerousness of this form of opium use and the subsequent breakdown of morality.

The public at large, believing the claims that only a small minority group would be affected, raised little opposition to this early piece of legislation, subsequent amendments, or the related broadening of police powers (Boyd 1984; Green 1979; Solomon and Green 1988). Indeed, racialized groups were easily targeted, and drugs associated with these groups increasingly came under attack (Boyd 1984, 1991; Comack 1986). Early arrest patterns in Canada suggest that between 1908 and 1930, Chinese and Black men were the ones singled out by the police for arrest. Clayton Mosher's (1998) study of systemic racism in Ontario's legal and criminal justice systems examines how Black and Chinese drug users were subjects of a "white paternalism" that was expressed in more lenient sentencing. In contrast, those convicted of selling to white people were sentenced harshly (Mosher 1998: 157, 159). Drug traffickers, especially people of colour, were depicted as preying on innocent white victims.

Before criminalization took effect, the prevailing profile of the opiate user was as a law-abiding, upper-class, Anglo-Saxon woman taking the drug for a variety of aliments ranging from reproductive problems to nervousness (Berridge and Edwards 1981; Gray 1999; Kandall 1996). Patent medicines containing opiates, cocaine, and cannabis (which were not included in early narcotic legislation) were advertised in Eaton's and Sears, Roebuck's mail-order catalogues. Given that most Canadian women lived in rural areas and could not afford the services of doctors, many of them relied on home remedies and patent medicines to treat themselves and the family members in their care (Kandall 1996; Mitchinson 2002: 31).

During the late nineteenth and early twentieth centuries significant historical, political, economic, and social shifts were occurring in Western nations. In Canada and the United States, industrialization, social unrest, and non-Protestant immigration threatened Protestant hegemony, and it was against this backdrop that the temperance and anti-opiate movements emerged in the nineteenth century, overlapping and intersecting with moral reform and social purity movements. Moral reform movements were both national and religious. Anti-opiate and temperance groups claimed that controlled use of opium and alcohol was impossible (Berridge and Edwards 1981), and by the early nineteenth century self-control, morality, and sobriety had become the template of white, Anglo-Saxon, middle-class respectability as well as the model for the imperial subject. Western Protestants adopted religious dedication and temperance as symbols of social status and self-control, and labour and material wealth were viewed as signs of "God's favour." As Max Weber (1976: 72) commented, the capitalist system "so needs this devotion to the calling of making money." The Women's Christian Temperance Union in Canada, for instance, regarded sobriety and morality as innate in the female gender; yet women could be easily corrupted because of their fragile characters. As a result, temperance and anti-opiate reformers constructed alcohol and the smoking of opium as two of the main culprits of many of society's ills — such as poverty, criminality, and violence. Moral reformers were concerned with what they perceived as the "breakdown" of the family and the abandonment of white, middle-class, Christian morality (Hannah-Moffat 2001; Valverde 1991). They thus set out to transform immoral individuals. Such practices were therefore intrinsically linked with the nation-building and state reform of the late nineteenth- and early twentieth-century period (Hunt 1999; Valverde 1991)

A Drug Policy for the Protection of White Women

Canadian views on certain drugs, and individuals and groups who used and sold drugs, would shift dramatically by the early 1920s, partially due to the efforts of moral reformers such as Emily Murphy. Hailing from Edmonton, Murphy was the first woman in Canada to be appointed a juvenile court judge. Along with other moral reformers, she produced and disseminated significant new materials about drug users and traffickers. In 1922 her book *The Black Candle* was published. Serialized in Canada's national *Maclean's Magazine*, the book was intended to educate Canadians about drug issues (Murphy 1973; Anthony and Solomon 1973).

Murphy's representation of the male drug trafficker is that of a non-white, deranged villain bent on destroying the Anglo-Saxon way of life, corrupting the morality of white women, and taking over the world. She targeted Chinese and Black men for enslaving white women and contributing to "race suicide." While Murphy (1973: 162) constructed male drug traffickers as devious people who were "active agents of the devil," the mixing of the races and the moral downfall of white women were central to her argument. Women's moral downfall was measured by their proximity to, and enslavement by, men of colour. Beneath a photo of a white woman and a Black man lying in what looks like an opium den, Murphy wrote, "When she acquires the habit, she does not know what lies before her; later, she does not care" (p.30). Murphy went on to assert that all women who are seduced by men of colour become addicted and degraded, and all of them also become liars. She claimed, "Under the influence of the drug, the woman loses control of herself; her moral senses are blunted, and she becomes 'a victim' in more senses than one" (p.17). For Murphy and others of her ilk the woman drug user was an immoral, promiscuous being who was contributing to the breakdown of the family and Anglo-Saxon society.

Canada's drug legislation, then, was grounded not only in the class interests of industrial capitalism, but also in the Eurocentric view of morality, gender, race, family, and nation-state. The image of white women as fragile and vulnerable to moral corruption sharply contrasts with the images of Aboriginal women as promiscuous, unruly, prone to public displays of drunkenness, and in need of confinement. What are the contemporary images of women in the drug trade and how do current socio-political agendas underpin the regulation of these women?

CONTEMPORARY REPRESENTATIONS OF THE DRUG TRAFFICKER: THE WAR ON DRUGS

Representations and Regulation

Contemporary representations of the drug trafficker have not strayed far from the writings of Emily Murphy. Indeed, drug laws in Canada have become increasingly severe, justified by police efforts to secure broader powers to capture and punish the drug trafficker and importer. Both the Opium and Drug Act of 1908 and the Narcotic Control Act of 1961 underwent many amendments (Giffen, Endicott, and Lambert 1991). Today certain drugs (excluding tobacco and alcohol) are regulated under the federal Controlled Drugs and Substances Act (1997). Few Canadians are aware of the content of this act and of the maximum penalties for possession, trafficking, and importation/exportation of drugs, which include: seven years for possession of drugs such as cocaine and heroin; life imprisonment for importing or trafficking these drugs; five years less a day for possessing less than 30 grams of marijuana; and life imprisonment for importing or trafficking more than three kilograms of cannabis. It is rare for a Canadian judge to impose a maximum penalty for a drug offence, especially because our legal system has first-time offence guidelines. Nevertheless, sentencing is not always lenient, especially in relation to importation charges. In addition, a series of minor offences or probation violations and failure to pay fines can snowball into a lengthy prison sentence.

Until the late 1950s and the emergence of the Beat and sixties countercultures, representations of illegal drug use and drug trafficking were constructed solely by police, judges, politicians, the medical profession, social workers, academics, and the media. The Beat writers of the 1950s and the political movement of the 1960s challenged official representations of the illegal drug user and, to a lesser degree, the drug trafficker. For millions of youth, use of drugs, especially marijuana and psychedelics, was considered to be a positive thing and a challenge to "rational consciousness" (Wagner 1997: 14). Illegal drug use was associated with altered states of consciousness and political dissent.

Despite these forms of resistance to dominant representations of drug use and users, several "drug scares" have been generated to rationalize increased drug regulation, including: heroin in the mid-1950s; marijuana and psychedelics in the 1960s; cocaine in the 1970s; crack cocaine in the mid-1980s; ecstasy in the 1990s; and, most recently, methamphetamine and marijuana grow-operations. Each drug scare has had a similar narrative, with similar actors: an epidemic of use that is spreading and in need of containment; criminal groups with links to organized crime (and now terrorist groups); criminalized spaces, such as inner-city neighbourhoods; vulnerable victims (especially youth) — and ruthless traffickers, importers, and producers.

Each drug scare embodies narrow representations of traffickers, importers, and producers as racialized, foreign Others operating outside the law. For instance, in a drug strategy recently adopted by the City of Vancouver, *A Framework for Action: A Four-Pillar Approach to Drug Problems in Vancouver*,[1] drug traffickers are racialized and seen as a threat. They are constructed as males who have ties to organized crime and cartels outside of the nation-state. In the report, drug traffickers are described as "masters of manipulation and impersonation, [who] can blend into mainstream society quite easily" (MacPherson 2001: 54). The report also singles out Asian, Colombian, and Italian-based groups that are thought to be active in the Canadian drug trade (although no evidence is provided). Since these groups are represented as being able to operate anywhere at any time, arguments are presented for the imposition of special police powers.

Like the earlier period, then, myths and narratives about the drug trafficker and importer continue. "Foreign" traffickers and importers are still seen as a threat to "Christian" nation-states. Since the terrorist attacks on the World Trade Center and the Pentagon on September 11, 2001, we have been told by the RCMP and politicians — particularly President George W. Bush and his supporters — that the war on drugs is linked to the war on terrorism. Both wars converge, instrumentally intensifying racial profiling and eroding civil rights. In Canada, 90 percent of all state funding for drugs goes to criminal justice (Nolan 2003: 187), and drug arrests continue to increase (Desjardins and Hotton 2004).

Drug Statistics
Historically, repressive drug laws have been supported by myths, narratives, and representations of the drug trafficker that intensify the regulation of women. We are told continually that the government, police, and drug agencies need more special powers, budgets, and repressive laws so that we can be "protected" and the drug trafficker can be caught. However, the statistics tell a different story about who is really using drugs and who is being profiled by the police.

Contrary to media, government, and enforcement claims, the drug user in Canada is most often using legal drugs such as alcohol, tobacco, prescribed drugs, and over-the-counter products (CCSA/CCLAT 2004; Gagnon 2002; Single et al. 1999). In 2002 Canadians spent $12.3 billion on prescription drugs (Gagnon 2002). In 2004 about 17 percent of women and 23 percent of men reported being current tobacco smokers (Health Canada 2004). In Canada's 2004 national drug survey, 79 percent of Canadians surveyed reported having used alcohol in the previous year. Women reported drinking slightly less than men (77 percent versus 82 percent for men).

Illegal drug use in Canada is primarily centred on cannabis use. In the 2004 survey, 14 percent of the Canadians surveyed reported using cannabis in the previous year. Women were less likely to use cannabis over the previous year (10 percent versus 18 percent for men). Contrary to depictions of illegal drug use by the poor, high income is correlated with a higher lifetime prevalence of cannabis use, and up to 70 percent of Canadian youth from eighteen to twenty-four years of age have tried cannabis at least once (CCSA/CCLAT 2004). Curiously, the national drug survey does not include usage rates for tobacco, our most toxic drug. However, it does include a conflated annual rate of 1.3 percent for speed, ecstasy, and hallucinogens. The survey gives a past year usage rate of 1.9 percent for cocaine/crack (CCSA/CCLAT 2004).

These statistics demonstrate that Canadians are drug users. Their drug use is most often confined to legal drugs — such as alcohol, tobacco, and prescribed drugs — and, to a lesser degree, illegal drugs such as cannabis. Yet the Canadian media, some politicians, and enforcement agencies would have us believe otherwise. We are inundated with representations of drug users as people who consume cocaine/crack, heroin, or methamphetamines, even though the statistics reveal that these users represent a small percentage of drug users.

Charges for drug offences increased steadily in Canada between 1981 and 2002, except from 1987 to 1989 (Dell, Sinclair, and Boe 2001: 60; Desjardins and Hotton 2004: 3). Cannabis offences increased by 81 percent between 1992 and 2002, most of them involving charges for possession (Desjardins and Hotton 2004: 1). In 2002 76 percent of all drug offences in Canada were for cannabis and 66 percent were for possession (Desjardins and Hotton 2004: 3). About 14 percent of all drug charges involved women. Yet, according to 2004 statistics from the Correctional Service of Canada, about 30 percent of female federal prisoners were serving time in federal prison for drug-related offences, compared to 18 percent of men.[2] The incarceration rate for women is higher than for men, even though men serving prison terms for drug offences such as trafficking and importation have "more extensive criminal history backgrounds" than do their female counterparts (Motiuk and Vuong 2001: 27). Importation offences make up about 1 percent of all drug charges, and more men than women are serving federal prison time for this offence. However, the total percentage of women serving time in federal prison in 2004 for importing charges is three times higher than it is for men. Similarly, the percentage of female federal prisoners serving time for drug trafficking is 11 percent, compared to 9 percent of male prisoners.[3]

Numerous Canadian studies point out that the female prison population has tripled since 1970 and that First Nations and Black women are overrepresented in federal prisons (Hannah Moffat and Shaw 2000b; Statistics Canada 2001a). According to the findings of the 1995 Commission on Systemic Racism in the Ontario Justice System, drug trafficking and importing dominate the increased number of admissions at the Vanier Centre for Women (VCW). White women made up the majority of women admitted for drug trafficking and importing charges in 1986/87, but by 1992/93 most of the women admitted were Black. White women and Black women admitted to VCW for drug trafficking and importing charges between 1986/87 and 1992/93 increased by 667 percent and 5,200 percent, respectively (Commission on Systemic Racism in the Ontario Criminal Justice System 1995: 25, 26). Similarly, research indicates a 20 percent increase in the number of female federal offenders serving drug-related sentences since 1997 (Correctional Service of Canada 2002-03).

Although state and police officials maintain that they are committed to arresting top-level drug traffickers, the makeup of the female prison population — the majority of whom are racialized, poor, undereducated, single parents — belies their claims. We need to ask, therefore, what is the current (neo-liberal) construction of women involved in the drug trade? How can we understand women's participation in the illegal economy in relation to a socio-economic context characterized by the disappearance of the social safety net, decreased opportunities for women, the increased stratification of social classes? And how are both women's engagement with the drug trade and the state response to that engagement shaped by race and class?

A FEMINIST ANALYSIS

One explanation for the increasing criminalization of women for drug offences lies in the economic, social, and political structures that shape women's lives (Wagner 1997). In these terms, the central factors in understanding rising incarceration rates and "coercive state violence against women" are the racialized feminization of poverty related to neo-liberal globalization, the tough-on-crime agendas of political parties, the transnational war on drugs, and the global prison-industrial complex (Sudbury 2005: 168). Feminist researchers have brought to our attention the situations of women around the world who are involved in the drug trade, imprisoned for drug-related crimes, and hurt in other ways by the war on drugs (Boyd 2004; Boyd and Faith 1999; DaCunha 2005; Diaz-Cotto 2005; Faith 1993, 2000; Green 1996, 1998; Heaven 1996; Huling 1992, 1996; Joshua 1996; Martin 1993; Roberts 2005; Sudbury 2005). They seek to situate women's involvement in the drug trade against the backdrop of international and national political, economic, and social factors that have an impact on the lives of women — an impact that has been experienced most acutely in the regulation of reproduction.

Bad Mothers
Historically, women who use, sell, and import illegal drugs have been constructed as being doubly deviant for transgressing both their proper gender role and the criminal law. They have been seen as a risk to themselves, their children, society, and the nation state. In more recent times, mothers suspected of using illegal drugs continue to be depicted as immoral, dangerous, and driven by their addiction (Boyd 1999, 2004; Campbell 2000; Humphries 1999; Martin 1993; Murphy and Rosenbaum 1999; Roth 2000). Indeed, women's bodies have become the newest ter-rain of the "war on drugs," as law and order pundits seek to criminalize maternal drug use. This situation has been further exacerbated since the 1980s by the intersection of the war on drugs and the war on abortion and women's reproductive rights. Drug policy has been shaped by dis-courses about good and bad mothers — about sexuality, reproduction, and morality.

Women's gains in reproductive autonomy, including legal access to birth control and abortion in Canada and other Western nations, were ac-companied by a counter-discourse about the fetus as a legal person who is separate from the pregnant woman and in need of protection. Feminist activists and researchers state that advances in fetal rights have culminated in a situation in which women's bodies are under attack (Boyd 1999, 2004; Paltrow 2001; Roth 2000). Unsubstantiated fears about maternal drug use have culminated in increased social-service, legal, and medical surveillance of women since the 1960s. The United States "crack scare" of the mid-1980s, for instance, centred on lurid, unsubstantiated tales about "crack babies" and unfit mothers (Humphries 1999).

In Canada social workers have expanded their domain of regulation through the regulation of drug use, including maternal drug use. A number of legal cases in the 1980s and 1990s highlighted their shifting practices to "apprehend" the fetus in order to protect it from suspected drug use by pregnant women (Maier 1992; Turnbull 2001). In challenging the legal definition of the term "child," these cases highlighted social workers' interest in expanding their domain and extending legal rights to the fetus. Anti-abortion and fetal-rights advocates have also been pressing for the fetus to be granted legal rights. They view the establishment of legal personhood as an important strategy toward criminalizing abortion and regulating women's activities during pregnancy and birth. Since the 1970s, neo-liberal discourses represent poor single mothers on public assistance as morally deficient and producing social problems, including damaged children (Bashevkin 2002: Boyd 2004). Individualized responsibility and self-sufficiency emerged as the neo-liberal solution to systemic poverty, social inequality, and racialized and sexualized welfare policy. Poor women were increasingly represented as draining the national coffers, and as immoral, promiscuous, dishonest, and unwilling to work. Further, they were depicted as a danger to their children and to the health of the nation. Negative representations of women on assistance were accompanied by cutbacks and shifts in social work practice. Rather than support, surveillance of families and accountability to management became central to social work practice (Bashevkin 2002). State apprehension of children is one of the most punitive practices that social workers employ against women who live in poverty, especially those mothers who are racialized (Swift 1995). The discourse centres on individualizing single mothers' personal behaviour, rather than on the impact of racialized and gendered welfare policy and the neo-liberal economic and social restructuring that shapes the lives of women and their children.

One 1996 case received considerable media attention, in turn illuminating the effect of negative representations of racialized single mothers on welfare who are suspected of using drugs. The case involved a young, pregnant First Nations woman who was being forced into treatment for solvent abuse by Winnipeg Child and Family Services. The media and the social workers involved argued that this woman had already had two damaged children due to her solvent use. They assumed, without evidence, that solvent use is linked to fetal damage during pregnancy (Medrano 1996). In hearing this case, the Supreme Court of Canada ruled that the courts cannot detain and order drug treatment for pregnant women to protect the fetus. The Court also ruled that the unborn child does not possess legal rights (*Winnipeg Child and Family Services [Northwest Area]* v. *G[D. F.]* 1997). This ruling has not stopped legal challenges from occurring, even though it did send an important message to legal, moral, and social service reformers who seek to limit women's reproductive autonomy.

The battle continues over women's bodies, drugs, and reproductive autonomy in the political arena as well. In 2002 Canadian Alliance MP Keith Martin (now a Liberal) introduced a private Member's bill, Bill C-233, to amend the Criminal Code. The bill — which was not ratified — was intended to amend the code to extend legal personhood to the fetus. It would have made it an offence for a woman who is pregnant to consume a substance harmful to a fetus that she does not have a fixed intention to abort. The bill sought to provide legal protection for the health of the fetus before it is born. It also "authorized" the courts to make orders to confine a woman in a treatment facility during her pregnancy, and to have her report to a physician weekly upon her release in order to protect the fetus. In the United States, over 200 women have been arrested and held criminally liable for the outcomes of their pregnancies (Paltrow 2001).

Such efforts to criminalize maternal drug use are shaped by discourses about unfit mothers, the dangerousness of certain drugs, and welfare moms who drain limited economic and social supports. Illegal drug use by mothers is viewed as placing the child at risk, thus as justifying state intervention. It is mistakenly assumed that drugs are the only variable that brings about negative pregnancy and maternal outcomes. The main problem with this is that moral panic about maternal drug use deflects our attention from poverty, one known social factor that has a negative impact on pregnancy. In Canada the numbers of poor women have been growing as social and economic supports decrease. Today more children live in poverty than was the case twenty years ago (Bashevkin 2002). The 1996 case in Winnipeg is a prime illustration of this point. Focusing attention solely on the culpability of a young, poor, Aboriginal woman to provide proper care for her fetus ignores the broader social and economic conditions that women in her situation confront in their struggle to make a life for themselves and their children.

Negative portrayals of mothers also ignore the wealth of research that clearly demonstrates that drugs are only one variable that influences pregnancy outcomes and that women who use illegal drugs can be adequate parents. In fact, when non-judgmental prenatal care and social and economic supports are provided, maternal outcomes improve (Boyd 1999; Colten 1980; Murphy and Rosenbaum 1999; Hepburn 1993). When these supports are in place, women using illegal drugs have had the same maternal outcomes as non-drug using women from the same socio-economic background (Hepburn 1993, 2002). Medical professionals maintain that while maternal drug use is a risk, it is a manageable risk.

Women, Drug Trafficking, and Importing

When we think about women who sell drugs, many of us think of women living in inner-city communities and working in the sex trade or selling drugs on the street to finance their addiction. While this may be true for a small percentage of women, the full picture is much more complex. Most women who use and sell illegal drugs are not driven by addiction. Economic factors such as cutbacks in housing and welfare assistance compel women to find alternative ways of making money. I am not suggesting that poor women are more involved in the drug trade than are middle- or upper-class women. Rather, I would argue that poor women are more likely to come into contact with the law due to their visibility, police-profiling, and increased intervention by social services and other state and non-state agencies that seek to regulate them.

Feminist sociological studies from Canada, Australia, the United States, and Britain tell a different story about women who traffic and import drugs. Marsha Rosenbaum's (1981) research in San Francisco provided the first feminist ethnographic sociological study of women heroin users, paving the way for other feminist studies about women who use and sell drugs. A growing body of research findings differs from conventional research that sees the female drug user and dealer as more deviant, immoral, pathological, and criminal than are male users and dealers. In contrast, critical and feminist research shows that many women "drift" into drug dealing, often pooling their money to get a better deal or to buy larger quantities (Waldorf, Reinarman, and Murphy 1991). Most women deal drugs in order to support themselves and their families, not to finance their addiction.

Patricia Morgan and Karen Ann Joe (1997), in their study of women who sell methamphetamine in three United States cities, found that women engage in drug selling and transporting in order to avoid dependency and to provide for their children in a world that provides few avenues of support for them. They challenge stereotypes of women who are involved in the drug trade, and argue: "Most women who use and sell illegal drugs are not from minority disenfranchised populations living in inner city communities, and most women who use and sell drugs have not, and will not engage in prostitution and other crimes outside of illegal drug sales" (Morgan and Joe 1997: 107).

An Australian study by Barbara Denton (2001) found that women's drug dealing was not driven by their drug use, but instead was seen by them as a viable way of making money. In my study on mothers (from diverse class and ethnic/race backgrounds) who use illegal drugs in Canada, the women revealed that they saw drug dealing as the most viable option for earning money to supplement inadequate incomes (Boyd 1999). However, Lisa Maher (1995) notes in her ethnographic study of women crack smokers in Brooklyn in the 1990s that for poor Black and Hispanic women, selling crack did not provide "equal opportunity employment." Women were more stigmatized and more subject to violence than were men (Maher 1995).

Women living within and outside of Canada have also been recruited or have chosen to import drugs into Canada. These women — labelled drug couriers or mules — are subject to long prison terms if they are caught — which sometimes happens in places where they do not speak the language and do not know the criminal justice system. They are more often than not imprisoned far away from their families. It is hard to conceive of anyone volunteering to carry or ingest drugs, because the profits are small and the risks are very high. Many women who "choose" this job are desperate. The research suggests that most women who are convicted of either importing drugs into or transporting within a nation rarely own the drugs they ingest or carry. They are paid a flat fee and most often do not share in the potential profits (Green 1998; Huling 1992; Wedderburn 2000).

Tracy Huling's 1992 study of female drug couriers who were arrested at the JFK airport in New York helped pave the way for a fuller understanding of women drug couriers by providing qualitative detail about the lives of the women involved. Huling noted that these women were sometimes used as decoys. They were usually first-time offenders, rarely released on bail upon arrest, and unable to develop an effective defence. The women in Huling's study were too poor to hire a lawyer, so they had to rely on court-appointed or legal aid lawyers with huge caseloads and limited budgets. Regardless of their innocence or guilt, the women were often advised to plea bargain to reduce their sentences — which meant an admission of guilt. Like other researchers, Huling (1992) found women drug couriers to be motivated by poverty and familial concerns rather than greed (see also Green 1996).

Between 1999 and 2001, Julia Sudbury (2005) interviewed twenty-four women in three prisons in Britain. Her findings confirm earlier studies about Black British women, Caribbean women, and working-class women serving sentences for drug-importing charges. While women are often naive about the drugs they carried, it would be a mistake to see all drug traffickers and couriers as lacking agency and being dupes of the drug trade. Rather, it is illuminating to look more closely at the ways in which women support themselves and their families when faced with social and structural inequalities, and state and male violence.

Despite this body of feminist research, misrepresentation of the female drug courier still persists. A British study of 1,715 drug couriers caught at Heathrow Airport between July 1991 and September 1997 asserted that female drug couriers carried more drugs "in terms of weight and value" than did their male counterparts (Harper, Harper, and Stockdale 2002). The women were also more likely to be carrying Class A (heroin and cocaine) than Class B (cannabis) drugs. Women made up 28 percent of the sample in the study. The authors expressed surprise that the female drug couriers appeared to be engaging in risk-taking and dangerous roles most often associated with criminalized men — thus subjecting themselves to greater penalties. They speculated that seeing women as risk-takers in these roles is counterintuitive to conventional gender stereotypes that construct women as subordinate dupes (Harper, Harper, and Stockdale 2002: 101, 106).

This study had several limitations, however. It provided no information about race/ethnicity or class, and no data indicating whether the women and men arrested at the airport were aware of the quality of the drugs that they carried. A number of other studies suggest that female couriers are usually unaware of the exact weight and quality of the drugs they carry, which become significant factors as trial evidence (see Green 1996). Further, the study offered no significant analysis as to why women are increasingly carrying Class A drugs. One might speculate that both cocaine and heroin, being less bulky than cannabis, are more easily transported and that flat rates for carrying cocaine and heroin are usually higher. It might also be the case that some women are more likely to be coerced to take more risks due to threats or intimidation.

When looking at women's involvement in the drug trade, we also need to examine the drug economy against the backdrop of the global economy. Poor women are exploited in both the drug economy and the global economy. They are the most "poorly remunerated" and the most "disposable of workers" (Sudbury 2005: 175). Neo-liberal economic structuring of the global economy ensures that some people will remain poor and exploited. Choices to participate in the drug trade are framed by global and national political and economic concerns, as well as by Western demand for and consumption of specific drugs. Poor women with little access to social and economic supports or to legitimate work with adequate wages may turn to the drug trade to provide for themselves and their families.

Although most drug traffickers and drug couriers are men, gender and racial profiling comes into play at a key entry point for illegal drugs: airports. Huling (1992) described how Black and Hispanic women were profiled by New York airport customs officers. The Drug Enforcement Agency (DEA) in the United States claims that Black women are ideal drug mules (Weich and Angula 2000: 3), and their profiling and enforcement practices are shaped by this belief. In 1999, Black women coming into a New York airport were nine times more likely to be X-rayed than were white women and two times more likely to be strip-searched than were other women (Ekstrand and Blume 2000: 2, 12). However, Black women were less likely than other women to be carrying contraband. In fact, Black women were half as likely as white women to have contraband on them. Only 4 percent of the total searches were successful, which means they had a 96 percent failure rate (Ekstrand and Blume 2000: 10). Since 2002 the war on terrorism has increased racial profiling by customs agents in the United States, Canada, and Britain.

The focus on drug couriers serves to deflect attention from the tons of drugs imported into Canada, the United States, and Britain via airplanes, ships, and trucks. These vessels hold significantly larger quantities of illegal drugs than those found on and in bodies. It also serves to deflect attention from the impacts of Western drug consumption and economic, military, and political initiatives on both Western and Third World nations and the people who live in them, especially poor women and women of colour.

In sum, narratives and representations of the drug trafficker and courier by criminal justice and moral reformers fail to capture the lives of most women in the drug trade. Feminist and critical drug research demonstrates that drug trafficking is not limited to the poor or people of colour. It is a normalized activity in many strata of society and can be found outside inner-city spaces. This research demonstrates that by expanding our analysis and challenging popular misconceptions, we can better understand how women in the drug trade — of all classes — derive rewards, especially monetary ones, from their work.

The makeup of our prison population demonstrates that race, class, and gender inequality do come into play for women who sell and import drugs by limiting their choices and closing avenues to legitimate work. These factors of inequality also come into play in relation to police-profiling, arrests, convictions, and sentencing. When poor women and women of colour — people who are the most vulnerable to arrest and conviction — come into contact with the drug economy, it is often at the lowest level, a position that mirrors their status in society.

THE CRIMINAL JUSTICE RESPONSE: *R. V. HAMILTON*

In Canada drug couriers are typically sentenced harshly, but two recent Canadian cases had a different outcome (see *Hamilton* 2004). In both cases, women were arrested at Toronto's Pearson International Airport after returning from visits to Jamaica. Marsha Hamilton was arrested in 2000, and Donna Mason in 2001. The trial judge sought to place the participation of both of these women as drug couriers against a backdrop of race, gender, poverty, and inequality. His analysis of the cases speaks to the social conditions that shape women's conflict with the law.

Marsha Hamilton is a Black woman with a grade 9 education. At the time of her arrest she was unemployed and living in Canada, with family in Jamaica. She was twenty-eight years old and a single parent with three children under the age of eight. She had made a trip home to Jamaica and, in preparation for returning to Canada, had swallowed ninety-three pellets of cocaine with an estimated $69,000 street value. She almost died on the trip because the pellets leaked cocaine into her body. Marsha had no prior arrests or police record, and she stated that she had committed the crime for financial reasons.

Donna Mason is a Black woman with a grade 12 education. At the time of her arrest she was thirty-three years old and living in Canada. She had three children whom she solely supported on a limited income. Prior to the birth of her third child, she had worked full-time at a Wendy's restaurant for $8 an hour, supplemented by welfare assistance. She was also the choir leader at her church. Before returning to Canada from Jamaica, she had swallowed under one kilogram of cocaine pellets. She had no prior arrests or police record, and she also said that financial hardship was the main reason she committed the crime.

Both women pleaded guilty to importing cocaine, in an amount of under one kilogram, from Jamaica. Both were Black women of limited economic means. Both had dependent children. Both were first-time offenders. Their "profile" is similar to that of other women in prison for drug importation in Canada, Britain, and the United States. In 2003 Mr. Justice S. Casey Hill of Ontario's Superior Court of Justice sentenced both women. Their cases are groundbreaking because both women were given conditional sentences and not sent to prison. Hamilton was sentenced to twenty months; Mason to twenty-four months less a day.

The defence in each of these cases highlighted the role of the judiciary, and specifically the sentencing judge, in addressing injustices against Aboriginal peoples in Canada — injustices recognized in *R.* v. *Gladue* (1999). The defence argued that Black women should be granted similar consideration when the evidence presented at the trial suggests a history similar to that of Aboriginal women — of poverty, discrimination, and overrepresentation of Black women in the criminal justice system (*R.* v. *Hamilton* 2003). In contrast, the arguments in the Crown's case drew from conventional law and order discourses related to concern for the protection of youth and narcoterrorism and organized crime. The Crown argued that cocaine is a dangerous drug and that schoolchildren in Canada would have been at risk if the cocaine that the women carried had reached the streets. They also noted the prevalence of narcoterrorism in Jamaica, stating that huge profits were to be made by gangs participating in the illegal drug trade.

In analyzing the two cases, Justice Hill did not confine himself to the arguments advanced by the Crown and the defence. Rather, the judge drew from his own observations in the courtroom, as well as the findings of the Report of the Commission on Systemic Racism in the Ontario Criminal Justice System (Ontario 1995) to explain how systemic social and economic circumstances shaped the lives of Hamilton and Mason and other Black women moving through the criminal justice system.

The judge's ruling and the defence lawyer's arguments suggest that some criminal justice professionals in Canada understand that women's lived experience and their conflicts with the law are shaped and defined by race, gender, and class. The *Hamilton* and *Mason* cases exemplify the "typical" situations of women involved in importing. Poverty, discrimination, and race and gender inequality shape women's lives.

Nevertheless, the Crown appealed the decisions. In August 2004 the Court of Appeal for Ontario ruled that the trial judge had erred in his sentencing decision and in his "holding that systemic racial and gender bias justified conditional sentences." However, the Court of Appeal declared that "the administration of justice would not be served by incarcerating the respondents for a few months at this time. They have served significant, albeit, inadequate sentences." Marsha Hamilton and Donna Mason were therefore allowed to complete their conditional sentences (*R.* v. *Hamilton* 2004: 34, 39).

Neither Marsha Hamilton nor Donna Mason fit mainstream media and law and order representations of the drug trafficker or importer. Representations of well-organized, male, high-level drug traffickers who

are a threat to the nation-state deflect our attention away from larger political actions and from gendered, racialized, and class-biased drug policy.
Conventional representations of the drug trafficker also ignore the plight
of women and the structural inequalities that shape their participation in
the drug trade. The *Hamilton* case, therefore, holds a potential for change.
Justice Hill's decision was significant for its recognition of systemic factors in the imposition of conditional sentences and for challenging the
representations of women in illegal drug trade discourse. However, the
Crown's successful appeal and the 2004 ruling of the Court of Appeal for
Ontario demonstrate that much more needs to be done to challenge the
law and order discourse of judges and prosecutors, as well as gendered,
racialized, and class-biased drug policies.

Furthermore, none of the legal decisions, including Justice Hill's
argument for leniency, challenged Canada's draconian drug laws and
the representation of cocaine as a "dangerous" drug.[4] Nor did the legal
decisions recognize the criminal justice system as a site of conflict and
oppression. However, Sophia Lawrence and Toni Williams (forthcoming) argue that the "criminal justice system is an agent" in these women's
subordination. They also note that in Justice Hill's argument, culpability
is reduced if Black women suffer from poverty and systemic racism and
gender bias. Such an argument, they claim, contributes to mythologized
negative representations of impoverished Black single mothers as "drug
criminals." They point out that Hill's argument builds on a discourse about
poor Black single mothers who are trapped by their social and economic
situation and thus pushed into crime. Black women are depicted as "prone
to swallowing and smuggling" illegal drugs.

PUBLIC IMAGINATION AND THE DECRIMINALIZATION OF DRUGS

To address issues relating to women and drugs, we have to look more
closely at the discourses that surround the drugs themselves, the user,
the trafficker and the importer, and how such discourses support the
criminalization of particular drugs and the expansion of police budgets
and power. Since the emergence of the anti-opiate movement and the
enactment of our first drug laws, drugs associated with racialized peoples
have been depicted as being "outside the border" and more "dangerous" and "evil" than are the drugs associated with white, Anglo-Saxon,
Christian, Western nations. Critical and feminist researchers point out
that legal categories are cultural and social fabrications. Most illegal
drugs are grown and produced locally (marijuana, for example) and
share the same pharmacology as legal drugs (morphine and codeine are

both opiates). Nevertheless, negative representations about criminalized drugs and the people who sell and import them continue to inform the public imagination. Those who engage in drug trafficking are depicted as the most dangerous, because they are seen as foreign, greedy, corrupt, and threatening the health and security of the nation. Women who use illegal drugs and those who participate in the drug trade are represented as being even more immoral and criminal than are their male counterparts for transgressing their gender role and the law. Racialized women, especially Aboriginal women, have historically been represented as being more easily led astray, and more desperate, immoral, and dangerous than their white counterparts. These negative representations inform and shape policy. Even as we explore the possibility of decriminalizing or legalizing marijuana in Canada, our discussions about drug reform are accompanied by arguments about the dangerousness of those involved in the drug trade and their perceived threat to the nation. Thus, harsher sentencing for trafficking and production (such as marijuana grow-operations) and increased law enforcement funding are recommended at the same time as decriminalization of personal use is considered.

Many feminist activists around the world oppose the so-called war on drugs. They consider criminal justice and military initiatives to be in direct opposition to peace and social justice. Drug wars are linked to domestic and international economic instability (Boyd 2004). One practical response would be to legalize drugs. Legalization can be regulated (as in the case of alcohol). We would thus see an end, or at least a decrease, in the illegal market and in drug-trade violence. Furthermore, women's bodies would no longer be used as the newest terrain for advancing the war on drugs. Legalization of drugs would also limit the number of overdoses and lower the transmission of infectious diseases such as Hepatitis C and HIV/AIDs. It would strip drug use of its pathologized, racialized, sexualized, and criminalized status. It would remove drug use from punishment industries and contribute to the emptying of prisons.

As we see more and more belt-tightening cutbacks to economic and social services, the criminal justice, the military, and the prison industries are all expanding. Legalizing drugs could save billions of dollars — dollars that could be diverted to socially beneficial services. Women like Donna Mason and Marsha Hamilton would be supported by a caring society, rather than left to fend for themselves in a free-market economy.

NOTES

I would like to thank Arlene Wells, Elizabeth Comack, Gillian Balfour, and an anonymous reviewer for their thoughtful editorial comments.

1. *A Four-Pillar Approach* is a compilation of data from a series of public forums in Vancouver and does not represent the author's opinion. It is interesting to note that the number of crime control "initiatives" increased between the first public draft and the final report.
2. C. McGregor, Media Relations Officer, Correctional Service of Canada (Personal communication March 18 and May 20, 2004).
3. Ibid.
4. See Coomber and South 2004, especially the editors' chapter, "Drugs, Cultures and Controls in Comparative Perspective" (pp. 13–26) and Alison Spedding's chapter, "Coca Use in Bolivia: A Tradition of Thousands of Years" (pp. 46–64). See also Morgan and Zimmer 1997.

For a long time she was ashamed of her past. She had these scars, they were luggage she carried everywhere. She had explained them so many times, trapped in long sleeves, self conscious. She learned how to maneuver without ever turning her arms over. She held them tightly to her chest to save her from telling. Why do people have to stare? Where do they get the nerve to ask me why or what? How do I respond? It's my mood, at times I tried to laugh it off, at times I've been direct. Other times I've been angry and ashamed. Should I tell the whole story, should I say what I know now,

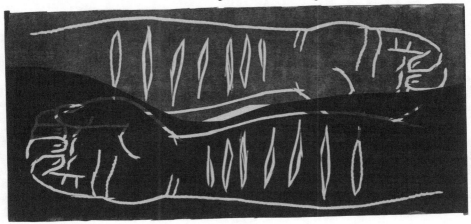

I didn't used to like myself? I was attacked by wild cats in the jungle. Or my favourite told to me by my uncle, "that's where the hawk landed and when he flew away." I loved to believe it because I admired him so much that I could actually forget that I had the same on my arms. But I don't ever recall any hawks. I didn't want to believe my uncle would do that. My scars. Self inflicted, self inflicted. They have held me captive for too long, held me Prisoner. Today I will wear what I want, go ahead, look, I am not ashamed any longer. I honour my Past. After all, it brought me here.

(Jackie Traverse, 2004)

Part III
REGULATING WOMEN AND GIRLS

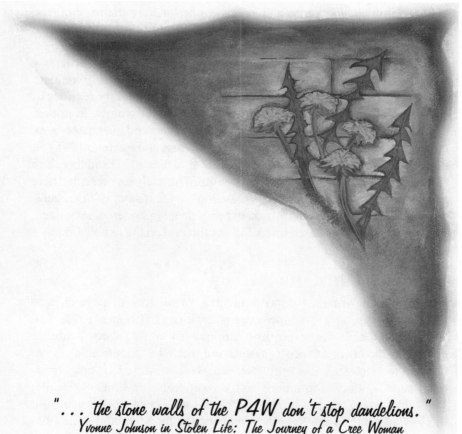

" . . . the stone walls of the P4W don't stop dandelions."
Yvonne Johnson in Stolen Life: The Journey of a Cree Woman

INTRODUCTION

Gillian Balfour

Conditions of poverty, racism, and misogyny very much characterize the lives of criminalized women — as we have seen in Part I of this book. The narratives of women's lives as sex-trade workers, gang members, and drug traffickers map out the connections between the choices that women make and how the conditions of their lives are and always have been linked to the socio-political context. In Part III our attention turns to how criminalized women and girls — as prisoners, patients, mothers, and victims — have been disciplined, managed, corrected, and punished through imprisonment, medicalization, and secure care.

The following chapters on the regulation of women reveal the legacy of moralizing discourses from the late nineteenth and early twentieth centuries — discourses that continue to shape contemporary regimes of control, such as the punishment and "correction" of women in prison. The more conventional view of criminalized women and girls casts them, historically, as "correctional afterthoughts" (Ross and Fabiano 1985) or, more recently, as "high need and high risk" (Laishes 2002) and therefore requiring intensive management and control. The analyses presented here provide a different view. Indeed, a close look at the history of the regulation of women and girls in Canada exposes deeply gendered, racialized, sexualized, and class-based interventions focused on the female offender as a failed citizen.[1]

THE IMPRISONMENT OF WOMEN

The history of women's imprisonment is "a mixture of neglect, outright barbarism, and well-meaning paternalism" (Cooper 1993: 33). Throughout the nineteenth century, criminalized women were oftentimes housed in the attics of men's prisons and treated as inconveniences or difficult to manage. These unruly women were subjected to "cruel treatment such as starvation and excessive corporal punishment" (Beattie 1977: 152-54). Canada's infamous Prison for Women (P4W) was built in 1934 adjacent to the Kingston Penitentiary for Men, and until 1995 was the only federal prison for women in Canada. Numerous government commissions — one of which, the Archambault Commission, reported only four years after the prison opened — denounced P4W. One of them said it was "unfit for bears, much less women" (Canada 1977). The facility was repeatedly condemned for closure, in part because of the cost of operating it for such a small number of women, but also because of the long-demonstrated low risk that the women housed there posed to public safety (Boritch 1997: 173).

Between 1920 and 1950 the criminalization of Aboriginal and white women for prostitution-related offences, vagrancy, and public drunkenness increased as part of a "broader web of gendered moral regulation articulated through law" (Sangster 1999: 34). By the 1950s 72 percent of all charges against Aboriginal women were alcohol-related. Between 1940 and 1950 the Female Refuges Act was more vigorously used to incarcerate Aboriginal women than it was for white women.[2] Joan Sangster (1999: 40) links this increase in the use of criminalization and incarceration of Aboriginal women to the migration of women in the 1950s into urban centres from reserves, leading to "spiraling economic deprivation and social dislocation." Reserve communities had been devastated by the impact of residential schools, which included physical and sexual abuse and the denigration of Aboriginal cultures and languages. This devastation was compounded by the lack of economic development and education on reserves. Young women fled the isolated reserves hoping to escape extreme poverty, only to find themselves facing racism, destitution, and homelessness in the city. Often they were charged with vagrancy or prostitution-related offences and sentenced to reformatories. Sangster suggests that policing and sentencing practices were informed by racialized and gendered images of the "drunken Indian," but were also deeply sexualized and class-based. Aboriginal women's public drinking and presumed sexual promiscuity offended middle-class sensibilities. Homeless and destitute Aboriginal women were viewed as "licentious wild women that symbolized sexual excess and need for conquest and control" (Sangster 1999: 44). Social workers and prison matrons described incarcerated Aboriginal women as "degenerate," "dirty," and "backward."

Although poor white women were also policed and imprisoned for similar types of offences — two-thirds of the women confined in the Mercer Reformatory in Ontario, for example, were convicted of public drunkenness and sexual promiscuity, and only 2.5 percent for assault — prison matrons and social workers responded much differently to them (Boritch 1997: 177; Oliver 1994). In contrast to the sexualized and racialized strategies of policing and punishment of Aboriginal women, white women received the "partial justice of degradation and humiliation and the positive elements of reform and discipline" (Dobash, Dobash, and Guttridge 1986). Poor white women were seen as unfortunate, childlike victims in need of protection. Nicole Rafter (1985b: 176) suggested, "Reformatories were designed to induce childlike submissiveness, and inmates were regarded as recalcitrant children." Prison programming of strict supervision and maternal care was intended to address women prisoners' lack of proper socialization and to instill proper virtues of domesticity and passivity.

Early feminist prison reformers were successful in achieving a separate prison system for women as well as gender-specific programming (such as training in homemaking skills and hairdressing). These reforms to women's reformatories were shaped by the broader socio-political context of moral regulation in the early twentieth century. Alan Hunt's (2002) study of social surveys from 1902 to 1919 shows how dance halls, movie theatres, ice cream parlours, skating rinks, department stores, and city parks were all sites of systematic disciplinary supervision. State and non-state agencies attempted to regulate the heterosexual lives of young working-class women and men — focusing, in particular, on the respectability of women — through the enforcement of by-laws and curfews. Interestingly, middle-class white feminists were instrumental in generating sexual purity campaigns to suppress prostitution and the spread of disease. These campaigns directly targeted young poor women and single women working as clerks in department stores (Hunt 1999a; see also Valverde 1991).

The early strategies embraced by prison reformers and feminist organizations such Elizabeth Fry Societies and the Women's Christian Temperance Society were rooted in the wider moral regulation. By the 1970s, however, explanations for the causes of women's lawbreaking as well as strategies for prison reform were being shaped by the liberal notion of formal equality to be achieved through legal challenges. A coalition of feminist academics and activists formed the group Women for Justice and launched a complaint with the Canadian Human Rights Commission to obtain equal treatment for women prisoners (Berzins and Hayes 1987). The Commission ruled that the Correctional Service of Canada had indeed discriminated against women prisoners. However, the solution to inequality was to make women's prisons more like men's prisons, despite the profound differences between men and women's offending histories and programming needs. In the end, women prisoners were to be treated like men and were bused into men's prisons for co-educational programs. Prison reformers quickly abandoned the strategy of formal gender equality because it had failed to achieve substantive equality or transformative justice for women prisoners.

In 1988 the tragic suicide of Marlene Moore inside P4W proved to be a profound moment in the history of the prison. Marlene had been raised in extreme poverty and was a victim of incest and rape (see Kershaw and Lasovich 1991). Institutionalized since the age of thirteen inside training schools and juvenile detention centres for status offences such as incorrigibility and running away, she eventually became the first woman to be declared a dangerous offender in Canada — even though she had never killed anyone. Rather, she was a repeat offender who was deemed not amenable to treatment. Marlene had attempted suicide many times and was a "cutter" — someone who uses self-injury as a way of managing profound emotional crises of fear or anxiety brought on by an overwhelming sense of powerlessness (Heney 1990; Fillmore and Dell 2001). A coroner's inquest was called to determine if prison protocols for the treatment of women in crisis contributed to Marlene's death. The Canadian Association of Elizabeth Fry Societies (CAEFS) was granted unprecedented legal standing at the inquest. Their strategy was to implicate the prison regime and staff in Marlene's suicide.

CAEFS believed that P4W had contributed to Marlene Moore's death by failing to provide her with the necessary therapeutic supports to prevent her from harming herself. The prison protocol at the time was to treat women who self-injure as threats to institutional security and to control women by segregating them. CAEFS, unfortunately, did not succeed in convincing the inquest's jurors that women in prison required therapy rather than control, but the media coverage of the inquest did draw attention to both the conditions inside P4W and the prevalence of sexual violence in the lives of criminalized women. Following the inquest, CSC announced the first-ever national Task Force on Federally Sentenced Women (TFFSW) to examine the conditions of women's imprisonment, their experiences in P4W, and their programming needs. The Task Force proved to be the most significant study of women's imprisonment in Canada, and served as a blueprint for unprecedented change in the treatment of criminalized women.

THE TASK FORCE ON FEDERALLY SENTENCED WOMEN

The striking of the TFFSW in 1989 was shaped by increased activism within the prison system by organizations such as CAEFS and its regional membership, Aboriginal women's organizations, and social justice groups. The socio-political context of the 1980s beyond the prison walls also reflected a broader awareness of issues affecting women's lives, an awareness underscored by the growing prevalence of feminist research in the areas of domestic violence, sexual assault, the feminization of poverty, single-parenting, and sexual harassment in the workplace. Feminist research methodologies began to reshape the analytical frameworks of activists and academics. Women's standpoint of their lived experiences of domestic violence, sexual assault, poverty, and racism began to define the agendas for change. In this way, the TFFSW was driven by a fundamentally new approach that called for the inclusion of women's experiences of criminalization and imprisonment, and emphasized the importance of community alliances in the development of a new, women-centred correctional model. A growing Aboriginal self-government political agenda also influenced the structure and aims of the TFFSW, illustrated by the inclusion of Aboriginal women (both prisoners and their advocates) on the task force and the commissioning of a survey of federally sentenced Aboriginal women in the community (see Sugar and Fox 1990).

The survey of federally sentenced women conducted for the Task Force (Shaw et al. 1991) was unlike most research on offenders in that it was a qualitative study that positioned federally sentenced women as experts. The women's narratives of their prison experiences provided a testament to the inadequate and damaging effects of a male model of corrections that "classified risk, prioritized needs, and fitted offenders into pre-structured programs" (Shaw et al. 1993: 55). From these narratives came the groundbreaking report *Creating Choices,* which revealed the prevalence of physical and sexual abuse in the lives of criminalized women and how abuse intersected with other difficulties such as drinking and drugging, violence, and mental illness (Shaw 1994a, 1994b). While many its recommendations focused on the immediate aims of addressing the therapeutic needs of women as victims, the report acknowledged the women's experiences as being compounded by the social context of poverty and racism. The relationship between women's victimization and their own use of violence — or what Karlene Faith (1993: 106) calls the "victimization-criminalization continuum" — was instrumental in defining a new gender-responsive correctional model.

Prior to the striking of the TFFSW, the federal government's correctional plan for the women prisoners had cycled through various configurations. Throughout the 1970s and 1980s, some women prisoners were held in provincial jails under exchange of service agreements so that they could remain close to their families and work towards their community reintegration; or they were confined in Kingston's Prison for Women and expected to participate in treatment programs based on a male prisoner model. Both approaches failed to meet the programming needs of women prisoners for gender-appropriate addiction treatment, educational and vocational training, and support in overcoming the trauma of abuse (Clark 1977; MacGuigan 1977; Needham 1978; Chinnery 1978; Canadian Advisory Council on the Status of Women 1981; Jackson 1988). Released in April 1990, *Creating Choices* called for the closure of P4W and the construction of four new regional facilities and a healing lodge for Aboriginal women. Programming within each facility would focus on a holistic, women-centred correctional model emphasizing five fundamental principles: empowerment to raise women's self-esteem; meaningful choices involving a variety of diverse programs in the prison and the community; respect and dignity to cultivate self-respect and respect for others; a supportive and nurturing environment; and shared responsibility amongst the woman prisoners, staff, and community. A series of key recommendations in the report also called for the development of a community release strategy that would offer increased resources for both the accommodation and treatment of women in the community.

THE IMPLEMENTATION OF CREATING CHOICES

While the federal government accepted in principle the report's main recommendations, the implementation of those proposals quickly deteriorated as CSC became more interested in a hierarchal top-down model as opposed to a tripartite consensus-building involving the community stakeholders, Aboriginal groups, and the government. Fears about public safety and a growing public backlash against prisoner rehabilitation also undermined the implementation process. CSC was required to enter into exchange of service agreements with the provinces where the regional facilities were to be built, and municipal and provincial governments were under increasing public pressure not to allow the construction of a women's prison close to their communities, especially without a perimeter wall, uniformed staff, or a traditional static security design. On one hand, the backlash from local communities was driven by wider neo-conservative political agendas of law and order and an increasingly vocal victims' rights lobby. On the other hand, neo-liberal economics had taken hold in most provinces, calling for fiscal restraint in the spending of public dollars (see chapter 8 here).

CSC further undermined the implementation of *Creating Choices* by excluding the Elizabeth Fry Societies from the National Implementation Committee, instead offering CAEFS a limited role in programming subcommittees. With this diminished status, Elizabeth Fry was quickly marginalized by the federal government, and less able to advocate for implementation of the recommendations of the Task Force report (Faith and Pate 2000). In 1992 CAEFS made the difficult decision to withdraw from the implementation process altogether to signify the organization's serious concerns over the CSC's shift in strategy in abandoning many of the principles of *Creating Choices*.

While the implementation process was underway, conditions inside the Prison for Women began to deteriorate. After the decision to close the P4W had been announced, the CSC's budget for P4W had been cut back to put monies into the new facilities, and senior staff had begun transferring out of the prison. These changes resulted in programming reductions and increased overtime hours for junior officers who had little knowledge of or experience in dealing with women prisoners. Meanwhile, the women prisoners were becoming increasingly frustrated with the inconsistencies in the prison's management and the absence of programming. They were also anxious about the lack of information related to their eventual transfer to another province.[3]

These conditions created a tense environment that sparked a confrontation between six prisoners and front-line staff in April 1994, resulting in the all-male Institutional Emergency Response Team (IERT) being sent into the segregation unit of P4W in riot gear to conduct "cell extractions" and strip-search the women (see Faith 1995; Pate 1999a; Shaw 2000; and also chapter 1 here). Shortly afterward, an internal Board of Investigation quickly produced a report, which included fifteen pages focusing on the profiles of the women prisoners involved in the incident, emphasizing their violent histories and institutional records. The report described the events inside P4W as "a planned attack on staff, perpetrated by a group of violent women who were attempting to escape" (Shaw 2000: 62), thereby justifying the use of force by male officers against women prisoners. The report made no mention of the strip-searching of the women prisoners by male guards or the IERT videotape made (as per "official policy") of the cell extractions.[4] Only after the CBC's *The Fifth Estate* obtained and aired a copy of the videotape were calls for a full inquiry into CSC's handling of the matter acted upon.

The report of the Commission of Inquiry into Certain Events at the Prison for Women in Kingston, headed by Madam Justice Louise Arbour (1996), described women in prison as "high needs/low risk." It also contained a critique of the Correctional Service for what Justice Arbour termed its violations of the rule of law. Arbour described the correctional system as being "out of control" and the behaviour of the male IERT as "cruel, inhumane and degrading." The CSC's response to the incident, according to Arbour, was to "deny error, defend against criticism and to react without a proper investigation of the truth." The report made some hundred recommendations, including the creation of the position of a deputy commissioner for women, stopping the practice of using male riot squads in women's prisons, and putting an end to the long-term segregation of women prisoners.

Between 1995 and 1997 the new regional prisons in Edmonton, Alberta, Kitchener, Ontario, Joliette, Quebec, and Truro, Nova Scotia, as well as the Okimaw Ohci Healing Lodge in Maple Creek, Saskatchewan, became operational. But it soon became clear that simply building new facilities was not enough to transform women's experiences of imprisonment. The CSC's response to several incidents involving suicides, slashings, walkaways, and disturbances at the regional prisons[5] was to implement a new agenda for the management of women prisoners — one that involved the reassertion of control and punishment (Shaw 2000). In 1996 the CSC announced that all women classified as maximum security would be moved to separate maximum-security units in three of the men's prisons, the P4W, or the Regional Psychiatric Centre in Saskatoon.[6] In 1997 it set up a new Mental Health Strategy for Women Offenders. The strategy adopted a broad definition of "mental illness" and "mental disorder." For instance, women could be identified as having mental health needs if they had a history of relationships characterized by abuse, dependent children, low educational attainment and limited job opportunities, or significant long-term substance abuse. In short, social marginalization was being transformed into a "mental health need" (Hannah-Moffat and Shaw 2001: 47). After commissioning a series of reports on the treatment and security needs of maximum-security women and those with acute mental health needs, CSC announced in 1999 the implementation of an Intensive Intervention Strategy for managing these two groups of women (see Laishes 2002).

Creating Choices took the position that women should not be held in the kind of secure environment that the P4W provided. It advocated cottage housing units, with an "enhanced" security unit to be used only on a temporary basis when required. Because women were seen as "high need/low risk" (Arbour 1996), they required support instead of security. Rather than classification, *Creating Choices* advocated an assessment of treatment needs and the use of a holistic as opposed to hierarchical model. Following the opening of the new facilities, however, CSC adopted an Offender Intake Assessment process. Initiated by cognitive psychologists for male prison populations, this scheme is based on an assessment of both risk and need, especially as these relate to rehabilitation prospects and the effectiveness of particular types of treatment. In addition to risk-based security placement and release decisions, the system assigns different levels and types of treatment based on a prisoner's "criminogenic needs." As Kelly Hannah-Moffat (2000) notes, what this approach does is redefine "need" as a "risk factor." Dependency, low self-esteem, poor educational and vocational achievement, parental death at an early age, foster care placement, constant changes in the location of foster care, residential placement, living on the streets, prostitution, suicide attempts, self-injury, substance abuse, and parental responsibilities: the system considers all of these as characteristics that give rise to criminogenic needs (Hannah-Moffat 2000: 37). The scheme also does not adequately take into account the gendered differences of need. For instance, women's pathways to substance abuse are different than men's, women's use of medical services and outpatient services are higher than men's, and women are less likely than men to have stable employment patterns.

Several of CSC's decisions also undermined the implementation of the healing lodge for Aboriginal women prisoners — and these decisions again violated the principles of *Creating Choices*. The initial plan for Aboriginal women at the healing lodge was to address the disconnection and dislocation experienced as a result of residential schools, child welfare apprehensions, and the Indian Act (Monture-Angus 2000). Instead, the healing lodge appeared to be governed by CSC's agenda of risk management through imprisonment, rather than the approved principles of healing and meaningful choices aimed at reconnecting Aboriginal women to their land, cultures, and communities (Monture-Angus 2000: 52). For example, because the healing lodge was deemed a minimum- to medium-security-level prison, Aboriginal women classified as maximum-security — who make up 46 percent of this group of women prisoners (CAEFS, 2003) — were denied access to the facility.

By 1998 it was clear that the programming for women prisoners was not going to be linked to a feminist analysis of the systemic nature of women's needs as envisioned in *Creating Choices*. Instead, CSC was implementing a system of cognitive behavioural programming, a therapeutic approach premised on the notion that "criminal offending is a result of the offender's inability to think logically, reason appropriately and to make rational decisions" (Pollack 2004: 694). Such an approach considered structural inequalities as irrelevant — it viewed any discussion of poverty, racism, or gendered experiences (such as rape) as the context of women's criminal behaviour as a denial of personal responsibility. Kathleen

Kendall (2002:183) argues that the cognitive behavioural paradigm of self-regulation "is consistent with neo-liberal strategies of individualizing social problems." Shoshana Pollack (2000b, 2004) found in her research that many Aboriginal and Black women prisoners rejected the cognitive behavioural paradigm as being irrelevant to their life experiences.

In 2003 the Correctional Investigator's Office (CIO)[7] reported on several key issues regarding the (mis)treatment of federally sentenced women. Access to programming and counselling remained abysmal due to long waiting lists and lack of services. Female offenders continued to be classified using inappropriate tools that translate poverty and lack of education into pathologies thereby justifying over-classification of most women, especially Aboriginal women, as maximum-security inmates. There was a chronic shortage of minimum-security facilities: for 101 minimum-security women, only 13 beds were available. The CIO also noted that there were virtually no community release facilities for women offenders, especially the women requiring mental health services. The Office reported that male guards held front-line positions at all regional facilities, despite continuing reports of sexual harassment, abuse, and assault. The CIO also condemned CSC's decision requiring all offenders serving life sentences to serve the first two years of their sentence in a maximum-security institution, regardless of their risk classification.

EMPOWERMENT AND RESPONSIBILIZATION

In 2004 CSC introduced a new correctional plan for female offenders that re-entrenched the view of criminalized women as being in need of cognitive therapy to address their criminal thinking. The plan considered women a greater risk because of their need for intensive treatment given the impact of severe childhood trauma of abuse and neglect upon their decision-making skills — causing them to "choose" drugs and alcohol, prostitution, and violence (see Fortin 2004). In short, women needed to learn how to take responsibility for their choices rather than challenge the conditions under which they must make such choices. Prisoners considered "difficult to manage" or unamenable to treatment because of their criminal personalities were to be managed under Dialectical Behavioural Therapy (DBT). In contrast to earlier feminist advocacy that sought to bring into a gender-responsive correctional programming an awareness of the broader social context of violence against women, DBT pathologizes women's experiences of victimization. It believes that women prisoners are not able to regulate their own emotions because of the impact of childhood sexual abuse. As such, their treatment needs are understood as being different than men's by virtue of the psychological damage of childhood sexual abuse and domestic violence (see chapter 9).

The complete erasure of structural inequality as a significant contextual factor in women's offending, together with the emergence of a risk-based discourse, signalled a dramatic shift in the regulation of women prisoners. How can we make sense of the more regressive and punitive response of CSC toward federally sentenced women — despite the progressive recommendations of *Creating Choices* and the dramatic findings of the Arbour inquiry? In part, it would seem that CSC was emboldened by an angry and fearful public, which was becoming increasingly influenced by media coverage of events such as the Homolka and Bernardo killings and was supposedly demanding protection through a punitive criminal justice response to crime. But in addition to such neo-conservative law and order sentiments, the dismantling of the welfare state under the sway of a neo-liberal rationality of governance had ushered in a new model of crime control whereby offenders were to be "empowered" to take responsibility for the consequences of their choices (O'Malley 1994; Hannah-Moffat 2000). Within this new model, terms such as empowerment — so central to the philosophy of *Creating Choices* — take on new meaning.

As Hannah-Moffat (2000) points out, feminist reformers invoked the language of empowerment as a way of recognizing women's power to make choices. The neo-liberal discourse, however, translates empowerment to mean holding women responsible for their own self-governance and calls for the minimization and management of their needs and their risk to themselves and the public. Hannah-Moffat (2000: 31) states:

> The responsibility of CSC is simply to facilitate this process. For example, if a woman is provided with a job-training program and completes the program, she is then seen as capable of obtaining employment upon release and is expected to do so. The current economic environment and rate of unemployment are not constructed as relevant, and in fact a woman's failure to secure employment and her reliance on social services is often interpreted as "irresponsible."

In short, under neo-liberal risk management schemes women are now being "responsibilized." This retreat by the federal government from its promise to implement the recommendations of *Creating Choices* becomes all the more concerning given that Canada — like other Western nations — has seen a large increase in the number of women denied bail and sentenced to custody for longer periods of time.

WOMEN IN CAGES

Public perception to the contrary, crime rates decreased over the decade from the early 1990s to the early years of the new century. In 2005 Statistics Canada reported that crime rates generally had been falling since 1991; the number of reported crimes in 2004 was down by 12 percent compared to a decade earlier. Most of the violent crimes reported were common assaults, and the rate of violent crimes in general was 10 percent lower than it had been a decade earlier. In 2004 the number of robberies fell by 4 percent — with half of the robberies committed without a weapon. The number of robberies involving a firearm was down by 3 percent; most robberies (35 percent) were carried out with other weapons, such as knives. The property crime rate, too, dropped by 3 percent and steadily decreased after 1991. The rate of break and enters fell by 4 percent — 36 percent lower than a decade earlier. With the increase of police crackdowns on marijuana grow-operations, the number of drug incidents grew by 11 percent in 2004, and over half of all drug offences reported by the police in 2004 were for simple possession of cannabis. The number of incidents involving young people reported to the police had also declined. The rate of violent crime among youth fell by 2 percent, including a 30 percent decrease in the youth homicide rate (Statistics Canada 2005).

While crime rates are down in Canada, worldwide women are the fastest-growing group of prisoners. The United States has seen an explosion in the number of women in prisons and jails: in 1970 5,600 women were incarcerated; by 2001 the number had reached 161,200 — representing a 2,800 percent increase. In Britain the annual average number of women in prison increased by 173 percent between 1992 and 2002 (Sudbury 2005: xiv). Julia Sudbury (2005: xvii) eloquently argues that the "global lockdown" of women inside immigration detention centres, psychiatric hospitals, and prisons is the manifestation of global capitalism's prison industrial complex, intended to "warehouse those surplus to the global economy and creating profits for private prison operators and corporations servicing prisons." Sudbury's analysis of this global lockdown reminds us of the many facets of the coercive power of Western capitalist democracies — such as the colonization (and criminalization) of indigenous peoples, the creation of legislation to combat the "war on drugs" that has incarcerated more women than men for trafficking of drugs, and the privatization of prisons to accumulate greater profits — and how these tactics aggressively affect women all over the world.

Although Canada has the third-highest rate of incarceration amongst

Western nations (116 adult and youth prisoners per 100,000 general population), criminalized women have long been considered "too few to count."[8] The Correctional Service of Canada reports that on April 11, 2004, federally sentenced women accounted for only 3 percent (379) of all penitentiary inmates. The vast majority of these women — 83 percent — were serving their first federal sentences (compared to 65 percent of male prisoners). Women were more likely than men to be serving shorter sentences (37 percent of women versus 23 percent of men were serving sentences of less than three years). In terms of the nature of their offences, the majority of federally sentenced women (58 percent) and men (64 percent) were serving time for Schedule I offences, although women were more likely than men to be serving sentences for drug trafficking and importing (Schedule II) offences (see Table 1). Women prisoners also tended to be younger than men prisoners; 29 percent of federally sentenced women were over the age of forty compared to 39 percent of men. While both Aboriginal men and women were overrepresented in prisons relative to their numbers in the general population, the percentages were even more severe for Aboriginal women: Aboriginal women made up 28 percent of the women's penitentiary population, while Aboriginal men comprised 18 percent of the men's.

Federal prisoners are classified at a minimum-, medium-, or maximum-security level in terms of their perceived security risk and programming needs. According to CSC, in April 2004, 37 percent of women prisoners were classified as minimum-security (versus 18 percent of men); 45 percent of women were classified as medium-security (versus 61 percent of men); and 9 percent of women prisoners were classified as maximum-security (versus 14 percent of men).[9] In part because of the small number of women prisoners, the costs of their incarceration are far greater than men's. Correctional Service Canada cites the average annual cost of incarcerating a female inmate to be $150,867, whereas the average annual cost of incarcerating a male inmate under medium security (where the majority of men are held) is $71,640 (Correctional Service of Canada 2005a).

The largest number of criminalized women in Canada languish inside provincial jails, sentenced for theft, impaired driving, fraud, shoplifting, prostitution-related offences, and other non-violent offences. In 2005, some 2,500 to 3,000 women were being held inside provincial jails, in addition to increasing numbers of women held in remand centres.[10] Studies of regional jail populations in the Prairie provinces reveal that nearly 90 percent of women prisoners in cities such as Saskatoon, Regina,

Table 1: Profile of the Canadian Federal Inmate Population, April 11, 2004

Length of sentence	Men (12,034)		Women (379)	
Under three years	2,746	23%	140	37%
Three to under six years	3,422	28%	117	31%
Six to ten years	1,679	14%	39	10%
Ten years or more	1,477	12%	15	4%
Life or indeterminate	2,710	23%	68	18%
Offence				
Murder–first degree	693	6%	16	4%
Murder–second degree	1,648	14%	50	13%
Schedule I* (excluding sexual offences	5,837	49%	214	56%
Schedule I (sexual offences)	1,814	15%	9	2%
Schedule II**	1,466	12%	74	20%
Non-scheduled	1,828	15%	44	12%
Serving a first federal sentence	7,796	65%	316	83%
Age				
Less than 18	5	0.04%	--	--
18–19	125	1%	6	2%
20–29	3,354	28%	125	33%
30–39	3,889	32%	138	36%
40–49	2,950	25%	73	19%
50+	1,711	14%	37	10%
Racial origin				
Aboriginal	2,193	18%	108	28%
Non-Aboriginal	9,841	82%	271	72%

Note: Individuals can appear in more than one category.
*Schedule I comprises sexual offences and other violent crimes excluding first- and second-degree murder.
** Schedule II comprises serious drug offences and conspiracy to commit serious drug offences.

Source: Correctional Service of Canada 2005a.

and Winnipeg are Aboriginal (Monture-Angus 1999).

While women have traditionally been sentenced to provincial incarceration for property offences and non-payment of fines (Johnson
and Rodgers 1993: 107), today more women are being criminalized for
domestic violence offences under mandatory charging and vigorous prosecution protocols in most provinces and territories (Pollack, Battaglia,
and Allspach 2005; Wood 2001). Changes in the response of the criminal
justice system to domestic violence have removed most judicial discretion to assess the context of a woman's use of intimate violence. Women
are therefore increasingly charged for using self-defensive violence or
are countercharged along with their spouses (Pollack, Battaglia, and
Allspach 2005; Wood 2001). (And as Susan Boyd outlines in chapter 5,
there has been a significant increase in the number of women charged
and incarcerated for drug-related offences.

The conditions of provincial lock-up also continue to deteriorate as
more provincial governments commit to a neo-liberal ethos — denouncing
the welfare state as too expensive while building prisons to increase jobs
in economically depressed voter-rich regions. For example, in Eastern
Ontario about thirty provincially sentenced women are held in the new
maximum-security superjail that incarcerates over 1,500 men. By 2005,
in Manitoba the Portage Correctional Centre for Women had been slated
for closure, but rather than reinvesting in community-based alternatives
(which are much more cost-efficient) the government was considering
building a new prison as part of a strategy to provide jobs in economically depressed rural regions of the province.

Prisoner advocate and feminist Kim Pate (2003) explains the connection between women's increased economic marginalization under
neo-liberal provincial governments and increased reliance by provincial
and territorial governments on prisons:

> We know the increasing numbers of women in prison [are] clearly
> linked to the evisceration of health, education and social services.
> We also know that the cycle intensifies in times of economic
> downturn. It is very clear where we are sending the people who
> are experiencing the worst in the downturn in the economy and
> social trends. Jails are our most comprehensive homelessness
> initiative. In terms of the rate at which women are charged, how-
> ever, there has been a 7 [percent] decrease overall in the number
> of women charged with criminal offences. In particular, we are
> seeing a decrease in the number of violent crimes committed
> by women [yet] there are increases in the number of women

in prison. These increases have occurred within the context of increased cuts to expenditures for social services, health and education throughout the country.

One of the consequences in Canada of the closure of the P4W and the construction of the healing lodge and regional prisons is that more women are being sentenced to longer periods of incarceration so that they can supposedly benefit from the treatment programs available. Prior to the closure of P4W, fewer women were receiving federal sentences, because judges were loath to send women to a prison so widely condemned. Ultimately, as more women are sentenced to prison "for their own good," the public will come to view criminalized women as being more and more dangerous (Shaw 1993).

BEYOND THE PRISON WALLS

Given the pathologizing of need as risk, and the socio-economic realities of neo-liberal economics, what do women's lives look like after they are released from prison?

In the early 1980s criminologists recognized that social-control mechanisms aimed at inducing conformity operated both inside and outside of the criminal justice system (Cohen 1985). These mechanisms are networks of professionals, such as social workers and counsellors, along with non-profit social service agencies, such as halfway houses, detox centres, and food banks. Each agency or expert engages in the supervision and reinsertion of the non-conformist (prisoner, addict, street person) back into the social control matrix of family and work.

Over time many of these agencies — such as church-based and charitable organizations — became an extension of the criminal justice and mental health systems, competing for operational funding to house, feed, treat, and supervise ex-prisoners and patients. Although neo-liberalism seeks to make individuals responsible for solving or handling their own problems, whatever they might be or wherever they spring from, it also seeks to put communities into the hands of "the market" for the delivery of social services. This approach to service delivery is seen as being more financially prudent and is rationalized as community capacity-building and empowering communities to take responsibility for their own problems and populations (Andersen 1999).

Critical criminologists such as Edwin Schur (1984) and Pat Carlen (2003) refer to the relocation of punishment into the community as "transcarceration." Feminist criminologists recognize that transcarceration regimes are also profoundly gendered. Through transcarceration women's and girls' relationships and bodies are governed "at a distance" through the reach of regulatory rather than criminalizing practices. Social-control networks of surveillance and observation within the community have expanded the gaze of the state through the use of halfway houses, shelters for battered women, food banks, probation officers, and community policing (Cohen 1985).

More recently criminologists have begun to take seriously the non-legal forms of governmentality — the process of social control in which the state works through civil society, not upon it (Garland 2001; O'Malley 1996). For example, low-income women on welfare are the target of moral scrutiny under the welfare laws of Ontario if they are deemed to be living in an unreported supportive relationship with anyone (the so-called "spouse in the house" rule) (Hillyard and Morrison 1999). According to governmentality theorists, the work of regulation is more diffuse across private and public domains; it involves technologies of surveillance and risk assessment that are often not administered by the criminal justice system (Ericson and Haggerty 1997).

INVESTIGATING THE REGULATION OF WOMEN AND GIRLS

The chapters that follow explore the historical and contemporary practices of the regulation of girls and women. In chapter 6 Robert Menzies and Dorothy Chunn tell us the story of Charlotte — a woman who defied many of the normative sexual and gendered expectations of the early twentieth century. Charlotte was imprisoned for most of her life as a patient/prisoner and was forced to endure brutalizing treatments for her undisciplined independence and resistance. Menzies and Chunn map out the gendered, class-based, and sexualized regulation of women that overshadows contemporary regimes of control inside and outside of the criminal justice system. Those regimes include risk-assessment technologies and gender-responsive treatment approaches, such as Dialectical Behavioural Therapy.

Turning to more recent times, Steven Bittle (chapter 7) focuses on how neo-conservative provincial governments have introduced coercive secure-care legislation to protect children from sexual exploitation. By embracing the discourses of victimhood and law and order, neo-conservative governments have furthered the neo-liberal interests of off-loading responsibility for the control and protection of at-risk youth onto families and communities. Developing a similar theme, Dorothy Chunn and Shelley Gavigan (chapter 8) outline the transformation of welfare laws in Ontario since the rise of neo-conservative politics and neo-liberal economic policies under Premier Mike Harris's government. Law and order rhetoric coupled with the individualism of neo-liberal economics resulted in the creation of new crime categories and a broadening of the regulatory powers of the state to properly discipline welfare recipients. Poor women with children were most vulnerable to these new policies, which ushered in a sharp reduction in welfare benefits, the ratcheting up of eligibility criteria, work-for-welfare policies, the creation of a welfare snitch line, investigations into the personal, intimate lives of welfare recipients, and the creation of welfare fraud as a criminal offence. In the end, neo-liberal governments — seemingly committed to smaller government — have increasingly relied upon the expansion of the criminal justice system to implement their policies.

Moving to inside the prison walls, Shoshana Pollack (chapter 9) argues that the gender responsivity in correctional treatment sought by feminist reformers in the 1980s and 1990s has been misused to reframe women's social exclusion as a psychological problem. Pollack takes specific aim at Dialectical Behavioural Therapy (DBT) — a regime introduced by CSC to treat women labelled as difficult to manage because of their aggression, independence, and defiant attitudes. Pollack suggests that DBT is an effective strategy in the governing of prisoners because it demands compliance and submission. Yet DBT is also complicit with the wider interests of neo-liberalism, as women must take individual responsibility for how they cope with the impacts of poverty, racism, and gendered violence.

Kelly Hannah-Moffat (chapter 10) also examines the interconnections between a women-centred correctional model and the trend toward governance through risk assessment. Through an analysis of decisions in 144 cases of federally sentenced women eligible for parole, Hannah-Moffat demonstrates how risk recidivism is assessed according to a gendered logic. Her data suggest that women's risk to reoffend is determined by their relational lives with their children and partners. Relationships are risky conditions unless women have received proper interventions, such as anger management or cognitive behavioural therapy to take responsibility for their relationship choices. Parole board members utilize records of women's past experiences of domestic violence — especially for those who have resisted abuse — as a possible predictor for future violence.

MaDonna Maidment (chapter 11) suggests that women living in the community after being released from prison can often re-experience their incarceration under the gaze of transcarceral strategies, such as home care or intensive supervision and support programs. Maidment argues that women experience such community release strategies to be as controlling and stigmatizing as imprisonment. In this way she demonstrates how transcarceration is particularly gendered as women are confronted with surveillance of their mothering, personal hygiene, and compliance with medication regimes.

The spaces and strategies used for the regulation of girls and women are hauntingly familiar. In the chapters that follow, historical sociologists, socio-legal scholars, and criminologists demonstrate how the state, through criminalization or treatment "for their own good," responds to women's and girls' resistance to their social isolation due to poverty/racism/maternalism/heterosexism. What emerges across all the narratives of criminalized and imprisoned women's lives is the profound impact of poverty and violence, and what happens to women when they choose to resist.

We are left to contemplate the words of Yvonne Johnson, a Cree woman who was arrested, convicted, and sentenced to life imprisonment for first-degree murder. Johnson offers a glimpse into the grief and loss she experienced as a mother separated from her young children — and her struggle to stay alive inside the belly of the beast.

NOTES

1. I use the term "female offender" — rather than woman prisoner — to intentionally draw attention to how women's identities are constituted by the "authorized knowers" (Snider 2003).
2. The FRA enabled the imprisonment of women aged sixteen to thirty-five, sentenced or even "liable to be sentenced" under any Criminal Code or by-law infractions for "idle and dissolute behaviour" (see Sangster 1996: 239–75, 2002; and chapter 2 here).
3. The government had announced in 1990 that the P4W would be closed by September 1994. P4W actually remained in operation until July 2000.
4. References to the women being strip-searched by male guards and the existence of the video had been edited out of the report. In addition, the report stated that the women had been given blankets and mattresses upon their return to their cells, which was untrue. The women were left for twenty-four hours dressed only in paper gowns.
5. For instance, between January and March 1996 there were two suicides and a series of slashings at the Edmonton Institution. In April 1996 seven women walked away from the Edmonton Institution. In a media release following the "escapes," CAEFS asserted that the women who had left the prison did so to see their families and were apprehended only a few blocks from the prison. There was also a disturbance at the Truro prison in September 1996 ("Problems Fester in New Women's Prisons," *Globe and Mail,* March 8, 1996; "Female Inmates Rampage," *Globe and Mail,* Sept. 7, 1996).
6. While this was to be a temporary measure (lasting eighteen months to two years), it was not until some six years later — in February 2003 — that women classified

as maximum-security were moved to "enhanced security units" inside four of the women's facilities.

7. "The Correctional Investigator is mandated by Part III of the *Corrections and Conditional Release Act* as an Ombudsman for federal offenders. The primary function of the Office is to investigate and bring resolution to individual offender complaints. The Office, as well, has a responsibility to review and make recommendations on the Correctional Service's policies and procedures associated with the areas of individual complaints to ensure that systemic areas of concern are identified and appropriately addressed." <www.oci-bec.gc.ca> (accessed Oct. 17, 2005).

8. Only the United States and England lock up more adults than does Canada. England imprisons 139 adults per 100,000 and the U.S. prisons hold a staggering 702 adults per 100,000 (Correctional Service of Canada 2005).

9. Some 5 percent of women prisoners and 6 percent of men prisoners had not yet been classified on April 11, 2004. See Correctional Service of Canada 2005.

10. Kim Pate, Executive Director of the Canadian Association of Elizabeth Fry Societies, personal communication, Oct. 3, 2005.

6. THE MAKING OF THE BLACK WIDOW: THE CRIMINAL AND PSYCHIATRIC CONTROL OF WOMEN

Robert Menzies and Dorothy E. Chunn

On an early autumn evening in the late 1940s, in a medium-sized city in British Columbia, thirty-three-year-old Charlotte Ross used a fourteen-inch carving knife to sever the jugular vein of her husband, Jimmy, as he sat sleeping in the living room of their fashionable duplex apartment.[1] She then turned the knife on herself, slashing her left wrist and throat, half-severing her trachea in the process. After an abortive effort to telephone the police, Charlotte slumped onto a sofa chair and gradually lost consciousness.

Hours later Jimmy Ross's son stumbled upon the macabre aftermath of the attack and called police. When officers arrived at the scene Jimmy was clearly dead. Charlotte's eyelids were fluttering and she was moaning softly. During the next two weeks, while Charlotte slowly recuperated from her wounds in the city's general hospital, police charged her with capital murder, and a string of local psychiatrists subjected her to a battery of mental assessments. When she was sufficiently recovered, Charlotte found herself in the city jail, alone in a cell, awaiting trial.

For more than two decades, as an "Order-in-Council" woman, Charlotte Ross would find herself trying to negotiate a psychiatry and law labyrinth and would experience the awesome powers of forensic justice in a more intensive and prolonged way, arguably, than has any other woman in B.C. history.[2] Her remarkable story poignantly reveals that the regulatory ideologies and practices visited upon supposedly "criminally insane" women who have transgressed the norms of womanhood far predate the neo-liberal era. Her sad journey illuminates the gendered operations of judicial and medical institutions during a key transformative era in the history of socio-legal responses to women's (and men's) madness and criminality. Her crime, mentality, intransigence, gender, and very identity combined to propel her into repeated conflict with the experts and officials who were striving to make sense of her — and to return her to what they considered a state of normalcy.

In the end Charlotte's tribulations can at least cast critically important light onto the dominant cultural understandings that constitute women's normative roles in law, science, and society, both in the context of her time and today. More generally, medicine and law often work in combination to pathologize women in conflict with the criminal justice system. In particular, in an intensive historical study that we undertook of Order-in-Council women like Charlotte, the medical and legal records and other materials reveal the dominant images of docile, responsible, sane womanhood that both frame the activities of psy-experts and, in turn, reflect wider understandings of gender, rationality, and order circulating globally through the public culture, then and now.

WOMEN, CRIMINALITY, AND MADNESS

From its inception in the early 1870s (Davies 1987; Kelm 1992; Menzies 2001), British Columbia's mental health system was a gender-stratified and segregated enterprise that initially interned far more men than women.[3] As in other jurisdictions (Brookes 1998; Finnane 1985; Geller and Harris 1994; Ripa 1990; Tomes 1990), female patients spent their days in women-only wards and/or buildings and engaged in forms of labour, leisure, and treatment that reflected deeply entrenched gender identities and expectations.[4] But while female matrons and nursing staff may have been omnipresent in the lives of these patients, the overarching authoritative identity of medical, legal, and administrative officialdom was unremittingly male.

On various levels of experience, the institutional careers in particular of Order-in-Council patients paralleled those of other women psychiatric inmates. They inhabited the same wards, supplied the same kinds of dreary domestic institutional service, were subjected to equivalent regimens of treatment and regulation, and endured the same long terms of confinement as did their civilly committed counterparts.[5] At the same time, their hybrid status as both criminal and insane conferred unique qualities on them, earmarking them as singular threats to an androcentric social, juridical, and scientific establishment. In contrast to "ordinary" madwomen, the "outwith" women (Carlen 1983: 155) who transgressed criminal as well as mental boundaries directly violated gender-identity standards of mind and action; in the eyes of authorities, they required exceptional measures of domestication.

Yet, notably, the crimes of most women considered to be criminally insane were then, and remain today, relatively minor. Among the thirty-eight B.C. cases in our study, thirty involved non-violent offences.[6] Only six Order-in-Council women during the period we studied, from 1888 to 1950, were charged with or convicted of murder. All killed family members, which is typical of women who commit homicide. All except Charlotte Ross took the lives of their own children, thereby inciting cycles of pathologization and pity that typically yielded comparatively lenient responses from the courts, and often diversion out of the criminal justice system altogether (Backhouse 1996; Bernier and Cellard 1996; Ward 1999; White-Mair 2000; Wright 1987).

Statistically, then, Charlotte Ross was an uncommon forensic specimen. But in the wider context of gender and power relations that infused mid-twentieth-century life, it is scarcely surprising that her case became by far the most infamous of these thirty-eight criminally insane women in British Columbia. The "black widows" (Skrapec 1994) who murder their husbands or male lovers are the embodiment of intimate danger. They have always precipitated reactions that are wildly out of proportion, given their miniscule numbers and the slight risk that they actually pose to men, society, and the state (Allen 1987; Chan 2001; Harris 1989; Hartman 1985; Jones 1996; Knelman 1998; Myers and Wight 1996).

While reactions were by no means uniform (Harris 1989), the black widow's liminal status was her defining attribute in the eyes of the community, science, and the law. She might be mad, but her insanity also expressed itself in calculated, "cold-blooded" crimes that were not fully female or male, willed or compelled, crazy or sane. According to official renderings (MacKay 1995; Moran 1981; O'Marra 1994; Walker 1968), many of these women knew right from wrong and were therefore legally accountable. Others, like Charlotte Ross, seemed to inhabit a medial mental zone between culpability and blamelessness, and arguably were all the more dangerous for their marginality. The urge to punish such women seeped through the languages and practices of modern psychiatry (Knelman 1998: 87).

Like other murderous women in Canadian history (Atwood 1996; Bernier and Cellard 1996; Kendall 1999; White-Mair 2000), Charlotte Ross was acting "against nature" or, rather, against the hegemonic, naturalizing images of a docile, nurturing, and subservient femininity. Moreover, in contrast to the conduct of many women who killed (Backhouse 1996; Dubinsky and Iacovetta 1991), Charlotte's seemed indefensible, and her inner motives opaque. Although her suicide attempt following Jimmy's murder — along with a record of prior psychiatric involvement — brought her mental capacity into question and justified the medical interventions that followed her arrest, to most observers at the time Charlotte Ross seemed the antithesis of a prototypical victim. Her husband had never been known to physically abuse her. He was a reliable breadwinner, and had recently been diagnosed with colon cancer. Thus, Charlotte's notoriety issued mainly from her positioning as a morally questionable and recalcitrant woman whose crime could not be attributed wholly to mental disease or defect. "The most sensational murderesses," writes Judith Knelman (1998: 121), "were spirited women who were a threat to the social order. Men and women alike were fascinated by [their] audacity and aggressiveness."

Throughout her many years of entanglement with the state's medico-legal apparatus, Charlotte Ross was, for all intents and purposes, on trial for moral turpitude. Her criminal and mental status were subsumed within, and inextricably bound up with, gender-laced assumptions about the quality of her character and her worth as a woman. In these respects, however atypical her case, the arc of Charlotte Ross's forensic career retraced the all-too-familiar contours of women's experiences with the criminal justice and mental health systems.

"AFRAID OF NO ONE": THE MAKING OF A BLACK WIDOW

Charlotte Ross grew up on a farm on the Canadian prairies, the oldest daughter among fourteen children in a poor family. According to the clinical records at Essondale, the provincial mental hospital, her father was a carpenter, a "short-tempered, aggressive, independent man... with deep religious convictions." He "could be physically violent... and dominated his passive ineffectual wife." As Charlotte said, *"He was like me — afraid of no one."*[7] Like many young women who came of age during the 1930s, Charlotte had an austere, arduous, and short-lived childhood. She was *"obliged and expected to terminate her schooling [at age thirteen] to help her mother look after the younger [children]"* as the family struggled to survive the onslaught of the Great Depression.

By age fifteen Charlotte had left home, but not her domestic service, finding work as a housekeeper. In the mid-1930s, while still in her teens, she met a man who was "apparently a drug addict, a dealer in narcotics, and a procurer of women." The man was said "to have seduced her," and she relocated with him to a small B.C. coastal town. He directed Charlotte to a local address that turned out to be the site of a "house of ill repute," where the proprietors seized her belongings. After some time Charlotte managed to escape from this sexual servitude, and she went on to obtain work as a waitress in what her physicians described as "one dive after another" in the Chinatown of a nearby city.[8] In the moralizing discourse of her clinical file, during that period in the later years of the

Depression, "Her dealings with men were on the basis of pick-ups and she indulged in some prostitution." She received treatment for venereal disease, became pregnant, and obtained an abortion.[9]

Charlotte Ross entered adulthood at an especially critical juncture in the history of Canadian working women. Although increasingly integral to the country's economy during the early twentieth century, young, single women who penetrated the public realm — through either choice or necessity — inevitably confronted the gendered forces of moral regulation. For the reigning state and civil agents and institutions of social purity, mental hygiene, eugenics, citizenship education, and other causes, the single, independent "working girl" of questionable repute was the embodiment of risk to traditional values of femininity, family, homeplace, and nation (Myers 1998; Sangster 2002; Stephen 1995; Strange 1995). Collectively, the "occupational wanderer,"[10] the "factory girl," the "pickup girl," and their ilk (Freund 2002; Roach Pierson 1990; Stephen 1995; Strange 1995) were the source of innumerable evils that represented an ominous trend in gender, race, class, and sexual relations. During World War II, when public panics targeting the evils of female promiscuity reached a crescendo in major cities, it was the transgressive and disreputable women like Charlotte Ross more than the professional sex-trade workers who were the main targets of moral enforcement sorties (Freund 2002). In these ways Charlotte's tale represents the experience of many Canadian women who breached the frontiers of normative family life as the twentieth century approached its midpoint.

Yet in many other respects the story of Charlotte Ross is unique. For one thing, she managed to extricate herself from her marginal life of waitressing and part-time prostitution and, as recounted years later by an Essondale social worker, she improved herself "as she went along." She "worked hard, saved her money and played the races." She took on a succession of jobs as a clothing store clerk, jeweller's assistant, and practical nurse and companion. One of her nursing assignments, involving an elderly salesman whom Charlotte tended through a fatal bout with cancer (authorities later described it as a "sugar daddy" experience), gave her economic stability. In partial payment for her services, he subsidized Charlotte's apartment and helped finance a coffee shop that she owned and operated through the war years.

Toward the end of the war Charlotte's life course took yet another turn when she met a prosperous local businessman, Jimmy L. Ross[11] — a seemingly sympathetic man in his late fifties. One of Charlotte's brothers would later affectionately describe him in court as "a prince."

At first Charlotte was a hired employee, but she and Jimmy were soon cohabiting, and within two years they had married while on vacation in the western United States. From the outset family and friends on both sides regarded the relationship with suspicion. During subsequent interviews with social workers, Charlotte's siblings depicted her as an aggressive and mercenary manhunter who had "been pursuing this wealthy man for a considerable period of time." As her sister put it, Charlotte "felt that she had made a 'good catch' in Mr. Ross and was rather inclined to look down on the rest of the family." For their part, Jimmy's business associates considered Charlotte a "gold digger" who had "taken in" their ingenuous, lovestruck friend.

Only weeks after the wedding, two shattering revelations punctured this already troubled domestic setting. First Jimmy divulged that he was suffering from cancer of the bowel and required immediate treatment. Then, while Jimmy was in hospital, Charlotte learned from her own family members that he had been leading two separate lives. Contrary to his many reassurances over the preceding three years, this "prince" had never finalized the divorce from his first wife. He also had an adult son who lived close to the Ross's home. When confronted, Jimmy claimed that he had no communication with his first wife and pleaded with Charlotte not to leave him. For a time, a conflicted Charlotte acquiesced.

It was then that Charlotte's immersion into the mental health system began. She precipitated her first psychiatric encounter by going to the city police and trying to lay an attempted murder charge against her brother. During her subsequent ten-day confinement on the psychiatric ward of the local general hospital, Charlotte accused Jimmy and her siblings of participating in a plot to poison her for her money. She threw her $1,500 diamond ring, a gift from Jimmy, down a ward toilet. During this and subsequent hospitalizations over the ensuing months, while Jimmy continued his cancer treatment, Charlotte endured insulin shock therapy and was eventually declared to be stabilized. One of her brothers advised that she be committed to Essondale, but Jimmy retorted, "I would not send a dog there."

The culmination of these events came six days after Jimmy's release from his latest hospital stay, during which doctors had performed a radical colostomy. By then Charlotte had decided to leave Jimmy because, in the later words of the Essondale social worker, "she could no longer place any trust or confidence in what he said." Moreover, after several days of nursing Jimmy and driving him to hospital daily, Charlotte's mentality was deteriorating. On the morning of Jimmy's death, Charlotte's brothers had visited the home, both later reporting (at Charlotte's preliminary hearing) that she had appeared "a wee bit sick mentally" and "seemed very strange at the time" and "she kept saying sarcastic remarks." That evening, after shepherding Jimmy through a further outpatient treatment session, Charlotte finally disclosed her intention to leave.

According to the clinical files, "an argument ensued, and she claims that she has no other recollection of what happened." When Charlotte next awoke, she was in a hospital bed. Jimmy was dead, Charlotte's slashed wrist and throat were stitched and bound, and her forensic "career" had begun.

UNFIT TO STAND TRIAL

Following her discharge from hospital, Charlotte Ross spent nine weeks in the women's wing at Oakalla, the province's largest prison and detention centre, located in the Vancouver suburb of Burnaby (Anderson 1993). Pending her murder trial scheduled for the spring assizes, Charlotte became the object of an intensive psychiatric inquiry. With three different medical experts involved, the inquiry was aimed at judging her state of mind at the time of the Jimmy's death, and her fitness to stand trial.

Charlotte Ross's legal predicament was clearly desperate. Charged with capital murder, and with all evidence pointing to her guilt, she faced very real prospects of execution by hanging (Anderson 1982; Hustak 1987; Strange 1996).[12] In theory, then, the involvement of medical experts should have been a godsend. A diagnosis of irresponsibility, incompetency, or general mental illness should have functioned to mitigate the charge or sentence, divert Charlotte out of the judicial system altogether, or — even in the worst-case scenario — support defence arguments for commuting a death sentence.[13]

Yet, as many observers (for example, Arrigo 2002; Coleman 1984; Menzies 1989; Sjostrom 1997) caution, the presence of clinical professionals does not necessarily dilute the power of criminal law. On the contrary, by supplying a pseudo-scientific rationale for penal sanctions, the forensic clinician functions to legitimize a powerful network of medico-legal control. Far from being diverted out of law's reach, those defendants deemed "mentally disordered" find themselves channeled into hybrid realms of regulation in which their characters and mentalities are as much on trial as are their criminal deeds.

Moreover, these mental health evaluations for the courts are intensely gendered (Allen 1987; Chunn and Menzies 1994; Kendall 2000; Menzies, Chunn, and Webster 1992). In ostensibly being "saved from law" (Smart

1989: 47), the woman defendant collides with a malestream system of forensic judgment that imperils her freedom, her state of mind, and her identity. The "doubly deviant" female forensic patient (Lloyd 2005) encounters a level of medico-moral scrutiny that often far exceeds that experienced by her male counterparts.

The three medical men who visited Charlotte Ross in Oakalla (two were Crown appointees, the other commissioned by the defence) produced virtually identical renderings of Charlotte's mind-state. Their assessments systematically replayed Charlotte's prior encounters with mental health professionals, her "paranoic" stance toward family and authorities, and the bizarre circumstances of Jimmy's death. These themes would become indelibly inscribed in Charlotte's official files and would register recurrently through her later encounters with psychiatry. The conclusions of one assessor — an eminent local psychiatrist — were typical. After three examinations (during the first of which Charlotte remained stonily silent), he wrote: " I am of the opinion that Mrs. Ross possesses delusions of a persecutory character which unfits her to stand trial from a mental standpoint as these delusions create such a personal fear that she seemed... duty bound to protect herself against such further occurrences."

Prior to Charlotte's assize trial for capital murder, the presiding judge held a hearing before a twelve-member jury to determine her mental competency. In their testimony, the three examining psychiatrists unanimously declared that Charlotte's delusions rendered her unfit to stand trial. Their opinion most likely gained support, in the minds of judge and jury, because Charlotte had discharged her lawyer on the very eve of the trial. On receiving this news, the judge had hastily summoned a substitute attorney from a local law firm, although the hearing was already in progress when the lawyer finally arrived. The jury deliberated for all of ten minutes before finding Charlotte unfit. Her automatic disposition under the Criminal Code was transfer to psychiatric hospital as an Order-in-Council patient, under a Lieutenant-Governor's Warrant, until she regained her fitness and could return to stand trial.

Charlotte's own memories of these events, conveyed to an Essondale physician two months following her admission, reveal much about her own experience of the trial, along with her abortive efforts to assume a measure of control over the proceedings and fend off a psychiatric commitment. She clearly wanted her day in court, but her limited knowledge of how law worked left her in an untenable position:

> I had an idea that this is what they were trying to do, to send me
> to this place ... so trying to stop that I used my own knowledge of

what I knew of the law, if I discharged my lawyer they wouldn't go on with the trial and I would be able to get another lawyer and have a trial, but apparently they still went on with the trial.... I was waiting for the judge to nod to me and say something to me to give me an opportunity to speak, I didn't want to jump up — I didn't know just the procedures to go through, which naturally I just sat there... and several times I had the opportunity to say something if I had known the right thing to say. Anyhow the jury went out and that was that.

Equally illuminating were Charlotte's reflections on the trial's aftermath. At a later Essondale case conference, she told the assembled hospital physicians and staff members, "*I didn't see [my lawyer] after my trial and I never saw him for seven weeks previous.*" Moreover, the evening before her trial, one of the appointed psychiatrists visited her for the first time in seven weeks. According to Charlotte, "*He said that I was looking very well and a few things and then left. He met [lawyer] in the hall and had a few words together, then [lawyer] came in to see me and proceeded to say what was going to happen.*" When one doctor asked, "Were you satisfied with that arrangement or would you have preferred to have gone to trial?" Charlotte replied emphatically, "*Well I would have preferred to have gone to trial for several reasons.*"

It is clear that Charlotte had accurately gauged the implications of her medical diversion to Essondale as an "unfit" criminal defendant. Her consignment to medico-legal limbo was an unwelcome, deeply resented intrusion. Her tireless protests against her mental confinement, her claims to be fit for trial, and her inexhaustible demands for access to justice rapidly emerged as the leitmotifs of her mental hospital experience. As Charlotte confided to her ward physician shortly after admission, commitment to Essondale was "*the very thing I didn't want to happen.... If I'm going to stand trial there is no reason why I can't stand now. Why didn't I stay in [gaol] and get my lawyer? If I was able to stay in [gaol] for nine weeks altogether, do my knitting, help the girls there, I don't know why I have to come here for treatment.*"

"UNDER CLOSE SUPERVISION"

Charlotte Ross spent thirteen years on the wards of the Essondale Women's Chronic Building. Like other women psychiatric inpatients (Davies 1987; Kelm 1992; Geller and Harris 1994; Reaume 2000; Ripa 1990), Charlotte found herself in a highly regulated institutional sphere in which the hierarchical doctor-patient relations were obvious and gender figured prominently in every minute detail of daily life. For many, isolation from the world beyond the walls was total and gender-segregated. Men rarely entered the East Lawn wards, particularly after the arrival of women psychiatrists at Essondale in the late 1940s. Moreover, contact between physicians and patients was sporadic at best. As Charlotte observed in a letter intended for her mother, but confiscated by staff, "*We had gotten so many Doctors in such a short time it was rather difficult to get an appointment with any of them.*"

Aggravating Charlotte's dilemma was her "criminally insane" status, which consigned her to a locked ward, restricted her comings and goings, disqualified her from grounds privileges, and inhibited her interactions with ward physicians. As Charlotte wrote in the same letter to her mother, "*I am an Order of council, and... I can not get a Doctor that will stay long enough to get interested in my case.*" But in contrast to her tenuous and often hostile relations with staff, Charlotte clearly took pleasure in the company of other women patients and benefited from the feminine culture prevailing on the wards. "*The ladies are very nice and very considerate,*" Charlotte observed in one case conference, "*because we realize we are all in the same boat so to speak, we are all rowing for one thing, and that is to get well physically and mentally and be able to live what is considered a normal life on the outside.*"

Charlotte's experience as an Order-in-Council patient at Essondale pivoted around the continuing efforts of medical authorities to appraise her mental competency and responsibility, to chart her moral biography of pathology and violence (Allen 1987; Carlen 1983; Chunn and Menzies 1994), and to identify the afflictions that had allegedly propelled her into hospital. As many feminist researchers and authors have observed (Becker 1997; Bordo 1988; Caplan 1995; Raitt and Zeedyk 2000; Stubbs and Tolmie 1999), psychiatric classification is highly gendered, as much concerned with women's moral transgressions and violations of normative femininity as it is with their supposedly defective states of mind. In Charlotte's case, she received a diagnosis of "Schizophrenic Reaction — Paranoid Type." "It is evident," physicians reasoned, "from her evasions and occasional blocking in her speech that she has systematized a delusional formation beginning at least as far back as the time of her marriage and involving ideas of jealousy, the police, and the idea that someone is after her money."

The psychiatric interviews that led to these conclusions were revealing in their own terms. Charlotte plainly took exception to the confessional, mind-probing qualities of her encounters with hospital staff. She especially resented physicians' efforts to elicit legally relevant information that, in her judgment, had no bearing on her medical status. One exchange with her first ward physician occurred shortly after her admission, and offers insight into the dynamics of these diagnostic "consults." The physician had also testified at Charlotte's fitness hearing.

> Q. What do you plan? You have arrived here and now what do you think is going to happen?
>
> A. *I just sit and wait on what you doctors say.*
>
> Q. You are quite content to abide by the decision of the doctors outside to have you here?
>
> A. *I certainly am not. There isn't anything I can do. I have fought and fought and everything I did — what did they do on Saturday — rushed in and said you are going and here I am. I fought about coming to this place ever since they started.*
>
> Q. The only way in which your present status can be altered is to talk to people on just [what] your future is.
>
> A. *If it didn't help me when I was there, how is it going to help me when I'm in here?*
>
> Q. It may not help you but it is the only possibility you have.
>
> A. *No. I did all I could to keep from coming in here. Now I'm here anyway. I don't see any sense in my taking up your time.*

Supplementing these interviews were periodic "case conferences," in which physicians, psychologists, social workers, nurses, and other staff members congregated to conduct group inquiries into Charlotte's mentality. These exercises invariably ended in frustration. Charlotte remained resolutely silent about her criminal charges. Claiming the protections of legal process, and citing the unhappy experience of her fitness hearing, she disputed doctors' claims to be acting in her best interests. In one such encounter Charlotte showed that she was more than a match for the assembled professionals. Stymied by her continuing intransigence, an exasperated head physician finally resorted to a thinly veiled threat — an ominous expression of his ultimate power to determine Charlotte's fate:

Q. All we are interested in is your own health, your mental health and physical health. We have no interest in the legal aspect of your difficulties, it is only in your personal health we are interested so if I ask you any question you would rather not answer you don't need to answer. I'll try to ask no question like that. In any case it is merely between ourselves from a doctor and patient angle.... Would you care to give any statements to me?

A. *I can't very well.*

Q. What transpires here is a confidence between doctors and patients and is never broken.

A. *Pardon me for saying so, Dr. [ ] said that to me and he is a doctor — it isn't that I doubt any doctors it has just made me a little wary of that fact.*

Q. It makes it [difficult] when you are not willing to discuss and talk freely with us very difficult for us to come to any conclusions to be of assistance to you. You can see that point?

A. *Maybe. On the other hand I don't need any assistance.*

Q. Well, you need assistance at least to get out of here.

A. *Yes, I understand that....*

Q. You tell me what you would like to do? What would you like us to do for you?

A. *Well, naturally I guess you are going to laugh at me, I would like to be left alone, let me go out and stand my trial and attend to my own affairs.... What point is my staying here? How long am I going to stay? Is there ever a chance of going out, or what is it?*

Q. You will have to stay here until we say you are ready to leave here.... And yet as you sit here not talking to me you are making it difficult for me to arrive at that conclusion are you not?

A. *Not in the way I look at it.... As I said before I talked to Dr. [ ] and he said he was going to help me and I still came here. I told him then and I told Dr. [ ] then. I still came here.*

Such unbending resistance could not be ignored. At Essondale, as in similar settings elsewhere, practitioners typically interpreted women's refusals of this sort as "pathologies of female protest" (Bordo 1988: 87), symptomatic of deep and dangerous mental aberrations. Following this interview, clinicians diagnosed Charlotte with paranoia and recommended insulin treatment.

Clearly, Charlotte was keenly aware of the price that she paid for refusing to assume the deferential patient role. In persistently rebuffing authorities and declining to address her charges and trial (because, in her words, *"that is legal, and that is personal"*), Charlotte confirmed the clinical impressions of her "paranoic" personality state. Following one such encounter, the presiding psychiatrist was led to opine that she "successfully retreats behind the defense that her lawyer had instructed her not to divulge this material as it pertains to the legal and not to the medical issues involved," and that "her defenses of denial and projection are inadequate methods of dealing with her difficulties."

But Charlotte's struggles extended beyond her resistance to interviews. Over the course of many years, Charlotte's transgressions violated nearly every aspect of the mandated role for women patients. She retained a lawyer. She wrote countless letters to governmental officials and potential advocates outside the hospital. She accused staff physicians of impeding the discharge of patients through their "professional and political influence." Moreover, she was not above mobilizing her reputation as an alleged knife-wielding murderess to advantage by approaching doctors she disliked and offering to cut their throats — behaviour that confirmed their view that "she must remain under close supervision." From Charlotte's perspective, the medical men were her sole adversaries. *"It is funny,"* she confided in one conversation, *"but I have never got mad at the patients or staff in hospital — it has always been doctors."*

In their efforts to manage Charlotte, the Essondale authorities relied mainly on the somatic therapies that were dominating institutional psychiatric practice through the post-war era. In the second summer of her detention, Charlotte endured more than two months of daily insulin injections. These treatments induced fifty-eight comas lasting several hours each morning, after which Charlotte returned daily to the ward sewing room for afternoon "occupational therapy" sessions. The effects of the insulin were immediate and profound. After a week of injections, Charlotte wrote a letter to a friend on the outside. The physicians (alarmed as much by the scarcely recognizable scrawl, no doubt, as by the contents) confiscated the letter:

Dear [ ]. since I have been taken treatment this past week I don't believe I have had a letter from you or have I written any. I really have been too sick this past week for the first time since I have arrived here. I was doing very well on my own so to speak, and everyone has been so surprise to see me on treatment, they say they don't understand because I was the last person they expected to see taken these treatments.... And apperetly it will take untell early this fall before I am through taken them. I am taken these treatments every morning.... And feel far worse since I have been taken them. I don't mind so much if they were doing me some good.... So would be pleased to see you any time you can get away. Your Loving Friend. Charlotte.

But Charlotte's treatment had scarcely begun. Doctors introduced electroconvulsive therapy (ECT) during her fifth year in hospital, and reintroduced the shocks intermittently thereafter. During one typical course of ECT, Charlotte experienced twenty-one grand mal seizures over a seven-week period. "*All this shock,*" as Charlotte described it, was devastating. In a note conveyed to the medical superintendent, written nine years after her admission, Charlotte declared that "*the word 'Shock Treatments' or 'E.C.T.' makes me ill to my stomack.... I'm off my food can not sleep, also have lost weight.*" Some three years later, after a great many more ECTs, her ward physician speculated that Charlotte had incorporated ECT into her paranoid belief system, since she had voiced the opinion "*that electroshock was a criminal procedure and... that it had its beginning some way that was not acceptable.*"[14] Despite her protests, the shocks continued. When anti-psychotic medications became available in the mid-1950s, doctors placed Charlotte on potent doses of largactil. When her blood pressure began to plummet dangerously, they shifted to riserpine. Afterwards, they reported, "She works in the laundry and is much more amenable." For Charlotte's treatment, it seemed that patient docility was the main arbiter of a successful regimen.

If compliance was the measure of recovery for women like Charlotte, it also offered the best available means of escape from the locked hospital wards. Whether induced by electricity, chemistry, burnout, or a genuine cure, Charlotte's conduct change by the late 1950s was conspicuous. Incrementally, in response, staff began to confer previously withheld privileges, such as bimonthly "comfort" payments of $50 (supplied by the attorney general's department). Correspondingly, in perceptible gradations, the psychiatric assessments began to change. "Mrs Ross," observed one physician:

has taken very responsible jobs in working in... the kitchen, helping recreation to supervise grounds picnics and she had free access to the gardens and to the picking of flowers to decorate her ward and the dining room. She has talked to me about the "poor patients" and she has told me how some of the patients are confused as to whether she is a patient or a staff member.

Near decade's end, Charlotte finally earned her transfer to an open ward. Her long-awaited emancipation from Essondale was apparently within reach.

"NOT UNFIT TO STAND TRIAL"

For Charlotte Ross, as for those in similar situations elsewhere, the law was a potential redeemer, and a valued alternative to the psychiatric purgatory that had entombed her for more than a decade. Charlotte was acutely aware of the inequities that she faced in being denied access to the courts. As her hospital experience attests, Charlotte showed both ingenuity and resolve in her efforts to enlist the protections of law. From her point of view, establishing mental competency before the courts was her best chance for escape from the asylum. But as ensuing events would affirm, Charlotte had failed to gauge the full extent of psychiatry's powers over her existence.

Toward the end of the 1950s, Essondale physicians were still resisting Charlotte's return to court. According to one psychiatrist, "In her present state of health... her personality would disintegrate in the court setting." In advising against a trial, this doctor reminded others that Charlotte faced execution if convicted on the capital murder charge. A colleague physician added that, even should Charlotte proceed to court and somehow be acquitted, she would still require further inpatient treatment under the Mental Health Act. When Charlotte protested angrily against this opinion, the doctor "told her that her response indicated that she may be ill still."

Nonetheless, as the 1960s dawned, the Essondale staff physicians, under relentless pressure from Charlotte and her lawyer — and perhaps impressed by her improved conduct on the wards — at last reported that she "had recovered sufficiently from her psychotic condition to be returned to court to stand trial." So advised, the provincial attorney general lifted Charlotte's warrant, and she returned to Oakalla pending her assize court trial in the spring.

When Charlotte Ross's day in court finally came to pass in the early 1960s, it rapidly mutated into a media circus for the local press, a field day for participating psychiatrists, and a topic of titillation for a captivated public. In the tradition of Victorian murderesses, about whom much has been written (Knelman 1998), Charlotte came to be portrayed as the quintessence of the crazed and lethal black-widow temptress whose warped mentality and morals had exploded into untold mayhem (Shipley and Arrigo 2004; Skrapec 1994). With all context and nuance purged from her story, Charlotte found herself reduced to a cipher for the objectifying, cautionary tales that issued forth in the courtroom, medical science, media discourse, and public culture about the dangers and disorders of femininity gone wrong.

After the jury's double-negative declaration that Charlotte was "not unfit to stand trial" (despite her diagnosis by three prosecution psychiatrists as a "paranoic schizophrenic"), the trial proper began. Under the headline "Hidden Fears Beset Once-Happy Woman," one journalist's account described "a comely brunette on trial for her life." She looked "haggard and drawn after nearly three days in the prisoner's box, the last two listening to testimony surrounding the... knife-slaying of city car dealer Jimmy L. Ross." According to this rendering, "Mrs. Ross sat with downcast eyes as one of her brothers described her sudden change of character... how she suddenly became transformed from a cheerful, happy, normal person to an individual beset by nameless fears and suspicions — an individual who secreted a gun in her bedroom and who obtained cartridges to fit it." Charlotte's union with Jimmy devolved, in her brother's testimony, into a "supposed marriage" to a "common law husband" — an invalidating theme subsequently reinforced by both prosecution and state-appointed psychiatrists. Then medical witnesses for both defence and Crown offered a litany of evidence attesting to Charlotte's mental state at the time of the killing, and her resulting incapacity to distinguish right from wrong under the Canadian Criminal Code's version of the McNaughten rules.[15] One expert testified, "she was... upset by the prospect her common law husband was jilting her, or about to jilt her." Another, who had treated her two months before the murder, revealed that Charlotte had "thought her food was poisoned by Jimmy Ross. She had said 'they wanted to kill me because I was not good enough for the social position.'"

On the fourth and final day of the trial, Charlotte herself took the stand. "Dressed in black, with black and white gloves," as one newspaper reporter recounted, "she hesitated before answering questions from counsel, and gave her replies quietly. During her testimony, the spectators in the public gallery were so quiet the rustle of counsel's gowns sounded unnaturally loud. She denied any recollection of events leading up to the death of Jimmy Ross." Unsurprisingly, Charlotte's version of events did not go unchallenged. "Crown prosecutor," the reporter continued, "submitted Mrs Ross to a searching cross-examination of her life leading up to the time she met Jimmy Ross and went through a form of marriage with him."

When the trial ended, the assize court jury deliberated for all of thirty-four minutes before rendering a verdict of "not guilty by reason of insanity."[16] Initially Charlotte was relieved to hear the presiding judge order her returned to Oakalla. In a subsequent visiting-room conversation (surreptitiously recorded by the prison matron) with her brother-in-law, a protestant minister, Charlotte confided that "she had asked to be sent back here, as she felt that she just could not face Essondale again, and her lawyer had told her that she would only be here for about a week." It was with shock and disbelief, then, that Charlotte learned about the provincial attorney general's decision to issue a second Order-in-Council, which called for her return to Essondale for another indeterminate term of confinement. For Charlotte, this double jeopardy outcome was the worst-case scenario. The Oakalla prison matron reported that when she broke the news, Charlotte "raved" about the attorney general, "said she came her[e] at the Lieutenant Governor's pleasure and Mr. [Attorney General Robert] Bonner had stepped in and taken over and he was doing everything to suit himself...."

AFTERMATH: STILL AFRAID OF NO ONE

In the wake of her insanity acquittal, Charlotte, now forty-eight years old, incredibly found herself back on the closed wards of Essondale. At first defiant, Charlotte "refused physical examination" at readmission "on the grounds that she no longer came under the jurisdiction of the hospital authorities." But she quickly realized the grim realities of her plight. And while even the physicians acknowledged the folly of her continuing detention, they stopped short of conceding that her protests might be entirely rational under these surreal circumstances. "She presents a most difficult problem," wrote her presiding psychiatrist, "in that her very real and justified resentment at being detained in hospital indefinitely is difficult to distinguish from her morbid state of paranoid schizophrenia." Ambivalently, he and his colleagues petitioned the provincial attorney general, Robert Bonner, to vacate this new Order-in-Council, but he refused. Meanwhile Charlotte began to deteriorate and, during the following winter, doctors subjected her to two months of sleep therapy[17] followed by another course of chlorpromazine.

A year later, authorities at last deemed Charlotte Ross sufficiently sane to exit Essondale on leaves of absence. On the outside Charlotte reverted to working variously as a housekeeper, waitress, and domestic under the long arm of an indeterminate Order-in-Council that placed strict conditions on her freedom. But, true to form, Charlotte resisted supervision. As her caseworker complained, "After Care appointments and visiting as a part of hospital service were dismissed scornfully as she has 'never received any treatment or service'…. She repeatedly said she would not be 'snooped upon'…. and that I must not show my face around the motel again." Charlotte continued to evade social workers and miss appointments until the Essondale administrators finally placed her on AWOL and notified police. By the mid-1960s, Charlotte was again back in Essondale, now called Riverview,[18] where physicians reaffirmed her diagnosis of "schizophrenic reaction paranoid type." She spent another three months on the wards, still *"Waiting to get my final release from the Attorney General."*

Release came the following autumn when Attorney General Bonner grudgingly lifted Charlotte's Lieutenant-Governor's Warrant. Three days later, Riverview Hospital medical staff discharged her. There was no follow-up, for, in the words of the discharging physician, "Mrs. Ross is so evasive that it is almost a physical impossibility to keep in touch with her. Her employment has been sporadic and the hours irregular and she will not make an effort to arrange appointments. She has not once given a change of address. We know of no community agency who would give service to so unreasonable and paranoid a client."

Charlotte Ross had one further encounter with medico-legal authority — a voluntary admission toward the end of the 1960s after her employer, for whom she was working as a domestic, reported to police that she was voicing delusions. Now considered a hopeless case, Charlotte received short shrift from hospital staff: "Despite an attempt to dissimulate and play the role of a normal person," doctors wrote, "she betrayed her basic condition and personality on several occasions evidencing extreme verbal hostility with slight provocation." Charlotte's continuing truculence also earned her a new label as a "Personality Pattern Disturbance — Paranoid Personality." Physicians also made several references to the pathological condition of her entire family. Yet, ironically, they discharged her into the arms of these same relatives.

Sadly, Charlotte's life continued to spiral downward after this last official encounter with the provincial mental health system. In the early

1970s a public health officer in another region of British Columbia contacted Riverview Hospital for information about a new patient, Charlotte Ross. She was living alone in a farmhouse eking out a marginal existence on unemployment insurance and was afflicted with "many problems, both physical and mental." After that, the files tell us nothing more about her.

Some might argue that Charlotte Ross was the architect of her own fate. As medico-legal officialdom would have it, Charlotte's downfall was best understood as a cautionary tale about the ravages of a disordered mind, the perils of a woman's promiscuity, and the end that awaits those misguided or diseased female mental patients who fail to yield to the reasoned ministrations of therapeutic science. But such an account — replicated again and again throughout the historical clinical files of female mental patients in British Columbia, as elsewhere — represents at best a partial and refracted rendering of women's experiences with the state's psychiatric apparatus. Charlotte Ross's melancholy tale reveals just how tenuous and open to challenge were the psychiatric lines of demarcation between defect and reason, madness and sanity, good and evil. If Charlotte did leave a legacy, it lingers in the fallacies, hypocrisies, and contradictions that she managed to expose in the state's relentless efforts, through its public mental health enterprise, to domesticate "criminally insane" women.

Her ultimate decline and fall in no way detract from Charlotte Ross's exceptional capacity — despite her status as a reputed madwoman and murderess — to contest the androcentric, normalizing practices of constituted medico-legal authority. After many, many lost years, she arguably had wrested back her right "to be left alone," and she was still "afraid of no one."

NOTES

For a longer version of this chapter, see Menzies and Chunn 2005. For their valued comments and support we are grateful to Elizabeth Comack, Gillian Balfour, Wendy Chan, and the two chapter authors who reviewed an earlier manuscript draft. All errors and omissions are, of course, our own.

1.   To safeguard confidentiality, we withhold and/or alter dates and place names throughout the chapter. Charlotte Ross, like all other names mentioned in the chapter, is a pseudonym.

2.   Order-in-Council women included those considered unfit to stand trial, or not guilty by reason of insanity, or transferred from prison because of mental disorder. Charlotte Ross was one of thirty-eight Order-in-Council women whose clinical files we surveyed in a project on the experience of gender, crime, and "insanity" in British Columbia's mental health system between 1888 and 1950 (Chunn and Menzies 1998; Menzies and Chunn 1999).

3. The main institutions were the Victoria Lunatic Asylum (1872–78) and its successors — the Public Hospital for the Insane opened in 1878 and the Provincial Mental Hospital, Essondale, in 1913. The percentage of women in mental hospital admission registries and provincial census statistics were, respectively: 23 percent and 25.6 percent in 1881; 22.6 percent and 29.1 percent in 1901; 30.7 percent and 41.5 percent in 1921; 42.2 percent and 46.0 percent in 1941; and 45.7 percent and 48.6 percent in 1951 (Menzies and Chunn 1999: fn 17; see also Labrum 2005).

4. During the early twentieth century, the facilities of the Public Hospital for the Insane were reserved exclusively for women. The gendered deployment of patients shifted again in 1930, with the opening of the Women's Chronic Building (later East Lawn) at Essondale.

5. Through the first century of British Columbia's public mental health operations, the vast majority of individuals entered hospital as involuntary civil commitment patients, under the province's Mental Hospitals Act, following an application by a family member, other citizen or authority, with certification by two physicians and ratification by a magistrate or justice of the peace (Davies 1987; Kelm 1992).

6. These non-violent offences included vagrancy (nine in total), public intoxication, incorrigibility, defamatory libel, public nudity, and causing a disturbance. One case involved self-injury, bringing an attempted suicide charge.

7. Unless otherwise indicated, the passages quoted in the chapter are taken from Charlotte Ross's Essondale clinical record. We reproduce all excerpts from letters and other documents verbatim, with no corrections of spelling or grammar errors.

8. On racialized images of white women living and working in Chinese communities, and efforts to regulate them, see Anderson 1991 and Backhouse 1994. On the events and aftermath of the 1924 Janet Smith case, which involved a Chinese houseboy falsely accused of murdering his white female co-worker, see Kerwin 1999, and Macdonald and O'Keefe 2000.

9. See Chunn and Menzies 1994, Sangster 2002b, Stephen 1995, and Strange 1995 on the moral regulation of young Canadian women during this era; Freund 2002 and McLaren 1987 on campaigns against prostitution; Cassel 1987, Chunn 1997, and Mawani 2002b on venereal disease control; and McLaren 1993 and McLaren and McLaren 1997 on abortion.

10. This term originates with the prominent Ontario psychiatrist, medical professor, and mental hygienist C.K. Clarke (Stephen 1995).

11. By coincidence, Charlotte and Jimmy shared surnames.

12. While a short-lived unofficial moratorium on the capital punishment of women had prevailed earlier in the century, by the 1940s Canadian women murderers were again, albeit infrequently, being condemned to the scaffold (Dubinsky and Iacovetta 1991; Greenwood and Boissery 2000; Kramer and Mitchell 2002).

13. From Canadian Confederation in 1867 through to the abolition of capital punishment in 1976, the federal cabinet in Ottawa undertook an automatic review of all capital sentences, commuting about half of these cases to life imprisonment (Strange 1996; Swainger 1995).

14. Charlotte had a point. Ugo Cerletti pioneered the ECT after witnessing how electrical shocks had a calming effect on pigs in an Italian slaughterhouse. On the origins of ECT see Breggin 1993, Frank 1978, and Valenstein 1986.

15. On Canadian adaptations of the cognitive "knowing right from wrong" test derived from the 1843 McNaughten case, and still enshrined in s.16 of the Criminal Code, see Eaves, Ogloff, and Roesch 2000 and O'Marra 1994.

16. Possibly the jury decision was influenced by the knowledge that a guilty verdict might lead to a capital sentence.
17. Historical accounts of prolonged sleep therapy and other somatic "treatments" include, in Canada, Collins 1988, and elsewhere, Breggin 1993 and Valenstein 1986.
18. In 1964, in the wake of revisions to the British Columbia Mental Hospitals (thereafter Mental Health) Act, the Provincial Mental Hospital, Essondale, became Riverview Hospital.

7. FROM VILLAIN TO VICTIM: SECURE CARE AND YOUNG WOMEN IN PROSTITUTION

Steven Bittle

The last fifteen years of the twentieth century brought fundamental changes in official discourses about youth prostitution in Canada. Beginning primarily with the work of the Committee on Sexual Offences Against Children and Youth (Badgley Committee 1985), there was a growing perception that young prostitutes should be treated as victims in need of assistance and "distinct from being treated as offenders" (Federal-Provincial-Territorial Working Group 1998: 74). This "victim not villain" transformation propelled a variety of government-sponsored initiatives that contemplated measures to protect youth who are sexually exploited through prostitution (see, for example, Alberta Task Force on Children Involved in Prostitution 1997; Federal-Provincial-Territorial Working Group on Prostitution 1998). A recent and controversial measure in response to this discourse on sexual abuse and exploitation is the enactment of secure care in the province of Alberta. Discussion has also begun around implementation of similar legislation in British Columbia and Ontario.

On the surface, secure care represents a decisive move by the state to take responsibility for combating the youth sex trade. It announces that state officials recognize the harms associated with youth prostitution and that they have initiated legislative measures to address this form of abuse. Although it is difficult to question the state's efforts to protect an obviously vulnerable segment of the population (cf. Phoenix 2002b: 361), critics argue that secure care represents an unduly harsh measure that will only serve to control "where and how the business is conducted," while also driving young prostitutes "further from real help" (Highcrest 2000: A1; see also Busby 2002; Martin 2002). Secure care also represents much more than a right-wing attempt to control the youth sex trade. Underlying this policy approach is a complex of power relations in which the state's limiting of an individual's freedom — particularly that of young women — is part of an overall series of interdependent and interrelated methods of control. In this sense secure care represents both an advance and a

195

retreat of state control over young women involved in prostitution.

Revealing the relations of power embodied within secure care requires an examination of this legislation within a broader understanding of emerging methods of governance and control — how, in essence, secure care represents a neo-liberal response to the (re)conceptualization of youth prostitution as a form of sexual abuse and exploitation.[1] Secure care reinforces and advances neo-liberal strategies of control, and of particular interest is how this legislation embodies various "responsibilization strategies" or techniques of the state to "devolve responsibility for crime prevention on to agencies, organizations and individuals which are quite outside the state and to persuade them to act appropriately" (Garland 1996: 452, 2001). Indeed, secure care effectively supports market conditions, activates community partnerships, befriends the family, throws responsibility for the youth sex trade onto the individual prostitute, and focuses on risk situations.

The net effect of the various responsibilization strategies is that the youth prostitution "problem" is governed at a distance, the youth sex trade is individualized, and the meaning of success in addressing youth prostitution is redefined. In the process, relations of power — or the conditions that make prostitution a "choice" for some young women — remain unchallenged. Secure care, and its underpinning of neo-liberal principles, ignore very important material and social factors that contribute to youth involvement in prostitution.[2]

Before proceeding, I want to raise two caveats. Here, in focusing on the philosophical underpinnings of secure care in Alberta and British Columbia, I am not concerned with empirically evaluating secure care — although this represents an important and largely unexplored line of inquiry — but with interrogating the "cultural assumptions that animate" (Garland 2001: xi; also see Phoenix 2002b: 353) this response strategy.[3] Second, in many respects it might appear misguided to criticize initiatives to protect young women involved in prostitution. I do not suggest that young women are not harmed or victimized through their involvement in prostitution, and I do not intend to challenge efforts to create conditions within which young people can choose to participate in healthy and age-appropriate lifestyles (cf. Phoenix 2002b: 361). Instead, I examine not only how the "rhetoric of victimhood" becomes incorporated into government policy, but also the impact that these choices have for young women involved in prostitution (Phoenix 2002b: 363). Borrowing from Joanna Phoenix (2002b: 363), I suggest that "recognizing that young people are... victimized in prostitution and lead lives shattered by the aggregate effects of poverty is not the same as constituting them in policy as always and already victims of child (sexual) abuse and the violence of men."

FROM VILLAIN TO VICTIM

The Emergence of Sexual Abuse Discourse

The emergence of the sexual abuse and exploitation discourse to describe youth involvement in the sex trade created a frame of reference (or way of knowing) that made new strategies of control possible. A detailed analysis of this discursive transformation is beyond the scope of this chapter, but we do need to at least briefly examine this "renaming game" (cf. Phoenix 2002a: 69). As Richard Ericson and Kevin Haggerty (1997: 84–85) suggest, "Discourse constitutes practice and is, in the very same process, constituted by practice."

The history of prostitution-related legislation reveals a marked difference in the treatment of female prostitutes and their male customers. Regardless of age, female prostitutes have been subjected to discriminatory legislation and unequal law enforcement (Sullivan 1986: 11; see also Martin 2002). During the early twentieth century, for example, when reformers lobbied for greater protection of young women and children involved in prostitution, law enforcement officials focused their efforts primarily on women involved in the trade (Backhouse 1985, 1991; McLaren 1986). During this period, several child-protection statutes were enacted to prevent young women from entering the life. Government officials had the power to detain children who were "wandering" or without a "settled place of abode" (Backhouse 1985: 243) and whose parents were deemed to be involved in sexually inappropriate behaviours (Sullivan 1986: 180). Many youth found themselves serving lengthy prison sentences under the guise of rehabilitation (Sullivan 1986: 180). The powers that be largely ignored the actions of male customers and the conditions that led to youth prostitution, including male sexual socialization and female poverty.

More recently, during the 1980s, attempts to combat street prostitution in various Canadian cities focused on the public nuisance aspect of the trade. As John Lowman (2001: 3) puts it: "Street prostitution was the breakdown of law and order, and most of the talk was about how to restore order." In the course of removing prostitution from certain locales, citizens and police harassed both adult and youth prostitutes. In Vancouver, for instance, city officials bowed to public pressures to do something about the street sex-trade "problem" by initiating court injunctions that restricted prostitutes from working in the city's West

End (male clients were not subject to this injunction) (Lowman 1992: 8). Community groups demanded the removal of street prostitution from their neighbourhoods, with no regard for where the trade would end up. Youth prostitutes were not immune from these various nuisance-based complaints (see, for example, Lowman 1986, Brock 1998).

The 1980s also brought renewed concerns with youth involvement in prostitution, primarily through the work of the Committee on Sexual Offences Against Children and Youth (Badgley Committee 1985).[4] The Badgley Report represented a "decisive point in the Canadian literature because it helped introduce the idea that although the Canadian age of consent is 14, prostitution involving 14 to 17 year-olds is a form of sexual abuse" (Lowman 2001). The victim discourse set the tone for a range of new sexual offences that hinged on differentiating between adults and youth (Brock 1998: 5). To uphold its protectionist mandate, the Badgley Committee recommended extending the use of criminal law and social service, despite evidence that questioned the ability of these strategies to provide for young prostitutes (Brock 1998: 5).

In 1986, in response to Badgley, the federal government introduced legislation to address the apparent increase of sexual offences against children and youth. The new law was designed to help protect victims of child sexual abuse, increase the number of prosecutions of child sexual abuse cases, increase the severity of sentences, and improve conditions for child victims and witnesses (Hornick and Bolitho 1992: xiv). As per Badgley's recommendation, the legislation criminalized purchasing or attempting to purchase the sexual services of a youth. What is now section 212(4) of the Criminal Code of Canada came into force on Jan. 1, 1988, marking the first time that the federal government had enacted specific legislation to criminalize the sexual procurement of youth.

Despite legislative condemnation of customers who purchase sex from youth, this new legislation was rarely enforced (Hornick and Bolitho 1992: xxix). John Lowman and Laura Fraser's (1996: 100) research found, "During the first six years of the new law's existence, there were apparently only six charges in Vancouver for offering to purchase the sexual services of a youth."[5] However, regardless of the lack of section 212(4) charges, it was becoming increasingly apparent that many government officials, services providers, and police agencies no longer deemed young prostitutes to be criminals, but rather victims of sexual exploitation who needed protection.

The "villain not victim" (O'Neill 2001: 98) transformation further surfaced through the actions of service providers and community members, who questioned the virtual immunity from the law enjoyed by men who purchased the sexual services of youth and initiated efforts to better protect sexually exploited youth, in cities like Vancouver (Bittle 1999). Data produced by the Canadian Centre for Justice Statistics also indicated that young prostitutes were not being charged with communicating as frequently as they had in the past (Duchesne 1997), indicating a growing acceptance that processing young prostitutes through the criminal justice system was inappropriate.

The 1990s witnessed municipal task forces and numerous provincial and interprovincial undertakings that examined the issue of youth sexually exploited through prostitution (see, for example, Alberta Task Force on Children Involved in Prostitution 1997; British Columbia Ministry of Attorney General 1996; Manitoba Child and Youth Secretariat 1996) or included it as part of their overall mandate (Federal-Provincial-Territorial Working Group on Prostitution 1998) (cf. Lowman 2001). In 1999 a joint statement by premiers and territorial leaders expressed their commitment to recognize and respond to youth prostitution as a form of child abuse (Child Prostitution press release, 40th Premiers Conference 1999).

Overall, a discursive shift occurred in which youth prostitution was problematized as a form of sexual abuse and exploitation. A new conceptual space or "field of experience" emerged, involving new "ways of objectifying and speaking the truth" (Burchell 1996: 31). In addition to providing a powerful impetus for politicians to take action (that is, it is politically untenable to be seen avoiding measures to protect child victims), the victim discourse has gained privileged status in accounting for and developing responses to youth prostitution (Phoenix 2002a: 69). It has created an atmosphere in which "help at almost any cost" becomes the slogan (cf. Hannah-Moffat 2000: 520). Victimized in their homes and, once on the streets, victimized by men who seek their sexual services, young women involved in prostitution need help to change their circumstances (cf. Hannah-Moffat 2000: 512). Unfortunately, regardless of this conceptualization, the underlying socio-economic conditions associated with youth prostitution remain untouched.

Although various psychological and social factors contribute to a young woman's decision to become a prostitute, research identifies several common material and social experiences that mediate this choice (O'Neill 2001: 83). For example, many young women involved in prostitution ran away or were "thrown away" (Highcrest 2000; Lowman 1987) from their home environments — including foster care and other state-sponsored settings — in which they experienced physical, sexual, and emotional abuse. With few opportunities for food, clothing, and housing — basic needs for subsistence that have become increasingly scarce in neo-liberal times — life on the streets becomes one of the few options that many young women have to choose from upon escaping abusive and dysfunctional settings (Sullivan 1986). In Canada these challenges are even greater for many Aboriginal youth, who end up on the streets as a result of the considerable inequalities that they have experienced in the wake of colonialism (Lowman 1986; Webber 1991). Once young women are on the streets, the poverty that many of them experience (little education, lack of employment, poor social services), coupled with a steady male demand for sexual services, makes prostitution a viable option (Lowman 1986; see also Badgley 1984; O'Neill 2001). The failure to address these fundamental issues is a reflection of the "masculinist" (O'Neill 2001: 118), racist, and class-based nature of the state.

The Advent of Secure Care
In May 1996 the government of Alberta convened the Task Force on Children Involved in Prostitution (see Forsyth Report 1997) to examine concerns with children and youth involved in prostitution, explore effective intervention programs, and recommend actions to the minister of Alberta family and social services. The Task Force's philosophical framework, as outlined in what is known as the Forsyth Report (1997: 3) conformed to the growing recognition that youth prostitutes are victims of child sexual abuse: "These children should be seen as victims of abuse. The children, if not abused while at home, are certainly victims of sexual abuse when they are used by either a pimp or john." A corollary of this position was the Task Force's belief that prostitution is not a "choice that children make from a healthy vantage point" (p.3).

The Task Force made several recommendations to address the sexual exploitation of children involved in prostitution, including the need for "collaborative case management," more charges under section 212(4) of the Criminal Code, a media campaign to raise awareness, and improved prevention and intervention techniques. Its most significant recommendation was to introduce secure-care legislation that would provide "legislative support for a continuum of services for children involved in prostitution."[6]

The Alberta government responded by introducing, on Feb. 1, 1999, the Protection of Children Involved in Prostitution Act (*PCHIP Act*), a child welfare response aimed at protecting child prostitutes from abuse by helping them end their involvement in prostitution. The law defines young prostitutes as "victims of sexual abuse" who require "victim support and services" (Deis et al. 2000), and empowers police and child welfare workers to detain children whose safety is "at risk" and yet will not cease their involvement in prostitution (Alberta Government press release 1999). The youth can be held in protective confinement for a seventy-two-hour assessment, during which they receive emergency care and treatment, with additional provisions that allow authorities to apply for a maximum of two more periods of detainment of up to twenty-one days each if child-care workers need more time to help the youth end their involvement in prostitution. The law also empowers police to arrest pimps and johns who purchase sexual services from a youth.[7]

In 1998 the B.C. minister of children and families launched a working group to examine whether that provincial government should implement a secure-treatment approach for dealing with high-risk youth. The Secure Care Working Group (SCWG) advocated a safe-care strategy that would allow officials to detain youth to make assessments, provide services, and develop plans of care (such as harm prevention strategies). The SCWG (1998: 6) argued:

> Holding children and youth against their will is not a comfortable prospect for anyone. At the same time, however, the harming of children and youth through abuse of alcohol and other drugs and sexual exploitation cannot be tolerated. The working group agrees that the problems of high-risk children and youth need to be addressed.

The B.C. government followed the SCWG's recommendation to introduce the Secure Care Act, giving "parents and authorities the power to get help for high-risk children and youth who are unable or unwilling to help themselves." The law is not limited to youth prostitution and includes other forms of "self-harm," such as drug addiction (British Columbia press release 2000). The legislation empowers a parent, guardian, or director of secure care to make an application for having a child apprehended into secure care for up to thirty days, although it is possible through renewal certificates to detain a youth for up to one hundred days (*Safe Care for British Columbia's Children: A Discussion Paper* 2004).[8]

While the B.C. legislature passed the Secure Care Act in July 2000, it was never enacted. A change in government (in spring 2001 the New Democratic Party lost the thirty-seventh provincial general election to the Liberal Party), along with concerns about the scope of the proposed legislation, prevented it from becoming law. Supportive of secure care, the Liberal government began work on a new law to address the needs of "young people who are commercially sexually exploited and for whom the safeguards of family, school and community have broken down" (*Safe Care for British Columbia's Children* 2004). [9]

In 2002 the Ontario government introduced An Act to Rescue Children Trapped in the Misery of Prostitution and Other Forms of Sexual Exploitation and to Amend the Highway Traffic Act (Bill 86, chapter 5, Statues of Ontario, 3rd Session, 37th Legislature, Ontario, 51 Elizabeth II, 2002), providing authorities with the power to detain children who are sexually exploited for commercial purposes.[10] A child is considered to be sexually exploited if she or he "engaged in or will engage in a sexual activity, for the financial gain of the child or another person," and the grounds include prostitution, adult entertainment facilities (such as massage parlours), escort services, "communications of a sexual nature," and appearing in pornographic images.[11]

The advent of secure care in Alberta, along with consideration of similar legislation in British Columbia and Ontario, represents a new regime of governance and control of youth prostitution. Unlike previous initiatives that treated young prostitutes as deviants in need of punishment, secure care begins from the premise that youth involved in prostitution are victims in need of protection.

NEO-LIBERAL CONTROL STRATEGIES

Considerable evidence suggests that secure care advances various neo-liberal strategies of responsibilization (Garland 1996, 2000, 2001). Instead of the state accepting responsibility for tackling the youth prostitution "problem," it is young women involved in prostitution, along with individual families and communities, who must take responsibility for changing their social circumstances and acting in more "age-appropriate" and acceptable ways. Secure care responsibilizes youth prostitution by philosophically and economically supporting a particular kind of secure care, relying on communities and families to address the youth sex trade when they have questionable capacity to do so, individualizing the "choice" to prostitute, and ignoring the broader context within which youth prostitution occurs.

Market Conditions

Secure care supports market conditions by emphasizing the need for cost-effective, private-sector services to protect young prostitutes. The Forsyth Report (1997: 4) argues that government departments and private agencies should "work together within available resources, systems and programs" and advocates cost-sharing agreements between governments, community agencies, and the private sector. Its recommendations include support for appropriate and efficient use of funds, with a focus on "reducing gaps, ensuring value for dollar, quality services, and accountability to outcomes aimed at assisting youth to leave prostitution" (p.28).

What is important in terms of secure care is that service agencies are forced to adhere to market conditions in two ways. First, they must compete for resources within an open market economy. With an emphasis on dollar value and accountability to outcomes, agencies that best reflect an economic model will be the most likely to receive government funding. Second, they must provide services that adhere to the state's secure-care philosophy — that is, to receive government funding they must offer protective services within a secure-care environment. In this respect, the concept of market within neo-liberalism means much more than privatizing strategies for addressing youth prostitution. When it comes to secure care, unfortunately, the range of options is limited. The overall message is that the government supports — both philosophically and financially — a particular kind of secure-care framework, and agencies seeking funding must compete for these resources.

This market environment leaves uncontested the questionable adequacy of these services for helping young prostitutes as well as the competitive tensions among service providers, and concerns do exist about the adequacy of service agencies to meet the needs of young prostitutes (Brock 1998: 5). For example, social services focus upon the individual actor, without consideration of the broader social conditions within which the individual acts. As Deborah Brock (1998: 134) notes, "Social service provision will always be stressed beyond the system's ability to function effectively as long as the structural problems inherent in Canadian society and the 'traditional' family (for example, chronic unemployment, family violence, racism) continue unabated." Indeed, most young prostitutes report negative experiences with child welfare services, experiences that have left them "suspicious of any helping agency" (Nixon et al. 2002: 1039). Placing young women in confinement therefore only serves to drive them further away from seeking the help of service providers (Busby et al. 2000: 13) and unwittingly drives the youth sex trade further underground, where young women will be even more vulnerable to the violence and exploitation of male pimps and customers (Busby 2002: 120).

Research also reveals fierce competition over the limited resources available to provide services to the youth prostitution population (see Bittle 1999). Tensions in that regard among service agencies have been exacerbated following years of "growing poverty and a shrinking social safety net" (Webber 1991: 243; see also Martin 2002). Massive cuts to social assistance beginning in the 1980s were aimed at discouraging young people from leaving their families, where it was believed that the responsibility for the provision of care and support resided (Martin 2002: 356). As a result, young people who leave home today at a young age find themselves with very few choices when it comes to food, clothing, and housing (Martin 2002: 378). As Diane Martin (2002: 398) argues:

> While both prostitution and the exploitation of children have long been with us, the numbers of homeless street youth vulnerable to that exploitation are a product of government and corporate strategies, both recent and historic. The strategies that have generated unprecedented disparities between rich and poor have consequences — and we see those consequences sleeping under bridges, begging on the street, and selling their bodies every day.

Activating Communities

Neo-liberal control strategies also stress the importance of communities taking upon themselves "the responsibility for the security of their property and their persons, and for that of their own families" (Rose 2000: 327). Included are strategies in which the state "backs off" its claim to be the sole provider of safety and security by recasting crime control as something that must be addressed through community partnerships (Garland 2000: 8). As David Garland (2000: 348) suggests, the state acts "through civil society and not upon it."

Secure-care strategies help the state act through civil society by advocating community responsibility and partnerships. For example, the Secure Care Working Group in British Columbia argues that in addition to parents and families, "communities and society as a whole" have the responsibility "to protect and care for our children" (SCWG 1998: 6). Its report further notes that a "child or youth's family and community are of great importance in addressing the problems of children and youth admitted to secure units" (p.16).

Contrary to the mid-1980s, when police were the main actors in controlling the sex trade, the secure-care framework emphasizes the inability (or refusal?) of the state to address, on its own, this complex social issue. Instead, it encourages strategies that develop community partnerships to address the victimization of young prostitutes, supporting what Jacques Donzelot calls "procedures of contractual implication" (cited in Burchell

1996: 29) or the idea that collectivities (and individuals) should assume responsibility for what was once the state's bailiwick. Still — and similar to concerns about the appropriateness of service agencies — what exactly constitutes the community and whether it has the capacity to address the complexities of youth prostitution are questions that remain unanswered.

Befriending the Family

A related responsibilization strategy is the state's engagement of the family in addressing youth-related problems. Vikki Bell (1993: 390) suggests that attempts to champion the "right of the mature child to autonomy" represent part of a neo-liberal trend in which the state befriends individuals and their families in the process of governing childhood. A key basis of this approach is that the family "has been downtrodden by welfarism and needs to become both independent and responsible once more" (Bell 1993: 395).

Both secure care in Alberta and the proposed legislation in British Columbia include strategies to befriend the family. The Forsyth Report (1997: 9) and the SCWG (1998: 6) argue for the inclusion of the family in protecting youth and developing methods and programs for removing children from the sex trade. A similar tone is evident in an Alberta government press release, which emphasizes that parents of youth involved in prostitution need to be active in "ensuring the safety of their children" (Alberta Government press release 1999).

An important strategy in befriending the family in a secure-care environment is to empower parents to control and change their children's circumstances. As the Forsyth Report (1997: 29) argues, "Parents wishing to help and support their children to leave prostitution often feel powerless and at the mercy of social service agencies and police…. This is not helpful or supportive of families." Similarly, the SCWG argues that parents have no rights "in regard to their children and to protecting them from harm" (SCWG 1998: 5) but still suggests that "high-risk" youth strategies should involve parents as an integral component in planning and delivering services to the youth (p.37).

The ultimate goal is to return young women to the family, thereby minimizing the state's responsibility to address youth prostitution and making the family the primary control mechanism. This approach, however, ignores the reality that many young women experience a range of threats to their safety and well-being within the home environment, whether it is the traditional family or a state substitute (such as foster care), including cases of frequent physical, sexual, and emotional abuse (see Badgley 1984). Therefore, in advocating the centrality and supremacy of the family, the gender-based power imbalances within the family setting — relations of power that give rise to the violation of youth — remain uncontested.[12] As Martin (2002: 361) points out, secure care, and neo-liberalism more generally, attempt to reaffirm the family as the "idealized white, Christian, heterosexual, bourgeois, patriarchically organized" site that is most appropriate for preventing and controlling deviant behaviour.

Individualizing the Problem of Prostitution

Secure care individualizes youth involvement in prostitution in three ways: providing help for the purpose of self-help; focusing on self-esteem as a prerequisite to full citizenship; and supporting and authorizing normative behaviour. In each case, responsibility for addressing the youth sex trade falls to the individual and, in the process, draws attention away from the broader social conditions that make prostitution a choice for some young women.

Referred to as "prudentialism," help for self-help means that individuals are no longer managed through the concept of collective risk (that is, prostitutes as a risk population); rather the approach "throws back upon the individual the responsibility for managing their own risk'" (Hannah-Moffat 2000: 522). Nikolas Rose (2000: 327) argues that prudentialism prevents individuals from turning to the public realm, including police and the courts, to provide help and protection. Instead, individuals need to self-educate and accept the helping hand of "experts" as a means of fending off threats to their individual security. Consumers of government-related services, in this instance the young women who consume secure care, must therefore make "rationalized" decisions (Rose 1993: 57).

Secure care embraces prudentialism in that the youth who makes the "appropriate" decision will no longer have to endure her victimization (Hannah-Moffat 2000: 522). As the Forsyth Report (1997:11) states: "Although these youth are seen as victims, the Task Force believes they must still take *responsibility* for their actions and accept the consequences. Youth must be *responsible* and *accountable* for their own involvement in crime — sometimes associated with the street life — and for the decision to leave the street" (emphasis added). The SCWG also espouses an individualized, prudential approach to secure care, arguing:

> The working group learned that there is a small group of children and youth in B.C. — it is not yet clear exactly how many

— who are placing *themselves* at a great risk of harm.... The risk is further increased by the fact that many of these children and youth resist whatever help is made available to them when they are ready for it....

Service providers in all three locations told us that there is a growing number of children and youth who are *out of control*, and that these children and youth are both younger and more seriously out of control than ever before. (SCWG 1998: 5, 16; emphasis added)

Implicit in these statements is the idea that the decision to leave the sex trade is primarily an individual choice, something that is further emphasized through the Forsyth Report's (1997: 19) recommendation for a continuum of services approach, in which differing programs and levels of service are provided to those wanting to leave and those not wanting to leave prostitution.

A second individualizing aspect of secure care is that it portrays self-esteem as a prerequisite to full citizenship. "High self-esteem is linked to power to plan one's life as an orderly enterprise and take responsibility for its course and outcome" (Rose 2000: 335). This empowerment tactic emphasizes "'tough love,' 'compassion with a hard edge'" (Rose 2000: 335) and aims at providing individuals with opportunities to participate fully in "a moral community, and to adhere to the core values of honesty, self-reliance and concern for others" (Rose 2000: 335). The Forsyth Report (1997: 8) emphasizes that a lack of self-esteem and dysfunctional family ties mean that young prostitutes have little hope for exiting the streets. The SCWG (1998: 37) infers that many youth are not "ready" or do not have the necessary self-esteem to use the services provided to them and, as a result, strategies for dealing with "high-risk" youth must presume that they will resist any attempts when offered services.

In her analysis of neo-liberal strategies of control within Canadian women's prisons, Kelly Hannah-Moffat argues that, "empowerment" (which can be linked to self-esteem) "can mean 'the development of individual autonomy, self-control, and confidence' and/or the 'development of a sense of collective influence over social conditions in one's life.'" However, as she reveals, the positive meanings of empowerment are lost in a prison environment — "the flexibility to make choices and control one's surroundings does not exist" (Hannah-Moffat 2000: 521). A similar argument can be made about secure care. Young women involved in prostitution do not have control over a secure-care environment, and they cannot control the conditions that made prostitution a choice in the first place. To borrow a familiar Marxist adage, people choose, but not under conditions of their own choosing.

Finally, secure care individualizes the decision to prostitute by attempting to "normalize" the behaviour of young female prostitutes. Secure care supports and authorizes normative behaviour (Rose and Valverde 1998: 548) by emphasizing the dangers associated with youth prostitution and the importance of developing "healthy" lifestyle choices. In a position paper on the proposed secure-care legislation in British Columbia, the B.C. Civil Liberties Association argues,

> Civil libertarians have traditionally treated children as a special case recognizing that they do not enjoy the same autonomy as adults and that parents/society may limit their "freedom" and impose requirements on their behaviour so that they can mature to make informed choices about their private lives and participate meaningfully in civil society. (BCCLA 1999: 6).

In short, citizenship for young people is "conditional upon conduct" (Rose 2000: 335).

Amendments to the Alberta legislation permit authorities to detain a youth for a longer period to "break the cycle of abuse" and start recovery in a safe and secure environment (Alberta Government press release 2000). During this time, treatment plans and programs are made available to the youth as a means of helping them end their involvement in prostitution (Deis et al. 2000). Similar to Hannah-Moffat's (2000: 524) analysis of women's prisons, "By attending programmes such as parenting, life skills, substance abuse, anger management and vocational classes women are expected to conform to a series of normative standards." Secure care therefore directs youth to conform to "acceptable" gendered behavioural standards.

The normalizing impact of secure care confirms the gender-based assumption that young women must remain virtuous to be considered "normal" — it feeds into a good girl/bad girl dichotomy. It is here that secure care hearkens back to the child-saving rhetoric of the early twentieth century (see Backhouse 1991; McLaren 1986). As Martin (2002: 364) argues, "The language (or goal) of child protection notwithstanding, surveillance and coercion of women and girls have increased, echoing regimes of long past."

Overall, the individualizing aspects of secure care fit well with middle-class values in that the option of self-governance seems "obvious" and "natural"; it seems almost commonsensical to suggest that any young woman presented with the means to end her involvement in prostitution will make the prudent choice (Garland 2001, as discussed in Carlen 2002b: 230). All that is needed is for the youth to be provided with an opportunity to see the error of her ways. "Change their *beliefs* about the world; the problem is in their heads, not their social circumstances" (Carlen 2002b: 235).

Although secure care is meant to protect youth involved in prostitution, it reinforces the fundamental distinction between a deserving victim, who recognizes her victim status and is willing to accept help, and the undeserving victim who refuses to acknowledge the involuntary nature of her behaviour (Phoenix 2002b: 368). Young prostitutes are therefore "known oppositionally as either victims *or* as offenders and *not* both" (Phoenix 2002a: 69). For the individual young prostitute who does not embrace her victim status, if she "chooses" to remain in prostitution, then by default she cannot be a victim and must therefore be a deviant and be treated as such. As Phoenix (2002a: 75) notes, "if they are not victims, then they are offenders."

In the end, young women involved in prostitution are still treated as criminal subjects, despite the rhetoric of victimization. Further evidence for this comes from how young prostitutes continue to be arrested for prostitution-related Criminal Code offences, even if less frequently than was the case previously, as well as for various offences commonly associated with life on the street (Busby 2002: 104). It is a routine part of living on the streets to be subject to ongoing police surveillance and harassment — in short, to be treated as a criminal (Martin 2002: 392). As Karen Busby (2002: 104) argues, "Girls involved in prostitution have always occupied a curious and contradictory place in criminal law because they are treated as both perpetrators and victims." The advent of secure care has done nothing to transform this position.

Risk Reduction: Governable Spaces
One final responsibilization strategy found within secure care deals with the notion of "governable spaces." While it is up to the individual to address her own behaviour, the state's role is to address risk situations (Garland 1996: 451). Nikolas Rose and Mariana Valverde (1998: 549) refer to the process of controlling situations as "spatialization" or "governable spaces." Instead of dealing with the causes of crime, the state instead deals with the consequences or effects of crime, the situations within which an event occurs (Garland 2001: 121).

Governable spaces relate to secure care in that the focus has shifted from legislation that criminalizes prostitution-related activities (for example, the communicating legislation) to reducing the risks associated with sexual exploitation and abuse. As the B.C. framework notes, "providing 'secure care' generally refers to the detainment of a child in a lockable setting with the purpose of removing the child from a dangerous situation and stabilizing the immediate crisis" (British Columbia Ministry for Children and Families 2001a). Similarly, parents surveyed in British Columbia agree that secure care is necessary to remove youth from the environment that is causing the harm (SCWG 1998: 15). The state helps the individual to "help themselves" by providing an alternative environment or, as the B.C. secure-care framework advocates, a "'time out' from high risk, potentially fatal circumstances" (British Columbia 2001b). And while secure care does remove young women from the risks associated with life on the street and in prostitution, at least temporarily, it cannot be seen as anything more than a form of incarceration, as well as a troubling indication that there is a serious lack of alternatives for addressing the prostitution of some young women (Phoenix 2002a: 91). In the end, the state focuses on risk situations and not contexts; spaces are governed, not transformed.

GOVERNING AT A DISTANCE

These various responsibilization strategies contribute to a new form of governance at a distance. As Barbara Hudson (1998: 557) states, "The contraction of the state reflects… the 'death of the social': we are an increasingly individualized population, with a diminished notion of 'society' and a greatly reduced expectation of what the state will do on our behalf." Secure care mixes the public and the private and, in the process, continues the trend of devolution of the state from its role as primary provider of safety and security (Hudson 1998: 557). However, the emergence of these strategies does not signal a process of totally downsizing state institutions, and it is more than simply a privatization of crime-control processes (Garland 1996: 454).

What is interesting in the secure-care scenario is that the fundamental machinery of "traditional criminal justice responses" remains largely untouched (Phoenix 2002b: 355). Whether it is apprehending young women for their own protection or because they are deviant, the net effect remains the same: power and control over young women involved in prostitution. In this respect there is nothing particularly novel or revolutionary about secure care in that welfare officials and police continue to do essentially the same type of control work that they have always done, albeit under the guise of protection instead of punishment. The introduction of the victim discourse and secure care has not ended the criminalization of youth involved in the sex trade; it has simply repackaged the concept of punishment under the guise of protection — it's the same foot, just a different shoe.

Secure care de-emphasizes the role of the state by stressing the importance of individual choice and partnerships (such as family and community involvement). The state becomes only one of many sites of responsibility for addressing the youth sex trade, thereby allowing the state to act through civil society. Secure care represents a renewed agenda whereby the state forges allies with other groups and seeks to create "responsibilization" and "empowerment" in sectors that are not directly linked to the central bureaucracy but are nonetheless connected though a "complex of alignments and translations" (Barry, Osborne, and Rose 1996: 12).

The Redefinition of Success
Governance at a distance also contributes to a new definition of success in that the state remains in the best position to govern, but it governs in a different way. As Rose (1996: 53) argues, "Neo-liberalism does not abandon the 'will to govern': it maintains the view that failure of government to achieve its objectives is to be overcome by inventing new strategies of government that will succeed." Instead of espousing the ability of the state to control youth prostitution through a law and order agenda, the secure-care discourse shifts responsibility for youth prostitution to the individual victim or community (Garland 1996: 458). In the process the inability of some young women to exit prostitution can be explained away through a victim/offender binary. Those who continually offend through their continuing involvement in prostitution do so, "despite the best efforts of those welfare-based organizations that are trying to 'exit' them from prostitution" (Phoenix 2002a: 76). Not only does this approach deflect the focus of responsibility away from the state (it is doing its best to help individuals to help themselves), but ignores the larger structural issues that make prostitution a choice for some young women.

Decisions Made out of a Larger Context
Overall, the victim discourse as it relates to youth prostitution — and secure care — effectively ignores the broader social context within which youth prostitution flourishes. As Garland (1996: 466) suggests, new strategies for addressing crime and deviance — such as secure care — have

no broader agenda, no strategy for progressive social change and no concern for the overcoming of social divisions. They are, instead, policies for managing the danger and policing the divisions created by a certain kind of social organization, and for shifting the burden of social control on to individuals and organizations that are often poorly equipped to carry out this task.

Secure care identifies change, help, or support as being associated with "responsibility," not relations of power (cf. Hannah-Moffat 2000: 525). As Hannah-Moffat (2000: 529) argues, "One reason why an empowerment strategy can be incorporated by the state is because it does not represent a significant challenge to existing relations of power, in fact it re-enforces them." The same can be said of secure care. Young women involved in prostitution continue to be held accountable for their non-normative sexual behaviour, while male (hetero)sexuality goes unchecked. The conditions that lead to prostitution — such as male sexual socialization, intrafamilial violence, the colonization of Aboriginal peoples, and youth poverty — go unchallenged.

Phoenix (2002b: 354) argues that starting from the perspective that young women involved in prostitution are "always and already victims" creates a context in which the totality of a young woman's experience can only be understood through her victimization. If she does not embrace her victim status she runs the very real risk of being labelled by authorities as troublesome, uncontrollable, even criminal. Most concerning is that the "material and social conditions" that give rise to the youth sex trade are obscured, effectively marginalized from the dominant discourse about youth prostitution and related policy decisions. As Phoenix (2002b: 366) suggests:

> Put very simply, these young people are no longer "prostitutes"; they are victims of child abuse. And with that, the experiences of poverty, homelessness, drugs, social isolation... are also erased. The space is foreclosed in which to recognize the compelling and subtle ways in which a young person's socioeconomic circumstances condition their survivalism

It is in this context that simply redefining youth prostitution as a form of sexual abuse and exploitation has failed to substantially improve the lives of young women involved in prostitution.

WHERE TO FROM HERE?

What does this analysis mean in terms of better understanding and responding to young women's involvement in prostitution? I would argue for creating spaces for, in the words of Pat O'Malley (2000: 164), "relational politics, hybridization and government innovation." Although the victim discourse appears to be firmly entrenched in the contemporary youth prostitution legal and policy lexicon, it should not be treated as infallible. As O'Malley (2000: 162) points out, "The ascendancy of neo-liberalism is by no means secure, let alone inevitable." Nor is the language used to support these control strategies.

Questions have started to surface about the wisdom of using the victim discourse to characterize young women's involvement in prostitution (see, for example, Busby 2002; Martin 2002; Phoenix 2002a, 2002b). Phoenix (2002a: 77) argues that youth prostitution and child sexual abuse are "sociologically distinct phenomenon." While child sexual abuse is something that typically occurs within particular relationships between adults and children, such as intrafamilial sexual abuse, the exchange of sex for money has little meaning outside of that commercial transaction. Phoenix does not deny that young women are subjected to abuse through their involvement in prostitution, but that "it cannot be conflated with that abuse without erasing the wider material, economic and ideological processes that make either prostitution possible or people's involvement in it plausible" (Phoenix 2002a: 78). Analyses like this are necessary for better understanding that for many young women, the choice to prostitute stems from their social conditions, not from some pathological decision-making process (see Brock 1998: 133).

Another possibility is to consider a social harm perspective. According to Paddy Hillyard and Steve Tombs (2004: 19), social harm refers to a range of events that happen to people and the conditions within which those events emerge throughout a person's life-course. Although social harm is a broad concept, and no less vulnerable than other language (such as victimization) to definitional power struggles, it provides an opportunity to think about a range of events that people experience in life, including their material and social conditions, and not just a particular instance as it happens in one place and time (see Hillyard and Tombs 2004: 19–24). A social harm perspective in reference to youth prostitution might further illustrate the limitations of a policy response that is based on apprehending young people in protective confinement *for their own good*. Clearly, as this chapter illustrates, there is much more that must be done to adequately address young women's involvement in prostitution.

Finally, challenging the victim and secure-care discourse means giving youth a significant voice in the process of understanding and responding to youth prostitution. Government and non-governmental organizations must move beyond consultation — which typically results in the selective use of information to legitimate certain strategies, such as secure care — to build effective partnerships. To do this we must be ready to allow youth to gain more control over their lives (including freedom from their families), help end "young people's secondary social and legal status" (Brock and Kinsman 1986: 125), and address the social conditions that make prostitution a viable means of subsistence for some young women.

As Deborah Brock and Gary Kinsman (1986: 124) argue, "We must develop state and social policies which focus on empowering young people themselves (as well as other oppressed groups), and on measures which address the roots of the problem in patriarchal social relations." The alternative is a continued proliferation of neo-liberal strategies that make young women responsible for their own social circumstances, without any recognition of the broader societal factors that help to propel youth prostitution in its current forms.

NOTES

This chapter is an updated and revised version of a paper first published as "When Protection Is Punishment: Neo-liberalism and Secure Care Approaches to Youth Prostitution," *Canadian Journal of Criminology and Criminal Justice*, 44, 3 (2002): 317–50. I would like to thank the editors at the CJCC for permission to use sections of the original publication for this collection. An earlier version was also presented at the Canadian Law and Society Conference, Laval University, Quebec City, May 28, 2001. I would also like to thank Elizabeth Comack, Gillian Balfour, and an anonymous reviewer for their helpful comments and feedback on this chapter.

1. This chapter focuses on young women's involvement in prostitution. Although much of the analysis it contains also applies to young male prostitutes, this population has not been the primary target of secure-care legislation in Alberta. For example, Justice for Girls reports that, since its enactment, 99 percent of youth detained under Alberta's PCHIP Act have been young women (Justice for Girls, year unknown).

2. Throughout this chapter I use the term "young women involved in prostitution" in reference to the youth who are subject to secure-care legislation. I use the term "young women" instead of "girls" in an effort to avoid feeding into any socially constructed age dichotomy in which "girls" (those under the age of eighteen) are deemed to have entered the sex trade for different reasons than "women" (those over the age of eighteen). In particular, this dichotomy potentially negates how some women of all ages choose to become involved in prostitution because of their similar material and social conditions. As Phoenix (2002b: 366) argues, an individual's socio-economic conditions, including "experiences of poverty, homelessness, drugs, [and] social isolation" makes prostitution a viable option for some young people.

3. There has yet to be an evaluation of Alberta's PCHIP legislation. In October 2004

the Ministry of Children's Services released a review of the safe houses used as part of this legislation (see Alberta Children's Services 2004), but this report does not examine the effectiveness of the law in response to the youth sex trade. Interestingly, the report notes that protective safe houses used within the secure-care framework have not been cost-effective due to the low number of apprehensions ("low occupancy rates"). The report recommends an education campaign aimed at child welfare workers and police officers so that they are better aware of PCHIP and more youth can be detained and placed in protective confinement. Busby (2003) also provides important insights about the perception of PCHIP from interviews she conducted with young prostitutes, but only in the context of a larger study on girls involved in prostitution.

4.   Although the initial mandate of the Badgley Committee did not include youth prostitution per se (it focused broadly on sexual offences against children and youth), the apparent growth of youth prostitution generated enough concern to have the issue included as part of the mandate (Lowman 1986: 195). Overall, the Badgley Report (1984) evoked considerable debate within the academic literature (see Lowman et al. 1986).

5.   Data produced for the federal Department of Justice suggested that police officers across Canada experienced difficulty enforcing the new youth procurement law (Hornick and Bolitho 1992: 65). Police officers argued that section 212(4) was difficult to enforce because "to achieve a conviction a youth who had been propositioned would have to testify against the accused. Youths would be reluctant to do this (why would they alienate their potential source of income?)" (Lowman and Fraser 1996: 100). Since the person who sexually procured a youth had to be "caught in the act," many commentators concluded that "traditional policing methods" were inappropriate for enforcing section 212(4) (Hornick and Bolitho 1992: xxv).

6.   An important issue that is beyond the scope of this chapter is the number of youth "at risk" of sexual exploitation through prostitution and the use of secure care to stop this form of abuse. For example, reports from both the Alberta Task Force on Children Involved in Prostitution (1997) and the Secure Care Working Group (1998) do not document the number of youth involved in prostitution as a basis for justifying the introduction of secure care. This lack of empirical data is part of a larger debate within the youth prostitution literature about the ability to document the number of youth involved in the sex trade, including whether the numbers are growing. As the Federal-Provincial-Territorial Working Group on Prostitution (1998: 15–16) notes, one problem with "profiling" youth involvement in prostitution is the lack of "reliable estimates," which vary widely depending on how researchers define youth prostitution (for example, is a young prostitute under the age of sixteen, eighteen, or twenty?), when they consider a youth to be prostituting (for example, if the youth only occasionally exchanges sex for food or shelter, as opposed to full-time prostitution), and whether they rely on official police data or estimates from primary research. For further reading, see the debate about the nature and prevalence of the youth sex trade between Brannigan and Fleischman (1989) and Lowman (1991).

7.   In response to a lower court decision (*Alberta* v *K.B. and M.J. 2000*), which ruled that the legislation was unconstitutional, the Alberta government tabled amendments to the PCHIP Act to ensure that "children's rights are protected and enable them to receive additional care and support" (Alberta Government press release 2000). In addition to extending the confinement period from seventy-two hours to five days, the amendments empower child welfare authorities to apply for a maximum of

"two additional confinement periods of up to 21 days each." As the press release announcing the amendments states: "This additional time will enable social workers to stabilize the child, help break the cycle of abuse and begin the recovery process in a safe and secure environment" (Government of Alberta 2000). Following the introduction of PCHIP Act amendments, a judicial review, *Alberta* v *K.B. and M.J.* (see *Director of Child Welfare* v *K.B. and M.J. [2000] ABQB*), overturned the lower court decision and ruled the objective of protecting children from sexual abuse meets the requirement of proportionality. (For a detailed review of these court decisions, see Busby 2002, Martin 2002.)

8. With the consent of the Ministry of Children and Families, a Secure Care Board can issue a secure-care certificate if the youth has an "emotional or behavioural condition" that puts them in harm or if they are "unable or unwilling to take steps to reduce risk," and if "less intrusive" measures are unavailable. In emergency situations, a young person can be detained without a certificate for up to seventy-two hours to be assessed and to arrange for treatment and support services (*Safe Care for British Columbia's Children* 2004).

9. In 2005, British Columbia's Liberal government was consulting with various stakeholders about its secure-care strategy. According to the Ministry of Children and Family Development (MCFD) website, the proposed Safe Care Act was to be tabled during the spring 2005 legislative session <www.mcf.gov.bc.ca/safe_care/> (accessed Aug. 20, 2005). However, as of fall 2005 this law had yet to be introduced, and a revised tabling date had not been announced.

10. Amendments to the Highway Traffic Act would permit authorities to suspend the driver's licence of a person who committed a prostitution-related office (sections 211–213 of the Criminal Code of Canada) while driving a motor vehicle.

11. Most child and family services acts (CFSAs) across Canada already include provisions for the detention of youth involved in prostitution. Although the law is slightly different in each province, the common thread is the power that authorities have to apprehend a child whose "life, health or emotional well-being is endangered," which necessarily includes children in the sex trade (see Busby et al. 2000: 11; also see Martin 2002: 369). Although young women involved in prostitution could be detained under CFSAs, since prostitution fits squarely within its definitional mandate, it is not a strategy that has been used frequently (Martin 2002: 370).

12. Proponents of secure care would note the safeguards within the legislation to protect youth from violence and exploitation within the family. For instance, the proposed secure-care approach in British Columbia includes a safeguard to "protect" children from being returned to "unsuitable" family situations (British Columbia 2001b). However, this does not undermine the overall goal of returning youth to their families and placing part of the onus for change within the family environment.

8. FROM WELFARE FRAUD TO WELFARE AS FRAUD: THE CRIMINALIZATION OF POVERTY

Dorothy E. Chunn and Shelley A.M. Gavigan

In Canada and elsewhere, attacks on the policies and practices of the Keynesian welfare state since the late twentieth century have led to the dismantling and massive restructuring of social security programs for the poor. These sweeping welfare reforms, which intensified through the 1990s — aptly characterized by some as a war on the poor — have a disproportionate impact on poor women (see, for example, *Falkiner* v. *Ontario* 2002; Klein and Long 2003; Little 2001; McMullan, Davies, and Cassidy 2002; Mosher et al. 2004; Savarese and Morton 2005). As Lynne Segal (1999: 206–7) argues: "The continuing offensive against welfare provides, perhaps, the single most general threat to Western women's interests at present — at least for those many women who are not wealthy, and who still take the major responsibility for caring work in the home." Indeed, it is no exaggeration to say that welfare law is primarily (and ideologically) concerned with the lives and issues of poor women, especially lone-parent mothers.

Welfare "fraud" occupies a central place in this attack on the poor. "Fraudsters" have always been a state concern in most liberal democracies, but the contemporary preoccupation with welfare "cheats" is unprecedented. Moreover, it is only the most visible form of assault. In Ontario, for instance, the attack on welfare has included deep cuts to the level of benefits (*Masse* v. *Ontario* 1996; see also Moscovitch 1997: 85), an expanded definition of "spouse" (*Falkiner* v. *Ontario* 2002), restructuring of the legislation from "welfare" to "work,"[1] mandatory drug testing, the introduction of a "quit/fire" regulation (which requires the cancellation or suspension of assistance to a recipient who resigns employment without just cause or is dismissed with cause),[2] the implementation of biometric finger-scanning (Little 2001: 26), anonymous snitch lines designed to encourage individuals to report suspected welfare abuse by their neighbours (see Morrison 1998: 32; Morrison and Pearce 1995), and zero tolerance" in the form of permanent ineligibility imposed upon anyone convicted of welfare fraud (see *Rogers* v. *Sudbury* 2001: 5; *Broomer* v. *Ontario* 2002).

This restructuring of welfare has shifted and been shifted by public discourse and social images (see Evans and Swift 2000; Golding and Middleton 1982; Misra, Moller, and Karides 2003; Mosher 2000). Few people, it seems, qualify as "deserving" poor anymore. Welfare fraud has become welfare *as* fraud. Thus poverty, welfare, and crime are linked.[3] Simply to be poor is to be culpable, or at least vulnerable to culpability.

Two Ontario women convicted of welfare fraud offer case studies of the culpable poor in this new era. In 1994 Donna Bond, a single mother of two teenaged children, was charged with welfare fraud in the amount of $16,477.84 over a sixteen-month period — she had not disclosed a bank account in her annual update report.[4] At trial, Bond testified that she had saved, and deposited, all the money she had ever received from her part-time employment, baby bonus, child tax credits, and income tax refunds (all of which she had disclosed in her annual reports to welfare). Initially she had planned to buy a car with this money, but then realized that her children would "require financial assistance to deal with [their serious health] problems in the years ahead" (*R*. v. *Bond* 1994: para.8). So she decided to set the money aside as a trust fund for them. Bond said she had "honestly believed that she did not have to report the savings because they were for the children" (*R*. v. *Bond* 1994: para.13).

The trial judge admitted to a dilemma:

> I was very impressed by the sincerity and achievement of the accused and troubled by the paradox of criminalizing the actions of this woman who scrimped as a hedge against the future financial health needs of her children. If she had spent this money on drinking, or drugs, or in any other irresponsible way, there would be no basis for any criminal charge. A conviction seems to send the message it was wrong to be conscientious about the welfare of her children and foolish to be frugal. (*R*. v. *Bond* 1994: para. 14)

Convict he did, however. And he was neither the first nor last "sympathetic" judge to enter a conviction for fraud against a welfare mother (see Martin 1992; Carruthers 1995). Arguably, this case is one in which reasonable doubt as to guilt ought to have existed. Had she not been convicted of welfare fraud, this normatively perfect mother might well have been a candidate for "Mother and Homemaker of the Year." Yet the trial judge found Bond culpable: "Her commendable frugality and her selfless motives for committing the offence [were only] matters for consideration on sentencing" (*R*. v. *Bond* 1994: para 14).

Some seven years later, in the spring of 2001, Kimberly Rogers pleaded guilty to welfare fraud that involved receiving a student loan and welfare assistance at the same time (previously but no longer permitted by Ontario's legislation).[5] Because she was pregnant, and had no prior criminal record, the judge sentenced her to six months of house arrest. However, as a result of the Ontario government's zero tolerance policy, which then stipulated three months, and later permanent, ineligibility of people convicted of welfare fraud, Rogers had no source of income (Keck 2002; MacKinnon and Lacey 2001: F1, F8). Seeking reinstatement of her benefits, she wrote in an affidavit to the court: "I ran out of food this weekend. I am unable to sleep and I cry all the time" (cited in Keck 2002). Through a court order, she did receive interim assistance pending the hearing of a challenge to the constitutionality of the new ineligibility rules (*Rogers* v. *Sudbury* 2001), but her rent ($450.00 per month) consumed the bulk of her monthly cheque ($468.00 per month). As a friend later observed, "no one can stretch $18.00 for a whole month" (MacKinnon and Lacey 2001: F8).

Isolated, in her eighth month of pregnancy, and confined to her tiny apartment, Kimberly Rogers died of a prescription drug overdose during a sweltering heat wave in August 2001. The circumstances of her death gave rise to a coroner's inquest in the fall of 2002. The coroner's jury made fourteen recommendations for changes in government policies and practices, including the repeal of the zero tolerance lifetime ineligibility for social assistance as a result of welfare fraud (Ontario 2002; see also Eden 2003). Following their defeat of the Harris Conservatives in October 2003, the newly elected Ontario Liberal government did repeal the lifetime ban.[6] This was a welcome reform, but it is important to note that Kimberly Rogers would still be liable to a welfare fraud conviction today and, if living under house arrest, she would still have only a pittance to live on after her rent was paid.

In our view, the *Bond* and *Rogers* cases raise many theoretical and empirical questions related to regulation, law, and morality, and the relationship between them at particular historical moments. We draw on these cases to analyze the intensified criminalization of poverty signified by the shift from welfare fraud to welfare *as* fraud. We argue that the shift reflects a reformed mode of moral regulation in neo-liberal states.

The concept of moral regulation was developed initially during the 1980s by Marxist-influenced theorists (see Corrigan and Sayer 1981, 1985; Hall 1980) who linked it to processes of state formation. Through the 1990s a number of Canadian scholars pointed to the importance of non-state forces and discourses in moral regulation, arguing that the state does not hold a monopoly on "social" and "moral" initiatives (Valverde and Weir 1988: 31–34; Strange and Loo 1997; Little 1998; Valverde 1991, 1998; see also Dean 1994, 1999; Hunt 1997, 1999b). In our view, however, the state never ceases to be a player, even when benched, ignored by some, or outmanoeuvred by others. Thus, it remains important to identify the links, forms, and sites of state action and inaction.

We draw on a large body of socio-legal scholarship that has advanced this form of inquiry and analysis and illustrate our examination of shifting modes of moral regulation with reference to the historical treatment of poor women on welfare (see Little 1998).[7] We focus in particular on the always precarious position of such women within the overarching (apparently anachronistic) category of the "deserving poor" through the example of welfare legislation and policy.[8] The recent welfare law reform and preoccupation with welfare fraud — the redefinition, restructuring, harassment, and disentitlement, coupled with the ever present threat of criminal prosecution — suggest that the state and its coercive apparatus continue to play an important role that requires close analysis.

THE DOUBLE TAXONOMY OF MORAL REGULATION: COMPULSION AND SELF-REGULATION

Moral regulation has no agreed upon meaning, but most scholarship in the area begins with the collaborative work of Philip Corrigan and Derek Sayer. In *The Great Arch: English State Formation as Cultural Revolution*, they linked moral regulation to the "cultural" project of English state formation:

> Moral regulation: a project of normalizing, rendering natural, taking for granted, in a word "obvious," what are in fact ontological and epistemological premises of a particular and historical form of social order. Moral regulation is coextensive with state formation, and state forms are always animated and legitimated by a particular moral ethos. (Corrigan and Sayer 1985: 4)

While Corrigan and Sayer placed the moral regulation project squarely within the realm of state actions and legal relations, other scholars theorizing regulation and control through the 1990s maintained that the state must be decentred (Valverde 1991), or its relationship with non-state agencies better appreciated (Valverde 1995), or erased as a significant player altogether (Valverde 1998). For Mariana Valverde, the heart of moral regulation or moral reform in a "moral capitalist setting... is not so much to change behaviour as to generate certain ethical subjectivities that appear as inherently moral" (Valverde 1994: 216; see also Weir 1986). The focus is less on the material consequences of regulation or reform than it is on the discursive context.

Although sympathetic to this "decentring" emphasis, we want to argue for a renewed focus on social and state forces, and in particular on the contradictions and contributions of forms of law and state to gendered and anti-racist class struggles in the realm of moral regulation. Moral regulation must be situated expressly within the context of capitalist class relations and struggles — not least of which is capital's globalized attack on the "straw house" of the Keynesian welfare state. In developing our position, we draw on Stuart Hall's early work on law, state, and moral regulation; specifically, his analysis of the reformist sixties era of the "legislation of consent" in Britain, when laws relating to divorce, homosexuality, abortion, and prostitution were liberalized (Hall 1980).

Hall's (1980: 2) organizing question is: "What was it about the shifts in the modality of moral regulation which enabled this legislation, plausibly, to be described as 'permissive'?" He notes that "the legislation of consent" contained "no single uncontradictory tendency" (p.7). By way of illustration, he looks at the influential Report of the Wolfenden Committee on prostitution and homosexuality and argues that it "identified and separated more sharply two areas of legal and moral practice — those of sin and crime, of immorality and illegality" (p.11). As a result, Wolfenden created "a firmer opposition between these two domains" and "clearly staked out a new relation between the *two modes of moral regulation — the modalities of legal compulsion and of self-regulation*" (Hall 1980: 11–12; emphasis added).

Wolfenden recommended decriminalization and "privatisation of selective aspects of sexual conduct" (Hall 1980: 13), notably off-street prostitution and homosexual relations between consenting adults in private, and increased regulation of visible sexual activities such as "street-walking" and "male importuning" that were "offences against [the] public sector" (pp.10–11). Hall identifies the "double taxonomy" of the Wolfenden recommendations: towards stricter penalty and control, towards greater freedom and leniency (p.14). Here, then, was the core tendency of the permissive legislation of the 1960s: "*increased regulation* coupled with *selective privatisation* through contract or consent, both in a new disposition," a "more privatised and person-focused regulation, tacit rather than explicit, invisible rather than visible" (p.21; emphasis added). In short, a clearer distinction was made between "public" and "private," state and civil society (p.13).

In identifying the double taxonomy of control and penalty and freedom and leniency, or simultaneous deregulation and increased regulation, Hall reminds us of the complexity of the unity of the 1960s reforms. The state was pulled back and reinserted in different ways in the same pieces of legislation; its invisibility in one area was reinforced by its visibility in the other. Thus, "self-regulation" was inextricably related to increased "public" regulation. The lines between unacceptable public and permissible private conduct were more sharply drawn. In this way, two modalities of moral regulation, legal compulsion and self-regulation, one neither displacing nor transcending the other, co-existed in a complex unity.

Before applying this conceptualization of moral regulation to our exemplar of welfare fraud, we first examine welfare reform during the 1990s in order to consider the increased interest and legal shifts in the area of welfare fraud.

REFORMING WELFARE IN THE 1990s

Although concern about welfare fraud is not a new phenomenon, the unrelenting punitiveness of the crackdowns under neo-liberalism is. Anti-fraud campaigns during the 1970s and early 1980s (see Golding and Middleton 1982; Rachert 1990) led to the review and total restructuring of welfare policies in Canada and other Western countries through the 1990s (see Bashevkin 2002; Moscovitch 1997). Here we focus primarily on Ontario reforms to illustrate the shift from welfare fraud to welfare *as* fraud.

A pivotal moment in the welfare history of Ontario occurred in 1988, when the Social Assistance Review Committee (SARC) released *Transitions*, a six-hundred-page report with 274 recommendations on Ontario's social assistance system (Ontario 1988). The report devoted only seven pages to issues of "system integrity" and "welfare fraud" and yielded but two recommendations, which were motivated not out of any belief on the part of the Committee that fraud was rampant, but because they wanted to address and instil "public confidence" in the system (Ontario 1988: 384–86):

> We have no evidence to suggest that fraud in the social assistance system is greater than it is in the tax system or the unemployment insurance system. Nevertheless, because public confidence in the social assistance system depends in large part on the belief that the funds are being well spent and that abuse is being kept to a minimum, we accept that some of the measures adopted to

control social assistance fraud may need to be more extensive
than they are in other systems. (Ontario 1988: 384)

Notably, however, the report identified adequacy of benefits as the
"*single most important weapon in the fight against fraud in the system*"
(p.384).

Responding to the recommendations concerning "system integrity,"
Dianne Martin (1992) criticized the Committee for abandoning its own
guiding principles, in particular its commitment to the creation of a
welfare regime based on the dignity and autonomy of social assistance
recipients. Martin (1992: 93) pointed out that the most reliable indicator
(conviction rate) placed the incidence rate of welfare fraud in Ontario
at less than 1 percent. She was particularly concerned about the dispro-
portional criminalization and punitive treatment of women on welfare
(p.91). The guiding sentencing principles stressed deterrence as "the
paramount consideration" even where the case was "pitiful" (p.66; see
also *R.* v. *Thurrott* 1971; Carruthers 1995).

From an almost insignificant place in *Transitions*, the fight against
welfare fraud emerged as a centrepiece of provincial welfare policy in
Ontario during the 1990s, irrespective of governing political party (see
Moscovitch 1997; Little 1998: 139-63; Morrison 1995). However, in
the implementation of their election platform, "The Common Sense
Revolution," the Conservatives under Premier Mike Harris introduced
changes that were more neo-liberal than conservative (see Cossman
2002), including the most draconian welfare reforms of any Canadian
province.[9] Taking their cue from the Klein administration in Alberta (see
Denis 1995; Kline 1997), the Harris government made welfare — and in
particular a vow to "crack down" on "fraud" — the core of its welfare
policy (Ontario 2000a, 1999).

Almost immediately after its election in 1995, the Harris government
implemented a 22 percent cut to welfare rates and redefined (that is,
expanded) the definition of spouse in welfare law in order to disentitle a
range of previously entitled recipients (see Gavigan 1999; Mosher 2000).
All of Canada's welfare poor live on incomes that are thousands of dollars below the poverty line, but in post-1995 Ontario the welfare-rate cut
widened the "poverty gap" even further (National Council of Welfare
2005: 87, Figure 5.2; see also Little 2001; McMullin, Davies, and Cassidy
2002). Between 1995 and 2004, the household income of a single employ-
able recipient of social assistance in Ontario fell from 48 to 34 percent of
the federal government's low-income cut-off measure; the income of a
single parent with one child dropped from 76 to 56 percent of the poverty

line; and the income of a couple with two children on welfare fell from 67 to 50 percent of the poverty line (National Council of Welfare 2005: 66, Table 5.1; see also Gavigan 1999: 212–13). Likewise, the impact of the expanded definition of spouse on single mothers was "devastating" (Little 2001: 27). In the eight months following this reform, according to Margaret Little (2001: 26), "More than 10,000 recipients were deemed ineligible under the new definition and cut off social assistance." Some 89 percent of those were women.

Further to these measures, the Harris government proudly announced its stance on welfare fraud: "The new zero tolerance policy is the first of its kind in Canada, and a key step in Ontario's welfare reforms."[10] Zero tolerance meant permanent ineligibility for anyone convicted of welfare fraud, an exceptionally severe consequence given that the discourse and politics of welfare fraud have obscured the imprecision of what is considered to be fraud, and by whom. In Harris neo-liberal discourse, "fraud" came to encompass all forms of overpayments, whether resulting from administrative errors or not, including people in jail whose welfare should have been terminated upon incarceration, as well as formal fraud convictions. The government's own "Welfare Fraud Control Reports" tended to collapse categories, frequently failing to distinguish between benefit "reduction" and "termination," and the reasons therefore (see, for example, Ontario 2003). Yet, as the coroner who presided at the Kimberly Rogers' inquest observed of the evidence that had been presented during the two months of hearings: "While overpayments are common, overpayments due to fraud are very uncommon" (Eden 2003). Indeed, recent research into abused women's experience of welfare within this discursive practice of welfare fraud (Mosher, Evans, and Little 2004) as well as research into the nature and extent of welfare fraud (Mosher and Hermer 2005) reconfirms both the problem with definition and the sharp drop between "allegations" and actual convictions:

> The number of convictions [in Ontario] for 2001-02 (393 convictions) is roughly equivalent to 0.1 percent of the combined social assistance caseload and one percent of the total number of allegations. Statistics from the Municipality of Toronto for 2001 provide a similar picture: *80 percent of 11,800 allegations made against recipients were found to be untrue, in 19 percent of the remaining allegations there was no intent to defraud,* 117 cases were referred to the Fraud Review unit, of these 116 were reviewed by a special review committee, 95 were referred on to the police and charges were laid or pending in 91 (less than one

percent of the total allegations). (Mosher and Hermer 2005: 34; emphasis added)

One reason that 99 percent of the allegations of welfare fraud were unfounded may be that the "overwhelming majority of the \$49 million [trumpeted in the Ontario Welfare Fraud Report for 2001–02 as going to undeserving recipients] can be attributed to errors, mistakes, oversights of one form or another, made by applicants and by administrators and not to fraud" (Mosher, Evans, and Little 2004: 51).

The complexity of the rules and the reporting requirements facing welfare recipients have also become more difficult and intrusive in the time since the *Transitions* report was released (Morrison 1995: A12–A14; Mosher, Evans, and Little 2004), thereby increasing the likelihood that a recipient may unintentionally commit "fraud." For instance, the previous legislation permitted a welfare recipient to receive social assistance as well as an income-based student loan in order to attend college or university. Now, as Kimberly Rogers learned, someone doing that runs the risk of a welfare fraud conviction (Keck 2002; MacKinnon and Lacey 2001).

Far from addressing a residual concern triggered by a few "cheats" (McKeever 1999: 261–70), policies of "enhanced verification," zero tolerance and permanent ineligibility illustrate a significant shift in the conceptualization of welfare. Along with ever more intrusive measures to ensure recipients' eligibility (Little 2001), a snitch hotline was created to encourage the anonymous reporting of suspected fraud and abuse by neighbours. Rather than instilling public confidence in the social security system (Ontario 1988), however, these initiatives encourage and maintain a lack of public confidence by conveying the impression that fraud was and is rampant, and that every person on welfare needs to be watched and reported on and tested.

The shift in the direction of increased surveillance and criminalization of welfare recipients — notably women on welfare — illustrates too that the coercive form of criminal law and the regulatory form of welfare law are inseparable. The Criminal Code continues to be used to prosecute welfare recipients when fraud is suspected, and even "sincere, devoted mothers" like Donna Bond find themselves at risk of prosecution and conviction. Yet for all the heightened intensity and investigation of welfare fraud, the convictions boasted by the Ontario government in its own statistics have amounted to no more than 1.36 percent of the total number of welfare recipients in the province and less than 1 percent based on statistics from the National Council of Welfare (2000).[11]

WOMEN, WELFARE, AND THE "NEVER DESERVING" POOR

Despite the contemporary shift in the prevailing mode of moral regulation, the welfare reforms of the 1990s did not mark a complete departure from past practices. On the contrary, Canadian welfare legislation and policy show important historical continuities (Abramovitz 1996; Little 1998; Mosher 2000). First, welfare policy has always been premised on the separation of the "deserving" from the "undeserving" poor. Second, the social support accorded to the deserving was, and continues to be, based on "the principle of less eligibility" — or the assumption that welfare recipients should not receive more money than the worst paid worker in the labour force. Third, the "deserving" always have been at risk of falling into the ranks of the "undeserving." Single mothers on social assistance have been and are subjected to intrusive and "moral" surveillance of their homes, their cleanliness, their child-rearing abilities, and their personal lives (Little 1998; see also Buchanan 1995: 33, 40). Fourth, there have long been criminal prosecutions for welfare fraud (Rachert 1990; Martin 1992: 52–97; Evans and Swift 2000).

What made the 1990s different from earlier times, then, was the ideological shift from welfare liberalism to neo-liberalism (see Stenson and Watt 1999; Clarke 2000). It is a shift that, however, still requires a major state presence and resources. On one hand, the state is ideologically de-centred but no less present (Denis 1995). The form of the state and its social policy has shifted; social programs designed to ameliorate or redistribute have been eroded, laying bare a heightened state presence that condemns and punishes the poor. On the other hand, the effect of this ideological shift has been a huge expansion in the category of "undeserving" poor. Virtually everyone is considered as "never deserving"; even those who do receive social assistance are viewed as temporary recipients who must demonstrate their willingness to work for welfare and who ultimately will be employed as a result of skills and experience gained through workfare and other government-subsidized programs.

Thus, lone-parent mothers who historically were more likely to be deemed "deserving" than were childless men and women are now no longer so "privileged" (Buchanan 1995; Moscovitch 1997; Little 1998; Mortenson 1999; Mosher 2000; Swift and Birmingham 2000; Bashevkin 2002), as even Canadian courts have begun to acknowledge that, as in *Falkiner* v. *Ontario* (2002: 504, para. 77), "the statistics unequivocally demonstrate that both women and single mothers are disproportionately adversely affected by the definition of spouse" in welfare law. As that case found, "Although women accounted for only 54% of those receiving

social assistance and only 60% of single persons receiving social assistance, they accounted for nearly 90% whose benefits were terminated by
the [new] definition of spouse" (p.504, para.77).

Similarly, Janet Mosher and her colleagues (2004: 56–59) found
that welfare reforms have made women more vulnerable than ever to
abusive men. Deep cuts to benefits increase women's dependence on
material assistance from others to supplement their welfare cheques, and
that assistance most often goes unreported. The expanded definition of
spouse also makes it more likely that women will violate the "spouse
in the house" rule. Abusive men take advantage of women's heightened
vulnerability by reporting or threatening to report their current or past
partners to welfare authorities, alleging fraud. As a result, women are
trapped in abusive relationships. As one such woman said:

> *It was all to do with welfare. I just got into an abusive relationship
> that I could no longer get out of because now someone could
> accuse me of fraud.*
>
> *Um, it's like... if he gave me some money and we had an
> argument, he'd say something like, "I'm sure you didn't tell your
> worker that I gave you two hundred dollars the other day. You
> know, you could get in trouble for that." (Cited in Mosher et al.
> 2004: 58)*

The contemporary expansion of the "undeserving poor" has required a
massive redeployment but, arguably, not a reduction in the allocation
of state resources to welfare. The downsizing of social assistance payments is accompanied by a concomitant increase in state-subsidized
make-work and workfare programs that will ostensibly return participants to the labour force. There has also been a dramatic increase in the
state-implemented technologies and programs aimed at ferreting out and
punishing the "undeserving" poor (Mosher 2000; Swift and Birmingham
2000; Mosher et al. 2004; Savarese and Morton 2005). For instance,
the Harris Tories' lifetime ban following a conviction for welfare fraud
ensured both a lifetime of (secondary) punishment (without parole) and
unameliorated poverty.

The past and the present contexts in which welfare and welfare fraud
are being framed, then, show important differences. We are witnessing a
profound attack on the "social" — indeed, the erosion of social responsibility — and the "authoritarian" neo-liberal state is a key player in this
attack. Despite the apparent transcendence of social relations and state

forms (in favour of dispersed pluralities of power), moral regulation must be understood in relation to state and social policy.

MORAL REGULATION REVISITED

The increased emphasis on welfare and welfare fraud is tightly linked to the process of state re-formation in liberal democracies. We concur with (moral regulation) scholars who argue that the success of the "new right" in Ontario and elsewhere cannot be reduced to economics and globalization. Rather, restructuring and the decline of the "social" must

> be understood in the context of a vast cultural offensive to transform society [in which] the ability to wield state power is essential.... Far from losing its sovereignty, the state reasserts its power over the lives of citizens.... It turns itself into the "authoritarian state," one of whose main characteristics is to usher in a new, more intense regime of moral regulation. (Denis 1995: 373; see also Hall 1988)

Again, as Hall (1980: 7) argued, the "legislation of consent" was shot through with contradictory tendencies, which made the "unity" of the various statutes involved "a necessarily complex one." Those contradictory tendencies are apparent in the welfare reform in Ontario and elsewhere during the 1980s and 1990s, a reform that restructured the relation between the two modes of moral regulation — self-regulation and compulsion. Specifically, the welfare reforms show a "double taxonomy" in the movement toward both expanded privatization and increased regulation. For one thing, they show the intensified individualization of poverty through the emphasis on personal responsibility, the imposition of self-reliance, and the relegation of former welfare recipients to the market (see also Cossman 2002). The slight and grudging acknowledgement of social responsibility for the poor that marked the Keynesian state was rescinded. Now, as in the nineteenth century, poverty is a problem of individuals in civil society, and the solution to poverty is an individualized matter to be found principally in the labour market and/or marriage.[12]

This intensified individualization of poverty has major implications for lone-parent women. Historically, the "deserving" mother on welfare may have been "hapless" (Evans and Swift 2000) and "pitied, but not entitled" (Gordon 1994), but she was also a public servant of sorts so long as she was considered to be (morally) fit. During the 1990s, Ontario and other governments began divesting themselves of public servants, including "welfare moms," and placed the emphasis on creating choices to work and become self-sufficient. Now work is strictly confined to the (private) market, and mother work no longer receives even the tacit recognition that it was accorded by Keynesian states. The promotion of individual responsibility and self-reliance and the equation of work with paid, private-sector employment are very clear in the statement of key principles underpinning Ontario's reformed welfare system: "Doing nothing on welfare is no longer an option.... Participation [in Ontario Works] is mandatory for all able-bodied people, including sole-support parents with school-aged children" (Ontario 2000b; see also Lalonde 1997).

Defining work as paid employment means that women who do unpaid work can no longer be dependent on the state, but they can work for welfare or be dependent on an individually responsible, self-reliant, employed spouse. The Harris government underscored this point by refining and expanding the "spouse in the house" rule on the ground that "no one deserves higher benefits just because they are not married."[13] Thus, while "welfare dependency" has become a form of personality disorder signifying inadequacy, and has been "diagnosed more frequently in females" (Fraser and Gordon 1994: 326), the "approved" alternative, or perhaps supplement, to the market for lone-parent women is marriage and the family (Murray 1990). As Segal points out: "This is why single mothers can be demonized if they *don't* work, even while married women with young children can be demonized if they *do*"(Segal 1999: 206).

Concomitant with the emphasis on an intensified individualization of poverty is the intensified state regulation and surveillance of dwindling numbers of public welfare recipients, now redefined as individuals who need "temporary financial assistance... while they satisfy obligations to becoming and staying employed" (Ontario Works Act 1997, s. 2). Since welfare "is temporary, not permanent," according to the Ontario Works Act (s. 2), the state must ensure that public money is not being wasted on "fraudsters." The Ontario legislation invokes the neo-liberal language of self-reliance through employment, temporary financial assistance, efficient delivery, and accountability to taxpayers.[14] As noted earlier, however, Ontario has poured extensive resources into the establishment of an elaborate and constantly expanding system of surveillance aimed at detecting and preventing fraud and misuse of the social assistance system. Concomitant with massive cuts to welfare rates, the government allocated considerable money for special staff with expanded powers to investigate welfare fraud: three hundred such investigators were hired in

1998–99 and the government later provided "additional funding for up to 100 more staff to do this work" (Ontario 2000b). Similarly, government resources were needed to create and maintain the Welfare Fraud Hotline and a province-wide Welfare Fraud Control Database, to implement biometric finger-scanning (Little 2001: 26), and to prosecute alleged "fraudsters." Clearly, the state will spend considerable public money to police welfare recipients — but not to provide for them.

Of course, if we move beyond what government authorities themselves say, it becomes evident that the moralization and criminalization of the poor in general and "welfare moms" in particular are far from seamless. Contradictions are evident both among those who apply welfare law and policy and among those who are the targets of moralization. Judicial decision-making, for instance, is not uniformly punitive in cases involving mothers charged with welfare fraud. Some criminal cases in which women were convicted of welfare fraud for "spouse in the house," and hence of not living as a single person, do illustrate the neo-liberal ideological shift from bad mothers to bad choices (see *R*. v. *Plemel* 1995; *R*. v. *Jantunen* 1994; *R*. v. *Slaght* 1995; and *R*. v. *Sim* 1980)

But not every woman charged with welfare fraud is convicted, or if convicted, sent to jail. Some judges go to lengths to ensure this. Donna Bond received a conditional discharge, fifty hours of community service, and six months' probation, all of which left her without a criminal record upon successful completion of the conditions.[15] In another Ontario case, Trainor J. refused to convict a battered woman for welfare fraud (*R*. v. *Lalonde* 1995; see also Carruthers 1995). Finally, the coroner's jury at the inquest into the house-arrest death of Kimberly Rogers made fourteen recommendations aimed at eliminating or softening the harsh welfare reforms that were implemented in Ontario during the 1990s.[16]

Accounts of "welfare mothers" also reveal diversity in practices among financial aid and front-line workers (Mortenson 1999). Some workers are empathetic and supportive; in *Lalonde*, for instance, welfare authorities had acquiesced to the man's presence in the home and only charged the woman after her partner "self-reported" his presence (*R* v. *Lalonde* 1995). Others are punitive and controlling of their "clients" (Little 2001; Mosher et al. 2004). Likewise, the poor, including "welfare mothers," are far from constituting a homogeneous category (Swift and Birmingham 2000; see also Gavigan 1999: 213-18). While welfare recipients arguably have a common class position, the ways in which they acquire that class position are diverse and mediated by other social relations of gender, race, sexual orientation, and ability or disability that in turn influence how and the extent to which mothers on welfare, for instance, are active agents in shaping these relations. Many women live in constant fear of scrutiny that may result in the loss of welfare assistance for not reporting income, having partners stay overnight, or being reported for child abuse and losing their children (Mortenson 1999: 122–23; Little 1998, 2001; *Falkiner* v. *Ontario* 2002: 515, paras. 103, 104). As a result, they engage in continual "self-censorship" of their activities (Little 1998: 180). Others resist or challenge welfare law and policy through the establishment of and participation in informal support networks of "welfare moms" and/or anti-poverty agencies and organizations (Buchanan 1995; Little 1998; Mortenson 1999).

Interview studies also reveal ideological contradictions among "welfare mothers." A few espouse the social Darwinism of neo-liberal law and policy. They see themselves as short-term, "deserving" welfare recipients who through workfare programs and/or their own hard work will become "contributing" members of society again (Mortenson 1999). Some also feel resentful of and more "deserving" than other mothers on welfare, whom they believe are "faring better in the distribution of scarce resources, including jobs" (Swift and Birmingham 2000: 94–95). In contrast, others strongly reject the neo-liberal thrust of welfare legislation and policy, equating workfare programs and the rationales for them as government propaganda. One woman interviewed by Mortenson said she went to a workplace orientation and found that "it was unbelievably stupid." She added: "You have to be gung ho about making nothing and not getting any benefits or security, is basically what they're telling you in so many words…. It's a cheap labour strategy" (cited in Mortenson 1999: 66).

The regulation/deregulation contradiction in the area of welfare legislation and policy reforms aimed at the poor also should be viewed in the context of government actions related to the welfare of the affluent and the regulation of capital. Increased criminalization and punishment of welfare fraud have occurred simultaneously with the deregulation and "disappearance" of corporate crime (Snider 1999; see also Pearce and Tombs 1998: 567–75; Tombs 2002; Glasbeek 2002). Massive welfare cuts targeting poor people are implemented at the same time as huge corporate tax cuts, which, together with direct fiscal subsidies, arguably are forms of social welfare for the rich (see, for example, Young 2000; Abramovitz 2001; Klein and Long 2003). The deregulation and de facto decriminalization of corporate wrongdoing benefit a minority of (primarily) affluent white men, while the criminalization of poverty and the intensified prosecution of welfare fraud punish the poor disproportionately (see Beckett and Western 2001).

As Laureen Snider (1999: 205) points out, the disappearance of corporate crime does matter:

> Abandoning state sanctions has far-reaching symbolic and practical consequences. State laws are public statements that convey important public messages about the obligations of the employer classes.... The situation is paradoxical indeed: while crimes of the powerful were never effectively sanctioned by state law, such laws are nonetheless essential to the operation of democratic societies.

The concomitant deregulation of corporate crime and increased punitiveness toward welfare fraud (and "street crime" more generally) suggest that in an authoritarian form of liberal-democratic state, government interventionism is redirected, not eliminated (Denis 1995: 368; see also Hall 1988). State withdrawal from Keynesian social programs and the economy occurs in tandem with government activism around issues such as youth crime and "terrorism" (Denis 1995: 369; see also Hermer and Mosher 2002). This shift in the focus of state interventionism has important implications for the regulation of the poor, and in particular, of lone-parent women.

"A BAD TIME TO BE POOR"

The reformed mode of moral regulation in Canada and elsewhere during the late twentieth century typified the reformed relationship between public and private under neo-liberalism. In Keynesian states a prevailing ideology of welfare liberalism provided a rationale for at least limited (public) state intervention to assist the "deserving" poor. In "authoritarian" neo-liberal states, a discursive shift to an emphasis on formal equality (sameness) has informed a new rationale for valorizing the (private) market as the only solution to poverty. As a result, to protect the public purse anyone who asks for state assistance must be scrutinized carefully, and welfare can only be a stopgap measure prior to the recipients' entry into paid employment. Therefore, while non-state practices play a role in moral regulation, the state clearly continues to be a major player as well.

The ideological and discursive shifts from welfare liberalism to neo-liberalism have also had a drastic material impact. They have exacerbated the poverty of all welfare recipients, but particularly lone-parent women who historically were among the most "deserving." In some contemporary moral regulation scholarship, "poverty" is a discursive construct displacing the class analysis that characterized the Marxian-informed literature of the early 1980s (Corrigan and Sayer 1981, 1985; Hall 1980). Our analysis of the shift from welfare fraud to welfare *as* fraud supports those who continue to argue for the interconnectedness of the material, social, and cultural and the need to look at the political and economic issues of redistribution as well as identity/self-formation (Fraser 1997; see also Roberts 1997; Segal 1999).

Some might argue that welfare law and policy have shifted again, away from the excesses of the 1990s toward more "humane" treatment of the poor. After all, the moral regulation of the poor under neo-liberalism is not uniformly oppressive. Courts sometimes refuse to convict, and some welfare workers are empathetic. Some governments are even proclaiming a "kinder, gentler" approach to the poor. Following the election of the Ontario Liberals in 2003, for instance, Sandra Pupatello, the new minister of community and social services, said that the Harris Tories had treated people on welfare as "a typical punching bag," and she expressed the new government's commitment to a "series of reforms" so that "the system actually works for people."[17] The Liberal government subsequently eliminated the lifetime ban, increased welfare rates by 3 percent, and implemented several of the forty-nine recommendations contained in a government-commissioned report on ways of improving the province's welfare system (Matthews 2004).

Although the Matthews Report (2004) incorporated the views of some low-income people and their advocates,[18] the Liberals did not follow up immediately with anything that would fundamentally change the legacy of the Harris Tories. The new mode of moral regulation exemplified by the conceptualization of welfare *as* fraud remained in place. The Liberal government stated its commitment to "no tolerance" for welfare fraud (see Galloway 2004: A9). Likewise, it retained the conviction of successive governments that "employment provides an escape out of poverty," an especially problematic assertion "in the context of a labour market that is characterized by precarious, low-waged work" (Income Security Advocacy Centre 2005: 6). In turn, the overweening focus on paid employment militates against any significant increase in what the Liberal government acknowledged are "unacceptably low" rates of assistance (Income Security Advocacy Centre 2005: 8). At the moment, it is truly "a bad time to be poor" (Klein and Long 2003), especially for the many lone-parent women and their children who have been newly relegated to the ranks of the "never-deserving."

NOTES

Special thanks to Elizabeth Comack and Gillian Balfour for their comments, support, and forbearance. We also want to acknowledge Steve Bittle for his thoughtful feedback and express our appreciation to Laura Lunansky and Yui Funayama for research assistance. This chapter is a revised, edited version of Chunn and Gavigan 2004.

1. General Welfare Assistance Act, R.S.O. 1990, c. G.6, as rep. by Social Assistance Reform Act, 1997, S.O. 1997, c. 25 enacting Ontario Works Act, 1997, S.O. 1997, c. 25, s. 1 [OWA] and Ontario Disability Support Program Act, 1997, S.O. c. 25, s. 2 [ODSPA]. The purpose of the Ontario Works legislation is to establish a program that, as expressed in s.1:
    (a) recognizes individual responsibility and promotes self-reliance through employment;
    (b) provides temporary financial assistance to those most in need while they satisfy obligations to become and stay employed;
    (c) effectively serves people needing assistance; and
    (d) is accountable to the taxpayers of Ontario.
2. Ontario Works Act, 1997, O.Reg. 134/98, Reg. 33.
3. See Hermer and Mosher 2002 for commentary on Ontario's Safe Streets Act 1999, S.O. 1999, c. 8. This legislation renders illegal the street activity of "squeegee kids" and panhandlers.
4. Welfare recipients were then required to report annually on their circumstances, in order to ascertain continued eligibility for assistance. In Ontario financial eligibility is now "reverified" on at least an annual basis, and ongoing "verification" and reporting requirements have intensified. A recipient is obliged to self-report any change in circumstances immediately.
5. Ontario Works Act, 1997, O.Reg. 134/98, Reg. 9 (a) and (b), provide that no single person who is in full-time attendance at a post-secondary educational institution is eligible for assistance if the person is in receipt of a student loan or is ineligible for a student loan because of parental income.
6. The permanent ineligibility sections of the Regulations were repealed by O. Reg 456/03 made under the Ontario Works Act, 1997.
7. For a political economy approach to these issues, see Fudge and Cossman 2002.
8. The racist dimensions of welfare law should be emphasized. Historically, welfare legislation excluded (implicitly or explicitly) lone-parent, racialized, and ethnic minority women. More recently, they have been disproportionately represented among the "undeserving" poor (see Roberts 1997; Chunn and Gavigan 2005).
9. See *Masse* v. *Ontario* (1996); *Rogers* v. *Sudbury* (2001); *Broome* v. *Ontario* (2002). The more recent initiatives of the Campbell provincial government in British Columbia promise to surpass the dubious record of the Harris Tories (see Klein and Long 2003).
10. Ontario Progressive Conservative government policy statement, Jan. 18, 2000, Ontario PC News and Headlines <www.mikeharrispc.com>. (Accessed Aug. 1, 2001.)
11. The statistics available from the Ontario Ministry of Community, Family and Children's Services reveal a steady decline in criminal convictions for welfare fraud: 1123 in 1997–98; 747 in 1998–99; 547 in 1999–00; and 393 in 2001–02 (Ontario 1999a, 2000a, 2000b, 2002, 2003: Table 1). With respect to the zero tolerance lifetime ban, the Income Security Advocacy Centre reported that a total of 106 individuals

became permanently ineligible to receive financial assistance due to welfare fraud offences committed between April 1, 2000 (when the ban took effect) and Nov. 27, 2002 <www.incomesecurity.org> (accessed June 23, 2003).

12. This is illustrated clearly by the repeal of the General Welfare Act in Ontario, and the introduction in its place of Ontario Works legislation.

13. The Ontario Court of Appeal struck down this expanded definition of spouse for "its differential treatment of sole support mothers on the combined grounds of sex, marital status and receipt of social assistance, which discriminates against them contrary to s. 15 of the Charter" (*Falkiner* v *Ontario* [2002]: 515 para. 105). Significantly, a person is deemed to be a spouse after three months' cohabitation; this is a much shorter time period of cohabitation (about two years and nine months shorter) than is required under Ontario's provincial family law legislation before spousal support obligations and entitlements are triggered.

14. See Ontario Works Act, 1997, s. 1 (a), (b), (c) and (d).

15. Sentencing took place on Sept. 19, 1994. *R.* v. *Bond* (1994), certificate of conviction (on file with the authors).

16. See "Verdict of Coroner's Jury into the Death of Kimberly Ann Rogers," released on Dec. 19, 2002. The coroner's inquest, which lasted two months, involved eight parties with standing, all represented by counsel, and forty-one witnesses. The jury heard that of the five thousand or so welfare recipients in Kimberly Rogers's home community of Sudbury, there were at most one or two convictions for welfare fraud annually. Evidence before the jury showed that "the Crown and the Courts were unaware that upon conviction the accused would be subject to a suspension of benefits." Recommendation 14 called for ongoing professional training of criminal justice personnel in this regard. The fourteen recommendations form part of a letter dated Jan. 17, 2003, sent by the presiding coroner, Dr. David S. Eden, to the chief coroner of Ontario (on file with the authors).

17. Ontario, Legislative Assembly, First Session, 38th Parliament, Official Debates (*Hansard*), no. 17A Wednesday Dec. 17, 2003, at 868.

18. Significantly, Aboriginal Peoples were not consulted about their social service needs (Income Security Advocacy Centre 2005: 8).

9. THERAPEUTIC PROGRAMMING AS A REGULATORY PRACTICE IN WOMEN'S PRISONS

Shoshana Pollack

The past decade has seen significant reforms in the housing of federally incarcerated women in Canada: the Kingston Prison for Women, once the only federal penal institution for women, was closed down, and five regional prisons, including an Aboriginal Healing Lodge, opened across the country. Changes in correctional policy identify program approaches and philosophy as being women-centred and gender-specific in order to better meet the needs of women prisoners.

Despite a shift in rhetoric, however, women-centred prisons have helped to consolidate the logics of women's corrections rather than offer substantial change (Hannah-Moffat and Shaw 2000a). Although *Creating Choices,* a key policy document guiding prison reforms, attempted to highlight the victimization experiences of women prisoners and how their needs differ from their male counterparts, it did not challenge the underlying principles and assumptions of imprisonment as a response to social exclusion; rather, it contained a sense of optimism that women's prison programming could help women to become empowered and to heal from the effects of experiences of victimization.

The Correctional Service of Canada (CSC), along with prison practitioners in Britain and the United States, promotes psychologically based gender-specific programming for criminalized women. But these correctionalist approaches, by focusing on the psychology of imprisoned women, have diluted the socio-cultural and political components emphasized in feminist accounts of women's victimization experiences. Essentially these therapeutic interventions are closely connected to neo-liberal governance strategies — and a case in point, considered here, is Dialectical Behaviour Therapy, which is built upon assumptions about a "criminal self" and women's inability to regulate their own emotions. To counter this direction we need to consider alternative formulations of gender and punishment drawn from feminist theories of state process and critiques of neo-liberal governance, providing a framework that moves beyond accounts of criminalized women based on their personal psychologies.

236

FEMINIST CRIMINOLOGY:
THE VICTIMIZATION-CRIMINALIZATION CONTINUUM

Until the 1980s criminology largely ignored the situation of women in conflict with the law. When women were the topic of mainstream criminological research, the approaches simply applied the theories that had been developed about men. Feminist criminologists have, not surprisingly, challenged this androcentrism, and they have been pivotal in bringing to the forefront the bias against women in the field of criminology — as well as the criminal justice, legal, and correctional systems (Rafter and Heidensohn 1995). The theoretical and empirical contributions of feminist criminologists over the past several decades have advanced our understanding of women's involvement in crime and the gender differences in men's and women's experiences of the criminal justice and correctional systems (see, for example, chapter 1 here; and Flavin 2004 for an elaboration of the contributions of feminist criminology to the study of gender and crime).

In their studies of women in conflict with the law, feminist criminologists have highlighted the social factors that have an impact on women's involvement in crime. In particular, a wealth of empirical scholarship now documents how a great majority of imprisoned women in North America have histories of childhood abuse and have experienced violence in their intimate relationships with men (Comack 1996; Richie 1996; Gilfus 2002; Owen 1998). This research, often referred to as the "pathways to crime" literature, illustrates that attempts to cope with victimization experiences, such as childhood abuse and male violence used against them, propel many women into situations that put them at risk of being criminalized. For example, Mary Gilfus (2002) identifies six interrelated pathways that many women travel from victimization to incarceration. These pathways include running away from home to escape abuse and living on the streets. They include addictions, poverty and homelessness, being abused by male intimates, and state violence.

This body of work has heavily influenced contemporary understandings of the experiences and needs of women prisoners and the factors that influence their involvement in the criminal justice system. Feminist criminologists have also successfully highlighted the importance of women's agency or resistance to oppressive social conditions, and how those resistance strategies are often criminalized (Comack 1996; Gilfus 2002; Owen 1998). As well, feminists have helped to develop gender-specific prison and community services for criminalized women.

Feminist studies of the lives of criminalized women have tended to privilege gender as an analytic category. As a result, feminists have been challenged to develop approaches that address the intersections of gender, race, class, sexual orientation, culture, nature, and (dis)ability in their analyses of gender and crime (Flavin 2004; Sudbury 2004); for examples that take this approach, see Daly and Stephens 1995; Richie 1996; Ross 1998.

THE PATHWAYS APPROACH AND CORRECTIONAL PRACTICE: PSYCHOLOGIZING WOMEN PRISONERS

In recent years, then, the discourse, programs, and policies of the Correctional Service of Canada have incorporated the recognition that imprisoned women have experienced high levels of victimization (Laishes 2002; Fortin 2004b) — a co-optation of feminist notions that has been duly noted (Hannah-Moffat 2001; Pollack 2000b). A central focus of correctional policy with federally incarcerated women is the idea that women's life experiences, involvement in crime, and program needs are different than those of incarcerated men. The CSC therefore states that "gender-specific" programming is necessary to help women heal from past abuses and become empowered to make changes in their lives (Task Force on Federally Sentenced Women 1990). Writing for the Correctional Service, Jane Laishes (2002: 6), for example, states that women prisoners differ from their male counterparts in that they have higher incidences of mental illness due to their experiences of abuse. She asserts, "Some mental health problems experienced by women offenders can be linked directly to past experiences of sexual abuse, physical abuse, and assault."

Although Canada is considered an international leader in gender-sensitive approaches to the imprisonment of women (Carlen 2002c), the implementation of gender-specific approaches in prisons has its strong contradictions and challenges. The logics of imprisonment, the correctional mandate to punish, and the "psy-sciences" (psychiatry, psychology, psychotherapy) have been implicated in transforming the ideals of empowerment and healing into strategies for governing women prisoners (Canadian Association of Elizabeth Fry Societies 2003; Carlen 2002c; Faith 1999; Hannah-Moffat and Shaw 2000a; Hannah-Moffat 2001; Pollack 2000b; Pollack and Kendall 2005; Snider 2003). The Canadian Human Rights Commission has stated not only that women's prisons are neither empowering nor healing, but also that women federal prisoners are discriminated against on the basis of race, culture, gender, and ability (Canadian Human Rights Commission 2003; see also chapter 12 here).

When incorporated into correctional logics and discourses, the abuse/

victimization narrative becomes psychologized; that is, the approach tends to focus upon the psychological/emotional impact of women's experiences and how impaired thinking, decision-making, and emotional control lead them to commit crimes. Consequently, programs link their outcomes to emotional/personal factors such as raised self-esteem, ability to make "better choices," improved reasoning skills, and engagement in therapy. In other words, correctional programming focuses almost exclusively on the "mind" of women prisoners while largely ignoring socio-economic factors — in addition to raising serious questions regarding coercive participation in therapy (see Pate 2005).

The minds, souls, and/or personalities of prisoners have always been a focus of correctional regimes (Foucault 1977; Hannah-Moffat 2001), but the most recent rendition of this focus in women's corrections has turned feminist therapeutic discourses into techniques for governing women prisoners. For example, an article published in *Forum on Correctional Research* (CSC's own research journal) outlines a gender-specific correctional program strategy for women. The article states that prison interventions must take into account the social, political, and cultural conditions that are unique to women in society, but then argues that this consideration means "understanding the psychological development of women" (Fortin 2004b: 38). The author draws on a branch of feminist psychology called "relational psychology" to substantiate the assertion that an understanding of women's psychology should be the foundation upon which gender-specific programming is built.

Relational psychology was developed by feminist psychologists at the Stone Centre at Wellesley College as a way of understanding how women's psychological development differs from the traditional male model of psychological development. Traditionally, developmental psychological theories have posited that the journey toward mature development is one that culminates in autonomy, independence, and separation (Jordan 1997). Relational theory asserts that women's sense of self is cultivated through connection rather than separation — and that it is in fact damaged by disconnections (such as abuse, violence, and incarceration). Central to its orientation is the development of "growth-enhancing" non-violating relationships characterized by mutuality (Miller et al. 1997).

Relational theory is a psychological theory that may offer helpful directions for therapeutic programming, but its application in gender-specific programs in prisons — in a context characterized by forced confinement, surveillance, and relationships of power — is counterproductive. Imprisoned women's lives tend to be characterized by relational disconnections and violations that render the women susceptible to drug abuse, street life, and criminalization (Covington and Bloom 2004): results that are the very antithesis of the end goals of relational theory. There is thus a contradiction in using this theoretical approach in prison without also dramatically altering the relations of power and control that exist there. Rather than being a constructive tool, the approach misuses a feminist-informed treatment model to solidify the logics of incarceration and perpetuate an individualistic focus on women's psychology. Moreover, the discursive sleight of hand that states the importance of understanding the socio-political context of women's lives (Fortin 1994) through treatment programs reframes social marginalization as a psychological problem. This conversion paves the way for the individualization of social problems and keeps the focus firmly fixed on the subjectivity of criminalized women. As the Canadian Association of Elizabeth Fry Societies (CAEFS) (2003: 39) notes, "By translating social disadvantage into mental health needs, CSC pathologizes a significant portion of federally sentenced women and subjects them to a greater degree of control based on the attribution of mental disability."

Kelly Hannah-Moffat (2005b; see also chapter 10 here) illustrates how the victimization/abuse narrative is connected to mental health issues and used in parole decisions to assess women's risk to reoffend. Her work demonstrates that a history of abuse/victimization, engagement in programming/therapy, and risk discourse are infused into decisions about whether or not an imprisoned woman may be released. Since a history of abuse or victimization is considered a "criminogenic" factor (that which is thought to be directly linked to criminal behaviour), these experiences render women more "risky." Again, violence against women becomes individualized, as the discourse of risk and responsibility frames much of correctional policy and practice. For example, if women have previously used force within an intimate relationship in which they were abused, they may be considered at risk of being violent in the future (Hannah-Moffat, 2005b). However, research shows that it is abusive men who in fact increase the risk to women's safety and the likelihood that abused women will be criminalized. For example, abused women are often charged in domestic violence situations for fighting back against abusive partners (Pollack, Battaglia, and Allspach 2005). Further, research shows that during domestic violence situations, women use available items, such as scissors, dishes, and TV remote controls, more often than men do. As a result of gender differences in strength and size, women incur a charge of "assault with a weapon" much more often than their male counterparts do (Comack, Chopyk, and Wood 2000). A psychologized victimization/abuse narrative used to assess imprisoned women's risk level thereby decontextualizes such things as gender-neutral domestic violence policies and their relationship to the criminalization of abused women.

NEO-LIBERAL CONTROL STRATEGIES AND IMPRISONED WOMEN

The Psy-Sciences and Acting Upon the Self

In addition to ensuring the security and stability of the prison, the correctional mandate is to assess, manage, and reduce the risk that prisoners pose to the institution, themselves, and the community. The primary purpose of prison programs is to reduce the likelihood that an individual will commit an offence after being released from prison. Therefore, programming targets the factors that are considered to be "criminogenic" — aspects of the individual that are viewed as causing crime and that are amenable to change.

These processes of normalization and responsibilization are often manifested through therapeutic programming designed to discipline, regulate, and reform "criminals" (Foucault 1977; Fox 1999; Kemshall 2002; Kendall and Pollack 2003; McCorkel 2003; Pollack and Kendall 2005). The "psy sciences" or professions play a significant role in these normalization and moralization projects, as "experts" employ normative classifications and categories to assess, diagnose, and treat. Imprisoned populations are especially susceptible to programs of self-regulation aimed at decreasing their risk to the security of the prison and to the outside community. Imprisoned women, in particular, are subject to the normalization processes of the psy sciences as their "selves" are assumed to be inherently disordered (McCorkel 2003; Haney 2004; Pollack and Kendall 2005).

The Risk Gaze

Another key principle of neo-liberal strategies of governance is "risk-thinking" (O'Malley 1996; Rose 2000; Baker and Simon 2002; Kemshall 2002). According to Nikolas Rose (2000), the contours of risk-thinking shape strategies for controlling socially excluded populations whose risk is managed by a myriad of control professionals. The risk gaze is most often aimed at those who are most socially excluded — those who experience poverty, homelessness, addictions, mental illness, and criminalization — and is thus fundamental to the regulation of social exclusion. Actuarial instruments used to measure and predict an individual's risk to commit a criminal offence further disadvantage impoverished and racialized communities, since such things as insecure housing, receipt of social assistance, and precarious labour-market attachment are viewed as increasing risk (Hudson 2002). In relation to imprisoned women, technologies for assessing and classifying levels of risk conflate risk with need, thus constructing such things as experiences of abuse as risk factors that lead women to criminal behaviour (Hannah-Moffat 2004). Therapeutic services — despite the good intentions of the individual therapist — become part of the risk-reduction apparatus; assessment, treatment, and documentation use correctional categories to evaluate such things as risk of violence and psychological and behavioural function-ing. As Rose (2000: 333) points out, the demands and objectives of risk management determine the very gaze of the control professional and the nature of that professional's encounters with clients, patients, or suspects. Thus, discourses about risk reduction and risk management proliferate throughout the correctional system and form the foundation upon which all programming is built.

Dependency Discourse
The notion of (in)dependence provides part of the ideological and discur-sive cement that binds together a variety of technologies for regulating social exclusion (particularly as they apply to women, and criminalized and racialized populations) (Cruikshank 1996; Rose 1996a; Pollack 2000a; Haney 2004; McCorkel 2004). Lynne Haney (2004) illustrates that the discourses of responsibility, accountability, and dependency are not unique to women's imprisonment policy and practice, but are part of a new gendered way of governing both the welfare and penal systems. For example, in an ethnographic study of a U.S. women's prison, Jill McCorkel (2004) traces how the importation of dependency discourse from the welfare arena into women's prisons — where it is used in therapeutic programming — creates the construct of "the criminally dependent" woman.

A similar process is evident within Canadian federal corrections, where *Creating Choices* identifies women's dependency (upon men, the state, and drugs/alcohol) as a primary factor in the lives of criminalized women (Task Force on Federally Sentenced Women 1990). A particularly potent illustration of how notions of dependency are both racialized and gendered comes in a Task Force assertion: "Dependency is a particularly relevant issue for Aboriginal women who have been historically streamed into dependence on non-Aboriginal institutions. Research indicates that culturally relevant programs are essential to help Aboriginal women to work through their dependency" (Task Force on Federally Sentenced Women 1990: 56). This therapeutic/psychological discourse effectively divests dependency of its social, racialized, and economic origins (Fraser and Gordon 1997). Instead, the discourse constructs dependency as a character trait that can be addressed through therapy and programming. The framing of dependency "as a problem of the will" (Rose 2000: 335) readily collapses into gender-specific therapeutic discourse and intervention, with a focus on women's psychology and self-esteem.

These technologies — self-regulation, risk-thinking, and dependency discourse — converge to create a heterogeneous network of control strategies used to act upon the individual and govern social exclusion. These strategies of neo-liberal governance signify a retreat from notions of social responsibility and a change to personal/individual blame and self-regulation (Kemshall 2002). Therapeutic programming, such as CSC's adaptation of Dialectical Behaviour Therapy, functions as a technology for the *responsibilization* (Rose 2000) of failed citizens — women prisoners.

GENDER-SPECIFIC PROGRAMMING? DIALECTICAL BEHAVIOUR THERAPY

The emergence of gender-specific programming within women's prisons is illustrative of the techniques of neo-liberal governance. A growing body of critical feminist literature demonstrates how programming in women's prisons relies upon a notion of a "criminal self" that includes faulty thinking, an inability to handle "freedom" properly, low self-esteem, and poor decision-making skills (Fox 1999; McCorkel 2003; Kendall and Pollack 2003; Pollack and Kendall 2005). At the core of this approach is the notion of a criminal mind or personality. These programs focus on restructuring how women think about themselves as a means of preventing them from reoffending. Such approaches pathologize women's lawbreaking by implying that criminal activity is the result of impairments in cognitive processes (Kendall and Pollack 2003). Women's attempts to discuss their experiences of trauma and/or marginalization are often viewed as denials or rationalizations of their offence (Fox 1999; McCorkel 2003). Instead, women are encouraged to internalize this "criminal personality" script in order to change their behaviour and prove their self-transformation.

In tandem with the concept of a criminal mind is the proliferation of a discourse that constructs women prisoners as emotionally unruly and psychologically disordered (Pollack and Kendall 2005). The CSC considers women prisoners' inability to emotionally self-regulate as the cause of problems in "cognitive functioning and/or substance abuse"

(Fortin 2004b: 39). The notion of "emotional deregulation" underpins the psychiatric diagnosis of Borderline Personality Disorder (BPD), a condition often attributed to women in prison (Pollack and Kendall 2005). Characteristics of those diagnosed with BPD are extreme emotionality, impulsivity, aggressive behaviour, dichotomous thinking, confused identity, self-injurious behaviour, and suicidal ideation. The BPD label is generally pejorative, both because the behaviours exhibited by those given this diagnosis are often difficult for others to deal with, and because BPD has traditionally been thought to be permanent and untreatable.

Recently, to deal with the "extreme" behaviours of women prisoners the CSC has implemented a new form of treatment called Dialectical Behaviour Therapy (DBT), which was originally developed by Marcia Linehan (1993) as a less stigmatizing cognitive-behavioural treatment model for women diagnosed with Borderline Personality Disorder. Although both men and women may acquire this psychiatric label, by far the majority of people diagnosed with BPD are women (Wirth-Cauchon 2001) — and a high percentage of those have a history of childhood trauma. Many mental health workers are reluctant to work with women diagnosed with BPD, because the subjects are often thought to be untreatable and unpleasant (Rivera 2002) and can exhibit behaviour that is challenging for therapists to deal with. Sam Warner (1996: 65) suggests that this label is applied to women who do not fit into gender role stereotypes, and that it is "a new name for an old 'problem'; disorderly women."

DBT is most often used with women whom the correctional system finds challenging; those who outwardly express their anger, distrust, or resistance to prison authority and/or who have developmental delays. These women are considered to be not only disordered, but also disorderly (Pollack and Kendall 2005). The main goals of the DBT program are to change a prisoner's "rigid ways of thinking" (Sly and Taylor 2003) and to teach women emotional regulation skills (Fortin 2004b). Although DBT has gained popularity as a non-pejorative cognitive-behavioural treatment model for women diagnosed with BPD, researchers have noted problems around the implementation of this program in prisons. Kim Pate (2005) argues that the used of DBT in women's federal prisons fosters a dependency of prisoners upon staff and disregards the practical needs of women who are returning to the community (the need for housing, job skills, education, and training, for example). She also states her concern that DBT represents a coercive approach to therapy, a concern that appears to be substantiated by CSC's own evaluation of the therapy. CSC found that 30 percent of the women participating in DBT did not volunteer to do so and said they had been "forced" into the program (Sly and Taylor 2003).

One of the problems of using DBT in the correctional system is the role it can play in perpetuating the prison mandate and ensuring prisoner compliance (Pollack and Kendall 2005). Treatment techniques — such as learning "distress tolerance" — have the potential to punish and discredit women's resistance to unjust or harmful practices by encouraging them to "bear pain skilfully" (Pollack and Kendall 2005: 79). Skills for learning distress tolerance (Linehan 1993) are used to help people manage heightened emotions, such as anger, frustration, and fear. However, within prisons this technique can readily carry the potential to silence protest against unfair or unjust assertions of authority. The intent of teaching the skill of distress tolerance is to help women who may have experienced violating and/or abusive childhoods to manage intense emotions. It is not meant, however, to help women to more skilfully bear the violations of imprisonment. The research conducted by the CSC itself states that one of the goals of DBT is to teach participants how to function in an institutional setting and to "reduce incidents" (Sly and Tayler 2003: 5). It seems that DBT as a therapeutic treatment program plays a significant role in regulating prisoner compliance and in "taming" women whose unruly emotions may interfere with the smooth operation of the prison.

Another technique adapted from Linehan's work is the "behavioural chain analysis," which is a written exercise in which women identify a problem, its causes, factors that interfered with the resolution of the problem, and methods of resolving the problem (Linehan 1993). In Linehan's model it is supposed to function as an aid to assist women in being less overwhelmed by their challenges, but in CSC's rendition the behavioural chain analysis appears to function as a means of regulation and punishment because it is used to detail, in writing, how an "egregious" behaviour occurred (McDonagh, Taylor, and Blanchette 2002). Although the behavioural chain analysis is ostensibly part of a therapeutic support, CSC reports that prisoners find this aspect of the treatment "aversive," and as a result a protocol has been established "to assist in managing the contingencies around its completion, including a 24-hour rule for the completion of the first draft [of the written report]" (McDonagh, Taylor, and Blanchette 2002: 38).

On the surface, DBT seems to provide an answer to "managing" women whom the correctional system is ill equipped to support. Prisons are not supportive environments, nor are there the available resources and qualified personnel to support women with mental health issues. The mandate of the correctional system to punish and control and the perspective that criminalized women have "criminal minds" and an inability to regulate their emotions transform even the most well-intentioned treatment approaches into control strategies. Feminist-informed treatment modalities cannot be successfully implemented behind prison walls if the hostile and punitive climate remains unaltered. Central to these approaches are notions of creating healthy environments and healthy relationships, which cannot be accomplished within a setting characterized by strip searches, constant surveillance, handcuffs and shackles, and control of daily movement and basic needs. Efforts to support women who have experienced abuse and other violations will only be effective if community alternatives to custody are made available so that punishment is not disguised as treatment.

BEYOND THE BARS OF INDIVIDUALISM: THEORIZING STATE REGULATION OF SOCIAL MARGINALITY

Correctional systems have semi-permeable boundaries, which means that they can be responsive to prison reform discourses, particularly if those discourses are compatible with the system's overarching logics. Reform efforts that infuse individualistic, gendered understandings into pre-established social control regimes can consolidate, legitimate, and strengthen the regulation of social marginality; and these individualistic perspectives on women's imprisonment tend as a matter of course to avoid larger questions of the state, racialization, immigration policies and practices, and the political economy. Although women prisoners are overwhelmingly poor, and racial and cultural minorities are overrepresented in prisons, women's victimization and emotional/psychological needs remain at the centre of much theorizing about women and punishment. Rachel Roth (2004) points to this very issue, arguing that feminist theorists of women's imprisonment do not frequently offer a rich analysis of state power (beyond a few claims about patriarchy and medicalization), but rather focus on women's personal feelings and behaviour. Consequently, Roth (2004: 417) states, "Studies emphasizing how women can develop their own inner resources but not how the state creates barriers will inevitably be theoretically and practically incomplete."

This omission may in part explain why some correctional systems have been open to efforts to reform women's prisons; liberal feminist efforts do not often challenge the overall correctional discursive framework or the legitimacy of imprisonment as a response to social exclusion (Sudbury 2004), thereby assisting in the perpetuation of subjectivity as the site of change for women prisoners.

Some scholars have challenged the discursive and theoretical limitations of the victimization/abuse narrative as applied to criminalized women. One of the emerging critiques is that despite attempts at incorporating the broader social context into analyses of women's crime and imprisonment, the pathways literature is often individualistic and positivist in its focus on explaining the cause of women's "criminality." Consequently, this discursive framing assumes that crime is a fact rather than a social construction (Snider 2003: 362). Accepting normalized criminal justice concepts and categories and the widespread use of such terms as "women's criminality" and "female offenders" helps to consolidate the deficit-based individualism characteristic of penal-welfare approaches. The label of "offender" operates within a criminal justice and correctional script and relies upon an Othering process that separates offenders (those Other women) from those writing about and working with them. Not only does this dualism stigmatize and create artificial boundaries and hierarchies, but it also reifies women's identity as permanently criminal or offending. Moreover, the use of the very term offender is imbued with the dynamics of power and can be used to rationalize unjust correctional practices (Canadian Association of Elizabeth Fry Societies, Guidelines for Advocacy).

Both mainstream and feminist-oriented criminologists also commonly invoke the well-worn phrase "what works with female offenders." Although used to signal that mainstream criminology and correctional practices transfer male norms and practices into women's prisons and that responses to imprisoned women need to be gender-specific, this phraseology perpetuates the idea that something must be *done to* criminalized women. Again, this discourse — and the related policy and programming it spawns — accepts individualized understandings of criminalized women and is directly linked to interventions aimed to "fix/cure/change" women who have been criminalized.

Scholars working from interdisciplinary perspectives have illustrated that the process of labelling something or someone as "criminal" is inherently political (Chan and Mirchadani 2002:15; Mauer and Chesney-Lind 2002; Sudbury 2005b) and have emphasized the significance of understanding processes of criminalization, rather than criminality. A discursive shift from "women's criminality" or "women offenders" to *criminalized women* is more than simply semantic; it signals the socially constructed nature of crime, provides space for analyses of state actors in the criminalization process (for example, policing practices, immigration laws), and allows for a more complex understanding of how processes of racialization, poverty, gender, nation-state governance, globalization, and violence function to shape and regulate social marginality.

MOVING BEYOND WOMEN'S PSYCHOLOGY AS A "CAUSE"

Both within and outside the disciplinary boundaries of criminology there is now a plethora of evidence that socio-economic marginalization, racialization, globalization, privatization, violence against women and children, policing practices, and community impoverishment contribute to the ever expanding prison-industrial complex (Mauer and Chesney-Lind 2002). Scholars and activists have noted that we are witnessing an unprecedented rise in the incarceration of both men and women, and that in particular there appears to be a worldwide "women's imprisonment boom" (Chesney-Lind 2002: 80). Are we really witnessing a worldwide epidemic of "criminally minded" women who cannot regulate their emotions?

To better respond to the expanding prison-industrial complex and the rising numbers of incarcerated women worldwide, feminist scholars have argued for a new paradigm that relies less upon individualized accounts of women's imprisonment. Julia Sudbury (2005b: xv), for example, argues that using victimization/abuse narratives to understand why women come into conflict with the law without putting these experiences into a larger socio-economic framework "obscures the broader social disorder signified by mass incarceration, and it sidesteps the question of why the state responds to abused women with punishment."

In response analysts have made a number of recommendations for enhancing the theoretical rigour of studies involving women, crime, and punishment. The central thrust of these recommendations is the need for a comprehensive examination of state roles and processes in gender and imprisonment studies (McCorkel 2004; Haney 2004; Sudbury 2005a). Sudbury (2005b: xvii) argues for a new body of research that combines a political economy of prisons with a transnational feminist analysis of gender, race, class, and nation, and urges a study of imprisonment that makes linkages across nation-states — linkages that are all the more important when, internationally, welfare states are being dismantled while the prison-industrial complex expands.

Such an approach allows for an analysis of processes of state power and punishment and how the lives of criminalized women are influenced by globalization-informed policy shifts in the penal-welfare and immigration arenas. Making connections to the wider socio-economic context helps to shift the focus away from an exclusive view of psychological issues as being responsible for women's crime; and it allows for a deeper understanding of the complex intersections between gender, racial, cultural, immigration, class, state policies and processes, subjectivity, and theories about women's crime and punishment.

10. EMPOWERING RISK: THE NATURE OF GENDER-RESPONSIVE STRATEGIES

Kelly Hannah-Moffat

The pressure to be "gender responsive" — or to make what Pat Carlen (2002) calls "woman-wise" decisions that take into consideration gender-relevant criteria — dominates contemporary women's penal regimes. Recently a feminist literature on gender-responsive penal interventions (Bloom 2000, 2003a; Bloom, Owen, and Covington 2003, 2005) has pragmatically focused on the production of gendered justice, convincingly demonstrating not only that law and crime are gendered, but also that gender shapes criminal justice responses to women and results in differential effects of policies for women and men (Daly and Maher 1998; Bloom 2003b; Carlen 2002). It argues that women are "different" and that female offending and pathways into and out of crime are quantitatively and qualitatively distinct (Hannah-Moffat and Shaw 2001; Bloom, Owen, and Covington 2003).

Typically, this material — often premised on relational theory — focuses on the characteristics of women prisoners, the dissemination of research, and the production of guiding principles and strategies for improving the management of women offenders. For a variety of legal and humanistic reasons, correctional agencies have started to "take gender seriously." The logic of gender-responsive corrections, which is gaining momentum in the international penal community, offers the managers of women's prisons an alternative regime.

Notwithstanding the proliferation of research on gender responsivity, well-intentioned policy-makers and academics have still not fully explored the assumptions and limitations of gender-responsive penality, or possible (inevitable) contradictions that exist between pre-existing penal logics (such as risk/need approaches) and gender responsiveness. What is even less certain is what gendered responsiveness "in practice" means in terms of how practitioners interpret and deploy gendered information in an effort to be more responsive.

Canada was one of the first countries to draw attention to the unique needs of women prisoners and to attempt to design a culturally sensitive, women-centred model of punishment. The reforms inspired by *Creating Choices,* the renowned report of the Task Force on Federally Sentenced

Women, established Canada as an international model of women-centred penality. The Task Force's recommendations, which were accepted by the federal government, enabled a gendered knowledge of punishment and offending to filter from feminist critiques into Canadian penal policy and, over time, into the managerial regimes governing women's prisons.

When Canada undertook the restructuring of women's prisons in the early 1990s, there was little empirical research on how gender ought to inform penal programs. The adoption and creation of gender-responsive policies were hasty and initially based on little research. The ad hoc operational definitions and interpretations of gender-responsiveness that emerged continue to be in a constant state of evolution and revision. In some cases, the emergent operational understandings are a product of empirical research and evaluation, but often gender considerations are undermined by wider organizational agendas (Hannah-Moffat 2002). The Correctional Service, regional prison administrations, parole boards, and correctional staff continue to grapple with the development and implementation of gender-responsive policy and practices, as well as with the operational relevance of the five guiding principles outlined in *Creating Choices* — empowerment, meaningful and responsible choices, respect and dignity, supportive environment, and shared responsibility. A number of organizational impediments to gender responsivity exist (Carlen 2002; De Cou 2002; Hannah-Moffat 2002) and have, in the Canadian case, contributed to the redefinition and erosion of gender-responsive programming and decision-making.

The recent interpretations and shifts in gender-responsive penality raise broader questions about the future governance of women prisoners — in particular, how the trend toward risk/need governance is combined with the ideal of women-centred correctional interventions, and how this particular gendering of risk essentializes gender, reframes victimization, and produces contradictory interpretations of choice and responsibility. Indeed, as we shall see, data from federally sentenced case files and the National Parole Board's decision registry indicate how the correctional staff and Parole Board members — operating in a broader culture of gender-responsive policy and cultural sensitivity — construct and use gendered understandings of risk to interpret women offenders' experiences when making conditional release decisions. The new international emphasis on gender responsivity and risk-based offender management in correctional and parole policy enables new (and problematic) ways of thinking about women's relationships, agency, and responsibility.[1]

Not just the gendered nature of risk (Stanko 1997; Walklate 1997) but also the difficulties associated with the operationalization of gender-responsive ideals are at question here. More specifically, risk, operating as a gendering strategy, differentially affects (often negatively) women, youth, and ethno racial groups — and, indeed, interacts with the gender-responsive strategies.

THE 2004 PROGRAM STRATEGY FOR WOMEN OFFENDERS

The 2004 Program Strategy for federally sentenced women (Fortin 2004a) provides an example of how the meaning of gender-responsive programming has developed and of the existence of conflicting and contradictory messages about gender. It is one example of how policy-makers constrained by wider managerial agendas have attempted to reform corrections to make it more gender responsive. The revised 2004 Program Strategy replaces the 1994 strategy (Federally Sentenced Women Program 1994). It suggests that the now muted five principles introduced in *Creating Choices*, and which formed the foundation of the 1994 strategy, continue to be of importance, but that the 1994 strategy is outdated.

The revised 2004 strategy is based on four new principles: women-centred, holistic, supportive environment, and diversity. However, these principles appear secondary to the dominant correctional logic — principles of risk, need, and responsivity — highlighted at the beginning of the document. The structure of the document implies that risk, need, and responsivity are of greater organizational significance than are the principles that follow, even though the logic and empirical basis of the risk/need/responsivity principles and ensuing correctional practices have yet to be vetted for their gender and cultural appropriateness.[2] The 1994 and 2004 strategies show several notable differences, one of which is that the new strategy frames gender responsivity relative to risk/need principles and redefines "need," placing a new emphasis on criminogenic needs and women's relationships.

The Impact and Proliferation of Risk/Need Approaches

The emphasis on assessing need (dynamic risk factors) reflects a much broader shift in penalty.[3] Donald Andrews and James Bonta's (1989/1994) principles of risk, need, and responsivity underline the Correctional Service of Canada's approach to classification and correctional programming. These principles are at the forefront of the revised 2004 Program Strategy. The risk principle, as described in the 2004 Program Strategy, is "an assessment of the future probability of offending if identified treatment needs are not met" (Fortin 2004a: 5). It is an endorsement of the premise that criminal behaviour is predictable and that treatment services can be matched to an offender's level of risk. Thus, offenders who present a high risk are those who are targeted for the greatest number of therapeutic interventions.

The needs principle indicates that correctional treatment ought to target those dynamic (changeable) attributes of an offender that are related to criminal behaviour — attributes that are called a "criminogenic need." Typically, criminogenic needs include employment, marital/family, associates, substance abuse, community functioning, personal/emotional, and attitude. Meta-analytic studies of the majority male populations, which largely dismiss the effects of gender, diversity, and social and economic constraints, form the empirical basis of current understandings of the risk/need/responsivity principles. This general practice — of validating pre-existing risk and need criteria or scales derived from research and theories about men's crime for their reliability for use with female offenders — is theoretically and empirically problematic. Most risk/need assessments and prescribed interventions are predicated on middle-class normative assumptions that are highly gendered and racialized (Hannah-Moffat and Shaw 2001; Hannah-Moffat and Maurutto 2004).

The 2004 Program Strategy does not address evidence contrary to these risk/need principles; instead, it reaffirms them. For instance, the strategy discursively constitutes the targeting of criminogenic needs as being central to gender-responsive programming. Accordingly, the report notes, "Needs are dynamic in nature and measure a variety of interpersonal areas in an offender's life" and that "Assessing a woman's needs provides insight into life history and guides program requirements to ensure effectiveness" (Fortin 2004a: 6). Perhaps in an effort to address academic and institutional critics (Canadian Human Rights Commission 2003; Auditor General of Canada 2003; National Parole Board 2002; Thigpen et al. 2004), the document argues that the needs principle is applicable to women but that evidence suggests that certain factors are more relevant for women: emotional dysregulation, self-injurious behaviour, suicide attempts, and self-esteem (Fortin 2004a: 6).

The responsivity principle, according to Don Andrews and James Bonta (1998: 245), suggests that "treatment be delivered in a style and mode that is consistent with the ability and learning style of the offender." Interestingly, the Program Strategy suggests that gender, age, culture, disability, mental health, and victimization (Fortin 2004a: 6, 8) are simply responsivity factors.

In a more refined description of the needs principle, Andrews and

Bonta (1998: 243) extend the concern with empirical links to recidivism to include "intervenability." An intervenable need is not an individual's self-perceived need, but rather a characteristic that an individual shares with a population and that has been shown to be statistically correlated to recidivism. An intervenable need is defined not only through the availability of resources and structural arrangements that allow for intervention and possible amelioration, but also through statistical knowledge of that need as a variable that is predictive of an undesirable and preventable outcome: recidivism. Technical correctional definitions of need are legitimated and authorized by science, not by individuals' lay assessment of their circumstances. Needs are derived from a statistical knowledge of variables in a population. These definitional strategies make up needs, which correctional organizations can respond to in the name of "good corrections."

Andrews and Bonta note that many offenders, especially high-risk offenders, have a variety of needs. They need places to live and work, and/or they need to stop taking drugs. Some have poor self-esteem, chronic headaches, or cavities in their teeth. These are all needs. The needs principle draws our attention to the distinction between criminogenic and non-criminogenic needs. Criminogenic needs are the dynamic attributes of an offender that, when addressed, are associated with changes in the probability of recidivism. Non-criminogenic needs are also dynamic and changeable, but those changes are not necessarily associated with the probability of recidivism. As such, variables that are significant but not related to recidivism, yet require intervention (such as poverty and health), are deemed non-criminogenic needs and considered a low priority in terms of intervention, except for "humane" consideration.

The 2004 Program Strategy reinforces the importance of risk/need assessment. It distinguishes between correctional programs, mental health programs, and other programs (education, employment and employability, and social programs) and clearly defines correctional programming "as interventions that address the multiple factors that contribute directly to criminal behaviour" (Fortin 2004a: 7). The document argues that women prisoners have multiple and interrelated "difficulties," but that not all of these difficulties are criminogenic, and "to be effective, institutional and community interventions must focus on factors that contribute directly to offending" (p.7). Further, the report notes that women need to address "emotional regulation issues which underlie other needs such as cognitive functioning and/or substance abuse" (p.8). This passage reflects the concerns articulated earlier: needs are not self-reported or entitlements, as they were characterized in the 1994 Program Strategy. Here, as a result of the emphasis on risk/need principles, women's needs are relevant only if they are considered to be criminogenic. Non-criminogenic needs are addressed through an attentiveness to pathology, cognitive ability, and personal responsibility.

Risk/need thinking produces new responsibilities and patterns of action, as well as new strategies for the definition, control, and neutralization of risk. The overlay of risk-based concerns onto existing correctional structures has produced new concerns about women's needs as promising targets for correctional intervention. However, when needs are defined in this way, the system justifies additional and/or intensified interventions into the life or psyche of a woman in the name of prevention or reformation. Correctional researchers are quite clear that the purpose of assessing criminogenic needs is to develop more "precise intervention strategies" (Serin and Mailloux 2001). There is a new legitimization of treatment and a shift in how correctional treatment is delivered. In essence, correctional interventions are now *targeted*. Correctional program narratives speak of interventions that "target criminogenic needs" and stratify service delivery, not of empowering women or responding to their "needs." However, the current emphasis on criminogenic need may in fact disadvantage women. Recent evidence suggests that needs associated with female offenders — such as those related to children, past abuse, and trauma — are being reconfigured as criminogenic needs (dynamic risk factors), which are useful therapeutic targets because they are statistically linked to recidivism and can be addressed through available correctional programming

New technologies of needs management rely on the creation of responsible, autonomous subjects. Broader structural relations are either ignored or constructed as individual inadequacies (that is, emotional dysregulation). Offenders are encouraged to take responsibility for their offending, in other words, for their histories and problems. Offenders are seen not as victims of circumstance, but as individuals incapable of adequately managing their needs in a way that averts the seemingly foreseeable risks of crime, victimization, poverty, racism, and unemployment. Categorical definitions of risk/need discredit, exclude, and co-opt alternative interpretations of offender needs, and dissociate understandings of needs from broader social and political contexts. Individuals are positioned as potential recipients of predefined services, rather than as active agents involved in processes of self-identifying needs.

Only "manageable" problems are targeted for intervention.

Manageable criminogenic problems are the ones that can be resolved through behavioural or lifestyle changes that are seen as achievable with a positive attitude and amenable to normalizing interventions, programs, or therapists who provide tools for change and teach offenders to think rationally and logically. Structural barriers conveniently disappear. Systemic problems become individual problems or, more aptly, individuals' inadequacies. CSC's reintegration efforts are designed "to offer an increased number of pro-social choices to help women become law-abiding citizens" (Fortin 2004a: 5), indicating that women need to take responsibility for the "choices" they make.

Risk/need thinking produces new responsibilities and patterns of action, as well as new strategies for the definition, control, and neutralization of risk. The overlay of risk-based concerns onto existing women's correctional structures has produced and legitimated new targets for intervention. Offenders are placed in a variety of generic programs designed to target the need area, enhance their ability to self-govern, and prudently manage their risk of recidivism. The "new targeted intervention" project then involves the creation of not only a particular type of disciplined normative subject but also the construction of a prudent risk/need manager, who is responsible and able to identify risky settings, get access to resources, and avert situations that may result in criminal behaviour.

In the context of the risk/responsibility dualism, cognitive behavioural programs suggest that an offender can become a "rational decision-maker" who makes prudent choices that avoid recidivism (see chapter 9). This construction of the offender leaves intact the presumption that crime is the outcome of poor choices or decisions, and not the outcome of structural inequalities or pathology. The offender's poor decisions were, then, a consequence of an absence of or deficiencies in the requisite skills, abilities, and attitudes necessary for proper, informed decision-making — or, more aptly stated: "Crime was the outcome of insufficiently or unevenly developed rational or cognitive capacities. Criminals did not know how!" (Duguid 2000: 183). Techniques like cognitive therapy or other similar programs are vehicles through which offenders (transformative risk subjects) can learn how to manage their criminogenic needs and reduce their risk of recidivism by acquiring the requisite skills, abilities, and attitudes needed to lead a pro-social life.[4]

Taking Responsibility for Relationship Choices

Women's relationships are elevated in gender-responsive risk/need discourses.[5] The approach suggests that relationships are essential to women's lives and "when the concept of relationship is incorporated into policies, practices and programs the effectiveness of the system or agency is enhanced" (Bloom 2003b). Relational theory forms the basis of gender-responsivity literature.

Briefly, this theory, which focuses on the psychological development of women, suggests that the women "develop a sense of self and self worth when their actions arise out of and lead back into, connections with others" (Bloom, Owen, and Covington 2003: 53). Relational theorists argue that "such connections are so crucial that many of the psychological problems of women can be traced back to disconnections or violations within relationships, whether in families, with personal acquaintances, or in a society at large" (p.55). Proponents of relationship theory maintain that women offenders have experienced considerable marginalization, disconnection, and violation in their primary and social relationships, and that they are more likely than men to be motivated by relational concerns and situational pressures such as the threatened loss of valued relationships (Bloom, Owen, and Covington 2003: 55; Covington and Surrey 1997, 2000; Steffensmeier and Allan 1998; Bylington 1997; Miller 1986; Coll and Duff 1995). Consequently, they argue that "effective" gender-responsive correctional interventions must acknowledge and focus on women's relationships.

In an effort to be more gender-responsive, policy narratives such as the 2004 Program Strategy — as well as training materials and publications for the National Institute for Corrections (Bloom, Owen, and Covington 2003) — underscore the feminist literature on relational theory. For instance, the new Program Strategy states:

> Gender-specific programming must reflect an understanding of the psychological development of women. Current thinking in this area suggests that women place great value in the development and maintenance of relationships. Consequently, "situational pressures such as the loss of valued relationships play a greater role in female offending".... Some academics believe that relational theory is an approach that adds effectiveness to programming for women. Relational theory focuses on building and maintaining positive connections and relationships. The main goal is to increase women's capacity to engage in mutually empathic and mutually empowering relationships. To enable change, women need to develop relationships that are not reflective of previous loss or abuse. (Fortin 2004a: 5)

References to the significance of women's relationships are evident throughout this document. While it is obviously important to recognize the significance of relationships, on a practical level it is also important to think about how an emphasis on relationships is conflated with broader concerns about risk, need, and interventions.

PRACTICES OF GENDERING RISK

Gender-responsive literature typically advocates that training in which relationship issues are a core theme be developed for correctional staff. While such training exists, it does not explicitly show practitioners how they should use (or not use) information about women's relationships when they make administrative decisions. Consequently, practitioners often encounter gender-neutral policies (criteria for release or classification) that require "gendering" to be consistent with co-existing expectations of gender responsivity. The following observations — based on an analysis of qualitative data extracted from 144 federal female parole candidates' case files and the decision registry of the National Parole Board (NPB) — demonstrate that the practice of modifying neutral risk criteria to reflect the gendered nature of women's experiences are inconsistent, unstructured, and highly interpretive. The NPB strategically deployed facts about the female population to make its understandings of recidivism gender-specific. For instance, some Board members believed that it was critical to place women's offending in a broader socio-political context and thus to consider their histories of victimization and intimate relationships. Others adamantly rejected the relevance of victimization to a determination of recidivism, arguing that women needed to take responsibility for their offending behaviour, regardless of these experiences.

Accelerated Parole Review Cases
The case files of parole candidates are the same files used by Parole Board members to determine the risk of general and violent recidivism. Decision sheets, from the decision registry, provide a detailed rationale of the NPB's initial pre-release decision (grant or deny), a summary of the case, the risk factors, and the rationale for special conditions, if imposed. All of the cases examined for this study were Accelerated Parole Review (APR) cases,[6] in which the law mandates a presumptive release in the absence of evidence demonstrating a potential for violent recidivism. To be eligible for APR, an offender must be serving her first federal sentence for a non-violent offence. It is important to note that a woman serving her first federal sentence may have committed a previous violent offence for which she received a community sanction or custodial sentence of less

than two years. The primary question guiding my analysis is: how is the potential for violent recidivism established in women's APR cases? From a content analysis of APR decision sheets on 144 cases — particularly the twenty-one cases in which parole was not granted in the paper review and the twelve cases denied appeal after an additional full panel hearing — we can learn how various knowledges are assembled and used by the Board to interpret facts and establish risk of violent recidivism. We can further understand how a Board member's awareness of gender does (or does not) influence his or her stated rationale.

Discussions of women's relationships with violent men were widespread in federally sentenced women's case files and in parole-decision narratives, particularly in cases in which a woman's potential for violent recidivism was being evaluated. Multiple dimensions and perceptions of victimization are apparent in the case files. The case files reviewed by Board members discuss in considerable detail the level of victimization that the woman has experienced in her primary adult and childhood relationships. Women who had documented histories of violence are often linked to violent male partners as victims, aggressors, or co-accused. My case file data on the context of offences show that one-third (31.5 percent) of the women in this sample had a male co-accused, and most of these women were in an intimate relationship with the man. The presence of men in these women's lives is often associated with an increased potential for violent recidivism. Given that correctional officials often construct the men in women's lives as negative influences, women's relationships are heavily scrutinized. Sometimes a condition of release is the prohibition to contact intimate partners. One aspect of this scrutiny pertains to women's experiences in violent relationships.

Gender-sensitivity training stresses the role of abuse and trauma in women's prison experiences and the relevance of these experiences to holistic gender-responsive interventions. Board members, like correctional staff, receive gender- and cultural-sensitivity training that provides them with aggregate "facts" about the female offender population and their pre-prison and post-prison experiences. Typically, gender-sensitivity training outlines academic and correctional research findings that describe the characteristics of the female offender population, their self-reported needs and experiences, and qualitative and quantitative differences in female offending patterns and barriers to release or reintegration. Training manuals and supplemental documents dealing with risk assessment present standard descriptive information, such as history of abuse, maternal status, the feminization of poverty, and other issues. These practices are clearly intended to heighten decision-makers' sensitivity to women's experiences and the differences between men's and women's crime. However, broader mandated policies remain unchanged, leaving it to the discretion of individuals to either use or ignore gender information. The absence of concrete guidance on how to use and integrate gendered knowledge with existing law and policy produces inconsistencies and confusion (Hannah-Moffat 2004). Interviews (n = 50) with correctional staff and Parole Board members revealed considerable disagreement among Board members about the relevance of gendered histories, specifically the role of past victimizations, to an understanding of women's offending and potential recidivism. Some believed that past victimizations provided a broader context for understanding women's offence patterns, but others reasoned that this information led to the construction of a victim identity that mitigates women's responsibility for past and potential future criminal conduct.

Consistent with the feminist criminological literature, case files reveal that most federally sentenced women have suffered victimization in all of their primary relationships from the time they were children. Although childhood and adult victimization is a reality of women prisoners' lives, and there does appear to be a relationship between victimization and involvement in criminal activities, victimization has not been established empirically as a reliable discriminate predictor of women's recidivism (Girshick 2003). The link between victimization and women's risk to reoffend violently is even more ambiguous (Eljudpovic-Guzina 1999; Howden-Windell and Clark 1999; Girshick 2003; Leonard 2003). Although most feminist criminologists see victimization as a relevant and important component of women prisoners' lives — and one that requires programmatic attention — they characterize victimization as a need, not a risk factor. Still, the hegemonic, gender-neutral correctional research on risk that informs the wider decision field in Canadian corrections conflates need and risk through the concept of criminogenic need. Although the notion of need can be considered as distinct from that of risk, such distinctions are difficult to ascertain, in part because correctional research policy and training manuals present needs as dynamic risk factors and are combined with static risk factors under the umbrella of criminogenic factors.

Furthermore, parole policy directs Board members to review the offender's marital and family history when they examine the potential for violent behavior (NPB 2001, 4.3-2). Board members' gendered interpretations of risk are shaped by the notion of a criminogenic need, policy attention to marital and family relationships, knowledge of the prevalence of victimization, and the violent relationships in women prisoners' lives. Risk is gendered in that for women (but not for men) victimization and relationships become central to general and violent recidivism. As one decision narrative notes, "Your current relationship with your partner does not constitute sufficient motive to believe you would commit an offence accompanied by violence." Normative perceptions of legitimate victim behaviour and positive relationships, coupled with concerns about "mutual combat" and the view that women can be as violent as men in intimate relationships, produce a gendered understanding of risk. Though most practitioners acknowledge that women occupy the dual status of victim and offender, when characterizing the potential for violence, practitioners dichotomously construct female parole candidates as either victims of violence or victimizers of others (largely of abusive male partners) or themselves. We can divide practitioners' interpretations of victimization and relationship stability more generally into three subcategories: the absence of facts, passive agency, and resistant agency.

The absence of facts and information about women's relationships is documented at the beginning of the decision sheets, in sections titled "Stressors indicating a potential for violence" and "Stressors in the environment that could lead to the commission of a violent offence." In these sections, the Board member reviewing the case documents the presence or absence of a past violent relationship — making it clear that the reviewer looked for evidence of such in the case file. Decision narratives routinely contain statements such as: "No apparent history of domestic violence"; "there is no known history of potential for violence in relationships"; and "family interviews via community assessment suggest no potential for violence." It appears that the absence of domestic/intimate violence mitigates risk. The potential for violent recidivism diminishes if a woman has no history of victimization (either partner or familial). A woman's risk of being violent is also mitigated if past victimization was evident in the file but did not combine with evidence of previous convictions, acquittals, or withdrawn charges for violent or weapons offences.

The presentation of information that constructed the offender as a passive agent — a victim who did not appear to fight back or who exhibited a generally compliant attitude — also mitigated risk of potential violence. Decision narratives document how past victimizations occurred, but do not connect this record to a woman's potential for violence:

> While you experienced sexual and physical abuse at the hands of partners there is no indication that this has led you to become

> violent.... You suffered much abuse as a child, youth and later as
> a young adult and this has contributed to you engaging in a high-
> risk prostitution trade, you have not engaged in overt violence.

> The recourse to violence doesn't seem to be part of your habitual
> repertoire of behaviours and it is noted that during arguments with
> your partner you would leave and go to your mother's house.

In these instances, women conform to gendered victim stereotypes. It is
clear from these cases that the Board is not simply making a link between
violent relationships and violent offending, but rather among victim
agency, violent relationships, and potential for violence. This observation is confirmed in cases in which women are not released. Here, Board
members use knowledge of past victimization, along with women's active
resistance,[7] to substantiate concerns about potential future violent crime.
Normally, women's resistance involves the use of aggressive means for
self-defence. The reports do not mention more legitimate forms of resistance (such as leaving an abusive partner or calling the police) — even
if there is evidence that they occurred in the case file. On average, these
decision narratives de-contextualize women's self-defensive actions.
They focus on the potential and actual harm done to the male involved
and the women's responsibility for the harm perpetrated. For example:

> When you were involved in domestic disputes with your spouse
> you reportedly retaliated to his attack with a broken beer bot-
> tle.

> Your conviction relates to a domestic assault during the course
> of which you obtained a knife and used it to intimidate the vic-
> tim and when he tried to take it from you it caused a deep cut
> to his hand.

> Your record shows a 1991 conviction for assault, documentation
> on file indicates that you burned an abusive partner with a ciga-
> rette to defend yourself and were given an absolute discharge.

These passages show how Board members link a criminal charge resulting from a domestic incident with potential for future violence. Decision
narratives do not document in any depth the nature or length of these
relationships — nor do they discuss the harm experienced by the women.
The narratives isolate women's behaviour; they stress only the women's
verbal or physical aggression. These findings are significant when placed

in the broader organizational context: victimization is equated with responsibility and choice (of associates/partner).

The de-contextualization of a woman's actions emphasizes her personal failings and excludes mitigating factors, reassembling facts to make her responsible for bad choices — such as using a weapon, even if defensively. Significantly, Board members expressed minimal concern about the potential for the women to become victims of violence again if they were to re-establish past relationships after their release. The absence of concern is significant given evidence that women continue to struggle with abuse and trauma on release. Some may return to abusive relationships or high-risk environments because of difficulties associated with re-entering communities with limited financial and housing options.

Knowledge of victimization provides practitioners with a way of interpreting risk and making it gender-specific. In this context, penal officials have used knowledge of victimization to create a risk identity that restricts and de-contextualizes victim agency. Although the potential "complexities and subtleties of meaning in the data are compacted" (Hawkins 1983: 115) in parole decision narratives, the reductionist process of simplification has particular effects. The de-contextualization of women's violence in these incidents suggests that a woman's actions are, at best, equivalent to her partner's coercive act and, at worst, more calculated. These presumptions run contrary to literature showing that intimate partner violence is an asymmetrical problem because victims of the most severe and most frequent abuse are most commonly women, and perceptions of risk significantly shape a victim's responses and choices (Dobash and Dobash 2004; Leonard 2003: 102–3). Furthermore, one study (Comack, Chopyk, and Wood 2000) of violence perpetrated by men and women shows that in cases of intimate violence, differences in physical strength result in women using weapons more frequently than men do. Thus, when the police intervene in these incidents, women are more likely to be charged with the more serious offence of assault with a weapon. As Anne Worrall (2002: 48) convincingly argues, the modern "search for equivalence" in violence, sexual deviance, and instrumental lawbreaking tends to disguise the interplay of gender, class, race, and age in offending. It further serves to produce and reproduce a spurious categorical equality that renders women punishable. As well, Worrall observes that assumptions of gender neutrality (that is, that domestic violence can be perpetrated by men or women) contain an asymmetrical moral judgment — or a double standard — in which women who use violence are viewed as being worse than men because they violate legal and gender norms.

These narratives impose a gendered understanding of risk that mobilizes specific, normative assumptions about violent relationships and women's roles within them. The omission of an analysis of gender and power disadvantages women, misrepresents the nature of violent relationships, and formulates a spurious link between resistance and the potential for violent recidivism — all of which inform parole decisions. The polarization of victimization and offending restricts understandings of how they are intertwined in the lives of female offenders. The victim/ offender dichotomy also limits the ability to see how Board members use stereotypical notions of victimization to establish women's risk of violent offending.

GENDER RESPONSIVENESS: THE REALITY AND THE IDEAL

The attempt to meld a gender-responsive logic with a traditionally repressive, "masculine organizational logic" (Britton 1997) of imprisonment raises larger questions. The history of women's penal reform confirms that penal institutions have the ability to absorb, integrate, and temporarily silence critical discourses. Reform discourses — including the ideal of gender responsiveness — can be appropriated, redefined, and harmonized with the pre-existing and new managerial and political priorities of an organization. The examples of the 2004 Program Strategy and the APR cases clearly reveal structural impediments to the creation of truly effective gender-responsive regimes.

We need, then, to move beyond the disjuncture between the "intent" of gender responsiveness and its misinterpretations, and reflect on how gender-responsive punishment is conceptualized and practised. The articulation and interpretation of gender in social policies (such as gender-responsive programs) and parole narratives shape popular conceptions of women prisoners as well as women prisoners' perceptions of themselves. As Lynne Haney (2004: 344) notes, "These discursive projects mobilize powerful feelings and desires — thus helping solidify the meanings attached to specific behaviours, practices and identifications." The meaning, purpose, and impact of gender-responsive regimes and logics ought to be critically evaluated and debated. Serious consideration ought to be given to what and who defines gender and/or culturally relevant criteria, particularly given the punitive context in which this logic is mobilized. For example, if relationships are important to women's lives — as much of the relationship theory and the 2004 Program Strategy suggests — then what normative assumptions ought to inform the ideal of "pro-social" relationships (monogamy, heterosexuality)? Discursive constructions of gender responsivity have relied on an essentialized notion of gender that reifies socially constructed categories and ignores intersections of gender with race, ethnicity, class, sexuality, and other axes of difference (Hannah-Moffat 1995; Goodkind 2005).

Clearly, gender and gender-sensitive approaches are important. An attentiveness to women's differences is critical to the development of a humane and responsive penal system. That being said, the interpretations of victimization, relationships, and needs that are manifest in the penal system essentialize women's differences, disregard structural disadvantages, and impose white, middle-class normative criteria. The 2004 Program Strategy and NPB decision narratives further illustrate how the governance of women prisoners is changing with the combination and introduction of risk/need and gender-responsivity logics. As we've seen, well-intended, gender-responsivity approaches can reframe victimization, produce contradictory interpretations of choice, and enable new (and problematic) ways of thinking about women's relationships, agency, and responsibility.

The newly formed normative understandings of risk embodied in the 2004 Program Strategy and NPB decision narratives target women's victim identities in a way that simultaneously infers responsibility, choice, and the capacity to change. The notion of crime as a choice and of taking responsibility for offending — as well as stereotypical and dichotomous constructions of the passive versus resistant victim — conflate freedom and agency. They equate the capacity to choose one's actions without external constraints with the power to act. In these terms, women are attributed a degree of responsibility for their history and past victimizations in a manner that is inconsistent with the original intent of gender-sensitive policy.

The discourses of responsibility and dependency offer a template for understanding women's victimization and needs. The reinterpretation of needs as a consequence of a wider organizational emphasis on risk/need and responsivity principles demonstrates that broader organizational logics continue to be imposed on the management of women prisoners without consideration of their compatibility with and potential impact on the ideal of gender responsiveness.

NOTES

1. There is a growing body of interdisciplinary research theorizing and documenting the emergence of risk-based governing and how institutional structures "embrace risk" (Simon and Baker 2002) to profile and efficiently manage populations. While instructive, analyses of risk have yet to explore how risk-based policies are gendered

or racialized in terms of their conceptualization, legitimacy, and effects. As Pat O'Malley (2004: 6) cogently notes, most analyses "assume risk's unity, as if risk centered government can only be imagined as one thing, rather than a heterogeneous array of practices with diverse implications."

2. Even though the risk/need/responsivity literature and ensuing policies have been criticized by those concerned with the impact of gender-neutral risk/need logics on women and ethno cultural populations, it persists. Advocates of gender-responsive approaches to risk-based assessment and decision-making are calling for greater accountability, validity, and reliability in risk assessment and management for women prisoners, as well as for the development of concrete gender-inclusive risk policies (Canadian Human Rights Commission 2003; Auditor General of Canada 2003; NPB 2002; Thigpen et al. 2004). Some have argued that risk approaches ought to be abandoned in favour of strength models, which are more compatible with gender responsive programming (Bloom 2003b).

3. Portions of the argument in this section are taken from Hannah-Moffat 2005a.

4. In 1991, this logic resulted in CSC designating "cognitive skills" a compulsory core program for most prisoners.

5. Portions of this section are taken from Hannah-Moffat 2005b.

6. The APR decision process is different from regular cases because it uses different criteria and does not initially require a parole hearing. All APR cases undergo an in-office file review (paper review). A panel hearing is held in the event that an offender's release is denied at this time. One of the striking features of this sample is that the Board granted parole to most of the women after the paper review; 86 percent of women who met APR criteria were granted parole. Of those 14 percent (twenty-one cases) denied at the paper review, 43 percent (nine cases) were granted parole on an appearance before the Board, in most cases a month later. During the hearings, which are conducted by at least two Board members, the panel considers the reasons for the previous decision to deny, all case documentation and evidence, new information, and representations from the offender regarding factors that led to the refusal to grant release at the in-office review (NPB 2001, 4.3.2).

7. An alternative construction of resistant agency is evident in decision narratives. This form of resistance pertains to women's self-injurious behaviour and resistance to psychiatric intervention — particularly to the taking of medication. Board members interpret knowledge of a woman's mental health and, more specifically, her engagement in self-injurious behaviour as relevant to determinations of violence. For additional information, see Hannah-Moffat 2005b.

11. PASSING THE BUCK: TRANSCARCERAL REGULATION OF CRIMINALIZED WOMEN

MaDonna R. Maidment

One of the most striking things that women prisoners have in common is a history of often long-standing encounters with state agents of control in the years before they are incarcerated. Most women who end up in custody have been under state supervision from an earlier age, and usually for non-penal reasons (Eaton 1993; Carlen 2002a). This experience — what Pat Carlen (2002a) calls the "care/custody mangle" — runs through encounters with the criminal justice, psychiatry/mental health, social welfare, and "child protection" systems.

Just as significantly, though, similar patterns emerge on the flip side of women's pathways into prison, following their release from custody. Increasingly, women ex-prisoners who are in essence attempting to reintegrate in their home communities end up being bounced from one state agency to another, often at the local level, in an enforced process of social management called "transcarceration." By managing and regulating criminalized populations outside prisons, the penal apparatus expands beyond the direct state level (psychiatry/mental health, child protection, social welfare) to the state-sponsored local level (halfway houses, home care, treatment centres).[1] Locked into this help-control continuum, the women find themselves leading a precarious existence, to say the least, as one layer of enforcement succeeds another, seemingly without end, in what Stan Cohen (1985) calls "a hidden custodial system."

TRANSCARCERAL CONTROLS

The term "social control" has been bandied about in the sociological literature for decades and has been extensively critiqued as a vacuous term that fails to account for gender (Rothman 1983; Welch 1997; Carlen 2003). There is an obvious need to explore the nature and types of regulations applied to girls and women who end up as the targets of official/formal correctional[2] controls. Moreover, because such regulation extends far beyond the immediate boundaries of the criminal justice system, there is also a need to extend the empirical analysis to include not only women's entanglement in the criminal justice system, but also women "at risk" of criminalization and those for whom the criminal justice system represents only one force along a broader continuum of controls that have pervaded their total lives. In this regard Pat Carlen (2003: 119), in analyzing the controls experienced by women, employs the concept of "antisocial control," which she defines as

> a generic term for a variety of malign institutionalized practices that may either set limits to individual action by favouring one set of citizens at the expense of another so as to subvert equal-opportunities-ideologies in relation to gender, race, and class (or other social groupings), or (in societies without equal-opportunities ideologies) set limits to individual action in ways that are antisocial because they atrophy an individual's social contribution on the grounds of either biological attributes or exploitative social relations.

An antisocial definition of control takes into account the ideological, political, medical, and economic circumstances in which control is exerted. In particular, it enables a focus on control agents outside the superficial boundaries of the criminal justice system. These sites of control, therefore, include the "antisocial family," wherein women are expected to subject themselves first and foremost to the family based on the powerful ideology that "good mothers make good families make good societies." It also includes the "antisocial state," whereby defiance of the expected gender roles subjects women to exclusionary and more formal measures of obedience. Finally, it includes what Carlen calls "antisocial masculism," which is achieved by the physical exclusion of women from public spaces, public institutions, and workplaces, managed primarily through law, the economy, and tradition (Carlen 2003: 122–24). Additionally, a further subjection of women is achieved through antisocial sexuality, which targets physical beauty as a measure of women's value to men. For women unable or unwilling to conform, there are the overprescribed medications and the oversubscribed mental hospitals (Schur 1984; Conrad and Schneider 1985; Carlen 2003; Neve and Pate 2005). In these terms, official regulatory agencies (courts and prisons) are but the end result of the antisocial targeting of women's conformity, achieved through various other converging social institutions. The power of the courts, laws, and corrections system to criminalize women's "disobedience" thus needs to be expanded and placed into this wider framework.

A transcarceral model lends itself to an antisocial control analysis by capturing the competing interests of power structures in society to regulate women. Transcarceration, then, looks to cross-institutional arrangements between the systems of criminal justice, mental health, and social welfare, in which "clients" of the criminal justice system are shuffled from one section of the help-control continuum to another. By managing "clients" in or outside of the institutional setting, the correctional machinery *expands* to encompass health, welfare, social services, child protection, education, and housing — all of which translates into decentralized *control* and increasingly entails the fitting together of subsystems rather than the consolidation of one agency in isolation from its alternatives (Lowman, Manzies, and Palys 1987: 9).

Mechanisms for transcarceral controls are also inherently gendered. Sexist traditions and ideologies permeate both the formal and informal spheres of control (Davis and Faith 1987). Criminalized women continue to be penalized outside the prison walls for violating traditional sex roles and defying the maintenance of social order (Schur 1985). Patriarchal relations serve foremost as a basis for defining women as "deviant" in sexually demeaning and dependent ways (Davis and Faith 1987). Increasingly punitive, individualizing, and pathologizing controls are exerted over women for actions that run counter to patriarchal norms and associated forms of resistance. Neo-liberal ideologies further enable the blaming of an individual woman for her failure to conform to gender-based ideologies. Therefore, not surprisingly, single mothers become prime targets for cutbacks in social spending that essentially penalize their departure from traditional, heterosexual marriage norms. Moreover, certain groups, most particularly Aboriginal women (and men) in Canada, are more vulnerable to institutionalized controls. Aboriginal women continue to suffer the shameful effects of colonization, and are vastly overrepresented in institutions under state control (Hamilton and Sinclair 1991; Backhouse 1999; Canadian Human Rights Commission 2003).

In their attempts to "make it" on the outside, then, women ex-prisoners face not only the growing and largely neglected covert enhancement of direct state regulation, but also the more behind-the-scenes imperatives of fiscal management that increasingly heap the "burden" of dealing with criminalized women onto local, non-governmental agents.

REGULATORY (STATE) CONTROLS

In the 1970s a shift to deinstitutionalize the mentally ill and prisoners began, driven not only by advanced capitalist economies seeking to disaggregate control models that were far too costly, but also by the advent of the therapeutic millennium and psychoactive drugs, and by an alleged concern with the more humane provision of "treatment" services in the community (Scull 1977). This strategy, however, failed to bring about the desired goals of closing down institutions and locating "clients" in their communities. Since then, professions and experts have proliferated dramatically, with the result that society became ever more dependent on them. What was to be "an apparently radical decarceration strategy" ended up "only shifting custody from the state to the local level and becoming a revenue sharing carve-up between local agencies" (Cohen 1985: 96). One major result of this community downloading was that psychiatric and mental health professionals took on an ever more central role in maintaining the antisocial control of criminalized women.

Psychiatry and Mental Health Systems
Much has been written on the institutionalization and decarceration of psychiatric patients (cf. Goffman 1961; Ingleby 1983; Arrigo 2002), providing powerful evidence of the stakes that professional interest groups have in this domain and of the growth of entire industries in whose favour it is to keep the controlled numbers high. "Social control entrepreneurship" (Warren 1981: 724–40) describes the rationale behind this expansion. To keep your doors open, your programs running, and your funding sustained, you must keep on expanding. Psychiatry and mental health have become key sites of intervention into the lives of criminalized women. Of the twenty-two women interviewed for my study on the experiences of women ex-prisoners (Maidment 2005 and forthcoming), well over half had cycled through the "prison-psychiatry mangle." Despite correctional risk management literature on the factors that are likely to account for "successful reintegration" (for example, static versus dynamic factors), my findings revealed a radical departure from the well-established formula. Almost two-thirds of the women in this sample who had been "successful"[3] in staying out of prison had become tightly entrenched in local and/or institutional-based settings operated by psychiatric and mental health agencies. The penal industrial complex is by no means lost on these women, who recognize the incestuous business of corrections and psychiatry. This looping back and forth between prison and psychiatric hospitals is now a permanent trajectory in their lives. One of them, Rebecca, knows this cycle all too well:

> It's much more than the criminal justice system. It's the mental health system. It's social services. It's every other system that

plays into it. They got sick of them at the Waterford [a psychiatric hospital] and shoved them out. They didn't want to deal with them anymore. Those are people who can't cope and they keep throwing them in jail.

One way of maintaining the psychiatry/prison continuum is the practice of locking women up under a provincially legislated Mental Health Act. This is often the first course of action taken by the police in responding to a woman in crisis, as Olivia, a thirty-four-year-old single mother knows all too intimately.

I've had over 100 admissions to the [psychiatric hospital].... A few weeks back I went to the hospital to talk to a doctor because I was not feeling well and I was refused to be seen. And because I was refused to be seen the police came and took me to the lock-up and I was down there for 16 hours on a mattress and that same night I was refused treatment.... So that was when the police came and told me they had no other choice [but] to take me to the lock-up.

This dependency continuum is perpetuated for criminalized women through a corrections system that has the legal power to enforce mandatory drug treatment on women. The conferring of a psychiatric disorder often takes place initially in prison, and the regulation of that condition must then continue upon release. Prison psychiatrists labelled Angie, a young woman in her early twenties, as having a bipolar disorder. While she continued to resist this label, she ultimately had to comply with a conditional release order to take her medication or risk being sent back to prison.

I had to take my medication. That was part of my probation.... I had respite workers [from the halfway house] which I didn't want but I had to have them. They were like pill-pushers. I had to take my pills or they would put me back into prison. Part of the conditions.

In keeping with the blurring of corrections and mental health, an "assertive case management" approach has been popularized as the community dis/organization model for dealing with criminalized women who have a psychiatric label (Luther 2003: 165). Those with a mental health diagnosis (a label often acquired in prison) are seen as more "manageable" in the community through a team-based approach comprising a host of psy-professionals (Ingleby 1983; Kendall 2000), correctional workers, child-care staff, and localized state-funded agencies with a mandate to "treat" women coming out of prison. Commenting on her involvement in the assertive case management stream, Jennifer draws the ever present interconnection between psychiatry and prison that continues to pervade her life.

> *I don't know if you know this but I am the first one in Newfoundland that they tried this with [assertive case management model]. I don't consider myself a criminal half the time. I consider myself sick and I am being treated like a criminal. But you don't know where to turn…. You are never out of the system once you're in it. You are never ever out of it, I don't care what anyone says. Like I am out of it now but I am still not out of it. I am still doing time [on the outside].*

Child Protection Agencies

Criminalized women, many of them single mothers, are also routinely subject to the intervention of child protection agencies. Indeed, for many of them, child protection had already become a well-established layer of control in their lives before incarceration, due mainly to their dependence on social assistance. For others, their maternal fitness becomes the subject of ongoing intrusion and surveillance in their lives after prison. While incarcerated, women often have little choice but to place their children into temporary foster care. Following their release, mother-child reconciliation then becomes a source of constant antisocial monitoring by the state. Not surprisingly, relationships between women and child protection officials are marked by high levels of suspicion and mistrust. Child protection agents continue to invade women's privacy by dangling the "unfit mother" label to ensure conformity, and the monitoring of the motherhood role becomes another site of interference in women's lives. Lydia, a fifty-five-year-old woman with a lengthy history of institutionalization, explains the antisocial control of her mothering role.

> *They [child protection] say I was unfit but they were the ones who drove me there. I mean I used to wash out the clothes twice a day. You could be able to eat off that floor…. Social Services would get calls to come in and I was getting pissed off. And I had the house spotless. Spotless. And the next thing you know a knock comes on the door. Lord God. A knock comes on the door and that was Social Services. There was two of them there*

and they had a police officer and they said we are here after getting more calls again. "What now?" I said. Well, we got calls saying your child is sore and you got a hole in the mattress and a bucket beneath the bed and I said Lord God. I got fed up with it and I said come on in. By the time the week finished they had the house wrecked. I grabbed the sheets and throwed them on the floor, got the mattress and tore it off. I said, "Look. Do you see a bucket there?" They said "no." I took them into the front room. I took off the chesterfield cushions. I said, "Look do you see any buckets there?" Oh, my God, I tell you. It's wicked. It's worse than being in prison.

Despite being out of prison for well over two years, and still entangled in the control continuum, Glynes is also subjected to routine investigations by child protection officials to regulate her conformity to motherhood norms.

Child Protection is still involved with me today, of course, because of my past with [my daughter], but they don't have no reason to have any concerns at this point. I have been doing good. I haven't had any trouble with the law. I am basically going to my counselling appointments and I am showing no signs that I am starting to go back to my old self. Well, not to my old self but to them, getting in trouble [is my old self]. They don't have no risk concerns at this time.

Social Welfare Systems

Under neo-conservative policies, single mothers existing on welfare are increasingly demonized and stripped of privacy rights. The coveted divide between public and private space has been eroded, as targeted groups come under stricter enforcement and surveillance through mandatory drug/alcohol testing, unannounced home visits by welfare cops in search of violators, and other draconian policies that violate privacy rights. Against this tide women find themselves trying to negotiate a balance between their right to privacy and a dependence on the state for maintenance of their families. Failing to strike that illusory balance, women often find themselves in opposition to these structures — and criminalization results.

Entanglement in the criminal justice system then brings with it a whole other set of contradictions. Quite similar to the nature and extent of intrusion by child protection agents, welfare officers continue to play an important role in women's lives after their release from prison. Reliance on social assistance benefits keeps women entangled in a system of controls, wherein regular reporting and checkups are routine. One example of this level of control and intrusion takes the form of monitoring the prescription intake of welfare recipients through the state-endorsed surveillance of a drug card. Heather, a client of the assertive case management model, explains how enhanced regulation during her most recent release had "assisted" her in staying out of prison.

> *One thing that is probably keeping me out is finally after so many years of going to Social Services and getting a drug card and loading up on pills and overdosing they [government] finally realized I am costing them a lot of money. So now my drug card is restrictive and only my home-care workers can pick up my pills. My pills are locked in a safe so I cannot even access my pills. So I cannot overdose or anything like that. I guess in a way that is a big benefit.*

Additionally, the ex-prisoners have to report to welfare officers the generation of any income outside the regular welfare payments. They have to report to social services any change in address or conditions of control by parole services. Finally, recipients are subject to unannounced home visits and intrusion by welfare cops employed to detect any fraudulent activities. The work of these officers includes checking up on a woman to ensure that she is not cohabitating with a male partner (known as the "spouse in the house" rule) (see Little 2003; chapter 8 here). Breach of any one of these stringent regulations could result in criminal charges of welfare fraud and is understandably a constant source of stress and disempowerment for women.

REGULATORY (STATE-SPONSORED) LOCAL CONTROLS

There is widespread disagreement among policy-makers and the public about what the "community" in "community treatment" actually encompasses, and very little empirical support that this "community" is effective in meeting its intended goals of rehabilitation, cost-savings, and humanity. As Anne Worrall (1997) contends, the term community "has become a thoroughly promiscuous word, attaching itself to almost any activity formerly regarded as a responsibility of the state." In practice, community-based "alternatives" are ripe with euphemisms, such as "personal care homes" and "treatment centres," which effectively camouflage the reality of a precarious existence in the community. As Stan Cohen (1985: 57–58) states, "The term community treatment has lost all descriptive usefulness except as a code word with connotations of 'advanced correctional thinking' and implied value judgements against the 'locking up' and isolation of offenders." This regulatory community for women represents another layer of enforcement and compliance in their release from prison. Quite apart from the criminal justice system, the stream of state-sponsored, local regulators continues to play a major role in women's lives long after their sentences have expired.

For the most part, various agents at the local level now control the majority of women who have successfully stayed out of "trouble" and therefore not landed back in prison (see Cohen 1985; Scull 1997; Carlen 2003; Blomberg 2003). These local agencies, with their extended intrusion into the so-called private lives of women, receive their core funding from government sponsors and are expected to do more, with less. As Cohen (1985: 53) points out, the agencies are "co-opted into the criminal justice system (but less subject to judicial scrutiny), dependent on system personnel for referrals and using more or less traditional treatment methods." The community, then, becomes the site of offloading by the state and represents the further blurring of private/public space.

To finance their operations — just to keep their doors open — nongovernmental organizations increasingly rely on the state, and in doing so they become absorbed into the formal state apparatus. The end result according to Cohen (1985: 62) is "the creation of a hidden custodial system, under welfare or psychiatric sponsorship, which official delinquency statistics simply ignore."

> This is the real, awful secret of community control. Not the old closely guarded secrets of the penitentiary (the brutality, the chain gangs, solitary confinement). These things occur in the community — and this is, by any measure, progress. The secret is a much less melodramatic one: that the same old experts have moved office to the community and are doing the same old things they have always done. Once again, we do not know what they are doing, not because they are hidden behind walls but because they are camouflaged as being just ordinary members of the community. (Cohen 1985: 75)

Halfway Houses
The resistance strategies employed by middle-class and upper-class communities to housing the "mad" and the "bad" in their neighbourhoods
mean that these makeshift halfway residences have been forced to locate
in transient, deleterious urban locales. "Treatment" under these conditions
of restraint is no more conducive to well-being or empowering than it is
in the rightly criticized confines of the institution. The treatment services
and housing arrangements made available to ex-psychiatric patients
and ex-prisoners are heaped onto the private-sector agencies, which are
largely free of state regulation and inspection and are often co-opted into
conforming to state-based ideologies. It amounts to little more than the
"re-packaging of misery."

Upon release, women pose a relatively low risk to the safety of the
community, and they have proved to have lower recidivism rates (Bonta,
Rugge, and Dauvergne 2003; Canadian Association of Elizabeth Fry
Societies 2003; Eaton 1993). As a result, according to the Canadian
Association of Elizabeth Fry Societies (2003), many of the women being released from prison "do not require the structure of halfway houses
and day parole releases to their own homes should be recognized as an
appropriate option for them." Another option is the establishment of
satellite apartments.

When residency for a period of time in a halfway house is a condition of their release, the options (and chances of success) are severely
limited. In general there are far too few spaces available in women-only
halfway houses across the country — there are no halfway houses at all
for women in the Atlantic region, and few exist in the Prairie region. The
Canadian Association of Elizabeth Fry Societies (2003) states, "The lack
of spaces for women in halfway houses and residential facilities also further prejudices women with mental health and/or cognitive disabilities or
other special needs, who may require more support upon release to meet
the challenges of reintegrating into the community." One result of the
shortage of spaces is that many of these women are released to halfway
houses for men, which is wholly contradictory to the woman-centred
principles espoused by Correctional Service Canada. It is as inappropriate
to force women coming out of prison to reside in a male halfway house
as it is to turn women prisoners over to the men's penitentiaries. When
this happens, women are once again being forced to adapt to the needs
of the larger male population.

Home Care

My research with criminalized women on release revealed the emergence of "assertive case management" as the community model for dealing with the "complex needs" of women. This model is defined as "intensive supervision to those severely and persistently mentally ill persons whose needs are not met through regular case management" (Luther 2003: 165). For many criminalized women falling into this model, their lives are generally characterized by the continuous presence of "home support workers" to assist them with daily tasks and to ensure compliance with any conditions established by the criminal justice system or those developed by the case management team, typically composed of multidisciplinary psy-professionals, including people in psychiatry, social work, and psychology. Karen, an assertive case management "client," had been out of prison for almost four years when I talked to her. Her narrative reveals the dependencies created by this model of intensive regulation.

> *I won't even go outside now. Right now I am worried because I am that big now that when I go to the washroom I can't even wipe myself I am that fucking big. I get into the bathtub and I get stuck. I can't even wash myself down below. I can only wash up here. I can't wash my own back. I can barely wash my own head. It makes me depressed. So I run to the institution. The Waterford. Then they make me angry and upset. If they went to grab me and put me in TQ [Therapeutic Quiet] I am liable to hurt someone. I don't want to. I have no plan to hurt nobody but if they wants to calm me down by putting me in TQ then I will [resist]. Then they will think I had that planned and then the next thing you know I am behind bars again.... More than likely I am going to end up 102B. That's my parole number.*

Nina was also a "client" of the assertive case management model. She explained the rationale behind her most recent increase in "support staff."

> *The most hours I have ever had in home care is four hours and now I got fourteen hours a day, everyday. Ninety percent of my crimes were committed late in the night so now I have a worker with me every night so I am never alone.*

Belinda, a young woman in her mid-thirties who had been shuffled back and forth between prison and psychiatric hospitals for all of her adult life, talked about her involvement with the assertive case management team, which brings together a host of institutional and localized agencies.

> *I have five different home-care workers. I had a meeting yesterday and every week workers are given an opportunity to go to a meeting and discuss problems and concerns they are having. The only thing I got against me now is that I used the phone once too often (laughs). So if that's going to be the worse thing then I think I am going to do okay. I mean, I know there are going to be times when I am going to have to go back to the hospital for a couple of days or whatever, but the other part is I have a good doctor now and when I go in to see him he doesn't just spend five minutes with me and then that's it. I will spend an hour or so with him. I also have a case manager, which is something that I have never had.*

The community aspect of what Angela Davis (2003) has termed the "prison industrial complex" has largely escaped the scrutiny of prison abolitionists and other radicals who rightly resist the building and expansion of prisons fuelled by corporate profit motives. The fiscally motivated bottom line is increasingly being met by downloading the business of corrections onto community groups with inadequate resources to effectively target the needs of women ex-prisoners. The absence of women-only accommodations in the Atlantic region, for example, requires that women parolees accept space at co-ed residential centres, which foremost house criminalized men and deinstitutionalized psychiatric patients. In correctional discourse, the term "woman-centred" has become the guiding philosophy behind institutional and community-based corrections in Canada. As Kelly Hannah-Moffat (1995: 36) argues, this approach is fundamentally problematic because of its reliance on a monolithic category of woman, its insensitivity to relations of power, and its denial of the legal and material realities of prison. While such criticisms have rightly exposed the essentializing character of woman-centredness in prisons, comparable analysis has not even been contemplated in the community. Yet, just as it has been argued that the basic principles of "woman-centredness" are incongruent with correctional goals of punishment and surveillance, the same holds true in a community model that fails to prioritize the needs of women

Locally run programs, funded by the state, lack any accountability in terms of implementing a women-centred philosophy. However, there has been no debate or consensus on how the various stakeholders engaged in service delivery for women ex-prisoners contemplate the practice of empowering women on a local level. Arguably, this lofty goal of empowering women through a penal system driven foremost by security and punishment concerns is even more problematic in a local setting, which is open to a whole range of subjective interpretations by the government, service providers, and criminalized women themselves. Cognitive-based treatment and assertive case management approaches that psychologize and individualize women's lawbreaking are as disempowering in a home as they are in a prison. The same tensions are inherent in an assertive case management strategy that attempts to control women while at the same time purporting to empower them in an ultimately coercive and involuntary localized setting.

STRATEGIES FOR CHANGE

Based on their increasing poverty as single mothers, their histories of physical and sexual abuse (which result in a double victimization of women by the state), the layers of controls that characterize their lives, and the increasing criminalization of mental health, criminalized women are amongst the most marginalized people in our society. In many cases a simple defiance of gender norms is met with the resistance and punishment of the state.

Obviously, these problems are also part of a much wider system that is failing women, and any solution has to take into account the broader capitalist, racist, and patriarchal structures that characterize and subvert the lives of Canadian women. As Walter DeKeseredy and his colleagues (2003: 125) make clear, "Ideological hurdles rather than economic obstacles account for the failure to mount rational campaigns to bring about social justice," and in the case of criminalized women, given the myriad of socio-economic and cultural factors that converge to their further disadvantage, a solution to the issues raised by transcarceration needs to be based in a much more comprehensive platform built on social justice reform. Given the well-documented feminization and subsequent criminalization of poverty (Eden 2002; Ehrenreich 2001; Gilliom 2001; Hadley 2001; chapter 8 here), and given that the overwhelming majority of women's crimes are crimes of survival, the issues surrounding women's increasing poverty and economic marginalization need to be more closely addressed from the perspective of the conditions that propel women into conflict with the law in the first place. At the same time, women's chances of successful completion of their conditional releases have to be directly related to the conditions and role of their economic marginalization.

Underlying the narratives of women's pathways into prison and their continued struggle to stay out is the failure of social assistance to provide a decent living income. As Janet Mosher and her collaborators (2004: vi) remind us:

> What is needed most urgently and most profoundly is a fundamental paradigm shift; a shift from viewing poverty as the failing of individuals, and those who are lazy, unmotivated and deceptive. To the extent that the welfare system... continues to operate from such a paradigm, there is really little hope that it will offer meaningful support to facilitate women's safe exit from abusive relationships. Women will continue to be subjected to demeaning, humiliating treatment; will be constantly regarded with suspicion; and will be subject to the control and discipline of the state.

Along these same ideological lines, critics call for a trangressive criminology — one that begins from outside the mainstream criminological discourse. As Maureen Cain (1990: 10) contends:

> It simply has not proved possible to make adequate sense of what is going on in these areas of concern by starting from inside criminological discourse. Only by starting from outside, with the social construction of gender, or with women's experiences of their total lives, or with the structure of the domestic space, can we begin to make sense of what is going on.

If we start from a place that situates our social world as one that is shaped by class, race, and gender, then the driving forces behind women's oppression can be seen as being continually reproduced through the power-brokering of state regulators and reinforced through such institutions as marriage, child-rearing, and sexual practices.

Strategies for change then rest, for example, on the overthrow of patriarchal relations, which would permit women's sexual autonomy and obliterate the oppressive nature of sexual and familial relations for women. We need to move away from a preoccupation with the corrections system in and of itself to more fundamental issues affecting the lives of all women. Rather than narrowing our focus to those women who get caught up in the machinery of the criminal justice system, we need to focus attention on the unravelling of our social safety net under a neo-liberal government strategy that predominantly targets women and drives them further into poverty and despair.

Women's trajectories into (and out of) prison are clearly non-linear. That is, conditions of poverty, violence, abuse, addictions, histories of formal and informal controls, and defiance of gender norms intersect with one another to produce a lifestyle of (unwanted) dependencies on the state. In turn, these dependencies become further entrenched in a criminal justice system that fosters a culture of dependency and does nothing to contribute to women's economic and social empowerment. The compounding effects of incarceration on the lives of women who have, for the most part, been excluded by society based on their class, gender, race, sexuality, and cultural differences need to be a core focus of any reintegration efforts by the state and the community. Feminists have been vigilant in their efforts to expose the human rights violations of prisons. The same critical appraisal needs to take place in our communities, where the regulation of women begins and ends.

NOTES

1. This chapter draws on interviews with twenty-two women ex-prisoners in Atlantic Canada. A full account of this work can be found in Maidment 2005 and forthcoming.
2. The "corrective" nature of the competing goals of incarceration (for example, punishment versus rehabilitation) has been challenged. As Gayle Horii (2000: 107) argues, "Corrections is plainly a misnomer since reformatories, lockups, jails, prisons and penitentiaries correct nothing, rather they err."
3. Defining and operationalizing "success" is highly problematic because criminalized women do not define their own successes and/or failures in the same way as the official recidivism scales do.

12. LIFER'S THOUGHTS

Yvonne Johnson

(Saturday, October 30, 2004)

As I sit here, I am listening to "Mama I'm Coming Home" by Ozzy Osborne, followed up by "No More Tears." I recall a day back in September of 1989. We had just celebrated my eldest child's birthday. She just turned six years old. I recall how she already knew how to ride a bike without training wheels. When she got her new bike that birthday she was off and running, her long black hair flying behind her in the wind.

My eldest son did not live with us, as he lived with his mother's family. We had three maternal children at home living with us. My eldest was now six years old; the next boy would be turning three in the coming month of December. The baby girl was going to turn two come the next February. My eldest girl's birthday was the last birthday I would celebrate with my children — as my life became a sentence, as I was arrested for murder on September 14th, 1989.

I was waiting to celebrate my own birthday come October 4th, and at the point of arrest I was still only twenty-six years old. I instead had my twenty-seventh birthday in the Edmonton Remand Centre. Technically my eldest was seventy-two months old, my boy was thirty-one months old, the baby was twenty months old when I got arrested and separated from them for life.

I have been incarcerated now for fifteen years and two months. I am forty-three years old, my eldest maternal child is twenty-two years old, the boy will be turning nineteen, the baby will be turning eighteen years of age. People often ask me what it is that keeps me going on and through life, with the Life Twenty-Five sentence. My most common reply is, "Every day I just place one foot in front of the other." Another comment is, "I don't know, I guess I'm just a sucker for punishment." When things get extremely tough for me, where death seems an easier way to go, I remind myself of the promise I made to my boy.

When I was being carted off after being placed under arrest, I was able to talk to my boy briefly. He was such a little big man, as he was born ten and one-half pounds at birth. He was so square and huge and solid that people could not believe he was just a baby still. He was standing on the porch of the house, watching them take me away in cuffs. Standing only as high as the RCMP's knees, his big brown button eyes larger than usual. I can see his eyes squeeze together as the tears started to come, his bottom lip sticking out and curling down in a pout he was notorious for. The RCMP would not let me talk to him, so I broke away anyways and ran to him.

We had three small steps up our cement porch. I knelt down on the cement to be at eye level with my boy. I looked into his eyes, wanted to shield him from all the strangeness that was going on around him. My hands cuffed behind my back, I could not hold him one last time, so I choked back my tears so this would not be his last memory of me. I placed my forehead on his and looked into his eyes. I said, "My boy, these men said I did bad. I got to go with them till I can get things understood. Then I come back as soon as I can."

I saw my baby girl squeeze through the RCMP's legs to look at me and my boy. I was now losing ground very fast and barely could restrain myself. It was like someone hit my chest with a sledgehammer. I clenched my jaw, put my face to the ground, a heavy groan escaped from me. I said my last words through the sadness I could no longer hold down. I told my baby girl, "Baby, mama loves you." I looked into my son's eyes one last time for many years to come. I knew he was but a baby himself, but I told him "My little big man, you watch out for your sisters okay. Mama loves you."

It took getting angry to break myself away from my kids. I jumped up and told the police to take me away. I tried to walk and my legs came out from under me. I hit the cement hard, a mournful wailing came out, and I broke down.

As the cops mobilized to carry me away I saw my eldest girl coming back from school. She was bouncing through the trees in the yard and she froze in place when she saw me and what was happening, as they were dragging me off. Now in the throes of emotions, I struggled to stay calm. I turned back and yelled to her, "Tell them you want to go to Auntie Barb's. Tell them, tell them to get a hold of grandma. She is on the reserve Red Pheasant in Saskatchewan."

I now sometimes, sitting in the Private Family Visits with my children, say, "It is you guys that keep me going," as I recall my promise I made when they took me away: "I will deal with this and will be back as soon as I can." Well it is now fifteen years later and I am still always trying to deal with it, it's just been a very long and trying haul is all. I am as always trying to deal with it all, to eventually fulfil my promise that I will be coming back, just hold on. It's been a long wait and a long time coming but I am still in there swinging, one day to break to the surface.

People without knowing say to me, "If I was in your shoes I would have killed myself a long time ago. I don't know how you do it, and for so long." Things always change throughout a life sentence, so do reason and logic. I recall thoughts of things early into my sentence. I saw a documentary and Chief Dan George was in it. It was about a young Native man who was brought up in many foster homes. He was trying to recoup and reclaim his Native ways, and all the struggles he endured. In one scene in the movie, George speaks to the young boy. He told the boy he was swallowed up by the great white shark. Meaning the white society and the white society of foster care.

I do not recall much more than that, but I utilized this much in reference to myself. I in turn understood this as likened to myself. I also recall a bible story of a man swallowed by a whale, but he was spit out on the shore later. I also recall, I think it was Pinocchio, he was swallowed up, but he started a fire in the whale's belly and therefore got spit or sneezed out as well. I recall being preached at one time about the man who was swallowed by the whale, I recall the very vivid story of what the man could have looked like after being in a whale's stomach for so long.

I pictured myself swimming around an island, the island was my home before arrest. As I swam around, the cops grabbed me and threw me into the mouth of the great white shark, the mouth of the shark representing the place where courts are held. Just being swished around in the shark's mouth, its sharp teeth cutting into me. My skin turning white, once I was sentenced, the shark then did swallow me whole. The shark represented the whole white male justice system, the shark's belly represented the prison system.

Now here I sit inside the shark's belly, where it swims constantly, always moving or it will drown itself. It is an unfeeling, predatorial man/women-eating beast with its cold steel eyes. I can sit and wait for the stomach acids and steady crunching motions of the stomach as it attempts to break me down, so the fish could slowly and surely devour me just to expel me out. Or I can study why it even is, how it moves, thinks, feels, its motivations, its desires, its strengths and weaknesses alike.

Once I could understand and accept I was swallowed whole with no other way out, I decided to find a way out. I was lucky when I started my bit way back at P4W. I met a man named Tom French. He was the founder of Life Line, and at the time was the only in-reach worker and only in Ontario Region. I listened to this man long and hard, as he was a no beat around bull-shitter type person. In the short time that I knew him, I learned things that are vital for all lifers to understand and work toward in order to eventually get out.

Throughout my sentence and to date I still try to utilize things he spoke of and adapt them to my very life as an inmate with eventual insight and will to one day get out. One thing he told me was your sentence starts literally at the time of your arrest. If you cannot fathom this idea at the point of arrest, you better damn well want to understand it at the moment you first walk into a federal prison. As written information forever on your record and file starts instantaneously, and you will forever after always have to answer to this.

Part IV
MAKING CHANGE

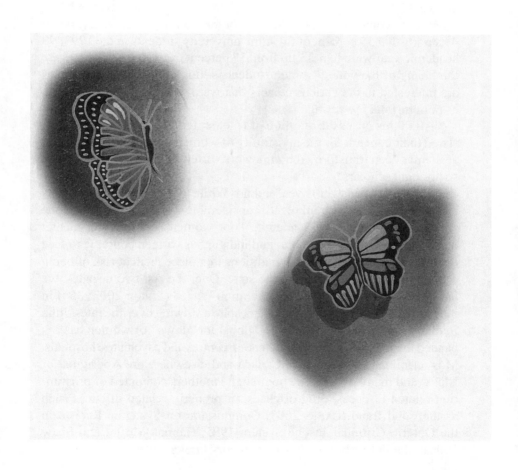

INTRODUCTION
Gillian Balfour

Today most Canadian university undergraduate criminology programs include courses with titles such as "Women, Crime, and Social Justice," "Women and the Criminal Justice System," or "Women, Law, and the State." These courses are offered either as special topics courses or as a part of the established curriculum. As well, more women academics are teaching in university classrooms,[1] and more classrooms are being filled with women students than ever before. Statistics Canada (2001a: 4) reports that 55 percent of full-time university students in the 1997–98 academic year were female, up from 37 percent in 1972–73. Chances are that many of the young women students sitting in criminology courses are interested in the various careers that were once male bastions, such as policing and lawyering.

All of this raises the question of whether feminist writers have overstated their concern for the invisibility of women in criminology. Hasn't academia been transformed by the work of feminist criminologists and socio-legal scholars?

In short, the answer is yes, and no. While these significant transformations should not be minimized, considerable work remains to be done — especially outside of academia. Poor women, women with mental health needs, women of colour, and indigenous women continue to face demoralizing and brutalizing conditions that place them at risk of being criminalized or disciplined by the state. Over the last two decades, we have seen an international "incarceration binge" (Snider 2003: 354) in the numbers of imprisoned women, despite a slowing of crime rates. Julia Sudbury (2005b) argues that this "global lockdown" of women has expanded to include immigration detention centres and psychiatric hospitals. Most criminalized women in Canada and elsewhere are Aboriginal or Black, and many of them are poor single mothers convicted of prostitution-related offences, drug offences, or property-related offences such as theft and fraud (CAEFS 2003; Commission on Systemic Racism in the Ontario Criminal Justice System 1995; Hannah-Moffat and Shaw 2000a; Manitoba Aboriginal Justice Inquiry Implementation Commission 2001).

Discussions of "how to" are critical in a time when the global rate of women's incarceration is rapidly increasing while closer to home the

welfare state collapses under the demand by the middle class and corporate elites for lower taxes. Meanwhile prison construction becomes a
job-revitalization strategy in voter-rich, economically depressed regions.
This final section of the book looks at the various feminist strategies that
have been used to address the conditions inside women's prisons, to defend criminalized women's human rights, to empower women prisoners,
and to draw attention to the systemic abuses against poor and racialized
women. It will also consider the more recent efforts of change-making
undertaken by former prisoners, prisoner advocates, and feminist academics. While there is certainly room for cautious optimism on these fronts,
there are lessons to be learned from the past that should frame how we
move forward in our efforts at making change — both inside and outside
the prison walls.

TRANSFORMING AND TRANSGRESSING CRIMINOLOGY: MAKING CHANGE WITHIN ACADEMIA

In chapter 1, Elizabeth Comack recounted how feminist criminology's
initial change-making strategy was to mount a substantive critique of
classical and contemporary criminological theories, revealing the striking inadequacy of malestream criminology to fully theorize criminalized
women. Feminist research pointed out that criminology has failed in a
number of ways. For one, conventional criminologists did not account
for the masculine norm of crime and deviance: that is, the gender-ratio
problem of why men make up the vast majority of those charged with
criminal offences. For another, the assumptions of criminological theory
unravelled when applied to the conditions of women's lives: women
experience far more severe conditions of economic marginalization and
lack of legitimate opportunities, yet commit fewer crimes than men.
Even the progressive critical theories of Marxist criminologists were
gender-blind and dismissive of the feminization of poverty, intraclass
violence against women, and the criminalization of women sex-trade
workers and not male customers or pimps. Finally, feminists pointed to
how contemporary criminology remains transfixed by classical notions
of biologism to explain women's "criminal mind."

By the 1980s, feminist critique gave way to a feminist criminology
that aimed to transcend the methodological and theoretical approaches of
conventional criminology. Also at this time, the striking overcriminalization of poor and racialized women further complicated how criminologists
should understand gender. Standpoint feminism was a strategy that made
the experiences of criminalized women visible. Through women's own

accounts of racism, poverty, and violence, a feminist criminology for, about, and by women was possible.

Maureen Cain (1990) suggested that by adopting a standpoint episte- mology, feminist criminology could transgress the very limits of criminol- ogy and attend to the complexities of race, class, and gender. Standpoint is more than a research practice; it is also a key political strategy that transforms theory into action, or feminist praxis. Liz Stanley (1990: 15) describes feminist praxis as "researching the world of women in order to change it, not only to study it." In this way, standpoint feminism in criminology challenged the disregard or distortion of women's gendered experiences of poverty and violence, and in doing so it advocating for significant social change. As Sandra Harding (1987: 185) understands it: "Standpoint never loses sight of women as actively constructing as well as interpreting the social processes and social relations which constitute their everyday realities, and which can only be achieved through engag- ing directly in the intellectual and political struggle."

Early standpoint epistemologies, however, tended to essentialize women, taking women's experiences as self-evident and the only basis of knowledge production (Smart 1990). In particular, the approach viewed women's victimization (sexual exploitation, domestic violence, rape) as a cause or pathway into violence, addiction, prostitution, or fraud. More recent feminist scholarship has challenged the overdetermined role of abuse in women's lives, cautioning that such a strategy renders women responsible for how they cope with abuse. It thus makes women risky subjects, to be imprisoned based on their assumed need for treatment (Pollack 2000a, 2004; Hannah-Moffat 2001, 2004a, 2004b). Margaret Shaw (1995: 448) points out that the continuum between victimization and criminalization is an essentialist understanding of criminalized women that rests upon a selective reading of women's own accounts of their lives:

> What is at issue here is not whether the women are right or wrong or politically correct in their judgements, but that there is in fact a range of views, and that some of these may be antithetical to a feminist viewpoint. They do not all hate men, or see themselves as victims. The plurality of their views needs to be recognized. We need also need to recognize that it is paternalistic to assume that they are necessarily "misguided," or want to have their consciousness raised.

Julia Sudbury (2005b: xv) asserts that standpoint epistemology follows the psychologizing and individualizing logic of the criminal justice system, and "sidesteps the question of why the state responds to abused women with punishment."

Regardless of its critics, at the time standpoint feminism did allow for the transformation of the discipline. Feminist criminologists were able to stake out a profoundly gendered space, no longer having to "add women and stir" into malestream criminology. Throughout the 1980s, groundbreaking research by feminists captured the voices of incarcerated and criminalized women in Canada and revealed the prevalence of sexual abuse and rape in the lives of many criminalized women (Shaw et al. 1991; Comack 1996). This research attempted to make important connections between victimization and criminalization, and to show how this connection was compounded by racism and poverty. Comack (1996) outlines that for some women, drinking and drugging, fraud, prostitution, violence, and self-harm are understood as strategies to help them cope with the sense of powerlessness and anger that comes from the experience of violence.

This ontology of experience opened up new strategies for making changes to the criminal justice response to women in conflict with the law, such as feminist therapy inside the Prison for Women.

FEMINIST THERAPY INSIDE THE P4W

Feminist therapy — based on the feminist principles of empowerment and advocacy — was introduced inside the Prison for Women in the early 1990s by local grassroots feminist organization volunteers in response to escalating rates of suicide and self-harm, especially amongst Aboriginal and maximum-security women. Feminist therapists worked to implement counselling programs that were informed by women's experiences of sexual violence, especially childhood sexual abuse. Instead of pathologizing and punishing suicide attempts, self-harm, eating disorders, or violence, feminist therapists understood such behaviours as signs of protest or resistance to conditions of powerlessness (Burstow 1992; McGrath 1992; Heney 1990). Counsellors taught women prisoners how to provide peer counselling for other prisoners, and worked to prevent the punitive use of segregation in cases of suicide or self-harm, instead providing crisis intervention supports to ensure women were not further isolated and disempowered.

The strategies of feminist counsellors to challenge the punitive treatment of women prisoners were met with deep opposition from the security staff at the Prison for Women (Kendall 1993). Counsellors reported experiencing harassment and accusations of unprofessional conduct when women committed suicide, or when counsellors hugged a woman prisoner or advocated for a prisoner's right to visit with her children (Balfour 2000). These responses were not surprising, given the "hegemony of correctionalism" underpinning paramilitary institutions that rely on domination and control (Balfour 2000: 102). The experience of feminist counsellors reveals that feminists working for change within the criminal justice bureaucracy must reconcile their principles with the conditions of the institutions in which they find themselves.

CHALLENGING THE CRIMINAL JUSTICE RESPONSE

Throughout the 1980s feminist activists undertook various attempts to challenge the criminal justice response to women, especially the treatment of women prisoners (see Introduction to Part III). Some of these strategies included a human rights complaint against the Correctional Service of Canada as well as participating in a coroner's inquest into the death of Marlene Moore. But little substantive change was achieved. The establishment of the Task Force on Federally Sentenced Women in 1989, however, held the promise of a transformative moment in the struggle for prison reform in Canada.

The problems involved in implementing the principles of *Creating Choices* revealed not only the barriers that feminists face in achieving full participation in the change-making process, but also the tightening grip of neo-liberalism in framing how women prisoners were to be managed. As Shoshana Pollack (chapter 9) shows, well-meaning feminist research and advocacy for women as victims of male violence have resulted in a gender-response program inside women's prisons that has absorbed the victimization discourse, but not in the way that feminists envisioned. The troubles of many Black women prisoners, for instance, emanate from their lack of independence and anger at not being able to provide for their children, not from the damage of sexual abuse. Kelly Hannah-Moffat's work (chapter 10) reveals how another unintended consequence of calling attention to women's victimization experiences has been the conflation of women's needs as security risks, thereby justifying a practice of overclassifying women. Hannah-Moffat also explains how women's abuse histories are arbitrarily used by prison and parole administrators to position women as potential recidivists in need of more intensive community supervision.

As MaDonna Maidment (chapter 11) discovered in her interviews with women in Atlantic Canada, a "care-custody mangle" of mental health and corrections experts and agencies transcends prison walls, reaching into the private lives of women well after their release from custody. Maidment describes how the transcarceration strategies — the spread of carceral tactics into the community under the guise of home care or intensive supervision and support — are not lenient measures of penality as women become more socially and economically marginalized. While Maidment suggests that the coercive powers of the state have widened to encompass the resources of social service agencies and experts — thereby governing women "at a distance" — what remains uncertain is if these transcarceral strategies are potentially positive alternatives for some women. For example, home care suggests a reinvestment in community-based alternatives to imprisonment and institutionalization, which could be interpreted as a progressive step. Nevertheless, in his review of Alberta's secure-care legislation for youth at risk of becoming involved in prostitution, Steven Bittle (chapter 7) is less optimistic about the role of the community in the regulation of at-risk youth. Bittle maintains that neo-liberal governments rely on rhetorical devices of protection and capacity-building to allow for an off-loading of state responsibility for the care of at-risk youth onto communities and families with already limited resources to cope. Clearly, while engaging with the state to achieve social transformation in the interests of women and girls, feminists have had to remain vigilant of the implications of criminal justice responses. Feminist advocates have also turned to law to hold the state accountable for its treatment of criminalized women and girls.

RESORTING TO LAW AS A STRATEGY FOR MAKING CHANGE

The resort to law has also been an important strategy in the feminist struggle for change. As a result of feminist lobbying, for example, legal reforms have taken place to address the prevalence of wife abuse (see Comack and Balfour 2004: ch. 6). In 1982 the federal solicitor general encouraged police departments across Canada to implement a "no drop" or mandatory charging policy for cases of domestic violence. Before that time wife abuse was generally considered to be a private matter between a husband and wife, and police were reluctant to intervene. Eventually, specialized prosecution policies were created to encourage women to report domestic violence and to provide evidence against their abusers, and several provinces established more rigorous zero tolerance arrest policies and specialized family violence court units (Ursel 2002).

In 1990 the Supreme Court of Canada recognized the battered women's syndrome in the case of *R. v. Lavallee* (1990). The Court accepted the expert witness testimony of a psychiatrist who claimed that Angelique Lavallee killed her abusive common-law spouse in self-defence because she suffered from learned helplessness as a result of living under the constant threat of violence. In the end, Lavallee was acquitted — a feminist victory of sorts. As feminist socio-legal scholars have argued, this Supreme Court decision did little to condemn male violence as a systemic problem, and it failed to recognize women's violence as a "rational" and "reasonable" action when located within the social context in which it occurs (Martinson et al. 1991; Comack 1993a; Noonan 1993).

Following the *Lavallee* decision, pressure mounted from advocacy groups — the Canadian Association of Elizabeth Fry Societies in particular — for the government to conduct a review of cases involving women who were convicted of murder or manslaughter but had been unable to use their history of abuse to prove that they were acting in self-defence. Consequently, Ontario Court Judge Lynn Ratushny was appointed in 1995 to conduct a review of ninety-eight cases. The *Self-Defence Review: Final Report* (Ratushny 1997) recommended law reform in the areas of self-defence and sentencing. Although that proposal itself seemingly represented another feminist victory, only seven of the ninety-eight cases were recommended to be granted relief, and the government agreed to this in only five of those cases. No women were released from prison as a result of the review.[2] Since this review was undertaken, researchers have noted that women are increasingly vulnerable to criminalization when they use violence in self-defence (Pollack, Battaglia, and Allspach 2005) and, under rigorous zero tolerance policies, women continue to be countercharged for domestic assault — even when they call the police for help (Comack, Chopyk, and Wood 2000).

It would seem that law has its limits. Nevertheless, feminist reformers and prison advocates have continued to resort to law as a strategy for addressing the discriminatory treatment of women within the criminal justice system. In March 2001 CAEFS and the Native Women's Association of Canada (NWAC) — along with twenty-seven other social justice groups — launched a human rights complaint with the Canadian Human Rights Commission (CHRC) based on the discriminatory treatment of federally sentenced women at the hands of the Canadian government. The complaint asserted that discrimination existed on three main grounds: sex (especially those women held in maximum-security units in men's prison); race (the treatment of Aboriginal and other racialized women); and disability (the treatment of those women with cognitive and mental disabilities).

In its written submission to the Human Rights Commission, CAEFS (2003) argued that the security classification system used by Correctional Service Canada is determined by an assessment tool that is fundamentally gender-biased and class-based. On the one hand, a woman is assessed according to criteria such as whether she has been a victim of spousal abuse, has "inappropriate sexual preferences," or has "sexual attitudes that are problematic" (CAEFS 2003: 24–25). On the other hand, middle-class norms infuse criteria such as whether a woman has a bank account, collateral, or hobbies, has used social assistance, lacks a skill or trade or profession, resides in a criminogenic area, or lives in a poorly maintained residence. CAEFS was also highly critical of the practice of confining those women classified as maximum security in segregated units inside men's prisons. As well, the Association pointed to the disproportionate classi-fication of Aboriginal women as maximum-security prisoners — which happens in large part due to the inappropriateness of the risk assessment tool that translates marginalization from systemic and historical practices into individualized risk. Aboriginal women were also granted conditional release at slower rates and later stages in their sentences, despite section 84 of the Corrections and Conditional Release Act, which is aimed at the reintegration of Aboriginal women into their communities. Similarly, CAEFS pointed out that the discrimination against women with mental and cognitive disabilities is built into the security classification scheme: those disabilities are one of the factors to be taken into account in assigning a prisoner's security classification. Associating security concerns with disability de facto constructs persons with a mental illness or disorder as "dangerous" (CAEFS 2003).

After extensive consultation and investigation, the CHRC released its report, *Protecting Their Rights*, in January 2004. In its profile of federally sentenced women, the report maintained, "The reasons why women offend, their life experiences and their needs are unique." Some two-thirds of federally sentenced women are mothers, and they are more likely than male prisoners to be the primary caregivers to their children. Federally sentenced women experience much lower employment rates than do their male counterparts. They have less education than the general Canadian population, and experience significant poverty. An "overwhelming" number — 80 percent — of federally sentenced women report histories of abuse. One of the "most disturbing" statistics cited by the Commission concerned the overrepresentation of Aboriginal women in maximum security: "Although Aboriginal women account for only 3% of the female population of Canada, they represent 29% of the women incarcerated in federal prisons and account for fully 46% of the women classified as maximum security" (CHRC 2004). As well, the report noted that federally sentenced women "are three times more likely than their male counterparts to suffer from depression. They also experience higher rates of mental illness, self-destructive behaviour such as slashing and cutting, and suicide attempts." Women with mental health issues are also disproportionately classified as maximum security.

The Commission identified systemic human rights problems in the Correctional Service of Canada's treatment of federally sentenced women, and made nineteen recommendations for immediate action to be taken on the part of CSC. In February 2005 CSC announced its response to the CHRC report — a multi-year action plan to implement the recommendations. The CSC acknowledged that the plan was not one that would "fundamentally challenge the concept of incarceration as applied to women offenders" because it only addressed "those suggestions which can be implemented within the legislative frame... of the Corrections and Conditional Release Act" (Correctional Service of Canada 2005b: 2). Nevertheless, while some of the CHRC recommendations were accepted in principle or in part, others — like the recommendation to change the blanket policy of not allowing maximum-security women at the healing lodge to one based on individual assessment — were not. In a press release issued the following month, CAEFS, NWAC, and other advocacy groups expressed their alarm over what they considered to be "the tacit acceptance by the Canadian Human Rights Commission of the relative inaction of the Correctional Service of Canada" on the issue of the systemic discrimination against federally sentenced women (CAEFS 2005c).

Confronted with a disappointing response by the CHRC to the inaction of CSC to address the discriminatory treatment of women prisoners, CAEFS and its coalition partners were not dissuaded from the importance of holding CSC accountable. To this end, the coalition made a formal submission to the United Nations Human Rights Committee to examine the federal government's claim that its treatment of women prisoners does not violate the United Nations Convention Against Torture and Other Cruel, Inhumane, or Degrading Treatment or Punishment (CAEFS 2005b). Utilizing the exhaustive research collected for the CHRC complaint, CAEFS and it partners argue that CSC violates UN Article 2 (prevention of acts of torture) in its classification and maximum-security units, its continued use of cross-gender monitoring and searching practices, its treatment of Aboriginal prisoners, its use of segregation, and the lack of gender-specific training, educational, and therapeutic programs (CAEFS 2005b).

Given the overincarceration of Aboriginal women, the conditions of their imprisonment, and the prevalence of violence against Aboriginal women, one of the key allies in the struggle for change has been the Native Women's Association of Canada.[3] In 2004 NWAC launched its Sisters in Spirit campaign across Canada to document the cases of Aboriginal women who had disappeared or died a violent death. NWAC estimated that five hundred Aboriginal women had gone missing over the past two decades (NWAC 2005). Amnesty International provided funding for the research and writing of a report presented at the United Nations Forum on Indigenous Peoples. In May 2005, NWAC received $5 million over five years from the federal government to assist in a number of projects, including the creation of a toll-free hotline for families to report their missing women; the creation of a national registry of missing Aboriginal women; and the implementation of a public awareness and education campaign. NWAC would also provide government with a policy analysis and recommendations to address violence against Aboriginal women (NWAC 2005).

One of the more troubling findings of the Sisters in Spirit campaign is the linking of violence against Aboriginal women with poverty and the failure of the criminal justice system to adequately protect Aboriginal women and girls from violence (NWAC 2005). NWAC draws parallels between the rape and murder of Helen Betty Osborne by four white men in The Pas Manitoba in 1971, and the unsolved murder of sixteen-year-old Felicia Solomon in Winnipeg in 2003. As Nahanni Fontaine (chapter 4) points out, it is only through the narratives of young women like Felicia that the connections between the legacy of colonialism and gang violence can be made. A key strategy for change is research for, by, and about Aboriginal peoples to expose the impact of racism.

SOCIAL EXCLUSION: THE DISCIPLINING OF WOMEN

Girls and women also experience another form of regulation: social exclusion. In recent years, feminist criminologists have recognized that girls and women today are likely to be managed by regulatory or "disciplining" forms of power outside of the criminal justice system. The auditor general of Canada reports that 77 percent of Canadians using social services such as shelters, income assistance, public housing, food banks, and day cares are women (Auditor General Canada 2003). As Shelley Gavigan and Dorothy Chunn point out (chapter 8), neo-liberal provincial governments have made significant clawbacks to these services, which has had a direct impact on women's vulnerability to domestic violence through dependency on abusive breadwinners and inadequate shelter spaces. Women also face increasing risks of criminalization for welfare fraud when they try to subsidize their meagre benefits with part-time work or student loans. It would seem that change-making strategies must attend to the complex interplay between poverty and violence.

As Robert Menzies and Dorothy Chunn (chapter 6) indicate, women's attempts to overcome poverty have always placed them at risk for criminalization and psychiatrization. Women such as Charlotte Ross actively resisted labels of mental illness and gendered methods of social exclusion, such as indefinite terms of institutionalization. Today we witness similar tactics of regulation in the lives of women such as Lisa Neve, whose 1994 dangerous offender designation (overturned in 1999) was linked to her resistance and keen sense of survival (Neve and Pate 2005). Another strategy of resistance used by criminalized women has been to seek financial compensation for the impact of their treatment while imprisoned. In 1998 Dorothy Proctor — a woman subjected to LSD treatments in the 1960s inside the Prison for Women — sued the federal government for $5 million. Her case sparked a Board of Investigation study into the use of LSD treatments on women prisoners. The results revealed that twenty-three women had been administered LSD without their consent, and numerous ethical research standards were compromised, such as the administering of LSD to inmates held in segregation as well as the sedation and isolation of prisoners after the LSD treatments (CAEFS 1998).

Dorothy Proctor and Lisa Neve, racialized women, were criminalized for prostitution and robbery. Joanne Minaker (chapter 2) describes how similar gendered, class-based, and racialized forms of censure were imposed upon poor and homeless white women by affluent women of privilege at the turn of the century. Wives of rich industrialists and politicians oftentimes led sexual purity campaigns against working-class women. However, racialized women were considered more dangerous than pitiful, and unworthy of salvation. Minaker rightly connects these regulatory practices to the wider historical practice of nation-building. In a more contemporary context, Susan Boyd's analysis (chapter 5) of the overcriminalization of Black women for drug-trafficking offences in Canada revealed how these women are not dangerous drug lords; rather, they are more often than not welfare-dependent single mothers who face systemic racism when they are trying to work or get access to affordable housing. The voices of the women captured in Chris Bruckert and Collette Parent's study of in-call sex-trade workers (chapter 3) indicated that these women share many of the same experiences as minimum-waged service industry workers such as waitresses, in that their work is sexualized labour intent on meeting the needs of customers. Like sex-trade workers, service industry workers have little job security and can face dangerous working conditions — and harassment. Throughout the narratives of the past and present, we witness how women face dire consequences if they resist the conditions of poverty.

MOVING FORWARD?

How then should we address the conditions of social exclusion (poverty, and racialized and sexualized violence) that appear to enable the regulation of women inside and outside of the criminal justice system? Recognizing the limits of law and the seemingly impenetrable prison bureaucracy, former prisoners and their advocates have begun to build strategic alliances with the international community. In chapter 13, Gayle Horii, a member of Strength in Sisterhood (a collective of federally sentenced women), Kim Pate (a prisoner advocate and executive director of the CAEFS), and legal scholar Debra Parkes write of their experiences in launching the human rights complaint in co-operation with other social justice groups across Canada. Although cautiously optimistic about the potential of law to transform the conditions of women's imprisonment in Canada, they recognize that the complaint process has been difficult. Nevertheless, one of the outcomes of the CHRC complaint process has been the creation of a global network of activists committed to addressing the conditions of social exclusion produced by neo-liberalism.

Like Horii and her collaborators, Laureen Snider (chapter 14) calls on us to fully appreciate the devastating impacts of neo-liberal economics on women — and how neo-liberal policies were put in place despite feminist claims-making and activism. Snider raises two vital questions for feminists in their pursuit of social change: first, is it even possible to make change in neo-liberal times; and second, are there ways of bringing the symbolic value of criminalization to bear while containing its harmful effects? In Snider's view, if substantive social change is to take place, feminist knowledge claims need to become a part of the "knowledge-power-change nexus."

Clearly, not all feminists agree on the necessary strategies for making change. Some believe that we need to engage with academia, law, and the criminal justice system to make it more responsive to women's needs, whereas others believe that advocates can only make change by working outside the criminal justice system. Most feminists would agree, however, that there remains a troubling disregard for feminist research in terms of political and public discourse about "what to do about crime." As feminist scholars struggle to be recognized as "authorized knowers," some of them, to further their access to government resources, have become entangled in unconventional alliances with neo-conservative interests (see Lacombe 1993). Feminist academics and activists are seldom a part of crime-control policy-making processes, which instead pay greater attention to the research and analytical frameworks of positivist criminologists who resolutely reject economic and social conditions as causes of crime. In the view of these criminologists, criminals are poorly socialized, impulsive, and have diminished cognitive functioning; criminals are unable to think logically, reason appropriately, and make rational decisions (Gorman 2001).

U.S. feminist criminologist Meda Chesney-Lind (2004) points to the importance of the conditions of change-making and activism as key strategic pieces in the struggle for significant change:

> Clearly, as professionals who study of the problem of crime, we should be able to claim a certain degree of credibility when it comes to public discussions of crime policy. Yet, when many critical decisions are made about these issues, we are almost never on the guest list. Why? It has been my experience that most academics, particularly in the United States, are wholly unplugged from the world of politics, particularly in their local communities, and are often completely unaware of what it takes to engage in pragmatic political activism. This situation is no accident, of course. Rather, it is the consequence of decades of political domination by conservative political leadership which, among other things, sought to shift the social sciences away from the activism that had characterized our fields in earlier decades.

What, then, are the challenges that now confront feminist criminologists? Throughout this book, we have suggested that women and girls are more likely to be criminalized today — labelled, processed, and punished — because of the ravages of a neo-liberal form of governance. How do we make sense of the trends towards a more punitive regulation of poor and racialized women? What are the sites and conditions of change-making? How can we best imagine our work to advocate on behalf of these women? These are the kinds of perplexing questions that feminist criminologists will continue to grapple with in the near future.

NOTES

1. Still, although there have been improvements in the hiring of women academics, women remain locked in the lowest ranks of academia (part-time instructors, untenured junior faculty). See Canadian Association of University Teachers, November/December 2002.
2. For a synopsis and commentary on the *Self-Defence Review*, see CAEFS, "Justice for Battered Women — Denied, Delayed... Diminished. Jails Are Not the Shelters Battered Women Need" <www.elizabethfry.ca/diminish.htm>. (Accessed October 15, 2005.)
3. The Native Women's Association of Canada is a national organization that represents the political, economic, and cultural interests of First Nations and Métis women. See <nwac-hq.org>. (Accessed October 15, 2005.)

13. ARE WOMEN'S RIGHTS WORTH THE PAPER THEY'RE WRITTEN ON? COLLABORATING TO ENFORCE THE HUMAN RIGHTS OF CRIMINALIZED WOMEN

Gayle Horii, Debra Parkes, and Kim Pate

In April 2005 a conference was held in Vancouver to commemorate the twentieth anniversary of the equality provisions of the Canadian Charter of Rights and Freedoms.[1] In planning a workshop presentation for this conference, the three of us had hoped to include Yvonne Johnson (who is serving a life sentence at the Edmonton Institution for Women) as a collaborator; but the Correctional Service of Canada was not willing to authorize her to attend and present with us in person. So before the workshop began we played the song "Ballad of Yvonne Johnson" as a way of making Yvonne's presence known to the audience.[2]

> my name is yvonne johnson, my native blood is cree
> i'm here to tell the story of the life stolen from me
>
> my grandfather's grandfather was the great war chief big bear
> and flora my grandmother worked with medicine and prayer
> my mother's from saskatchewan, my dad's u.s. marine
> and i was just a half-breed falling somewhere in between
>
> raised up in a reckless world of drugs and alcohol
> the police killed my brother earl, the only one who cared at all
> cleft palate split my face in two, my words came soft and spare
> i lived in shame and ridicule, foundations of despair
>
> daniel let the kids all watch when i was only three
> he threw me on the table, forced himself inside of me
> my brother leon learned from him what i learned not to tell
> cause when my daddy found out then he had his way as well,
> boys,

he took me down as well

i didn't have a language for the pain i suffered through
escaping into marriage, but your past just catches up with you
until i had three children and a ragged family
a desperate urge to keep them from the wolves that got to me,
boys,
wolves that got to me

i wish i could forget that night, the way the cards all fell
the deck was stacked against me and i played my part so well
three days on the party in a drunken revelry
shirley ann said chuck had plans to lure my kids from me

i wrapped the cord around him there, they beat him round the
head
they threw him down the cellar stairs and pulled the cord til he
was dead
courts set me up to take the fall, i went down silently
i'm doing life in prison now for murder first degree
while they got leniency.

grandmother, grandmother, send your prayers to me
protect me and my children, for i love them endlessly
creator, creator, i have come alive
medicine bear woman, doing life at 35, life at 35

i pray
help me to make my amends to those that i have harmed
grant them love and peace so they may understand i'm sorry
help me share my shame and pain so others they might do the
same
and so awaken to themselves and to all peoples of this world
hai hai
hai hai
aho

Yvonne continues to be an inspiration and collaborator with us in this
work.

   In the following pages we first locate ourselves and our relationship
to the struggle for equality and justice for criminalized women before
moving on to discuss the efforts to document the systemic and pervasive

discrimination experienced by criminalized women in Canada. We also outline our work as members of a coalition of social justice and equality-seeking groups that has used the Charter and human rights legislation to hold the Canadian government accountable for its failure to uphold the human rights of women prisoners; and we reflect on the possibilities, challenges, and future of such change-making collaborative work.

Gayle Horii: When I began my life sentence in 1986, I was a forty-two-year-old novice in the fields of criminal law and imprisonment. I first entered the (then) Lakeside Correctional Centre for Women, a schoolhouse-like building on the grounds of the old Oakalla Prison for Men in Burnaby, B.C. Condos now sit on those grounds, and all remnants of the prisons and executions by hangings at Oakalla are gone.

After four months in British Columbia watching young women come and go, I made the difficult decision to transfer three thousand miles away, to Kingston, Ontario, to what was then the only federal prison for women (P4W). I was told that I could have private family visits with my husband and obtain a university education there. Arriving at P4W, I was immediately reclassified to maximum security (max), the policy for lifers at P4W, and told that there was no use in being classified lower since — unlike a man serving a similar sentence — there was no lesser security prison I could be held in. The max level also ensured that I was ineligible for the busing program to the men's Collins Bay Penitentiary, where Queen's University professors conducted courses. Later, in the P4W library, I found the Commissioner's Directive (CD) that stated time served under another jurisdiction could be applied to the six-month waiting period for a Private Family Visit (PFV), but learned that this directive was not applicable to women. I vowed to fight back, albeit with my pen in hand and armed with the Charter of Rights and Freedoms and the non-gendered binders of commissioner's directives from the library.

Yet my first encounters with discrimination in the system were small compared to those suffered by many other women, women much younger and less able to withstand the emotional turmoil that accompanied one's every day at P4W. Many of these women were nearly illiterate, while many others illustrated their severely traumatized lives through the thickness and variations of scarring that covered their arms and their bodies.

I went on to serve two partial terms as chairperson of the Prisoners' Committee and was honoured to become part of an extraordinary time of solidarity and sisterhood among the women imprisoned there. Using group grievances and letters to members of Parliament and to women's organizations, and by reaching out to many others, we tried continuously to raise support to change policy and/or to obtain conditions more equitable to those of federally sentenced men.

In 1993 I was released to a men's halfway house, and in 1994 I reconnected with other federally sentenced women (FSW). Encouraged by Karlene Faith, a long-time prison advocate and criminology professor at Simon Fraser University (she donated the money from a prize awarded for her 1994 book *Unruly Women*), we incorporated the Strength in Sisterhood (SIS) Society. Our mandate is ensured via our constitution, which dictates that the SIS board must comprise a majority of FSW. We advocate for other FSW inside and outside the walls, speak on panels and in colleges and universities, and assist women in their efforts to gain liberty and to remain at liberty. Without the consistent support and mentorship of Kim Pate of the Elizabeth Fry Societies, we would not have been included in the many federal venues in which we have participated over these past ten years. Our voices would have remained as those inside the walls are — silenced. Kim, alone, has ensured that SIS is among the stakeholders at the table, and on behalf of FSW we are able to express their viewpoints and address their needs. Any success we have had is directly attributable to Kim's intrepid assistance.

Kim Pate: Anything Gayle attributes to me is actually a credit to her mentorship. When I joined the Canadian Association of Elizabeth Fry Societies in January 1992, I was a virtual neophyte. Although I had worked for about ten years with marginalized, criminalized, and imprisoned youth and men, and although I also worked (albeit in a voluntary capacity) with a number of women's groups, nothing had prepared me for the reality facing criminalized and imprisoned women. During my early days and weeks with CAEFS, I had the privilege of meeting Gayle and a number of other women in prison who, with patience and perseverance, undertook the task of assisting me to fulfil my personal and CAEFS' organizational mandate. As a working-class service brat, I had learned early about some forms of oppression. Thanks to the determination of many academics, my lived experiences are nuanced by the academic training I received in arts, education, and law. I owe the greatest debt to the many young people, men, and especially the women who have taught me the importance of knowing who I am and what I stand for, and demanded that I never shrink from the challenges that our struggles present. It is thanks to the courage and amazing resiliency and forgiveness of such women that we will realize our collective, inclusive, feminist vision of equality.

Debra Parkes: I consider it a privilege to work alongside these amazing activist women. I have come more recently to this work, having taught constitutional and criminal law at the University of Manitoba for four years while also being on the board of directors of the local Elizabeth Fry Society and the national board of CAEFS. I became deeply concerned about the discriminatory and unjust treatment of criminalized women while researching a law-school paper in 1996 about the Correctional Service of Canada policy and practice of incarcerating women in segregated units inside men's maximum-security prisons. In the course of that research, I had the privilege of interviewing two women imprisoned in men's prisons in Saskatchewan, and also of meeting Kim Pate. The two prisoners amazed me with their resiliency and courage. Kim motivated me to think more deeply and critically about the systemic and multidimensional nature of discrimination against women prisoners, including its relationships to sexism, racism, colonialism, and class oppression. I am also inspired by activist academics such as Angela Davis and Karlene Faith. Their work demonstrates the radical potential of critical, engaged, participatory research and scholarship to support social change movements such as penal abolition.

DOCUMENTING DISCRIMINATION: REPORT AFTER REPORT

Debra: I was a law student when Madam Justice Louise Arbour (1996) released her *Report of the Commission of Inquiry into Certain Events at the Prison for Women in Kingston.* Anyone who has read any of the many reports written over the years documenting the discrimination and deplorable treatment experienced by women prisoners in Canada knows that the women have long endured a system designed and managed for the over 95 percent of the prison population that is men. Women have been neglected as "too few to count" (Adelberg and Currie 1987a) and subjected to stereotypical assumptions about "female criminality" and women's gendered, classed, and racialized roles in society. It is well known that most women who are imprisoned do not pose a significant risk to community safety (Hannah-Moffat and Shaw 2001) — and yet, ironically, due to their small numbers relative to male prisoners, women often serve their time in more secure conditions and with fewer supports, programs, and services than do men.

In her report, Justice Arbour (1996: 200) noted:

Women also served their sentences in harsher conditions than men because of their smaller numbers. They have suffered greater family dislocation, because there are so few options for the imprisonment of women. They have been overclassified, or in any event, they have been detained in a facility that does not correspond to their classification. For the same reasons, they have been offered fewer programs then men.... They have no significant vocational training opportunities.

In the course of her investigation, Justice Arbour (1996: 239) found a culture of disrespect for the rule of law and a long history of unequal treatment of women prisoners characterized by "stereotypical views of women; neglect; outright barbarism and well-meaning paternalism." Among her long list of recommendations, she called for a focus on the release and reintegration of women in custody and concrete action toward that end. In addition to the women-focused recommendations, Justice Arbour called for an end to the practice of long-term confinement in administrative segregation for all prisoners (to be facilitated by a recommendation that segregation be subject to judicial supervision) and the expanded jurisdiction of judges to reduce sentences when there have been rights violations in the conditions of confinement. Almost ten years later, none of her most significant recommendations have been implemented.

It is worth noting that the events leading to the Arbour Report — the strip-searching of eight women prisoners by a male Institutional Emergency Response Team in full riot gear, the subsequent illegal and involuntary transfer of six women to a segregated unit adjacent to a "treatment" unit for men convicted of sexual offences in Kingston Penitentiary, and the further illegal detention in segregation for eight and a half months for two women and nine months for six women — took place less than four years after the release of *Creating Choices*, the ground-breaking report of the Task Force on Federally Sentenced Women (1990). *Creating Choices* called for a new approach to addressing the needs of women prisoners on the basis of research indicating that women were generally "high needs, low risk," as compared to male prisoners. The government was urged to abandon the traditional coercive regime in favour of smaller institutions with independent living units, no perimeter fences, security that was dynamic (that is, increased staffing) rather than static (fences, bars, cameras), and programming led and delivered by the local community. Concretely, the report proposed the closure of the Prison for Women and the construction, in its place, of four regional women's prisons as well as an Aboriginal healing lodge, recommendations that the federal government accepted.[3] The reason that these reports were written will not be forgotten. In each case, they were prompted by the tragic deaths or inhumane treatment of women in prison, events that Gayle remembers all too well.

Gayle: When I was in P4W, slashing was a common occurrence. We did our best to take care of our bleeding sisters rather than watch the guards take them, often by force, to segregation. It was only then that a nurse would be called to look at the wounds and determine their severity. I'm still haunted by the December 3, 1988, suicide of Marlene Moore (whom we knew as "Shaggy") (see Kershaw and Lasovich 1991), as the news spread on the range and the deputy warden (DW) decided that all of the lights should be shut off — as if that would contain the grief that spontaneously erupted. A few of us demanded to see the DW and bargained for the release of the twenty women being held in segregation, knowing that they too would hang themselves as soon as they heard that Shaggy was dead. Her suicide prompted the call by many feminists and women's organizations for a commission of inquiry or task force on federally sentenced women. That Task Force was established in March 1989.

A few weeks following the striking of the Task Force, a young Aboriginal woman at P4W was told that there was no bed for her in a woman's treatment centre and that she would need to seek treatment in a co-ed facility. She had been raped in a co-ed facility a few years before. With no place to go, on March 29, 1989, Pat Bear hung herself from a tree with her new shoelaces. The first meeting of the Task Force occurred a few days later. While the Task Force was beginning its work, Sandy Sayer hung herself from her bars in October 1989. Four months later, on February 27, 1990, Marie Ledeaux hung herself in the basement of the family visiting unit so that her dad could finally take her home to Manitoba. In April 1990, the Task Force produced its report, *Creating Choices.* And on September 15, 1990, while the Canadian government debated the costs of implementing the recommendations contained in the report, Careen Daigneault hung herself. Two months later, on November 16, 1990, Johnny Neudorf (Bear) also hung herself in her cell. Three months after that, on February 4, 1991, Lorna Jones strung herself up.

In two years seven women had taken their own lives rather than exist in P4W or face a release that promised a continuation of the violence, mistreatment, and exploitation that had contributed to their criminalization. Six of these seven young women were Aboriginal women. I repeat their names as I remember their faces so that you can all understand what it actually took to move the Canadian government to act on the recommendations made in *Creating Choices*. And although the barbaric conditions in P4W should have been clearly understood as causal factors that resulted in the suicides of seven women, the cruelties did not end there, and P4W remained open until 2000.

Although the decision to close P4W was heralded when it was announced in 1990, the mostly Aboriginal women left there throughout the 1990s suffered more brutal treatment, along with restrictions on movement and cutbacks to programs. Aboriginal women were confined to a special range that became even worse than segregation, with the final straw being the mysterious destruction of their Grandmother Drum in the women's sweatlodge. That epic event preceded the now infamous "Certain Events at the Prison for Women" in April of 1994 and the airing on the CBC's *Fifth Estate* of a videotape showing naked women kneeling in front of armed and masked men with batons, with the men tearing at the clothing of defenceless women while other women in uniform stood by and watched. It was Kim, as executive director of CAEFS, along with Ron Stewart, the (then) correctional investigator, who refused to cover up the abuses. And since that time, Kim has been a constant light for federally sentenced women at the end of a very long and very dark tunnel.

Kim: The virtual isolation of the mostly Aboriginal women on what was known as "B range" and the lockdown of that unit from September 1993 on — combined with incidents such as the destruction of the Grandmother Drum, the cancellation of private family visits of women with their children, mass punishments, and more — precipitated what have now come to be known as "the April 1994 incidents." Significantly, the CSC, and consequently the media, persist in referring to these times as a "riot," despite the repeated acknowledgements of correctional staff and administrators that the incidents did not meet the CSC definition of a riot. I visited with the women who were locked in their segregation cells — one still fully shackled because she had refused a body cavity search — almost two days after the male IERT stripped them and their cells. Yet, in meetings with the administration, I heard a litany of reasons as to why the women deserved the treatment they had received — such as, the women were lying or perhaps "out of it" when they told me they were strip-searched by men. The CSC boldly asserted that I must have been mistaken. No woman was forced to have body-cavity searches; no women were shackled or otherwise restrained in their locked segregation cells.

It was at that time that I realized it was one thing for the CSC to believe that they could get away with calling the women prisoners liars. It was quite another to realize that they were sufficiently confident of their control of the media and public perception and credibility that they could tell an outside person that she had not seen what she saw. Some have described this as perhaps my epiphany in relation to this work. For me, it was the moment of crystal-clear understanding: if I was going to continue to do this work, I needed to know and commit to never flinching from telling the truth — while recognizing that my legal education and position of employment would not shield me or anybody else from the personal and organizational attacks aimed at those who stand in alliance with the oppressed in order to challenge their oppressors.

After every other avenue had been attempted and failed to achieve adequate results, the eight women, in desperation, authorized the release in 1994 of the videotapes of the degradation they had endured to *The Fifth Estate*. More than a decade later, the abuse and revictimization of these women continue every time the videos are broadcast or viewed. Until the day I die, I will work to ensure that such abusive, tortuous, degrading treatment is prevented and, when we fail in this regard, that it is publicly exposed and redressed.

Despite this reality, everyone recognizes that without the videos, there would not have been an Arbour Commission, another woman would probably have been the director of CAEFS, and the exposure of the CSC's defensive culture of denial and disrespect for the rule of law may have faced few challenges. Debra has highlighted the significance of Justice Arbour's findings and recommendations. We, the women and their allies, applauded the report. In fact, a deputy minister later revealed that for several years running, it was the single most requested document available from the Ministry of the Solicitor General (as it then was). This reality notwithstanding, copies are rare and often difficult to obtain.[4]

GOING TO THE HUMAN RIGHTS COMMISSION

Kim: As the fifth anniversary of the release of the Arbour report approached, CAEFS, frustrated with the lack of implementation of the majority of the recommendations, started to examine the possibilities of proceeding to international forums. CAEFS had by then tried many other approaches, including attempts at partnerships, joint meetings, court cases, and lobbying. Concerned that we might be required to first exhaust all domestic or internal remedies, however, and since the last major human rights initiative on behalf of federally sentenced women (in 1982) predated the 1985 implementation of the section 15 equality provisions of the Charter, we determined that we should try one last domestic tool — a complaint to the Canadian Human Rights Commission on behalf of all women serving federal terms of imprisonment.

So, on March 8, 2001, CAEFS and the Native Women's Association of Canada requested that the CHRC conduct a broad-based systemic review and issue a special report, pursuant to section 61(2) of the Canadian Human Rights Act, regarding the treatment of women serving federal terms of imprisonment. This request was supported by twenty-seven other organizations.[5] The Commission decided to undertake a special report and issue recommendations to government based on its findings, addressing government policies and programs. This took the form of the special report, *Protecting Their Rights* (CHRC 2003).

The basis of the request for a special report from the CHRC was that federally sentenced women face discrimination throughout the criminal (in)justice system. This was, and remains, particularly true of Aboriginal and other racialized women, as well as women with mental and cognitive disabilities. Accordingly, as part of the process of developing our submissions to the Commission, CAEFS consulted with national women's, Aboriginal, and social justice groups. We also commissioned additional research and provided resources for as many groups as possible to make submissions directly to the Commission.

In October 2002 and February and May of 2003, CAEFS sponsored consultations with national women's and equality-seeking justice groups. Thanks to the resources we obtained from Status of Women Canada and the Voluntary Sector Initiative, we were also able to distribute resources to a number of groups to enable them to develop submissions to the Commission. Groups such as Strength in Sisterhood, Womyn4Justice (W4J), Native Women's Association of Canada, the Women's Legal Education and Action Fund (LEAF), the DisAbled Women's Network of Canada (DAWN), the National Association of Women and the Law (NAWL), Amnesty International, the National Council of Women of Canada (NCWC), the Canadian Federation of University Women (CFUW), and several other organizations provided input to the CHRC.

The submissions developed by all of the groups were of such a high quality that we also compiled them for publishing and made them available electronically as a collection. CAEFS' response to a discussion paper issued by the CHRC, as well as our submissions and those of other equality-seeking groups, have been circulated electronically to our membership, coalition partners, and many others nationally and internationally.[6] Hard copies were distributed to each local Elizabeth Fry Society and coalition partner, as well as prison libraries, organized groups, and individual prisoners. Additionally, the annual reports of the correctional investigator, the 2003 auditor general's report, and the Public Accounts Committee response to the CSC's submission regarding the auditor general's report revealed their alignment with our submissions.

Debra: Let me comment on the substantive arguments made to the CHRC in the systemic review process. Given the Commission's mandate to investigate discrimination on the basis of enumerated grounds, coalition members framed their submissions around discrimination on the basis of race, sex, and disability, and on the overlapping and intersecting nature of discrimination experienced by Aboriginal women and women with mental disabilities (Monture-Angus 2002). Key areas of inequality highlighted by coalition members and discussed by the Commission included discrimination in the security classification system (on the basis of race and mental disability), the lack of minimum-security conditions and community release options for women, the construction of maximum-security units within the regional prisons, which amounts to effective segregation, the continued use of male guards on the front lines in women's prisons, and the provision of essentially involuntary mental health treatment through a new regime — euphemistically called the "Intensive Healing Program." The tendency to rely on simple comparisons between federally sentenced men and federally sentenced women was resisted (Calder 2003) even though, for example, the minimum- and maximum-security conditions experienced by men and women reveal significantly more restrictive environments for women, despite the lower risk women tend to present. Clearly, male prisoners are not an advantaged group, and they should not be constructed as such.

In addition, the work of feminists and other equality-seekers for over twenty years demonstrates the importance of adopting a more nuanced, substantive equality analysis. As stated in the LEAF submission, "The danger of using men as the sole comparator group for analyzing the needs and treatment of federally sentenced women, is the reification of the needs and treatment of federally sentenced men as the standard against which all treatment should be measured" (Calder 2003: 4). Coalition members also took care to avoid proceeding on the assumption, wittingly or unwittingly, that "women's unique needs" could ever be addressed adequately in a prison environment, recognizing that some earlier efforts at "feminist prison reform" had led to unintended consequences (Hannah-Moffat

2001; see also chapters 9 and 10 here).

Therefore, while the legal basis on which the Human Rights Commission had jurisdiction to issue its report was the statutory obligation of the federal government to provide "correctional services" in a non-discriminatory manner (CHRC 2003:13), coalition members resisted the idea that prison was an inevitable government "service." Instead, the focus was on the need for effective remedies to redress known discrimination, including the allocation of resources to prevent and redress the overrepresentation of Aboriginal women in prison and the immediate return of incarcerated women to their communities, with adequate supports. The coalition made efforts to incorporate an analysis that would not lend legitimacy to the current structure (that is, simply reforming it would not be enough), and also to include strong calls for decarceration strategies, community programming, and supports for women (not to take for granted that programming would take place in the prison rather than in the community). For example, the DisAbled Women's Network argued that attempts to make institutional mental health treatment and programming responsive to the needs of women did not meet the government's substantive equality obligations to prisoners with mental disabilities; instead the organization advocated for community-based programming and supports (Peters 2003).

On the issue of discrimination on the basis of race, the tragic — and growing — overrepresentation of Aboriginal women in the criminal justice system, and particularly in prisons (CHRC 2003: 5, 28), is well known. On the one hand, advocates of change tend to cite the overrepresentation numbers and expect them to speak for themselves. On the other hand, the Correctional Service acknowledges the reality of overrepresentation yet increasingly seems to treat it as an intractable or inevitable problem that must be addressed with specialized programming, more secure environments, and token cultural activities for Aboriginal prisoners. Patricia Monture-Angus, a Mohawk woman, lawyer, academic, and member of the Task Force and the recent Human Rights coalition, has called overrepresentation merely the "first layer of discrimination" (Monture-Angus 2002).

In its submissions to the Commission the coalition made concerted attempts to delve underneath the numbers, to highlight the how and why of overrepresentation. One of the challenges of doing so is the reality that human rights law does not expressly acknowledge colonialism — much less the gendered nature of colonialism — as a form of discrimination (Monture-Angus 2002: 5). In light of this limitation, and in an effort to focus on the "degree to which repeated attempts to remedy the discrimination against federal prisoners has been [un]successful," Monture-Angus made the provocative and challenging argument that the federal government is in a fiduciary relationship with prisoners (in light of the exercise of power and corresponding vulnerability to that exercise in the jailer-prisoner relationship), and owes particular fiduciary duties to Aboriginal prisoners (Monture-Angus 2002: 43–46; McIvor and Johnson 2003; MacDonald 2003). We legal academics and lawyers need to do more of this kind of innovative thinking and refashioning of legal doctrines to address social justice ends.

On the topic of innovative legal arguments, I am reminded of the words of Sharon McIvor, one of the founders of NWAC, reflecting on the resistance with which substantive equality arguments were met: "In those early cases, we had to get up our courage just to make arguments that are now established principles in equality law. The first judges thought we were irrational, while today's judges use our language in their equality rights judgments" (cited in Lugtig and Parkes 2002: 17).

I also want to comment on the process of collaboration and formulating arguments in a context such as this one. That women should be involved actively in devising and pursuing legal and other strategies to redress the discrimination that they themselves have experienced is a central tenet of much feminist organizing and theory. Yet it is often difficult to make this happen in practice, particularly with women who are as marginalized as prisoners and former prisoners.[7] Sometimes, despite a professed commitment to that principle, the involvement of women with lived experience is little more than a token gesture or afterthought. To do more requires significant resources and a concerted effort to let the *real* experts — the women with lived experience (Faith and Pate 2000: 144) — speak and be heard throughout a process that can be dominated by lawyers or other educated activists and advocates.

In addition to this sort of involvement being vital to the legitimacy of the process, it can also assist in creating a culture of resistance and rights-claiming among the women inside. Regrettably, however, Corrections sees involving prisoners and former prisoners (not surprisingly) as problematic for the security of institutions, but perhaps more fundamentally, because it is inconsistent with the correctional goal of "responsibilizing" women. In the correctional view, a woman is not taking responsibility for her criminal behaviour if she is filing grievances or human rights complaints, resisting arbitrary or punitive exercises of power, or otherwise claiming her rights.

Gayle: In fact, participating in these activities can be used to assess a prisoner's "institutional adjustment" as poor, a negative connotation that will appear on any assessment-for-release decision. The culture of prisons as paramilitary institutions is one of control — not one of assisting, enhancing, or rewarding the critical thinking ability of prisoners. Women prisoners who want to speak of or write about the conditions inside prison walls require protection from CSC's coercive practices. One strategy is to bring guest lecturers from the community into prison, which could assist greatly in furthering the in-reach work being done to nurture confidence in the women inside, and to remind them that they are indeed part of the community of women.

My experiences with personal efforts to put into effect the application of the law and, in particular, the inherent rights of women for fair treatment promised under the Charter were not particularly productive. Throughout my seven-year period of incarceration, I filed numerous prisoner complaints and grievances for myself and on behalf of other women. This process was satisfying only in that it enabled comment when we believed our rights were violated. I was committed to following the process through to the end, without positive expectations of the outcome. I did this in order to compile a written record of the continuing and myriad abuses that occur within prison walls and, in this way, believed I was doing everything possible to deal in a positive manner with every matter that affected my and other women's waking existence.

Debra: The opposition and barriers experienced by women like Gayle who claim their rights in prison calls to mind the need for those of us with legal education to engage in "rebellious lawyering" with and on behalf of poor and otherwise disenfranchised individuals and groups. Rebellious lawyering has been defined as "a non-hierarchical relationship between lawyer and client; a true collaboration between them in identifying and addressing problems and solutions; a bipolar educational experience between lawyer and client and an exploration of non-legal collective action to fight oppression" (Diamond 2000: 107). U.S. rights lawyer Jessica Feierman suggests that such an approach holds particular promise in the prison context because of the degree to which prisoners are silenced and cut off from public view in a manner that perpetuates myths about crime and prisoners (Feierman 2004: 269–71). Prisoners are also cut off from their natural allies — other social justice groups such as anti-poverty groups, women's groups, and disability rights groups. Lawyers and established community organizations can act as resources to prisoners and former prisoners, as well as advocate for funding to prisoner organizations such as SIS and W4J.

THE CHRC REPORT AND ITS AFTERMATH

Kim: The CHRC report — released on January 28, 2004 — made nineteen recommendations for far-reaching changes with respect to the manner in which the Correctional Service of Canada might work to alleviate the systemic discrimination experienced by women serving federal sentences. Throughout the report, the Commission points to the tragic consequences that result from the defective manner in which women are initially assessed (as minimum, medium, or maximum security). Aboriginal women and women with mental disabilities are especially overclassified, often kept in segregated, isolated living conditions. Fewer women classified as maximum-security prisoners would mean that more women could be reintegrated into the community in a much shorter time. Therefore, CAEFS continues to work to urge the minister of public safety and emergency preparedness to act to introduce a new classification system as well as the decarceration strategies that such a new approach to assessing and classifying women would necessitate. CAEFS strongly supports the proposal for independent monitoring and accountability mechanisms found in the CHRC report. The call for judicial oversight reiterates the recommendations of Justice Arbour. In 1996, Justice Arbour reported on the failure of the CSC to follow the law and its own policies in dealing with women prisoners. Now, more than ever, we see that many people recognize the vital need for an independent body to monitor CSC's adherence to principles of justice, fairness, and the rule of law.

In February 2005, we received the final version of CSC's response to the report of the Canadian Human Rights Commission. Suffice it to say that the entire coalition was disappointed — albeit not surprised — by that response. As we have unfortunately experienced far too many times, the response was primarily symbolic and inadequate.

What the coalition was not prepared for, however, was the alarming abdication of its role by the Canadian Human Rights Commission. CAEFS, NWAC, and SIS publicly expressed our collective shock in relation to the response of the CHRC to the non-response of the Correctional Service of Canada to their recommendations with respect to the urgent remedial action required to address the systemic discrimination experienced by women prisoners in Canada. As disability and other groups have also experienced of late, the CHRC seems to be more interested in appeasing the government than in fulfilling its own mandate to protect Canadians from the discriminatory treatment of human rights violations.

When the report was released, we believed that the Commission clearly understood the urgency of the need to address the human rights violations experienced by women prisoners. Nobody from the Commission has visited the women's prisons since it released its report publicly in January 2004. Instead, its members appear to have relied upon what the Correctional Service of Canada says its plans to do, even where CSC's response to the CHRC's recommendation for immediate action received a response that action would commence within three years of the publication of the recommendations. The coalition believes that there have already been enough reports and enough inaction on the part of Corrections to explain why that body's commitment may be considered somewhat suspect, and why the working group was so insistent that the Commission fulfil its monitoring function to ensure that action flows from its review.

Gayle: Canada has in fact learned how to rely upon the methods that its own agents employ in ignoring recommendations made by official examiners of the treatment of federally sentenced women. The CHRC's nineteen recommendations that flowed from the systemic review now join a remarkable number of other recommendations made since the inception of women's prisons in Canada. The majority of recommendations made by previous commissions, parliamentary committees, and task forces have been nullified, often simply by a changing of the guard — the guaranteed-to-work "fallback" strategy of the CSC. This is possible because the CSC relies upon the knowledge that there will be little pressure from government to deal with any recommendations in a forthright and timely manner. In addition, the CSC's $1.5 billion (or more) budget includes funds for public relations managers, whose job it is to spin the harsh realities of prison conditions as being safe environments that are professionally staffed. For example, who knew that there had already been many regular lockdowns of federal prisons for women? In fact, they are so common that the women do not tend to report them, even to Kim. She recently raised the alert when women from three different prisons called her the same weekend to report that they were either in, or emerging from, institutional lockdowns. Who read about the suicide of a woman in the Structured Living Environment in the Grand Valley prison on December 20, 2003 — the "safe" environment said to be professionally staffed "24-7"?

Penal authorities simply co-opt human rights language and utilize it for their own purposes to further obstruct the ability of those on the outside to understand exactly what is going on inside the walls. In fact, they obstruct the course of justice, utilizing the language of the Charter and the Human Rights Act to assuage those outside the circle of knowing, to assure everyone of their humane treatment of prisoners and their respect for the rights of women — all the while increasing their budgets and (through increasing "correctional programming") their staff.

DEVELOPING, MAINTAINING, AND BROADENING COALITIONS

Kim: Despite our deep concern about the lack of implementation of the CHRC's recommendations, we have been encouraged by some of the ways that the analyses in the coalition's submissions to the CHRC have proven useful for human rights advocacy by other vulnerable populations, not only those who have been criminalized. For instance, anti-poverty and disability rights movements, as well as a number of racialized groups, have requested and been granted authority to quote extensively and otherwise utilize the arguments and references contained in the submissions of CAEFS and the other equality-seeking groups.

In addition, Amnesty International and Human Rights Watch have indicated a keen interest in participating in the next stage of our international efforts to ensure human rights protections for criminalized women and girls in Canada. Groups in Australia, Britain and other countries in the European Union, Africa, India, and the United States are using our work and the report of the Commission to foster support for similar processes that are being initiated in their international venues. For example, we are working with groups in Australia that are documenting the human rights abuses of women prisoners in Australian states. We also established a link with members of the Australian Human Rights and Equal Opportunity Commission and state anti-discrimination bodies. Our countries have a shared genocidal reality of the tragic and outrageous colonial legacy for Aboriginal women and a shared need to call our governments to account and to redress the systemic injustice and discrimination felt most acutely by Aboriginal women who have been criminalized.

As a further result of our domestic initiatives, CAEFS was invited by international feminist, anti-racist, and human rights NGOs to provide input to their respective submissions to the United Nations Committee for the Elimination of Discrimination Against Women and the Special Rapporteur on Contemporary Forms of Racism, Racial Discrimination, Xenophobia, and Related Intolerance of the UN Commission on Human Rights. As our international profile has grown, so too has our capacity to influence the agenda of policy-makers and politicians. Indeed, the various reports issued all reveal the impact of our submissions in respect of the systemic review by the CHRC.

Several other issues and initiatives have also arisen as a result of our initiation and involvement in the CHRC process. For example, CAEFS has been invited to participate in discussions with respect to restorative justice and the definition of and orientation of new Law Commission projects; discussions regarding the sexual exploitation of children and youth, trafficking of women and girls, and their relationship to women's equality; and several interorganizational and community meetings, consultations, and joint planning initiatives, particularly with regard to child protection, juvenile justice, decarceration strategies, anti-regressive law and order initiatives, immigration, pay equity, violence against women as a matter for the federal government, women's equality as an issue of human rights, and international trade and development. The overall results of the process of developing CHRC submissions point to the need and obligation of the Canadian government to continue to support such initiatives from the independent women's movement — and especially from equality-seeking organizations. The success of this process clearly demonstrated our capacity to mobilize and unify disparate branches of the movement to develop a collective effort to address fundamental issues of discrimination on the basis of sex, race, and disability.

Gayle: The filing of internal complaints, grievances, and CHR complaints are simply base-building steps. That being said, it is astounding to see how the 2001 CHR complaint process "morphed" into a social movement. It grew international arms at Kim's helm. Kim single-handedly utilized this process to motivate the growth of a massive coalition working now toward a global vision of human rights work. Through her own abilities to collaborate via international and professional organizations, Kim has created a network of workers, of people who will continue to put to use the compilation of documents and testimonials on the discrimination suffered by a few hundred women prisoners in Canada. In this light, all of the work and all of the efforts put into this project will continue to assist hundreds of women in their efforts to alleviate the discriminatory treatment that they suffer, whether it be at the hands of a bureaucracy, a government, a spiritual body, or a professional body.

Debra: As part of a broader, multifaceted advocacy agenda, CAEFS and NWAC continue to work in coalition to pursue other legal strategies to challenge, including at the pre-conviction stage, the criminalization of Aboriginal women and their strategies of resistance. For example, in March 2005, the two groups successfully sought intervenor status in a Manitoba case in which an Aboriginal woman was charged with manslaughter (the charge had recently been reduced from second-degree murder) (McIntyre 2005: A3). CAEFS and NWAC decided to intervene in an application for a stay of proceedings on the basis of systemic discrimination in the policing and prosecution of this case, amounting to an abuse of process.

In a related endeavour, CAEFS, NWAC, and SIS have identified a need to challenge the increasing labelling by Corrections of certain women — most of them Aboriginal — as "difficult to manage" and "dangerous." Such labels are often applied during the women's terms of incarceration due to failures of "institutional adjustment," rather than pre-existing "dangerousness." To that end, CAEFS, working with NWAC and SIS, has successfully sought funding to enhance existing supports and establish in-reach support work (by former prisoner peer advocates and Aboriginal women in the community) with individual women whom Corrections has characterized as the most dangerous and difficult to manage. This project, aptly named "Human Rights in Action," builds on the advocacy done with and on behalf of other women characterized as dangerous, most notably the ultimately successful effort to have overturned the "dangerous offender" designation applied to Lisa Neve, a young Aboriginal woman, in Alberta (Neve and Pate 2005). It is also evidence of a concerted, collaborative effort to change the status quo of human rights *inaction* and failure to implement the myriad recommendations made in various reports. When women's human rights are really *in action*, women will be claiming those rights and will be moving from prison into the community, with the social and material supports to which they are entitled.

In the recent Supreme Court of Canada decision declaring unconstitutional the federal ban on prisoner voting (*Sauvé* v. *Canada* 2002), Chief Justice Beverley McLachlin stated that prisoners are not "temporary outcasts from our system of rights and democracy" (para. 40). Yet many prisoners are either unaware of the rights they have or have no effective means of enforcing them. As Justice Arbour (1996: 181) commented darkly in her 1996 report, in prisons "the Rule of Law is absent, although rules are everywhere." CAEFS and its coalition partners have prioritized strategies that raise awareness among prisoners (as well as correctional staff) about the rights of prisoners and the legal limits on correctional power, while amplifying the prisoners' own voices and assisting to equip them and other supportive community members to advocate along with them.

RIGHTS AND REMEDIES: REACHING BEHIND PRISON WALLS

Kim: While we are pleased with the content of the Commission's report, the response of the Correctional Service of Canada was unfortunately another link in the chain of inability or unwillingness to admit, evaluate, or address the issues outlined. As we have all seen in far too many cases in the past, their response is once again that they plan to study the recommendations and report further in the next few years.

At this stage, having exhausted all internal remedies, we are now looking forward to the opportunity to once again present material to Madam Justice Arbour, but this time in her new capacity as the United Nations High Commissioner on Human Rights. The work we are doing with our international partners to prepare for our ventures at the United Nations has been progressing very well. Consequently, in addition to continuing to work in coalition with our international sisters, we have also continued to partner with NWAC to follow up the recommendations of the Canadian Human Rights Commission.

The law must not merely persist as a paper tiger. Feminist lawyers and academics must assist us in reaching behind prison walls. How else can we expect those locked away from public view to experience the protection and promotion of their human rights?

Gayle: In conclusion, I believe it is important to utilize whatever processes exist to move forward — with the necessary caveats that none of them alone will result in a change of bureaucratic behaviour, and that an effective enforcement of rights and remedies is required. As Justice Arbour observed almost ten years ago, prisons will continue to be lawless environments if there is no effective judicial oversight to realize and implement the promises of the Charter. Laws must be changed. And, due to the immense power and wealth backing this particular elitist bureaucracy, it is only with a collaborative feminist effort that the possibility of successful legal changes and challenges can be fulfilled. If the rights of criminalized women can be served, all human rights will be raised.

NOTES

1.   The conference, "Women's Rights & Freedoms: 20 years (In) Equality," was hosted by the National Association of Women and the Law and the West Coast chapter of the Women's Legal Education and Action Fund.

2.   Yvonne Johnson co-wrote the lyrics of "land of milk and honey" with Eliza Gilkyson

(Red House Records, St. Paul, Minn., 2004).

3. Kelly Hannah-Moffat (2001) discusses the frustration experienced by key Task Force participants, such as the Canadian Association of Elizabeth Fry Societies, at the degree to which the implementation process was directed and controlled by the Correctional Service of Canada, with little significant community involvement. Patricia Monture-Angus (2000) further argues that the Healing Lodge has become a prison, rather than the place of healing envisioned by the Aboriginal women on the Task Force.

4. The Ministry only distributed the initial print run of the Arbour report and has never reprinted it. In addition, it apparently disappeared from the CSC website at one time, but was eventually reinstated. The report is also available via Professor Michael Jackson's web site <www.justicebehindthewalls.net>. (Accessed January 13, 2006.)

5. Including, among others, Amnesty International, Canadian Bar Association, Canadian Federation of University Women, DisAbled Women's Network of Canada, Women's Legal Education and Action Fund, National Association of Women and the Law, National Council of Women of Canada, Human Rights Watch, Strength in Sisterhood, Women 4 Justice, Joint Effort, West Coast Prison Justice Society, National Association of Friendship Centres, Assembly of First Nations, Metis National Council of Women, National Organization of Immigrant and Visible Minority Women of Canada, Sisters Inside, and Victoria Community Legal Centres.

6. All of these submissions are available on CAEFS' website <http://www.elizabethfry. ca>. (Accessed January 13, 2006.)

7. The Task Force on Federally Sentenced Women also made this commitment — and many prisoners and former prisoners did speak out in that process. However, the Task Force had substantial government resources behind it. Most advocacy efforts, such as human rights complaints or court cases, are made *against* the government and, therefore, usually with very few resources to involve those with lived experience.

14. MAKING CHANGE IN NEO-LIBERAL TIMES

Laureen Snider

Making change in neo-liberal societies is not difficult. The air fairly bristles with "reform chatter" as entrepreneurs keen on privatizing chunks of criminal justice jostle with experts from ever-widening groups of disciplines, subdisciplines, and specialties eager to offer themselves as consultants and reap lucrative fees. What *is* difficult is making change that matters to disempowered, marginalized people, change that provides tools they can use to lessen oppression, challenge repression, and change the relations of power.

Many critics have argued that the reliance by some feminists on criminal law and institutions of criminal justice is misguided — bad policy, bad praxis, a theoretical and intellectual dead end (Snider 1994, 1998; Smart 1989, 1995; Comack 1993; Razack 1991). Criminal law individualizes and disempowers those it is supposed to help — as illustrated by the epidemic of countercharges against women defending themselves against violent partners, or contempt of court charges against women who refuse to testify against their partners. Widespread zero tolerance provisions, inserted into domestic violence statutes to stop state officials from ignoring women's pleas for help (or so we thought) have intensified state surveillance over women already victimized by violence, racism, and poverty. They have forced progressive feminist movements into alliances with neo-conservative groups lobbying for more state coercion. And they have become tools to incarcerate ever increasing numbers of (primarily) poor, young Aboriginal and Black men (Comack and Balfour 2004).

These are not the only problems in a reliance on criminal justice "remedies." The criminal justice system in the modern democratic state is structurally ill equipped to deliver empowerment or amelioration (Snider 1994). Even goals of ameliorative policies such as restorative justice take second place to the priorities of security and are thus only applied to offenders classified as low risk. Criminal justice does not have a Janus-like quality, a legitimating, positive or life-affirming mission to balance its repressive side. The official role of institutions of criminal justice is to discipline those designated as lawbreakers, to control them legally and equally, regardless of race, class, or gender. This means that institutions of criminal justice are not like other state institutions — schools, for example, are charged with educating, hospitals with healing — because they are charged only with delivering "equal-opportunity" social control. The favoured consciousness-raising strategy of progressive groups — calling institutions to account for not delivering on their official promises — has limited potential here. Police, prisons, and courts cannot be named, blamed, or shamed for failing to empower women or failing to provide them with more life-affirming choices. They can only be castigated for failing to punish women and men equally. (Note: the comparator group, the flip side of the binary, is always man.)

Lobbying for equal-opportunity repression, not a progressive goal under any circumstances, is particularly problematic when evidence indicates (Hannah-Moffat 2002; Rafter 1985a; Zedner 1998) that when some differences between male and female punishment were gender-sensitive, they worked to the advantage of (some) women and girls.[1] Moreover, in a neo-liberal, punishment-obsessed culture, any evidence of "leniency" will instantly be seized by sensationalistic media eager both to foment and capitalize on anti-feminist backlash. And the policy lesson taken from evidence of male-female difference will always be interpreted as a call to punish women more, not to equalize by punishing men *less*. This and similar iatrogenic consequences of feminist-inspired initiatives have led many of us to argue that, instead of focusing on obtaining punishment and revenge for the very real injuries that women suffer at the hands of men, feminists should concentrate on changing the social conditions that make women and children easy and legitimate targets of male rage. This means spending more time and effort on struggles to attain equal resources for women and children, working for more public services, for universal state-subsidized child care, and for income equality. The ultimate goal must be to establish social and cultural conditions that create and sustain less desperate populations — of men, women, and children — for only by doing this can we build less violent societies (Snider 1998).

The purpose of this chapter is to advance that goal by using the lessons of the past as guidelines for the knowledge work, resistance, and praxis of the future. The discussion is organized around two broad questions. First, is it possible to make significant ameliorative change in neo-liberal times? At the present time progressive groups are forced to spend inordinate amounts of energy and money on defensive battles just to prevent powerful neo-liberal and neo-conservative forces from reversing feminist victories won decades earlier on everything from abortion rights to equal pay for work of equal value. Second, what about institutions of criminal justice? Should strategies using criminal law be completely abandoned, or are there ways of maximizing the symbolic impact of criminalization while minimizing its inhuman consequences? The chapter begins by incorporating a factor that for the most part has gone unnoticed in feminist discussions: the pivotal role of knowledge claims. Understanding how change is forged requires, first and foremost, dissecting the role of experts, of expertise, and of authorized knowers and knowledge claims. It is essential to examine the impact and results of feminist and non-feminist claims that have constituted woman as victim and as offender. Only by analyzing how feminist knowledge claims and expertise become part of the knowledge-power-change nexus is there any hope (there is never any guarantee) of fashioning research and praxis with truly counterhegemonic potential.

GAINING GROUND:
RECONSTITUTING WOMAN AS OFFENDER AND VICTIM

The first and most obvious lesson of the reform efforts of the past is that making change is a complex and complicated activity. The belief that we can either control or predict the future is a modernist dream.[2] Trying to control change is an impossible task because we are describing in static terms an evermoving, constantly reconstituted social reality (Foucault 1977, 1978b). Our knowledge claims transform the objects we are writing about. This does not happen in ways that we can predict, or have consequences we necessarily desire. Feminist and non-feminist research, evaluations, and critiques continuously inspire new belief systems, policy initiatives, and procedural reforms, which constitute new and different social and cultural situations out of which come the next set of evaluations and changes, simultaneously responding to and constituting yet another distinct set of conditions. Ad infinitum.

To interrogate the knowledge/power equation, then, we must ask how feminist knowledge has been fed back into Canadian society. This means treating knowledge produced by feminist and non-feminist criminologies as productive and constitutive, as an essential component of changes in the conception of woman as victim and as offender, and in the policies devised to simultaneously control and assist her. Our claims as authorized knowers and our actions as reformers have become integral parts of a complex process that has transformed the entire landscape of criminal justice, from the belief systems of police officers to black letter law. Most crucially, they have transformed and reconstituted the subject of feminist reform efforts: the battered wife, the rape victim, the prostitute, the criminalized and incarcerated woman. Thanks to feminist "discoveries" about her, she has become a different kind of subject than she was in 1955 (Heidensohn 1994; Snider 2003).

However, to say that feminist knowledge claims are an important part of the power/knowledge nexus, and that we cannot understand the process of change without looking at "our" part in it, is not to say that feminist claims were automatically integrated into state policy. Far from it. To understand the reception of knowledge claims, how they are interpreted, received, and publicized, we must shift analytical focus from knowledge produced to knowledge heard. Knowledge claims are bids to power, bids that work to the benefit of some parties and the detriment of others. Those with power to set institutional agendas — players with superior economic, political, social, and moral capital — are therefore able to influence which/whose claims are heard and listened to. There are two essential differences between claims that get written up in *Globe and Mail* editorials and inserted into the briefing notes of cabinet ministers, and those that languish on life-support in intensive-care units (a.k.a. Sociology and Women's Studies departments). Knowledge claims with "legs" are those that resonate with dominant cultural agendas (Garland 2001), and those that promise economic and/or political rewards to groups that matter. Most critical feminist claims demand a redistribution of income, power, prestige, and benefits from the most powerful groups in the society to the least. It is hardly surprising that much more work — more research, more activism, and time — is required to get these claims heard. And if getting an audience for critical claims is difficult, getting them translated into workable and ameliorative policies is even tougher.

As suggested in Elizabeth Comack's chapter 1, the goals of second-wave feminist criminology were to study the forces that maintained female inequality, and to change them. The defective, inferior woman constituted by nineteenth-century criminologists was revealed as a product of the patriarchal lenses of the "scientists" who "discovered" her (Lombroso and Ferrero 1895; Goring 1913; Pollak 1950; Hooton 1939). Early feminist studies replaced these gender-biased views and knowledge claims with ours (Smart 1976; Morris 1987; Bertrand 1969). Gender bias and misogyny were not restricted to positivist criminology, or to the nineteenth century: 1970s labelling and "new criminology" perspectives depicted rebellious boys as heroes resisting the yoke of capitalism and conformity while rebellious girls, if mentioned at all, were either promiscuous copycats or victims of their hormones and pathologies

(Becker 1967; Taylor, Walton, and Young 1973).

The resulting feminist criminologies — liberal, radical, and socialist — were critiqued by the next generation of feminist knowers (Daly and Chesney-Lind 1988), and in many cases by the original authors as well. Feminist knowledge claims of the 1980s were castigated for failing to take differences between women into account. By attempting to speak "truth" in the name of *all* women, researchers inadvertently privileged the perspectives of the white, upper-middle-class, educated woman. Poststructuralist/postmodern perspectives today incorporate race, class, sexual orientation, and other differences between women and men into their accounts (Smart 1995; Bosworth 1999; Worrall 1990, 2002).

In the 1970s and 1980s, feminist work attracted considerable public attention. Patriarchal and discriminatory practices in every profession and occupation were unearthed and publicized. Components of feminist arguments migrated from position papers and articles in obscure journals into people's heads, belief systems, and institutions. Overt gender bias gradually became unfashionable. In this process, science and scientific expertise came under attack. Feminists (and environmentalists and other critics) deconstructed the expert, as scientific studies in a number of arenas were shown to be wrong. The cumulative effect of these knowledge claims was to destabilize expertise. Outsiders (that is, the great majority who are not credentialed as scientific "experts"), saw that expertise is fallible. Scientists see the world and interpret their experiments through culturally formed prejudices and biases, which often include male-gendered glasses. Equally credible experts disagree. "Scientific knowledge," once considered unchallengeable, was revealed as a human — and largely male — creation. Through destabilizing expertise, the *fallible expert* was constituted. In criminology, questioning the mainly male "experts" meant showing that the emperors of science had no clothes. One important effect was to open the door for those seen as victims and offenders, equipping them with evidence and language to resist scientific knowledge/power claims about their lives, their motivation, their realities (Snider 2003).

A second and more direct result of feminist research was the constitution of *woman as victim*. Quantitative and qualitative research in the 1970s and 1980s revealed that women were regularly beaten and abused by their male partners, and harassed or assaulted by males in positions of power over them, by employers, brothers, and fathers (MacKinnon 1987; Marsh, Geist, and Caplan 1982; Matthews 1994; Stanko 1990). Police were unlikely to respond when called for help because they classified such calls as domestic disputes, private issues best settled between the couple — which meant, by the male partner. In police subcultures husbands were seen as having the right and duty to control their wives. "Everyone knew" a wife was emotional, often unreasonable, nagging her man until he (understandably) lost control. As long as male discipline did not go "too far," such practices were tacitly accepted (Dobash and Dobash 1979). This research evidence persuaded many feminists that zero tolerance provisions were the only way to make police and courts take "wife-battering" (as it was then called) seriously.

Feminist research on sexual assault followed a similar trajectory. It showed that rape was much more common than was previously thought, and that women who reported rape were either not believed, or were blamed for failing to prevent it (Brownmiller 1975). If charges were laid, victims were forced to endure nothing less than a second assault in court — and beyond it in the court of media-driven public opinion. As Carol Smart (1989) pointed out, the rape trial became a "pornographic vignette" in which victims were forced to relive the attack to establish their own credibility. Feminist researchers interpreted sexual assault as an important mechanism of patriarchal dominance. Well-founded fears of rape kept women docile, "in their place," under male control. Women ultimately, always, bore the blame, the shame, and the baby. To change this situation, feminist claims-makers lobbied for laws that replaced rape statutes with "sexual assault" laws emphasizing the violent nature of the act, and for new laws of evidence to lessen victim trauma on the stand and increase chances of convictions (Ruebsaat 1985; Snider 1985; Mohr and Roberts 1994).

Women serving time in reformatories, jails, and prisons — formerly depicted by Lombroso as "worse than any man," as defective and therefore in need of treatment and/or containment (Adelberg and Currie 1993) — were reconstituted as needy and victimized. Second-wave feminist research highlighted differences between male and female prisoners. The female prisoner became "the woman in trouble" (Comack 1996), less violent, less dangerous, a woman deserving "help" rather than punishment. The violence women did commit was more likely to be familial and defensive, not aggressive and stranger-oriented. Female prisoners had different demographic characteristics: they were more likely to have suffered physical and sexual abuse (especially the latter), to be custodial parents, and to come from an ethnic/racial minority — Aboriginal in Canada, Australia, and New Zealand, Black or Hispanic in the United States, Caribbean/Black or Asian in Britain (Carcach and Grant 2000, 1999; Finn et al. 1999; Canadian Centre for Justice Statistics 1997, 2000;

Bureau of Justice Statistics 2000; British Home Office 1999). Despite this, fewer programs were offered to female prisoners, who were incarcerated for acts overlooked or celebrated in males, such as sexual "promiscuity," and kept inside longer and at higher security levels than their offender profile would dictate (Carlen 1983, 1988; Chesney-Lind 1981, 1987, 1988a; Hannah-Moffat 2002).

The most significant and important result of such feminist claims has been the constitution of a new subject, a female offender who "knows" at some level of her identity that women are victimized by men, and that this is socially and legally censured. She also "knows" that experts who diagnose and proclaim the "truth" of female prisoners make mistakes. Thus, we see the emergence of the prisoner "with attitude," the woman who enters prison equipped with new tools of resistance. This subject draws from this culturally available knowledge store to develop strategies of resistance and to maintain less censured individual selves and identities (Bosworth 1999; Worrall 1990).

The woman victimized by physical or sexual assault occupies a different discursive space than the criminalized woman, though she may be the same person.[3] Knowledge claims have constituted her, at least in the Western world, as the Believable Victim. The female victim of domestic or sexual assault is today seen as deserving assistance from the state, action from the police, and accountability and revenge from the criminal justice system. Expectations about what criminal law can accomplish have been raised, as has consciousness. Though research documenting this is hard to come by, popular culture and survivor reports indicate that women today are less likely to blame themselves if they are physically or sexually attacked. Middle-class and working-class women are more likely to have the resources — psychological, political, and economic — to escape violent partners and demand redress for their victimization. Upper-middle-class women have benefited from feminist efforts to compel the state to take attacks on women seriously.

If the criminal justice system is called in, however, all women lose control of the process. Decisions about how the attack should be treated and what should happen to the offender are out of a woman's hands. She becomes "the complainant," and is henceforth a legal category, a statistic, a good or bad witness, a "case" to be processed in the most "efficient" manner (see Comack and Peter forthcoming). For the institutions and actors of law and criminal justice, only certain victims are deserving; they distinguish between the good victim and all others. The faithful wife, the good mother, the gainfully employed, and the teenager living with

parents — in general, women who are acting out conventional patriarchal scripts — fall into the "good victim" category. The single mother
on welfare, the Aboriginal woman on a reserve, the runaway street kid,
the prostitute — women without the moral, social, and economic capital
to force criminal justice to take them seriously — are relegated to the
"other" category. This woman becomes the subject who is, literally and
figuratively, hard to believe.

One caveat: it is ontologically and epistemologically impossible to
find linear cause and effect links between knowledge claims, feminist or
otherwise, and changes in cultural climate, law, and policy. Cause and
effect is complex and overdetermined, an intricate and massive series of
feedback spirals and loops as factors constitute each other. Nor is this
process conspiratorial, directed by all-knowing, all-powerful classes or
groups. Knowledge claims and dominant discourse seep into individual
consciousness and personalities to different degrees and in different ways.
The argument, rather, is that the common-sense beliefs of Canadian society about victimized and criminalized women have changed. Female
offenders and victims increasingly make their own claims, adapting cultural resources (knowledge claims and morality tales) to their individual
or collective advantage.

Overall, the knowledge that women in the past have been victimized by men in every dominant institution — family, school, church,
and workplace — is now widespread. The very success of the feminist
movement in getting women's complaints taken seriously is a major factor
generating resistance, in the form of counterclaims, countercharges, and
backlash. This "push-back" has also become part of the feedback loop.

LOSING GROUND: NEO-LIBERAL REALITIES

Many women today are worse off materially than they were thirty years
ago. Welfare and (un)employment benefits are harder to obtain and retain,
education and day care are more expensive and increasingly unavailable.
Those in the bottom third of the income pyramid face more intrusive
surveillance and greater demonization if they are perceived as stepping
out of line. In neo-liberal societies, those unable or unwilling to meet
the stepped-up demands of neo-liberal societies, the "flawed consumers"
(Bauman 1997), are constituted as "risky subjects," feckless inadequates
who must be forcibly "responsibilized" or punished, preferably both. The
failures of feminist change-making efforts must be located in the context
of the dismantling of the Keynesian welfare state and the allied rise of
anti-feminist backlash.

The Gendered Impact of Dismantling the Welfare State
Canada, with its export and resource-based economy, has always been particularly vulnerable to global economic conditions (Fudge and Cossman
2002: 13). In the 1970s mounting inflation, government deficits, and
intensified global competition, spurred by new technologies that freed
capital from the geographic constraints of the nation-state, undermined
the economic, political, and intellectual viability of the Canadian welfare
state. The transformation in government personnel, thought, policy, and
rhetoric was quick and profound (Cohen 1997). Priorities such as fighting
unemployment, inflation, and poverty disappeared. Cutting government
deficits, freeing business from the "yoke" of government, tax cuts, and
privatization became the new priorities. With the acceptance of doctrines
proclaiming markets as the only legitimate regulatory mechanism, policies aimed at protecting citizens from the harsh realities of profit maxi-
mization weakened and disappeared. "Labour-market flexibility" became
the new mantra, and policies were tailored to meet that goal (Fudge and
Cossman 2002: 14). Responsibility for individual welfare became "less
a matter of collective, social or public obligation" (Fudge and Cossman
2002: 3–4); producing the self-reliant citizen became the ultimate goal of
government and the ultimate achievement of the responsible citizen.

The gendered impact of this shift has been documented by a host of
scholars (see Brodie 1995; Bakker 1996; Bashevkin 1998). Judy Fudge
(2002) traces the history of federal civil servants in Canada, 60 percent
of whom are women in low-level clerical positions. The rise and subsequent decline of the women's movement can be traced from its nadir
in 1944, when all married female civil service employees, seventeen
thousand of them, were fired to provide jobs for returning World War II
veterans, to its peak in the late 1970s. Several things came together for
the women's movement during that time. The Liberal government created the Royal Commission on the Status of Women (1967), accepted
its major recommendations, and set up the Office of Equal Opportunity
(1971) and the National Commission on the Status of Women (1972). All
three government-funded bodies pushed hard to secure equality, in areas
from divorce law to pension reform. Liberal feminism — predominantly
middle-class, educated, and white — became a force to reckon with. In
the federal civil service, with studies showing that formal equality had
not produced substantive equality, the principle of equal pay for work
of equal value was adopted (Fudge 2002), and a fifteen-year battle for
compensation and back wages ensued. With the media fanning the flames
and conditions in the private sector deteriorating, public servants were

demonized as overpaid, underworked fat cats. This massive resentment meant that gender equality could not be achieved by paying women more; equity would have to be achieved by paying men less. Thus the wages and working conditions of both sexes deteriorated. Ironically, on October 29, 1999, the Treasury Board agreed to pay compensation to women for past injustices. But the wages and working conditions of both sexes deteriorated, a lose-lose solution indeed.

Other components of the welfare state were refashioned with similar effects, from the late 1980s on. Fudge (2002: 110) sees the free-trade election of 1988 as pivotal, arguing that it signalled "the loss of national sovereignty and dismantling of the Canadian welfare state." Working conditions in the public and private sectors deteriorated; job and wage cuts were common as out-sourcing and "just in time" management took hold. Increased levels of exploitation, increased income inequality, massive unemployment, and a general lowering of wages resulted. Tax law (Philips 2002), retirement income (Condon 2002), immigration (Macklin 2002), and health care (Gilmore 2002) were all subjected to the rigors of the free market. Services that delivered profits to the private sector were expanded; unprofitable services atrophied. Thus by the late 1980s feminist discourse morphed into gender neutrality, and social justice was replaced by market discourse. While these policy shifts have had an impact on men, women, and children, they hit certain groups much harder than others. The virtues of neo-liberalism — self-reliance, commodification, and market dependence — are harder to achieve if you are poor, uneducated, disabled, or marginalized by race or ethnicity. When governments turn their responsibilities for day care, elder care, and health care over to the private sector, those who cannot pay for services are punished. When retirement income is privatized, those who have been excluded from the labour market (traditionally mothers), and those who never earned much (also more likely to be women), suffer most.

The neo-liberal revolution, then, has altered the quality of life and life chances of all women. Throughout the 1990s, those at the top of the income distribution hierarchy saw their incomes grow exponentially; those in the bottom quintile suffered declines (Schrecker 2001). For middle- and working-class families, it now takes the combined wages of two breadwinners to provide the equivalent in purchasing power to the wage of one full-time, unionized breadwinner (usually male) in 1975 (Fudge and Cossman 2002). Although government programs in Canada have thus far prevented total destitution for those on the bottom (Sharpe 1998), inequality has risen sharply, within categories as well as between them. Wage distribution for women has become much more unequal. Women of the baby boom generation have, by and large, benefited from feminist struggles for access, wage, and pension equality. Younger women, particularly those with less social or racial/ethnic capital, face highly competitive labour markets that deliver few good jobs for anyone. Those dependent on the state and those unable or unwilling to take on "responsible," profit-maximizing roles are worst off, suffering not only loss of income and entitlement, but also intensified censure, surveillance, and incarceration.

These changes happened despite feminist struggle, knowledge claims, and lobbying. The forces that "caused" neo-liberal reform were basically economic and political. Foreseeing the spectre of declining profitability and defining this as a crisis of capitalism, captains of industry, political leaders, and state officials used Chicago-school economics ("science") to legitimize, publicize, and celebrate knowledge claims consonant with elite views of the world and elite priorities. Their actions as agents on all cultural and social fronts persuaded state elites to institute policy reforms that reduced the "burdens" — of employees, regulations, and taxes — on business. Their private troubles became national and international problems, because they had the structural and ideological power to make their claims into self-fulfilling prophecies. Neo-liberal reforms were sold to the populace — most of these changes were voted in — with promises of prosperity and wealth on the one hand and economic disaster on the other. Entrepreneurial citizens will get rich; the remainder will get intensified social, legal, and moral control. Not coincidentally, the resulting society has delivered disproportionately large benefits to the elites that sponsored these changes.

Anti-feminist Backlash and Punitiveness
Both backlash and accelerated punitiveness are intricately related, though not directly or in a linear way, to the material and ideological changes introduced by neo-liberal policies. The consequences are particularly dire for the most marginalized women. Some of the most dramatic and far-reaching effects have been on the lives of "woman as offender" and "woman as victim."

While rates of incarceration for both women and men have increased, women have experienced the most dramatic growth. This is glaringly obvious in the most neo-liberal Anglo-American democracy, the United States, where the number of male and female prisoners rose from under five hundred thousand in 1980 to nearly two million in 2000, and still it grows. As one study concluded, "Approximately one-third of all Black males will experience state prison in their lifetime" (Austin et al. 2001: 14). From 1980 to 1999, rates for men increased 303 percent — but rates for women were up by 576 percent.[4] Not only that, the combined effects of zero tolerance, "three strikes" laws, and draconian anti-drug legislation have narrowed the long-standing gender gap: since 1995 women's rate of growth in incarceration has outpaced that of men (Austin et al. 2001). As always, the female offender is highly racialized. From 1986 to 1991 rates for African-American women for drug offences rose by 828 percent; for Hispanics, 328 percent, for white women, 241 percent (Chesney-Lind and Faith 2000). There is no comparable increase in female crime rates to explain or justify this mania for incarceration (Belknap 2001).

With the alpha power adopting intensified incarceration, other societies susceptible to its rhetoric and example both copied and resisted U.S. penal policies. In England and Wales the number of female prisoners tripled from 1970 to the late 1990s, with most of that increase occurring from 1993 on (British Home Office 1999). In Australia the prison population doubled from 1982 to 1998 (Carcach and Grant 1999, 2000). Although 95 percent of inmates are male, women, unfortunately, are increasing their market share. In recent years Canada's federal government has been trying to bring rates of incarceration under control, instituting restorative justice alternatives for juveniles and Aboriginal peoples and issuing directives advising judges to use non-custodial sentences wherever possible (*R. v. Gladue* 1999; Finn et al. 1999). Many provincial governments have been going in the opposite direction. Although the provinces only handle adult prisoners on remand and those serving sentences of less than two years, Alberta and Ontario[5] have made incarceration more certain and more punitive, setting up boot camps, cutting inmate pay, and banning smoking. (Because most inmates smoke, tobacco is an important currency of exchange inside the prison, and inmates do not have the option of stepping outside to light up.)

For woman as victim, the consequences of feminist-inspired reforms reshaping domestic and sexual assault have been, to say the least, mixed. Zero tolerance policies on spousal assault have, ironically, produced more female offenders, with women getting charged with contempt of court for their unwillingness to testify. Or they face criminal charges when their abuser claims, "She hit me too" (Snider 1994, 1998; Comack, Chopyk, and Wood 2000). Here too punishment is racialized and class-specific — most prisoners are young, poor, and from minority groups, and sharp increases in the incarceration rates of impoverished Aboriginal men have accompanied zero tolerance provisions (Comack and Balfour 2004).

Sexual assault laws have accomplished some of the goals that feminists had hoped for, namely more charges laid and higher conviction rates (Roberts 1991; Ursel 1991). But there is no evidence that women feel safer, or that they are safer. Despite extensive changes in laws of evidence, testifying in court is still an ordeal for the victim. As Elizabeth Comack and Gillian Balfour (2004) illustrate, the old defence practice of "whacking the complainant" — that is, destroying her credibility in every legal way — is alive and well in Canadian courts.

This result is not surprising. It is a natural consequence of seeking change through criminal justice and the adversarial system that the system employs. Moreover, it is hard to envisage an alternative within criminal justice institutions that would improve the process for the victim without assuming that every accused is guilty. Within institutions of criminal justice, then, neo-liberal governance has fashioned a new "common sense." Despite hard empirical evidence to the contrary (Carlen 2002; Comack, Chopyk, and Wood 2000), conceptualizations of domestic assault today portray men and women as being equally aggressive, as equally likely to bully and inflict damage on their partners. Gender-neutral policies and programs in institutions threaten gender-sensitive regimes, and feminist claims about gender and female equality have been muted.

Outside criminal justice, the anti-feminist backlash has invaded every institution, from education (where boys are now seen as victims of discrimination) to workplace harassment. The word "feminist" has been transformed from badge of honour to stigma (Masuch 2004). Canada's federal government, in 1998, cut subsidies to the National Action Committee on the Status of Women and awarded subsidies to the anti-feminist group Real Women (Fudge 2002). Fathers' rights groups, one component of the powerful men's movement, claim discrimination against fathers in family law and demand their "right" to sole custody of children (Menzies forthcoming). Intolerance of feminist positions and policy reversals are widespread — in the United States the right to abortion is threatened, pregnant cocaine addicts are charged with felonies against the unborn child (Tong 1996), and equal rights amendments are no longer even discussed. Moral panics about violent girls, female stalkers, and homicidal mothers fill newspapers and magazines, videos, and the Internet. Stories that reflect unfavourably on "feminists" receive prime time. The *National Post,* for example, ran a series of articles on shelters for abused women in 1998, portraying disputes between the women running the shelters and their clients and boards of directors as the result of self-serving attempts by power-hungry feminists to put "ideology" (another buzzword) ahead of abused women's needs. Selected interviews with shelter clients highlighted those (few?) who claimed that anti-male doctrines were being forced upon them (Mann 2000).

Neo-liberal governance has required the constitution of a new subject, the responsibilized individual. The goal of government became not to deliver social justice or full employment, or guarantee minimum standards of living to those on the bottom, but to enable citizens to become consumers who can fend for themselves. Everyone is to make prudent investments and put their faith in the private sector and in markets — outcomes delivered by the market are just and fair by definition. You get what you deserve. Consumers have been "set free" from the yoke of government — free to turn themselves into commodities, marketing their skills, wombs, genes, and identities. These measures were sold to the electorate, through knowledge claims, in three basic ways: they were argued as necessary (to cut government deficits), as beneficial (to ensure that citizens take responsibility for themselves), and as forms of freedom (delivering tax cuts and less intrusive government).

The result has been extensive privatization, the fraying of the social safety net, and sharply heightened levels of inequality (Cossman and Fudge 2002; Schrecker 2001). Increased inequality and more desperate, fearful populations have always gone hand in hand with greater punitiveness and higher levels of state coercion (Martin 2002: 355). As people on the bottom become more desperate, the privileged become more fearful. Both segments feel resentful, fearful, more victimized, and less well served by government. Insecure people in unequal societies consent to more state control over the people supposedly beneath them — the people with less income, power, and prestige. As long as "criminals," "welfare cheats," "violent girls," and "squeegee kids" are the object of repression, as long as these controls are directed against Them and not Us, coercion is legitimate and politically popular.

MAKING CHANGE IN NEO-LIBERAL TIMES

Clearly, attempting to change societies is a complex undertaking. In the process of change-making, feminist knowledge claims, like all others, become part and parcel of the reality they attempt to alter, thereby constituting a new reality. Once knowledge claims get published and known, the social environment is changed. One useful analogy might be to picture "society" as a complicated, humungous sweater made up of many different types and colours of yarn. Each new knowledge claim represents a stitch, a contribution to the shape and pattern of the whole, which changes the overall pattern, however slightly. Critical, barely heard counterhegemonic arguments may be represented by light-coloured, weak, or dead-end strands; hegemonic arguments from dominant groups, those picked up and celebrated, are fashioned in bold, bright colours, of tough sturdy yarn. Hegemonic claims are the most numerous, and basically determine the shape of the sweater. However, feminist knowledge claims are now part of the whole, and their presence therefore alters that whole.

While the first part of this chapter has shown where and how feminist claims were heard, the second part has illustrated where they were not heard, and why. To return to the sweater analogy, we have seen how dominant economic and political forces tore the Keynesian sweater apart, refashioning it to fit not the entitled or victimized woman, but the genderless — or male? — neo-liberal subject. Some feminist and some critical claims — those legitimating increased punitiveness and incarceration — were reworked and incorporated in this new design, and now strengthen neo-liberal motifs. The combined forces of capitalism in perceived crisis, acting in concert with the state, are sometimes too powerful for oppositional groups to overcome. In the last twenty-five years, agents who embodied capitalist interests, speaking in the name of prosperity and progress, proved figuratively and literally irresistible.

Thus policy shifted in directions that left women more equal before law in theory, but materially poorer. The picture is not all gloom and doom. Some women, primarily white, educated, and middle-class or above, reaped enormous benefits from feminist change-making initiatives. They (we) now enjoy legal rights to education and access into professions, top jobs in important institutions, and marriage to equally successful partners. Their children have the best of the public services that remain, in addition to gaining access to the best of the private sector. Even the double shift facing all employed mothers, where child care and household maintenance chores must be done on top of wage labour, has been lessened for these women because they can hire nannies and housecleaners (usually less privileged women). Many of the benefits of feminist change-making have been similarly class and race/ethnic specific. For women in the bottom 50 percent of the income pyramid and for racialized women, the consequences of some feminist claims, when joined with neo-liberal mentalities, sensibilities, and policies, have been dire.

What can we learn from this? Is it possible to make significant human-enhancing change in neo-liberal societies, or institute policies that are less likely to backfire? Yes. While we cannot control how our arguments are heard, or predict their consequences, we can make our messages harder to "mishear." This approach requires walking a fine line, because messages deemed "too radical" will never make it into political arenas, while those labelled "reasonable" may be incorporated and co-opted, sometimes with disastrous effects.

Women facing criminal charges, or incarcerated women, are a case in point. The consequences of feminist change-making efforts around women in prison have proved problematic because of how women's needs have been translated by politicians and correctional officials. Prison activists and feminist researchers (often the same people) argued for change in women's prisons that would empower inmates, helping them overcome the multiple victimizations most prisoners have endured (Task Force on Federally Sentenced Women 1990; Bertrand 1999; Hayman 2000; Gelsthorpe 1989; Hannah-Moffat and Shaw 2000a; Shaw 1993). The subject they constituted was the capable woman who needs more choices, better alternatives, and more humane, self-enhancing counsel. If it is now accepted that prisons cannot be abolished, at least not yet, this criminalized woman needs gender- and ethnicity-sensitive prisons. Instead, these claims were heard through discourses of risk and the language of risk assessment, in which women with multiple needs — the most traumatized, those with the least education and the worst backgrounds — become high-risk offenders (Hannah-Moffat 2001). With science unmistakeably "proving" that these women are the most likely to reoffend, the neediest and most dispossessed inmates get herded into maximum-security facilities where they are deprived of programs that inmates in the "normal" population receive. How, then, can messages of empowerment be made harder to "mishear"?

First and foremost, the dialogue, with criminalized women and with those paid to keep them inside, is of paramount importance. There will always be "better" and "worse" prisons; and with punitive neo-conservative and neo-liberal forces now in the ascendance, struggles for ameliorative change may, at the very least, stave off further regression. Going silent means that the only voices governments and correctional authorities hear are vindictive and fear-obsessed, which provides a certain recipe for longer sentences and meaner prisons. Moreover, though arguments of humanity cut no political ice today, working with inmates and officials to humanize prison environments and empower those inside is the decent option for people who care about prisoners.

Second, critique and policy are separate but equally necessary discussions. As Pat Carlen (2002: 19) points out, misheard messages may occur not because one party is sadistic or malicious, but because "different parties hear differently." Feminist objectives must be seen through the lens of prison managers, because these people have to translate them into operating procedures. They will therefore have different priorities, points of view, and ways of seeing the female prisoner. They must negotiate change through a myriad of complex and contradictory government regulations, keep unionized staff (who also see differently) onside, and prevent security lapses. Security trumps all other objectives in today's prisons, given vengeance-obsessed media and politicians constantly on the lookout for sensational items (Osborne 1995). It is essential to hear, respect, and understand the differences that parties bring to policy discussions without silencing any of the voices. As Carlen points out, unlike academics, senior administrators and prison staff have to act. They do not have the luxury of "talking off the top of their critiques" (Carlen 2002: 18).

From a praxis perspective, social action always starts with the obvious, which in this case is the uncontroversial, "common-sense" reality that punishment involves gendered bodies. Experience teaches us that seeking gender-sensitive regimes is less likely to backfire than is arguing for equality between male and female institutions. Women still make up a tiny percentage of prison populations (less than 5 percent in most countries), and the last thing that progressive forces want to do is increase those numbers. As we have seen, arguing for equal punishment in a punitive culture will be heard as wanting more women to be punished more, not as a call to punish men less. Seeking parity rather than formal legal equality is less likely to deliver "punishment in disguise" (Hannah-Moffat 2002; Carlen 2002: 13). Courtroom strategies that aim to widen law's understanding of "free choice" and of "rational behaviour" may decrease convictions because they require law to formally recognize the realities facing the abused wife or Aboriginal street prostitute. What is rational for the white, middle-class, middle-aged man is not necessarily rational for the woman escaping a man she thinks will kill her, or the runaway whose alternatives are turning tricks or going hungry (or going "cold turkey" from addictions, which many see as much worse).

Thus, progressives might fight for judicial instructions that ask courts to consider not what the classic "reasonable man" would have done, but "what was reasonable for this defendant under these circumstances?" (Hudson 2002). Interrogating the meaning of "real" choices is also essential: to choose the law-abiding options endorsed by corrections, people must be able to acquire the essential goods and services of life through legitimate means. Poverty and racism, sexism, and other "isms" prevent most marginalized people from doing this. Arguments such as these highlight the crucial link between inequality and criminality, a truth obliterated by the now dominant "science" of risk assessment.

Looking at sexual and domestic assault, how can we lessen the chances of mishearing here? First, we must recognize the very real victories that feminist activists have achieved. Definitions of domestic and sexual assault have been clarified and extended, and there has been real and significant progress at the all-important level of *habitus*. In all Anglo-America democracies, males who beat up or sexually assault women are now named, blamed, and shamed. Their behaviour is no longer normative or legitimate. "Common-sense" beliefs in mainstream culture have changed; offenders are more likely to be shamed by peers; some, if they define their offences as violent (which many do not) will even shame themselves. The symbolic stigma of criminal law accounts for an unknowable proportion of this crucial cultural shift, which is why criminal law "solutions" must remain in the policy mix at some level.

However, experience should teach us not to look to institutions of criminal law to improve the life of the female who is victimized. We need to devise ways of combatting the iatrogenic consequences of zero tolerance and similar "reforms" while retaining their symbolic impact. To prevent the widespread phenomenon of countercharging victims of domestic assault, "equivalence of violence" directives used by some jurisdictions are promising (Comack and Balfour 2004). In Manitoba, for example, police are told to consider, before laying countercharges, whether the complainant's violence was equivalent to that of the defendant. They are also directed to consider whether the aggression was offensive or defensive, aimed at self- preservation or at injuring the other party (Comack and Balfour 2004).

Seemingly intractable problems with change-making through criminal law remain. Institutions of criminal justice cannot deal with the material and social realities of offenders or victims; they can only offer equal punishment. Some knowledge claims heard in the past delivered increased punishment for the putative offender without producing empowerment for the putative victim. In most criminal events, "victim" and "offender" are one and the same; among the troubled populations that fill Canadian courts and jails, most have been both victim and victimized (Comack 1996). However, law, in statutes ranging from youth prostitution to break and enter, sees the two categories as binary opposites — an approach that ignores the material and social conditions of most criminalized populations and takes the spotlight off inequality and puts it onto punishment (Phoenix 2002a: 69). Change-making efforts should therefore concentrate less on improving criminal law and more on altering the material and social conditions of the most marginalized. As distinguished criminal lawyer and law professor Diane Martin (2002: 356) argues: "Regardless of the motives of those seeking new crime control methods, the end result is similar: status quo power relations and distinctions based on race, class, age and gender are preserved and reinforced."[6]

Outside criminal justice, institutions designed to nourish, educate, or heal have considerable counterhegemonic potential. No social order is static. Neo-liberal knowledge claims constitute new realities, and their consequences provoke resistance. Fudge (2002) argues that women's workloads, in both productive and reproductive spheres, have been dramatically increased by privatization, thereby creating an unstable gender order that is ripe for change. Researchers can take advantage of the world's three-decade experience with neo-liberal governance by designing research that highlights the often-tragic results of privatization and commodification. However, such consequences must be carefully connected to the neo-liberal practices that produced them, given the cultural eagerness to position disasters as the fault of the individual. The neo-liberal subject constructing blame will always gaze down, seeking out the proverbial bad apple, the incompetent Crown attorney, the careless employee, the neglectful mother. Revealing the structural sources of the social conflicts shaping individual circumstances does not make for an easy sound bite, but it is essential nevertheless.

Finally, knowing the class and race-biased consequences of past change-making efforts, progressives must propose solutions with the potential to benefit all women, not just the most privileged. Working with and incorporating the knowledge, perspectives, and experience of marginalized women are the only ways this can be done.

NOTES

1. This advantage was never universal. Historically, young, white working-class women were the main beneficiaries of institutions such as the reformatory movement (Rafter 1985a; Freedman 1981; Dobash, Dobash, and Guttridge 1986; Zedner 1998). Similarly today, it is primarily "good mothers," faithful wives, the chaste, young, white, and working class or above who are believable as victims or merit "less culpable" designations as offenders.

2. That dream is rapidly becoming a nightmare, with governments adopting proposals from right-realist criminology promising that the safety of the privileged can be ensured by surveillance and incarceration of the desperate; and with "scientific research" depicting "criminals" as morally flawed individuals unable or unwilling

to defer gratification (Gottfredson and Hirschi 1990).

3. As discussed in the last section of this chapter, actual female bodies are often both victim and victimized. However, formal law rigidly categorizes them as binary opposites.

4. Since there are fewer female prisoners than male, relatively small numerical increases translate into high percentages. All the same, a fivefold increase is huge.

5. Quebec is the dramatic exception to this wave of punitiveness; a distinct society indeed.

6. This is one of the problems with strategies of restorative justice and decarceration. The other is the monumental public opposition, from those who have accepted neo-liberal ideology, to any policy that appears to be "soft" on "criminals."

REFERENCES

Aboriginal Justice Implementation Commission. 2001. *Final Report*. Winnipeg: Manitoba Justice. Available at <www.ajic.mb.ca>. (Accessed January 14, 2006.)

Abramovitz, M. 2001. "Everyone is Still on Welfare: The Role of Distribution in Social Policy." *Social Work* 46, 4.

_____. 1996. *Regulating the Lives of Women: Social Policy from Colonial Times to the Present*. Second edition. Boston: South End Press.

Adelberg, E., and C. Currie (eds.). 1993. *In Conflict with the Law: Women and the Canadian Justice System*. Vancouver: Press Gang.

_____. 1987a. *Too Few to Count: Canadian Women in Conflict with the Law*. Vancouver: Press Gang.

_____. 1987b. "In Their Own Words: Seven Women's Stories." In E. Adelberg and C. Currie (eds.).

Adkins, L. 1992. "Sexual Work and the Employment of Women in the Service Industries." In M. Savage and A. Witz (eds.), *Gender and Bureaucracy*. Oxford: Blackwell.

Adler, F. 1975. *Sisters in Crime*. New York: McGraw-Hill.

Alberta Children's Services. 2004. "Protection of Children Involved in Prostitution: Protective Safe House Review." Available at: <www.child.gov.ab.ca/whatwedo/pcse/pdf/psh_report_Nov_7.pdf>. (Accessed April 20, 2005.)

Alberta Government. Year unknown. *Overview: Protection of Children Involved in Prostitution Act*. Available at <http://www.acs.gov.ab.ca/initiatives/prostitution/pros_main.htm>. (Accessed June 20, 2005.)

Alberta Government press release. 2000. *Government to Amend Law Protecting Children Involved in Prostitution* (November).

_____. 1999. *Protection of Children Involved in Prostitution Act* (March).

Alder, C., and A. Worrall. 2003. *Girls' Violence: Myths and Realities*. Albany: State University of New York Press.

Alexander, R. 1995. *The Girl Problem: Female Sexuality Delinquency in New York, 1900–1930*. Ithaca: Cornell University Press.

Aline. 1987. "Good Girls Go to Heaven, Bad Girls Go Everywhere." In F. Delacosta and A. Priscilla (eds.), *Sex Work: Writings by Women in the Sex Industry*. Pittsburgh: Cleis Press.

Allen, H. 1987. *Justice Unbalanced: Gender, Psychiatry and Judicial Decisions*. Milton Keynes: Open University Press.

Amir, M. 1971. *The Patterns of Forcible Rape*. Chicago: University of Chicago Press.

Amnesty International. 2005. "Stolen Sisters: A Human Rights Response to Discrimination and Violence Against Indigenous Women in Canada". Available at <http://www.amnesty.ca/stolen sisters>. (Accessed October 19, 2005.)

Andersen, C. 1999. "Governing Aboriginal Justice in Canada: Constructing Responsible Individuals and Communities Through 'Tradition.'" *Crime, Law and Social Change* 31.

Anderson, E. 1993. *Hard Place to Do Time: The Story of Oakalla Prison, 1912–1991*. New Westminster: Hillpointe.

Anderson, F. 1982. *Hanging in Canada: A Concise History of a Controversial Topic*. Surrey, BC: Heritage House.

Anderson, Kay. 1991. *Vancouver's Chinatown: Racial Discourse in Canada, 1875–1980.* Montreal-Kingston: McGill-Queen's University Press.

Anderson, Kim. 2000. A *Recognition of Being: Reconstructing Native Womanhood.* Toronto: Sumach Press.

Andrews, D., and J. Bonta. 1998. *The Psychology of Criminal Conduct: Theory, Research and Prictice.* Cincinnati: Andersen Publishing.

Anthony, B., and R. Solomon. 1973. "Introduction." In E. Murphy, *The Black Candle.* Toronto: Coles Publishing.

Arbour, The Honourable Justice Louise (Commissioner). 1996. *Commission of Inquiry into Certain Events at the Prison for Women in Kingston.* Ottawa: Solicitor General.

Armstrong, J. 2004. "'I am Not a Monster,' Ellard Says." *Globe and Mail* July 8: A7.

Arnold, R. 1995. "The Processes of Victimization and Criminalization of Black Women." In B.R. Price and N. Sokoloff (eds.), *The Criminal Justice System and Women.* New York: McGraw Hill.

Aronowitz, S. 1992. *Politics of Identity.* New York: Routledge.

Arrigo, B. 2002. *Punishing the Mentally Ill: A Critical Analysis of Law and Psychiatry.* Albany: State University of New York Press.

Artz, S. 1998. *Sex, Power, and the Violent School Girl.* Toronto: Trifolium Books.

Atwood, M. 1996. *Alias Grace.* Toronto: McClelland and Stewart.

Auditor General of Canada. 2003. *Report of the Auditor General to the House of Commons; Chapter 4 Correctional Services of Canada: Reintegration of Women Offenders.* Ottawa: Minister of Public Works and Government Services.

Austin, J., M. Bruce, L. Carroll, P. McCall, and S. Richards. 2001. "The Use of Incarceration in the United States." *The Criminologist* 26, 3.

Australian Institute of Criminology. 2004. *Australian Crime: Facts and Figures 2003.* Canberra. <http://www.aic.gov.au/publications/facts/2003/>. (Accessed January 14, 2006.)

Backhouse, C. 2002. "A Measure of Women's Credibility: The Doctrine of Corroboration in Sexual Assault Trials in Early Twentieth Century Canada and Australia." *York Occasional Working Papers in Law and Society.* Paper #1.

_____. 1999. *Colour-Coded: A Legal History of Racism in Canada, 1900–1950.* Toronto: University of Toronto Press.

_____. 1996. "The Shining Sixpence: Women's Worth in Canadian Law at the End of the Victorian Era." *Manitoba Law Journal* 23, 3.

_____. 1994. "White Female Help and Chinese-Canadian Employers: Race, Class, Gender, and Law in the Case of Yee Clun, 1924." *Canadian Ethnic Studies/Etudes Ethniques au Canada* 26, 3.

_____. 1991. *Petticoats and Prejudice: Women and Law in Nineteenth Century Canada.* Toronto: Women's Press.

_____. 1985. "Nineteenth-Century Canadian Prostitution Law: Reflection of a Discriminatory Society." *Social History* XVII (November).

Badgley, R. 1984. *Report of the Committee on Sexual Offences Against Children and Youths.* Ottawa: Minister of Justice and Attorney General of Canada.

Baker, T., and J. Simon. 2002. "Embracing Risk." In T. Baker and J. Simon (eds.), *Embracing Risk: The Changing Culture of Insurance and Responsibility.* Chicago: University of Chicago Press.

Bakker, I. 1996. *Rethinking Restructuring: Gender and Change in Canada.* Toronto: University of Toronto Press.

Balfour, G. 2000. "Feminist Therapy in Prison." In K. Hannah Moffat and M. Shaw (eds.), *An Ideal Prison? Critical Essays on Women's Imprisonment in Canada*. Halifax: Fernwood.

Bannerji, H. 2005. "Introducing Racism: Notes towards an Anti-Racism Feminism." In B. Crow and L. Gotell (eds.), *Open Boundaries: A Canadian Women's Studies Reader*. Second edition. Toronto: Pearson.

Barber, P. 1992. "Conflicting Loyalties: Gender, Class and Equality Politics in Working Class Culture." *Canadian Woman Studies* 12, 3.

Barron, C. 2000. *Giving Youth a Voice: A Basis for Rethinking Adolescent Violence*. Halifax: Fernwood.

Barry, A., T. Osborne, and N. Rose (eds.). 1996. *Foucault and Political Reason: Liberalism, Neo-Liberalism and Rationalities of Government*. Chicago: The University of Chicago Press.

Barry, K. 1995. *The Prostitution of Sexuality: The Global Exploitation of Women*. New York: New York University Press.

_____. 1979. *Female Sexual Slavery*. New York: New York University Press.

Bashevkin, S. 2002. *Welfare Hot Buttons: Women, Work, and Social Policy Reform*. Toronto: University of Toronto Press.

_____. 1998. *Women on the Defensive: Living Through Conservative Times*. Toronto: University of Toronto Press.

Batacharya, S. 2004. "Racism, 'Girl Violence,' and the Murder of Reena Virk." In C. Alder and A. Worrall (eds.), *Girls' Violence: Myths and Realities*. Albany: State University of New York Press.

Bauman, Z. 1997. *Postmodernity and Its Discontents*. Cambridge: Polity Press.

Beattie, J.M. 1977. *Attitudes Towards Crime and Punishment in Upper Canada, 1830–1850: A Documentary Study*. Toronto: University of Toronto, Centre of Criminology.

Becker, D. 1997. *Through the Looking Glass: Women and Borderline Personality Disorder*. Boulder, CO: Westview.

Becker, H. 1963. *The Outsiders*. New York: Free Press.

Beckett, K., and B. Western. 2001. "Governing Social Marginality: Welfare, Incarceration, and the Transformation of State Policy." *Punishment and Society* 3, 1.

Belknap, J. 2001. *The Invisible Woman: Gender, Crime and Justice*. Second edition. Belmont, CA: Wadsworth.

Bell, S. 2002. "Girls in Trouble." In B. Schissel and C. Brooks (eds.), *Marginality and Condemnation: An Introduction to Critical Criminology*. Halifax: Fernwood.

Bell, V. 1993. "Governing Childhood: Neo-liberalism and the Law." *Economy and Society* 22, 3 (August).

Benoit, C., and A. Millar. 2001. *Dispelling Myths and Understanding Realities: Working Conditions, Health Status and Exiting Experiences of Sex Workers*. British Columbia: PEERS.

Bernier, Joanne, and André Cellard. 1996. "Le syndrome de la femme fatale: 'Maricide' et représentation féminine au Québec, 1898–1940." *Criminologie* 29, 2.

Berridge, V., and G. Edwards. 1981. *Opium and the People: Opiate Use in Nineteenth-Century England*. London: Allan Lane.

Berry, J. 1994. "Aboriginal Cultural Identity." Report prepared for the Royal Commission on Aboriginal Peoples. Ottawa: Department of Indian and Northern Affairs.

Bertrand, M-A. 1999. "Incarceration as a Gendering Strategy." *Canadian Journal of Law and Society* 14, 1.

_____. 1967. "The Myth of Sexual Equality Before the Law." Fifth Research Conference on Delinquency and Criminality. Montreal, Centre de Psychologies et de Pédagogie.

CRIMINALIZING WOMEN

Berzins, L., and B. Hayes. 1987. "The Diaries of Two Change Agents." In E. Adelberg and C. Currie (eds.).

Bittle, S. 2002. "When Protection is Punishment: Neo-liberalism and Secure Care Approaches to Youth Prostitution." *Canadian Journal of Criminology and Criminal Justice* 44, 3.

_____. 1999. "Reconstructing 'Youth Prostitution' as the 'Sexual Procurement of Children'" M.A. Thesis. School of Criminology. Simon Fraser University, Burnaby, BC.

Blomberg, T. 2003. "Penal Reforms and the Fate of Alternatives." In T. Blomberg and S. Cohen (eds.), *Punishment and Social Control*. New York: Aldine de Gruyter.

Bloom, B. (ed.). 2003a. *Gendered Justice: Addressing the Female Offender*. North Carolina: Carolina Academic Press.

_____. 2003b. "A New Vision: Gender Responsive Principles, Policy and Practices." *Gendered Justice: Addressing the Female Offender*. Durham, NC: Carolina Academic Press.

_____. 2000. "Gender Responsive Supervision and Programming for Women in the Community." In M. Thigpen (ed.), *National Institute of Corrections Annual Issue 2000: Responding to Women Offenders in the Community*. Washington: National Institute of Corrections.

Bloom, B., B. Owen, and S. Covington. 2005. "Gender Responsive Strategies for Women Offenders: A Summary of Research, Practice and Guiding Principles for Women Offenders." Washington: National Institute for Corrections.

_____. 2003. *Gender Responsive Strategies: Research, Practice, and Guiding Principles for Women Offenders*. Washington: National Institute of Corrections.

Boe, R., M. Nafekh, B. Vuong, R. Sinclair, and C. Cousineau. 2003. *The Changing Population of the Federal Inmate Population: 1997 and 2002*. Ottawa: Research Branch, Correctional Service of Canada.

Bonta, J., T. Rugge, and M. Dauvergne. 2003. *The Reconviction Rate of Female Offenders*. Ottawa: Solicitor General Canada.

Bordo, S. 1988. "Anorexia Nervosa: Psychopathology and the Crystallization of Culture." In Irene Diamond and Lee Quinby (eds.), *Feminism and Foucault: Reflections on Resistance*. Boston: Northeastern University Press.

Boritch, H. 1997. *Fallen Women: Female Crime and Criminal Justice in Canada*. Toronto: Nelson.

Bosworth, M. 1999. "Agency and Choice in Women's Prisons: Towards a Constitutive Penality." In S. Henry and D. Milovanovic (eds.), *Constitutive Criminology at Work: Applications to Crime and Justice*. Albany: State University of New York Press.

Boyd, N. 1991. *High Society: Legal and Illegal Drugs in Canada*. Toronto: Key West Books.

_____. 1984. "The Origins of Canadian Narcotics Legislation: The Process of Criminalizaton in Historical Context." *Dalhousie Law Journal* 8.

Boyd, S. 2004. *From Witches to Crack Moms: Women, Drug Law, and Policy*. Durham, NC: Carolina Academic Press.

_____. 1999. *Mothers and Illicit Drugs: Transcending the Myths*. Toronto: University of Toronto Press.

Boyd, S., and K. Faith. 1999. "Women, Illegal Drugs and Prison: Views from Canada." *The International Journal of Drug Policy* 10.

Bradley, H. 1996. *Fractured Identities: Changing Patterns of Inequality*. Cambridge: Polity.

Brannigan, A., and J. Fleischman. 1989. "Juvenile Prostitution and Mental Health: Policing

Delinquency or Treating Pathology." *Canadian Journal of Law and Society* 4.

Breggin, P. 1993. *Toxic Psychiatry. Drugs and Electroconvulsive Therapy: The Truth and the Better Alternatives*. London: Harper Collins.

Brinkerhoff, M., and E. Lupri. 1988. "Interspousal Violence." *Canadian Journal of Sociology* 13, 4.

British Columbia. 2001a. *Secure Care*. Ministry for Children and Families. June 21.

_____. 2001b. *Secure Care and Secure Treatment: A Summary of Legislation and Services in Other Jurisdictions*. Ministry for Children and Families. February.

_____. 2000. *An Overview of the Secure Care Act*. Ministry for Children and Families.

British Columbia Civil Liberties Association. 1999. *News Flash: The Report of the Secure Care Working Group: A Response by the B.C. Civil Liberties Association*. Available at <http://www.bccla.org/positions/children/99securecare.html>. (Accessed January 14, 2006.)

British Columbia Ministry of Attorney General. 1996. *Community Consultation on Prostitution in British Columbia: Overview of Results*. Ministry of Attorney General.

British Columbia Ministry of Children and Family Development. Safe Care Consultation. Available at <http://www.mcf.gov.bc.ca/safe_care/>. (Accessed August 20, 2005.)

British Columbia press release. 2000. *New Law to Keep Young People Safe*. Ministry for Children and Families. June 21.

British Home Office. 1999. "Aim 4: The Government's Strategy for Women Offenders."

Britton, D.M. 1997. "Gendered Organizational Logic: Policy and Practice in Men's and Women's Prisons." *Gender and Society* 11, 6.

Brock, D. 1998. *Making Work, Making Trouble: Prostitution as a Social Problem*. Toronto: University of Toronto Press.

Brock, D., and G. Kinsman. 1986. "Patriarchal Relations Ignored: An Analysis and Critique of the Badgley Report on Sexual Offences Against Children and Youth." In J. Lowman, M. Jackson, T. Palys, and S. Gavigan (eds.).

Brodie, J. 1995. *Politics on the Margins: Restructuring and the Canadian Women's Movement*. Halifax: Fernwood.

Brodie, J., S. Gavigan, and J. Jenson. 1992. *The Politics of Abortion*. Toronto: Oxford University Press.

Brookes, B. 1998. "Women and Mental Health: An Historical Introduction." In Sarah E. Romans (ed.), *Folding Back the Shadows*. Dunedin: University of Otago Press.

Browne, A. 1987. *When Battered Women Kill*. New York: Free Press.

Brownmiller, S. 1975. *Against Our Will: Men, Women and Rape*. New York: Simon and Schuster.

Brownridge, D. 2003. "Male Partner Violence Against Aboriginal Women in Canada: An Empirical Analysis." *Journal of Interpersonal Violence* 18, 1.

Bruckert, C. 2002. *Putting it On, Taking it Off: Women Workers in the Strip Trade*. Toronto: Women's Press.

Bruckert, C., and M. Dufresne. 2002. "Reconfiguring the Margins: Tracing the Regulatory Context of Ottawa Strip Clubs." *Canadian Journal of Law and Society* 17.

Bryan, J. 1965. "Apprenticeship in Prostitution." *Social Problems* 12.

Buchanan, M. 1995. "The Unworthy Poor: Experiences of Single Mothers on Welfare in Chilliwack, British Columbia." M.A. Thesis, Simon Fraser University, Burnaby, BC.

Burchell, G. 1996. "Liberal Government and Techniques of the Self." In A. Barry, T.

Osborne and N. Rose (eds.).

Bureau of Justice Statistics. 2000. *Prison and Jail Inmates at Mid-Year 2000*. Washington, DC: U.S. Department of Justice, # 185989.

Burman, M., S. Batchelor and J. Brown. 2003. "Girls and the Meaning of Violence." In E. Stanko (ed.), *The Meanings of Violence*. London: Routledge.

Burstow, B. 1992. *Feminist Therapy: Working in the Context of Violence*. Newbury Park: Sage Publications.

Busby, K. 2002. "The Protective Confinement of Girls Involved in Prostitution: Potential Problems in Current Regimes." In K. Gorkoff and J. Runner (eds.), *Being Heard: The Experiences of Young Women in Prostitution*. Black Point, NS: Fernwood.

_____. 1999. "'Not a Victim Until a Conviction Is Entered': Sexual Violence Prosecutions and Legal Truth." In E. Comack (ed.), *Locating Law: Essays on the Race/Class/Gender Connections*. Halifax: Fernwood.

Busby, K, P. Downe, K. Gorkoff, K. Nixon, L. Tutty, and J. Ursel. 2002. "Examination of Innovative Programming for Children and Youth Involved in Prostitution." In H. Berman and Y. Jiwani (eds.), *In The Best Interests of the Girl Child: Phase II Report*. Ottawa: Status of Women Canada.

_____. 2000. *Examination of Innovative Programming for Children and Youth Involved in Prostitution*. Available at <www.harbour.sfu.ca/freda/reports/gc204.htm>. (Accessed April 20, 2005.)

Bylington, D. 1997. "Applying Relational Theory to Addiction Treatment." In S. Straussner and E. Zelvin (eds.), *Gender and Addictions: Men and Women in Treatment*. Northvale, NJ: Jason Aronson.

Cain, M. 1990. "Towards Transgression: New Directions in Feminist Criminology." *International Journal of the Sociology of Law* 18.

Calder, G. 2003. *Rethinking the Treatment of Federally Sentenced Women in a Substantive Equality Context*. Submission of the Women's Legal Education and Action Fund to the Canadian Human Rights Commission. Available at <http://www.chrc-ccdp.ca/legislation_policies/subcalder-en.asp>. (Accessed January 14, 2006.)

Califa, P. 1994. *Public Sex: The Culture of Radical Sex*. Pittsburgh: Cleis.

Campbell, N. 2000. *Using Women: Gender, Drug Policy, and Social Justice*. New York: Routledge.

Canada. 1977. *Report to Parliament by the Sub-Committee on the Penitentiary System in Canada*. Ottawa: Supply and Services.

Canada, Public Service Commission, Research Directorate. 1999. "The Future of Work: Non-Standard Employment in the Public Service of Canada." Ottawa: Policy, Research and Communications Branch.

Canadian Advisory Council on the Status of Women. 1981. *Women in Prison: Expanding Their Options*. Ottawa.

Canadian Association of Elizabeth Fry Societies (CAEFS). 2005a. Elizabeth Fry Week Fact Sheet. April 10th. Available at <http://www.elizabethfry.ca/eweek05/factsht.htm>. (Accessed October 4, 2005.)

_____. 2005b. *Submission of the Canadian Association of Elizabeth Fry Societies to the United Nations Human Rights Committee Examining Canada's 4th and 5th Reports Regarding the Convention Against Torture*. Available at <www.elizabethfry/ca/un/torture/pdf>. (Accessed October 15, 2005).

_____. 2005c. "More Promises to Women not Kept." Available at <http:www.elizabethfry.ca>. (Accessed October 17, 2005.)

_____. 2003. *Submission of the Canadian Association of Elizabeth Fry Societies*

(CAEFS) to the *Canadian Human Rights Commission for the Special Report on the Discrimination on the Basis of Sex, Race, and Disability Faced by Federally Sentenced Women.* May, 10, 2003. Available at <http://www.elizabethfry.ca>. (Accessed October 18, 2005.)

_____. 1998. *Another Bad Trip: CSC Malingering in the LSD Compensation Case.* Available at <http://www.elizabethfry.ca/areporte/pg20.htm>. (Accessed October 19, 2005.)

_____. "Guidelines for Advocacy." Available at <http://www.elizabethfry.ca/guidelin/guide03.htm>. (Accessed May 15, 2005.)

_____. "Justice for Battered Women — Denied, Delayed... Diminished. Jails are Not the Shelters Battered Women Need." <http://www.elizabethfry.ca/diminish.htm>. (Accessed October 15, 2005.)

Canadian Association of University Teachers. 2002. *Equity in the Workplace: A Better Environment for Everyone.* Faculty Association of the University of Waterloo (November/December).

Canadian Centre for Justice Statistics. 2000. *Juristat: Adult Correctional Services in Canada, 1998–99.* Ottawa: Statistics Canada, 20 (3).

_____. 1997. *Uniform Crime Reporting Survey.* Ottawa: Statistics Canada.

Canadian Human Rights Commission. 2003. *Protecting Their Rights: A Systemic Review of Human Rights in Correctional Services for Federally Sentenced Women.* Ottawa: Canadian Human Rights Commission. Available at <http://www.chrc-ccdp.ca/pdf/reports/FSWen.pdf>. (Accessed January 14, 2006.)

Canadian Panel on Violence Against Women. 1993. *Changing the Landscape: Ending Violence — Achieving Equality.* Ottawa: Minister of Supply and Services Canada.

Caplan, P. 1995. *They Say You're Crazy: How the World's Most Powerful Psychiatrists Decide Who's Normal.* Reading, MA: Addison-Wesley.

Carcach, C., and A. Grant. 2000: *Imprisonment in Australia: The Offence Composition of Australian Correctional Populations, 1998 and 1988.* Canberra: Australian Institute of Criminology, # 164, July.

_____. 1999: *Imprisonment in Australia: Trends in Prison Populations and Imprisonment Rates.* Canberra: Australian Institute of Criminology, 130 (October).

Cario, A. 1968. *This Was Burlesque.* New York: Grosset and Dunlop.

Carlen, P. 2003. "Virginia, Criminology, and the Antisocial Control of Women." In T. Bloomberg and S. Cohen (eds.), *Punishment and Social Control.* New York: Aldine De Gruyter.

_____. (ed.) 2002a. *Women and Punishment: The Struggle for Justice.* Cullompton, UK: Willan.

_____. 2002b. "New Discourses of Justification and Reform for Women's Imprisonment in England." In P. Carlen (ed.), *Women and Punishment: The Struggle for Justice.* Cullompton, UK: Willan.

_____. 2002c. "Controlling Measures: The Repackaging of Common Sense Opposition to Women's Imprisonment in England and Canada." *Criminal Justice* 2, 2.

_____. 1988. *Women, Crime and Poverty.* Milton Keynes: Open University Press.

_____. 1983. *Women's Imprisonment: A Study in Social Control.* London: Routledge.

Carrington, K. 1993. *Offending Girls: Sex, Youth and Justice.* Sydney: Allen and Unwin.

Carruthers, E. 1995. "Prosecuting Women for Welfare Fraud in Ontario: Implications for Equality." *Journal of Law* and *Social Policy* 11.

Carter, V. 2004. "Prostitution and the New Slavery." In C. Stark and R. Whisnant (eds.), *Not for Sale: Feminists Resisting Prostitution and Pornography.* North Melbourne:

Spinifex.

Cassel, J. 1987. *The Secret Plague: Venereal Disease in Canada, 1838–1939*. Toronto: University of Toronto Press.

CCPA Monitor. *2004. 11, 1 (May) Ottawa: Canadian Centre for Policy Alternatives.*

CCSA/CCLAT. 2004. *Canadian Addiction Survey (CAS). Highlights*. Ottawa: Canadian Centre on Substance Abuse.

Chan, W. 2001. *Women, Murder and Justice*. London: Palgrave.

Chan, W., and K. Mirchandani (eds.). 2002. *Crimes of Colour: Racialization and the Criminal Justice System in Canada*. Peterborough: Broadview Press.

Chan, W., and G. Rigakos. 2002. "Risk, Crime and Gender." *British Journal of Criminology* 42.

Chapkis, W. 1997. *Live Sex Acts: Women Performing Erotic Labour*. New York: Routledge.

Chesney-Lind, M. 2004. "Feminism and Critical Criminology: Towards a Feminist Praxis." Available at http://www.critcrim.org/critpapers/chesney-lind1.htm>. (Accessed September 10, 2005.)

_____. 2002. "Imprisoning Women: The Unintended Victims of Mass Imprisonment." In M. Mauer and M. Chesney-Lind (eds.).

_____. 2001. "Are Girls Getting More Violent? Exploring Juvenile Robbery Trends." *Journal of Contemporary Criminal Justice* 17, 2.

_____. 1999. "Review of 'When She Was Bad: Violent Women and the Myth of Innocence'." *Women and Criminal Justice*.

_____. 1988a. "Girls and Status Offenses: Is Juvenile Justice Still Sexist?" *Criminal Justice Abstracts*, 20.

_____. 1988b. "Doing Feminist Criminology." *The Criminologist* 13, 1.

_____. 1987. "Girls and Violence: An Exploration of the Gender Gap in Serious Delinquent Behavior." In D. Corwell, I. Evans, and C. O'Donnell (eds.), *Childhood Aggression and Violence*. New York: Plenum.

_____. 1981. "Juvenile Delinquency: The Sexualization of Female Crime." *Psychology Today* (July).

_____. 1978. "Chivalry Re-Examined." In L. Bowker (ed.), *Women, Crime and the Criminal Justice System*. Lexington, MA: Lexington Books.

Chesney-Lind, M., and K. Faith. 2000. "What About Feminism? Engendering Theory-Making in Criminology." In R. Paternoster (ed.), *Criminological Theories*. Los Angeles: Roxbury Press.

Chesney-Lind, M., and N. Rodriguez. 1983. "Women Under Lock and Key." *The Prison Journal* 63.

Chesney-Lind, M., and R. Sheldon. 1998. *Girls, Delinquency and Juvenile Justice*. California: Wadsworth.

Child Prostitution press release, 40th Premiers Conference. 1999. Available at <http://www.scics.gc.ca/cinfo99/850073021_e.html#850073026e>. (Accessed April 20, 2005.)

Chinnery Report. 1978. *Joint Committee to Study Alternatives for Housing Federal Female Offenders*. Ottawa: Ministry of Solicitor General.

Chunn, D. 1997. "A Little Sex can be a Dangerous Thing: Regulating Sexuality, Venereal Disease, and Reproduction in British Columbia, 1919–1945." In S. Boyd (ed.), *Challenging the Public/Private Divide: Feminism, Law and Public Policy*. Toronto: University of Toronto Press.

Chunn, D., and S. Gavigan. 2004. "Welfare Law, Welfare Fraud, and the Moral Regulation of the 'Never Deserving' Poor." *Social and Legal Studies* 13, 2.

_____. 1988. "Social Control: Analytical Tool or Analytical Quagmire?" *Contemporary Crises* 12.

Chunn, D., and R. Menzies. 1998. "Out of Mind, Out of Law: The Regulation of 'Criminally Insane' Women Inside British Columbia's Public Mental Hospitals, 1888–1973." *Canadian Journal of Women and the Law* 10, 3 (Fall).

_____. 1994. "Gender, Madness and Crime: The Reproduction of Patriarchal and Class Relations in a Pretrial Psychiatric Clinic." In R. Hinch (ed.), *Readings in Critical Criminology*. Scarborough, ON: Prentice Hall Canada.

Clark Report. 1977. *Report of the National Advisory Committee on the Female Offender.* Ottawa: Ministry of Solicitor General.

Clarke, J. 2000. "Unfinished Business? Struggles over the Social in Social Welfare." In Paul Gilroy, Lawrence Grossberg, and Angela McRobbie (eds.), *Without Guarantees: In Honour of Stuart Hall*. London: Verso.

Cohen, M. 1997. "From the Welfare State to Vampire Capitalism." In P. Evans and G. Wekerle, (eds.), *Women and the Canadian Welfare State: Challenges and Change*. Toronto: University of Toronto Press.

Cohen, S. 1985. *Visions of Social Control*. Cambridge: Polity.

Coleman, L. 1984. *The Reign of Error: Psychiatry, Authority, and Law*. Boston: Beacon Press.

Coll, C., and K. Duff. 1995. *Reframing the Needs of Women in Prison: A Relational and Diversity Perspective. Final Report, Women in Prison Pilot Project*. Wellesley, MA: Stone Center.

Collins, A. 1988. *In the Sleep Room: The Story of the CIA Brainwashing Experiments in Canada*. Toronto: Lester and Orpen Dennys.

Colten, M. 1980. "A Comparison of Heroin-Addicted and Nonaddicted Mothers: Their Attitudes, Beliefs, and Parenting Experiences." In *Heroin-Addicted Parents and Their Children: Two Reports*. (National Institute on Drug Abuse Services Research Report). Washington, DC: U.S. Department of Health and Human Services; Public Health Service; Alcohol, Drug Abuse, and Mental Health Administration.

Comack, E. 1996. *Women in Trouble*. Halifax: Fernwood.

_____. 1993a. *The Feminist Engagement with the Law: The Legal Recognition of the 'Battered Woman Syndrome.'* Ottawa: Canadian Research Institute for the Advancement of Women.

_____. 1993b. "Women Offenders' Experiences with Physical and Sexual Abuse: A Preliminary Report." Criminology Research Centre, University of Manitoba.

_____. 1986. "'We Will Get Some Good out of this Riot Yet': The Canadian State, Drug Legislation and Class Conflict." In S. Brickey and E. Comack (eds.), *The Social Basis of Law: Critical Readings in the Sociology of Law*. Toronto: Garamond.

Comack, E., and G. Balfour. 2004. *The Power to Criminalize: Violence, Inequality and the Law*. Halifax: Fernwood.

Comack, E., V. Chopyk, and L. Wood. 2002. "Aren't Women Violent Too? The Gendered Nature of Violence." In B. Schissel and C. Brooks (eds.), *Marginality and Condemnation: An Introduction to Critical Criminology*. Halifax: Fernwood.

_____. 2000. *Mean Streets? The Social Locations, Gender Dynamics, and Patterns of Violent Crime in Winnipeg*. Winnipeg: Canadian Centre for Policy Alternatives (Manitoba) (December).

Comack, E., and T. Peter. Forthcoming. "How the Criminal Justice System Responds to Sexual Assault Survivors: The Slippage Between 'Responsiblization' and 'Blaming the Victim.'" *Canadian Journal of Women and the Law*.

Commission on Systemic Racism in the Ontario Criminal Justice System. 1995. *Report of the Commission on Systemic Racism in the Ontario Criminal Justice System: A Community Summary*. Toronto: Queen's Printer for Ontario.

Committee on Sexual Offences Against Children and Youth (1984) (Badgley Committee) *Sexual Offences Against Children and Youth*. Ottawa: Department of Supply and Services.

Condon, M. 2002. "Privatizing Pension Risk: Gender, Law and Financial Markets." In B. Cossman and J. Fudge (eds.).

Conrad, P., and J. Schneider. 1985. *Deviance and Medicalization: From Badness to Sickness*. Columbus, OH: Merrill Publishing Company.

Cooke, A. 1987. "Stripping: Who Calls the Tune?" In L. Bell (ed.), *Good Girls, Bad Girls: Sex Trade Workers and Feminists Face to Face*. Toronto: Women's Press.

Coomber, R., and N. South (eds.). 2004. *Drug Use and Cultural Contexts: 'Beyond the West.'* London: Free Association Books

Cooper, S. 1993. "The Evolution of the Federal Women's Prison." In E. Adelberg and C. Currie (eds.).

CORP. 1987. "Realistic Feminists." In L. Bell (ed.), *Good Girls, Bad Girls: Sex Trade Workers and Feminists Face to Face*. Toronto: Woman's Press.

Correctional Investigator. 2003. *Response to the Canadian Human Rights Commission's Consultation Paper for the Special Report on the Situation of Federally Sentenced Women*. Available at <http://www.chrc-ccdp.ca/legislation>. (Accessed September 30, 2005.)

Correctional Service of Canada (CSC). 2005a. *Basic Facts About the Correctional Service of Canada*. Available at <http://www.csc-scc.gc.ca>. (Accessed July 6, 2005.)

_____. 2005b. CSC Action Plan in Response to the Report of the Canadian Human Rights Commission. Available at <http://www.csc-scc.gc.ca/text/prgm/fsw/gender4/CHRC_response_e.shtml>. (Accessed May 12, 2005.)

_____. 2002–03. *Department Performance Report, 2002–03*. Available at <http://www.csc-scc.gc.ca/text/pblct/dpr/2003/section_3_overview_of_changes_e.shtml>. (Accessed June 10, 2005.)

_____. 1995. *Board of Investigation — Major Disturbance and Other Related Incidents — Prison for Women from Friday April 22 to Tuesday April 26th, 1994*. Ottawa.

_____. 1990. *Creating Choices: Report of the Task Force on Federally Sentenced Women*. Ottawa: Solicitor General.

Corrigan, P., and D. Sayer. 1985. *The Great Arch: English State Formation as Cultural Revolution*. London: Basil Blackwell.

_____. 1981. "How the Law Rules: Variations on Some Themes in Karl Marx." In Bob Fryer et al. (eds.), *Law, State, and Society*. London: Croom Helm.

Cossman, B. 2002. "Family Feuds: Neo-Liberal and Neo-Conservative Visions of the Reprivatization Project." In Brenda Cossman and Judy Fudge (eds.).

Cossman, B., and J. Fudge (eds.). 2002. *Privatization, Law, and the Challenge to Feminism*. Toronto: University of Toronto Press.

Covington, S., and B. Bloom. 2004. "Creating Gender Responsive Services in Correctional Settings: Context and Considerations." Paper presented at the American Society of Criminology Annual Meetings, November 17–20, Nashville, Tennessee.

Covington, S., and J. Surrey. 2000. "The Relational Model of Women's Psychological Development: Implications for Substance Abuse." Working Paper Series (No. 91) Wellesley, MA: Stone Center.

_____. 1997. "The Relational Model of Women's Psychological Development: Implications for Substance Abuse." In S. Wilsnack and R. Wilsnack (eds.), *Gender and Alcohol: Individual and Social Perspectives.* New Brunswick, NJ: Rutgers University Press.

Cowie, J., V. Cowie, and E. Slater. 1968. *Delinquency in Girls.* London: Heinemann.

Criminal Intelligence Service Canada. 2004. *2004 Annual Report on Organized Crime in Canada.* Available at <www.cisa.gc.ca>. (Accessed September 1, 2005.)

Cruikshank, B. 1996. "Revolutions Within: Self-government and Self-esteem." In A. Barry, T. Osborne, and N. Rose (eds.).

Da Cunha, M. 2005. "From Neighborhood to Prison: Women in the War on Drugs in Portugal." In J. Sudbury (ed.), *Global Lockdown: Race, Gender and the Prison-Industrial Complex.* London: Routledge.

Dalpy, M. 2002. "Dark passage in Ontario's past: Until 1958, female minors deemed incorrigible could be put in jail: Velma Demerson was one." *Globe and Mail,* March 22.

Daly, K. 1998. "Women's Pathways to Felony Court: Feminist Theories of Lawbreaking and Problems of Representation." In K. Daly and L. Maher (eds.).

_____. 1992. "Women's Pathways to Felony Court: Feminist Theories of Lawbreaking and Problems of Representation." *Southern California Review of Law and Women's Studies* 2.

_____. 1989. "Rethinking Judicial Paternalism: Gender, Work-Family Relations, and Sentencing." *Gender and Society* 3, 1.

_____. 1987. "Discrimination in the Criminal Courts: Family, Gender, and the Problem of Equal Treatment." *Social Forces* 66, 1.

Daly, K., and M. Chesney-Lind. 1988. "Feminism and Criminology." *Justice Quarterly* 5, 4.

Daly, K., and L. Maher (eds.). 1998. *Criminology at the Crossroads: Feminist Readings in Crime and Justice.* New York: Oxford.

Daly, K., and D. Stephens. 1995. "The Dark Figure of Criminology: Towards a Black and Multi-Ethnic Feminist Agenda for Theory and Research." In N. Rafter and F. Heidensohn (eds.).

Dauvergne, M. 2004. "Homicide in Canada, 2003." *Juristat* 24.8. Ottawa: Canadian Centre for Justice Statistics.

Davies, M. 1987. "The Patients' World: British Columbia's Mental Health Facilities, 1910–1935." Unpublished MA Thesis, University of Waterloo.

Davis, A. 2003. *Are Prisons Obsolete?* New York: Seven Stories Press.

Davis, K. 1937. "The Sociology of Prostitution." *American Sociological Review* 2.5.

Davis, N.J., and Faith, K. 1987. "Women and the State: Changing Models of Social Control." J. In Lowman, J. et al., (eds.), *Transcarceration: Essays in the Sociology of Social Control.* Aldershot: Gower.

Dean, M. 1999. *Governmentality: Power and Rule in Modern Society.* London: Sage Publications.

_____. 1994. "'A Social Structure of Many Souls': Moral Regulation, Government and Self-Formation." *Canadian Journal of Sociology* 19, 2.

DeCou, K. 2002. "A Gender-Wise Prison: Opportunities for, and Limits to, Reform." In P. Carlen (ed.), *Women and Punishment: The Struggle for Justice.* Cullompton, UK: Willan.

Deis, M., K. Rokosh, S. Sagert, B. Robertson, and I. Kerr-Fitzsimmons. 2000. "A Historical Act — Bill 1: Protection of Children Involved in Prostitution." Unpublished background paper. Edmonton: Government of Alberta.

DeKeseredy, W., S. Alvi, M. Schwartz, and A. Tomaszewski. 2003. *Under Siege: Poverty and Crime in a Canadian Public Housing Community*. Lanham, MD: Lexington Press.

DeKeseredy, W., and R. Hinch. 1991. *Woman Abuse: Sociological Perspectives*. Toronto: Thompson.

DeKeseredy, W., and B. MacLean. 1998. "'But Women Do It Too': The Contexts and Nature of Female-to-Male Violence in Canadian Heterosexual Dating Relationships." In K. Bonnycastle and G. Rigakos (eds.), *Unsettling Truths: Battered Women, Policy, Politics, and Contemporary Research in Canada*. Vancouver: Collective Press.

Dell, C., R. Sinclair, and R. Boe. 2001. *Canadian Federally Incarcerated Adult Women Profiles Trends from 1981 to 1998*. Ottawa: Research Branch. Correctional Service of Canada.

Demerson, V. 2004. *Incorrigible*. Waterloo: Wilfred Laurier University Press.

_____. 2001. "The Female Refuges Act." *Opening the Doors: The Newsletter of the Council of Elizabeth Fry Societies of Ontario*. (Spring).

Denis, C. 1995. "'Government Can Do Whatever It Wants': Moral Regulation in Ralph Klein's Alberta." *Canadian Review of Sociology and Anthropology* 32, 3.

Denton, B. 2001. "Property Crime and Women Drug Dealers in Australia." *Journal of Drug Issues* 31, 2.

DERA-Dancers Equal Rights Association of Ottawa. Forthcoming. *Erotic Dancers' Labour Needs Assessment*. Ottawa.

_____. 2004. *Handouts: Roundtable of Regulation, Ottawa, January 27, 2004*, Unpublished.

Desjardins, N., and T. Hotton. 2004. "Trends in Drug Offences and the Role of Alcohol and Drugs in Crime." *Juristat* 24.1.

Devens, C. 1992. *Countering Colonization: Native American Women and Great Lake Missions, 1630–1900*. Berkeley: University of California Press.

Dhruvarajan, V. 2002. "Women of Colour in Canada." In V. Dhruvarajan and J. Vickers (eds.), *Gender, Race and Nation: A Global Perspective*. Toronto: University of Toronto Press.

Diamond, M. 2000. "Community Lawyering: Revisiting the Old Neighborhood." *Columbia Human Rights Law Review* 32.

Diaz-Cotto. 2005. "Latinas and the War on Drugs in the United States, Latin America, and Europe." In J. Sudbury (ed.), *Global Lockdown: Race, Gender and the Prison-Industrial Complex*. London: Routledge.

Dobash, R.E., and R. Dobash. 2004. "Women's Violence to Men in Intimate Relationships: Working on a Puzzle." *British Journal of Criminology* 44.

_____. 1992. *Women, Violence and Social Change*. London: Routledge.

_____. 1979. *Violence Against Wives: A Case Against the Patriarchy*. New York: Free Press.

Dobash, R.E., R. Dobash, and S. Guttridge. 1986: *The Imprisonment of Women*. Oxford: Basil Blackwell.

Dobash, R., R.E. Dobash, M. Wilson, and M. Daly. 1992. "The Myth of Sexual Symmetry in Marital Violence." *Social Problems* 39, 1 (February).

Doob, A., and J. Sprott. 1998. "Is the 'Quality' of Youth Violence Becoming More Serious?" *Canadian Journal of Criminology* 40, 2.

Dowbiggin, I.R. 1997. *Keeping American Sane: Psychiatry and Eugenics in the United States and Canada, 1880–1940*. Ithaca, NY: Cornell University Press.

Dubinsky, K., and F. Iacovetta. 1991. "Murder, Womanly Virtue, and Motherhood: The

Case of Angelina Napolitano, 1911–1922." *Canadian Historical Review* 72, 4 (December).

Dubois, E., and L. Gordon. 1983. "Seeking Ecstasy on the Battlefield: Danger and Pleasure in Nineteenth-Century Sexual Thought." *Feminist Studies* 9.

Duchesne, D. 1997. "Street Prostitution in Canada." *Juristat* 17, 2. Ottawa: Canadian Centre for Justice Statistics.

Duguid, S. 2000. *Can Prisons Work? The Prisoner as Object and Subject in Modern Corrections.* Toronto: University of Toronto Press.

Dumont-Smith, C. 1995. "Aboriginal Canadian Children Who Witness and Live With Violence." In E. Peled, P. Jaffe and J. Edeson (eds.), *Ending the Cycle of Violence: Community Responses to Children of Battered Women.* Thousand Oaks, CA: Sage.

Duncan, K. 1965. "Irish Famine Immigration and the Social Structure of Canada West." *Canadian Review of Sociology and Anthropology* 1.

Dutton, D. 1994. "Patriarchy and Wife Assault: The Ecological Fallacy." *Violence and Victims* 9.

Eaton, M. 1993. *Women After Prison.* Buckingham: Open University Press.

Eaves, D., R. James, P. Ogloff, and R. Roesch (eds.). 2000. *Mental Disorders and the Criminal Code: Legal Background and Contemporary Perspectives.* Burnaby: Simon Fraser University Mental Health, Law, and Policy Institute.

Eden, D. 2002. *Inquest into the Death of Kimberly Rogers: Jury Recommendations.* Sudbury, ON.

Eden, Dr. D.S. 2003. Letter to Chief Coroner of Ontario re: Inquest into the Death of Kimberly Rogers.

Edstrand, L., and J. Blume. 2000. *U.S. Customs Service, Better Targeting of Airline Passengers for Personal Searches Could Produce Better Results.* Washington, DC: General Accounting Office.

Edwards, S. 1985. "Gender Justice? Defending Defendants and Mitigating Sentence." In S. Edwards (ed.), *Gender, Sex and the Law.* London: Croom Helm.

Ehrenreich, B. 2001. *Nickel and Dimed: On (not) getting by in America.* New York: Metropolitan Books.

Eljdupovic-Guzina, G. 1999. *Parenting Roles and the Experiences of Abuse in Women Offenders: Review of the Offender Intake Assessments.* Ottawa: Correctional Service of Canada, Federally Sentenced Women Program.

Ericson, R., and K. Haggerty. 1997. *Policing the Risk Society.* Toronto: University of Toronto Press.

Evans, P., and K. Swift. 2000. "Single Mothers and the Press: Rising Tides, Moral Panic, and Restructuring Discourses." In Sheila M. Neysmith (ed.), *Restructuring Caring Labour.* Toronto: Oxford University Press.

Ewing, P., and S. Silbey. 1995. "Subversive Stories and Hegemonic Tales: Toward a Sociology of Narrative." *Law and Society Review* 29, 2.

Faith, K. 2000. "Seeking Transformative Justice for Women: Views from Canada." *Journal of International Women's Studies*, 2.1.

_____. 1999. "Transformative Justice versus Re-entrenched Correctionalism: The Canadian Experience." In S. Cook and S. Davies (eds.), *Harsh Punishment: International Experiences of Women's Imprisonment.* Boston: Northeastern University Press.

_____. 1995. "Aboriginal Women's Healing Lodge: Challenge to Penal Correctionalism?" *Journal of Human Justice* 6, 2.

_____. 1993. *Unruly Women: The Politics of Confinement and Resistance.* Vancouver: Press Gang Publishers.

Faith, K., and D. Currie. 1993. *Seeking Shelter: A State of Battered Women.* Vancouver: Collective Press.

Faith, K., and K. Pate. 2000. "Personal and Political Musings on Activism." In K. Hannah-Moffat and M. Shaw (eds.).

Federally Sentenced Women Program (FSWP). 1994. *Correctional Program Strategy for Women.* Ottawa: Correctional Service of Canada.

Federal-Provincial-Territorial Ministers Responsible for the Status of Women. 2002. *Assessing Violence Against Women: A Statistical Profile.* Available at <http://www.swc-cfc.gc.ca/pubs/0662331664/index_e.html>. (Accessed January 13, 2006.)

Federal-Provincial-Territorial Working Group on Prostitution. 1998. *Report and Recommendations in Respect of Legislation, Policy and Practices Concerning Prostitution-Related Activities.* Ottawa: Department of Justice.

Feierman, J. 2004. "Creative Prison Lawyering: From Silence to Democracy." *Georgetown Journal of Poverty Law and Policy* 11.

Feminist Review. 2001. "Sex Work Reassessed." (Special Edition) 67, 1.

Feree, M. 1990. "Between Two Worlds: German Feminist Approaches to Working-class Women." In J. Nielsen (ed.), *Feminist Research Methods.* Boulder: Westview Press.

_____. 1984. "Sacrifice, Satisfaction and Social Change: Employment and the Family." In K. Sacks and D. Remy (eds.), *My Troubles are Going to Have Trouble with Me.* New Brunswick, NJ: Rutgers University Press.

Fillmore, C., and C. Anne Dell. 2001. "A Study of Prairie Women: Violence and Self Harm." *The Canadian Women's Health Network* 4 (Spring). Available at <http://www.cwhn.ca>. (Accessed October 18, 2005.)

Finn, A., S. Trevethan, G. Carriere, and M. Kowalski. 1999. "Female Inmates, Aboriginal Inmates, and Inmates Serving Life Sentences: A One Day Snapshot." *Juristat* 19, 5. Ottawa: Canadian Centre for Justice Statistics.

Finnane, M. 1985. "Asylums, Families and the State." *History Workshop Journal* 20 (Autumn).

Firestone, S. 1970. *The Dialectic of Sex: The Case for Feminist Revolution.* New York: Bantam.

Flavin, J. 2004. "Feminism for the Mainstream Criminologist: An Invitation." In B.R. Price and N.J. Sokoloff (eds.), *The Criminal Justice System and Women: Offenders, Prisoners, Victims, and Workers.* Third edition. New York: McGraw-Hill.

Flexner, A. 1920. *Prostitution in Europe.* New York: Century Co.

Flowers, A. 1998. *The Fantasy Factory: An Insider's of the Phone Sex Industry.* Philadelphia: University of Pennsylvania Press.

Forsyth Report. 1997. "Children Involved in Prostitution." Edmonton, Alberta: Ministry of Family and Social Services.

Fortin, D. 2004a. *Program Strategy for Women Offenders.* Ottawa: Correctional Service of Canada.

_____. 2004b. "A Correctional Programming Strategy for Women." *Forum on Correction Research.* Ottawa: Correctional Services of Canada. Available at <http://www.csc-scc.gc.ca>. (Accessed October 18, 2005.)

Foucault, M. 1983. "The Subject and Power." In H. Dreyfus and P. Rabinow (eds.), *Michel Foucault: Beyond Structuralism and Hermeneutics.* Second edition. Chicago: University of Chicago Press.

_____. 1979. *History of Sexuality: An Introduction.* Vol. 1. London: Penguin.

_____. 1978a. "Governmentality." In G. Burchell, C. Gordon, and P. Miller (eds.), *The*

Foucault Effect: Studies in Governmentality. Chicago: University of Chicago Press, 1991.

_____. 1978b. "Politics and the Study of Discourse." *Ideology and Consciousness* (Spring).

_____. 1977. *Discipline and Punish: The Birth of the Prison*. New York: Vintage.

Fox, K. 2001. "Self-Change and Resistance in Prison." In J. Gubrium and J. Holstein (eds.), *Institutional Selves: Troubled Identities in a Postmodern World*. Oxford: Oxford University Press.

_____. 1999. "Changing Violent Minds: Discursive Correction and Resistance in the Cognitive Treatment of Violent Offenders in Prison." *Social Problems* 46,1.

Frank, K. 1998. "The Production of Identity and the Negotiation of Intimacy in a 'Gentleman's Club.'" *Sexualities* 1, 2.

Frank, L.R. 1978. *The History of Shock Treatment*. San Francisco: Self-published.

Fraser, N. 1997. *Justice Interruptus: Critical Reflections on the "Postsocialist" Condition*. New York: Routledge.

_____. 1989. *Unruly Practices: Power, Discourse and Gender in Contemporary Social Theory*. Minneapolis: University of Minnesota Press.

Fraser, N., and L. Gordon. 1997. "A Genealogy of Dependency." In N. Fraser (ed.), *Justice Interruptus*. New York: Routledge.

_____. 1994. "A Genealogy of Dependency: Tracing a Keyword of the U.S. Welfare State." *Signs* 19, 2.

Freedman, E.B. 1981: *Their Sister's Keepers: Women's Prison Reform in America, 1830–1930*. Ann Arbor: University of Michigan Press.

Freund, M. 2002. "The Politics of Naming: Constructing Prostitutes and Regulating Women in Vancouver, 1939–45." In J. McLaren, R. Menzies, and D. Chunn (eds.), *Regulating Lives: Historical Essays on the State, Society, the Individual, and the Law*. Vancouver: University of British Columbia Press.

Fudge J. 2002. "From Segregation to Privatization: Equality, the Law and Women Public Servants 1908–2001." In B. Cossman and J. Fudge (eds.).

Fudge J., and B. Cossman. 2002. "Introduction: Privatization, Law and the Challenge to Feminism." In B. Cossman and J. Fudge (eds.).

Gagnon, L. 2002. "Rising Drug Costs in Canada." *Federations* 2.4.

Galloway, G. 2004. "Liberals Scrap Lifetime Ban for Those who Cheat Welfare System." *Globe and Mail*, January 10.

Galton, F. 1907 (1883). *Inquiries into Human Faculty and its Development*. New York: Dent and Dutton.

Garland, D. 2001. *The Culture of Control: Crime and Social Order in Contemporary Society*. Chicago: University of Chicago Press.

_____. 2000. "The Culture of High Crime Societies: Some Preconditions of Recent 'Law and Order' Policies." *The British Journal of Criminology* 40, 3 (Summer).

_____. 1996. "The Limits of State Sovereignty: Strategies of Crime Control in Contemporary Society." *The British Journal of Criminology* 36, 4 (Autumn).

Gaskell, J. 1986. "Conceptions of Skill and Work of Women: Some Historical and Political Issues." In R. Hamilton and M. Barrett (eds.), *The Politics of Diversity: Feminism, Marxism and Nationalism*. London: Verso.

Gavigan, S. 1999. "Poverty Law, Theory and Practice: The Place of Class and Gender in Access to Justice." In E. Comack (ed.), *Locating Law: Race/Class/Gender Connections*. Halifax: Fernwood.

_____. 1993. "Women's Crime: New Perspectives and Old Theories." In E. Adelberg and C. Currie (eds.).

Geller, J.L., and M. Harris. 1994. *Women of the Asylum: Voices From Behind the Walls, 1840–1945*. New York: Anchor Doubleday.

Gelsthorpe, L. 1989. *Sexism and the Female Offender.* Aldershot, England: Gower.

Gelsthorpe, L., and A. Morris (eds.). 1990. *Feminist Perspectives in Criminology*. Milton Keyes and Philadelphia: Open University Press.

_____. 1988. "Feminism and Criminology in Britain." *British Journal of Criminology* 23.

Giffen, P., S. Endicott, and S. Lambert. 1991. *Panic and Indifference: The Politics of Canada's Drug Laws*. Ottawa: Canadian Centre on Substance Abuse.

Gilchrist, L. 1995. "Urban Survivors, Aboriginal Street Youth: Vancouver, Winnipeg and Montreal." Research Report presented to the Royal Commission on Aboriginal Peoples (January).

Gilfus, M. 2002. "Women's Experiences of Abuse as a Risk Factor for Incarceration." Available at <http://www.vaw.umn.edu/>. (Accessed March 12, 2004.)

_____. 1992. "From Victims to Survivors to Offenders: Women's Routes of Entry and Immersion into Street Crime." *Women and Criminal Justice* 4 (1).

Gilliom, J. 2001. *Overseers of the Poor: Surveillance, Resistance, and The Limits of Privacy*. London: The University of Chicago Press.

Gilmore, J. 2002. "Creeping Privatization in Health Care: Implications for Women as the State Redraws its Role." In B. Cossman and J. Fudge (eds.).

Girshick, L. 2003. "Abused Women and Incarceration." In B. Zaitzow and J. Thomas (eds.), *Women in Prison: Gender and Social Control*. London: L Reinner.

Glasbeek, A. 2003. "'A Justice of Their Own': The Toronto Women's Court, 1913–1934." Ph.D. dissertation. Toronto: York University.

Glasbeek, H. 2002. *Wealth by Stealth: Corporate Crime, Corporate Law, and the Perversion of Democracy*. Toronto: Between the Lines.

Glover, E. 1969 [1943]. *The Psychopathology of the Prostitute*. London: Institute for the Study and Treatment of Delinquency.

Glueck, E., and S. Glueck. 1934. *Five Hundred Delinquent Women*. New York: Alfred A. Knopf.

Goffman, E. 1961. *Asylums: Essays on the Social Situation of Mental Patients and Other Inmates*. New York: Anchor Books.

Golding, P., and S. Middleton. 1982. *Images of Welfare: Press and Public Attitudes to Poverty.* Oxford: Martin Robertson.

Goodkind, S. 2005. "Gender-Specific Services in the Juvenile Justice System: A Critical Examination." *Affilia* 20, 1 (Spring).

Gordon, L. 1994. *Pitied But Not Entitled: Single Mothers and the History of Welfare*. Cambridge, MA: Harvard University Press.

Goring, C. 1913. *The English Convict: A Statistical Study*. London: His Majesty's Stationery Office.

Gorman, K. 2001. "Cognitive Behaviorism and the Holy Grail: The Quest for a Universal Means of Managing Offender Risk." *Probation Journal* 48, 1.

Gottfredson, M., and T. Hirschi. 1990. *General Theory of Crime*. Stanford: Stanford University Press.

Gray, M. 1999. "Long Day's Journey into Night." *The Drug Policy Letter* 39.

Green, M. 1979. "The History of Canadian Narcotics Control." *University of Toronto Faculty Law Review* 37.

Green, P. 1998. *Drugs, Trafficking and Criminal Policy: The Scapegoat Strategy*. Winchester, UK: Waterside Press.

_____. 1996. "Drug Couriers: The Construction of a Public Enemy." In P. Green (ed.), *Drug Couriers: A New Perspective*. London: Quartet Books.

Greenwald, H. 1958. *The Call Girl: A Social and Psychoanalytic Study.* New York: Ballantine.

Greenwood, F. Murray, and B. Boissery. 2000. *Uncertain Justice: Canadian Women and Capital Punishment, 1754–1953*. Toronto: Dundurn.

Gunn, R., and C. Minch. 1988. *Sexual Assault: The Dilemma of Disclosure, The Question of Conviction*. Winnipeg: University of Manitoba Press.

Gunn Allen, P. 1992. *The Sacred Hoop: Recovering the Feminine in American Indian Traditions*. Boston: Beacon Press.

Hadley, K. 2001. *And We Still Ain't Satisfied: Gender Inequality in Canada: A Status Report for 2001*. Toronto: National Action Committee on the Status of Women.

Hagan, J., A.R. Gillis, and J. Simpson. 1985. "The Class Structure of Gender and Delinquency: Toward a Power-Control Theory of Common Delinquent Behavior." *American Journal of Sociology* 90.

Hagan, J., J. Simpson, and A.R. Gillis. 1987. "Class in the Household: A Power-Control Theory of Gender and Delinquency." *American Journal of Sociology* 92, 4 (January).

_____. 1979. "The Sexual Stratification of Social Control: A Gender-Based Perspective on Crime and Delinquency." *British Journal of Sociology* 30.

Hall, S. 1988. "The Toad in the Garden: Thatcherism Among the Theorists." In C. Nelson and L. Grossberg (eds.), *Marxism and the Interpretation of Culture*. Champaign: University of Illinois Press.

_____. 1980. "Reformism and the Legislation of Consent." In National Deviancy Conference (ed.), *Permissiveness and Control: The Fate of the Sixties Legislation*. London: Macmillan.

Hamilton, A.C., and C.M. Sinclair. 1991. *The Justice System and Aboriginal People: Report of the Aboriginal Justice Inquiry of Manitoba*. Vol. 1. Winnipeg: Queen's Printer.

Haney, L. 2004. "Introduction: Gender, Welfare and States of Punishment." *Social Politics* 11, 3.

Hannah-Moffat, K. 2005a. "Criminogenic Need and the Transformative Risk Subject: Hybridizations of Risk/Need in Penality." *Punishment and Society* 7, 1.

_____. 2005b. "Losing Ground: Gender Knowledges, Parole Risk and Responsibility." *Social Politics* 11, 3.

_____. 2004. "Gendering Risk at What Cost: Negotiations of Gender and Risk in Canadian Prisons." *Feminism and Psychology* 14,2.

_____. 2002. "Creating Choices: Reflecting on Choices." In P. Carlen (ed.), *Women and Punishment: The Struggle for Justice*. Cullompton, UK: Willan.

_____. 2001. *Punishment in Disguise: Penal Governance and Federal Imprisonment of Women in Canada*. Toronto: University of Toronto Press.

_____. 2000. "Prisons that Empower: Neo-liberal Governance in Canadian Women's Prisons." *British Journal of Criminology* 40, 3 (Summer).

_____. 1999. "Moral Agent or Actuarial Subject." *Theoretical Criminology* 3,1.

_____. 1995. "Feminine Fortresses: Women-Centered Prisons?" *The Prison Journal* 75, 2.

Hannah-Moffat, K., and P. Maurutto. 2004. *Youth Risk/Needs Assessment: An Overview of Issues and Practices*. Ottawa: Department of Justice.

Hannah-Moffat, K., and M. Shaw. 2001. *Taking Risks: Incorporating Gender and Culture into the Assessment and Classification of Federally Sentenced Women in Canada.* Ottawa: Status of Women Canada.

_____ (eds.). 2000a. *An Ideal Prison? Critical Essays on Women's Imprisonment in Canada.* Halifax: Fernwood.

_____. 2000b. "Introduction." In K. Hannah-Moffat and M. Shaw (eds.).

Harding, S. 1990. "Feminism, Science, and the Anti-Enlightenment Critiques." In L. Nicholson (ed.), *Feminism/Postmodernism* London: Routledge.

_____ (ed.). 1987. *Feminism and Methodology.* Milton Keyes: Open University Press.

Harper, R., G. Harper, and J. Stockdale. 2002. "The Role and Sentencing of Women in Drug Trafficking." *Legal and Criminal Psychology* 7.1.

Harris, R. 1989. *Murders and Madness: Medicine, Law, and Society in the Fin de Siècle.* Oxford: Clarendon Press.

Hartman, M. 1985. *Victorian Murderesses: A True History of Thirteen Respectable French and English Women Accused of Unspeakable Crimes.* London: Robson.

Hartnagel, T. 2004. "Correlates of Criminal Behaviour." In R. Linden (ed.), *Criminology: A Canadian Perspective.* Fifth edition. Toronto: Harcourt Brace.

_____. 2000. "Correlates of Criminal Behaviour." In R. Linden (ed.), *Criminology: A Canadian Perspective.* Fourth edition. Toronto: Harcourt Brace.

Hawkins, K. 1983. "Assessing Evil: Decision Behaviour and Parole Board Justice." *British Journal of Criminology* 23, 2.

Hayman, S. 2000. "Prison Reform and Incorporation: Lessons from Britain and Canada." In K. Hannah-Moffat and M. Shaw (eds.).

Hazelwood, R., J. Warren, and P. Dietz. 1993. "Compliant Victims of the Sexual Sadist." *Australian Family Physician* 22, 4 (April).

Health Canada. 2004. *Canadian Tobacco Use Monitoring Survey* (CTUMS). Summary of Results for the first half of 2004 (February to June). Available at <http:www.hc-sc.gc.ca/hecs-sesc/tobacco/research/ctums/2004/summary_first.2004.html>. (Accessed April 13, 2005.)

Hearn, J., and W. Parkin. 1995. *Sex at Work: The Power and Paradox of Organization Sexuality.* New York: St. Martin's Press

Heaven, O. 1996. "Hibiscus: Working with Nigerian Women Prisoners." In P. Green (ed.), *Drug Couriers: A New Perspective.* London: Quartet Books.

Heidensohn, F. 1994. "From Being to Knowing: Some Issues in the Study of Gender in Contemporary Society." *Women and Criminal Justice* 6, 1.

_____. 1985. *Women and Crime.* London: Macmillan.

_____. 1968. "The Deviance of Women: A Critique and an Enquiry." *British Journal of Sociology* 19, 2.

Heimer, K. 1995. "Gender, Race and Pathways to Delinquency." In J. Hagan and R. Peterson (eds.), *Crime and Inequality.* Stanford: Stanford University Press.

Heney, J. 1990. *Report on Self-Injurious Behaviour in the Kingston Prison for Women.* Ottawa: Solicitor General.

Henry, F., C. Tator, W. Mattis, and T. Rees. 2000. *The Colour of Democracy.* Second edition. Toronto: Harcourt Brace

Hepburn, M. 2002. "Providing Care for Pregnant Women who Use Drugs: The Glasgow Women's Reproductive Health Service." In H. Klee, M. Jackson, and S. Lewis (eds.), *Drug Misuse and Motherhood.* London: Routledge.

_____. 1993. "Drug Use in Pregnancy." *British Journal of Hospital Medicine* 49, 1.

Hermer, J., and J. Mosher (eds.). 2002. *Disorderly People.* Halifax: Fernwood.

Heyl, B. 1979. *The Madam as Entrepreneur: Career Management in House Prostitution.* New Brunswick, NJ: Transaction Books.

_____.1977. "The Training of House Prostitutes." *Social Problems* 24.

Highcrest, A. 2000. "When Protection is Punishment." *Globe and Mail*, August 14: A13.

Hillyard, M., and I. Morrison. 1999."The Pecker Detectors are Back: Regulation of the Family Form in Ontario Welfare Policy." *Journal of Canadian Studies* 34, 3 (Summer).

Hirschi, T. 1969. *Causes of Delinquency.* Berkeley: University of California Press.

Hochschild, A. 1983. *The Managed Heart: Commercialization of Human Feeling.* Berkeley: University of California Press.

Hogeveen, B. 2003. "Can't You Be a Man?" Unpublished PhD thesis. University of Toronto.

Hoigard, C., and L. Finstad. 1992. *Backstreets: Prostitution, Money and Love.* University Park: Pennsylvania University Press.

Hooton, E.A. 1939. *The American Criminal: An Anthropological Study.* Cambridge: Harvard University Press.

Horii, G. 2000. "Processing Humans." In K. Hannah-Moffat and M. Shaw (eds.).

Hornick, J.P., and F. Bolitho. 1992. *A Review of the Implementation of the Child Sexual Abuse Legislation in Selected Sites: Studies on the Sexual Abuse of Children in Canada.* Ottawa: Ministry of Supply and Services.

Houtman, I., and M. Kompier. 1995. "Risk Factors and Occupational Risk Groups for Work Stress in the Netherlands." In S. Sauter and L. Murphy (eds.), *Organizational Risk Factors for Job Stress.* Washington: American Psychological Association.

Howarth, D. 2000. *Discourse.* Buckingham: Open University Press.

Howden-Windell, J., and D. Clark. 1999. *Criminogenic Needs of Female Offenders: A Literature Review.* London: HM Prison Service.

Howe, A. 1994. *Punish and Critique: Towards a Feminist Analysis of Penality.* London: Routledge.

Hudson, B. 2002. "Gender Issues in Penal Policy and Penal Theory." In P. Carlen (ed.), *Women and Punishment: The Struggle for Justice.* Cullompton, UK: Willan.

_____. 1998. "Punishment and Governance." *Social and Legal Studies* 7, 4.

Hughes, K. 1999. *Gender and Self Employment in Canada: Assessing Trends and Policy Implications.* (Report N0 4W04) Ottawa: CPRN.

Huling, T. 1996. "Prisoners of War: Women Drug Couriers in the United States." In P. Green (ed.), *Drug Couriers: A New Perspective.* London: Quartet Books.

_____. 1992. *Injustice Will Be Done: Women Drug Couriers and the Rockefeller Drug Laws.* New York: Correctional Association of New York.

Humphries, D. 1999. *Crack Mothers: Pregnancy, Drugs, and the Media.* Columbus: Ohio State University Press.

Hunt A. 2002. "Regulating Heterosocial Space: Sexual Politics in the Early Twentieth Century." *Journal of Historical Sociology* 15, 1.

_____. 1999a. "The Purity Wars: Making Sense of Moral Militancy." *Theoretical Criminology* 13, 4.

_____. 1999b. *Governing Morals: A Social History of Moral Regulation.* Cambridge: Cambridge University Press.

_____. 1997. "Moral Regulation and Making-up the New Person: Putting Gramsci to Work." *Theoretical Criminology* 1, 3.

Hustak, A. 1987. *They Were Hanged.* Toronto: Lorimer.

Income Security Advocacy Centre. 2005. *The Matthews Report: Moving Towards Real Income Security*. Toronto. Available at <http://www.incomesecurity.org/index.html>. (Accessed July 5, 2005.)

Ingleby, D. 1983. "Mental Health and Social Order." In S. Cohen and A. Scull (eds.), *Social Control and the State*. New York: St. Martin's Press.

Jackson, Margaret. 1999. "Canadian Aboriginal Women and Their 'Criminality': The Cycle of Violence in the Context of Difference." *The Australian and New Zealand Journal of Criminology* 32, 2.

Jackson, Michael. 1988–89. "Locking Up Natives in Canada." *University of British Columbia Law Review* 23.

_____. 1988. *Justice Behind the Walls*. Ottawa: Canadian Bar Association.

James, J. 1977. "The Prostitute as Victim." In J. Chapman and M. Gates (eds.), *The Victimization of Women*. Beverly Hills, California: Sage Publications.

Järvinen, M. 1993. *Of Vice and Women: Shades of Prostitution* (translated by K. Leeander). Oslo: Scandinavian University Press.

Jarvis, E. 1979. "Mid-Victorian Toronto: Panic, Policy and Public Response, 1857–1873." Unpublished PhD thesis. University of Western Ontario.

Jeffreys, S. 2005. "Different Word, Same Dangers from Trade in Women." *Sydney Morning Herald*.

_____. 2004. "Prostitution as a Harmful Cultural Practice." In C. Stark and R. Whisnant (eds.), *Not for Sale: Feminists Resisting Prostitution and Pornography*. North Melbourne: Spinifex.

_____. 1985. "Prostitution." In D. Rhodes and S. McNeil (eds.), *Women Against Violence Against Women*. London: Onlywomen Press.

Jiménez, M. 1999. "The Law, Violence, and Lisa Neve." *National Post*. Saturday, April 3: B1, B5.

Jiwani, Y. 2002. "Erasing Race: The Story of Reena Virk." In K. McKenna and J. Larkin (eds.), *Violence Against Women: New Canadian Perspectives*. Toronto: Inanna Publications.

Johnson, H. 1996. *Dangerous Domains*. Toronto: Nelson.

Johnson, H., and K. Rodgers. 1993. "A Statistical Overview of Women and Crime in Canada." In E. Adelberg and C. Currie (eds.).

Johnson, M. 2002. "Jane Hocus, Jane Focus." In M. Johnson (ed.), *Jane Sexes It Up*. New York: Thunders Mouth Press.

Johnson, S. 2004. "Adult Correctional Services in Canada, 2002/02." *Juristat* 24, 10.

Jones, A. 1996. *Women Who Kill*. Boston: Beacon Press.

_____. 1994. *Next Time She'll Be Dead: Battering and How to Stop It*. Boston: Beacon Press.

Jordan, J. 1997. "A Relational Perspective for Understanding Women's Development." In J. Jordan (ed.), *Women's Growth in Diversity: More Writings from the Stone Center*. New York: Guilford Press.

Joseph, J. 2006. "Intersectionality of Race/Ethnicity, Class and Justice: Women of Color." In A. Merlo and J. Pollock (eds.), *Women, Law and Social Control*. Boston: Pearson.

Joshua, L. 1996. "Nigeria, Drug Trafficking and Structural Adjustment." In P. Green (ed.), *Drug Couriers: A New Perspective*. London: Quartet Books.

Justice for Girls. *Statement of Opposition to the Secure Care Act*. Available at <www.justiceforgirls.org/publications/pos_securecareact.html>. (Accessed April 20, 2005.)

Kandall, S. 1996. *Substance and Shadow: Women and Addiction in the United States*. Cambridge, MA: Harvard University Press.

Keck, J. 2002. "Remembering Kimberly Rogers." *Perception* 25. Available at <http://www. ccsd.ca/perception/2354/kimberly.htm>. (Accessed May 28, 2003.)

_____. 1996. "When Does the Speaking Profit Us?: Reflections on the Challenges of Developing Feminist Perspectives on Abuse and Violence by Women." In M. Hester, L. Kelly and J. Radford (eds.), *Women, Violence and Male Power*. Buckingham: Open University Press.

_____. 1988. *Surviving Sexual Violence*. Minneapolis: University of Minnesota Press.

Kelm, M-E. 1992. "'The Only Place Likely to do Her any Good': The Admission of Women to British Columbia's Provincial Hospital for the Insane." *BC Studies* 96 (Winter).

Kemshall, H. 2002. "Effective Practice in Probation: An Example of 'Advanced Liberal' Responsibilisation." *The Howard Journal* 41, 1.

Kendall, K. 2002. "Time to Think Again About Cognitive Behavioural Programmes." In P. Carlen (ed.), *Women and Punishment: The Struggle for Justice*. Cullompton, UK: Willan.

_____. 2000. "Psy-ence Fiction: Governing Female Prisons through the Psychological Services." In K. Hannah-Moffat and M. Shaw (eds.).

_____. 1999. "Beyond Grace: Criminal Lunatic Women in Victorian Canada." *Canadian Woman Studies* 19.

_____. 1993. *Program Evaluation of Therapeutic Services at the Prison for Women*. Ottawa: Correctional Service Canada.

_____. 1992. "Dangerous Bodies." In D. Farrington and S. Walklate (eds.), *Offenders and Victims: Theory and Policy*. London: British Society of Criminology.

_____. 1991. "The Politics of Premenstrual Syndrome: Implications for Feminist Justice." *Journal of Human Justice* 2, 2 (Spring).

Kendall, K., and S. Pollack. 2003. "Cognitive Behavioralism in Women's Prisons: A Critical Analysis of Therapeutic Assumptions and Practices." In B. Bloom (ed.).

Kennedy, L., and D. Dutton. 1989. "The Incidence of Wife Assault in Alberta." *Canadian Journal of Behavioural Science* 21.

Kershaw, A., and M. Lasovich. 1991. *Rock-A-Bye Baby: A Death Behind Bars*. Toronto: Oxford University Press.

Kerwin, S. 1999. "The Janet Smith Bill of 1924 and the Language of Race and Nation in British Columbia." *BC Studies* 121 (Spring).

Kesler, K. 2002. "The Plain-clothes Whore." In M. Johnson (ed.).

King, W.L.M. 1908. "The Need for the Suppression of the Opium Traffic in Canada." Ottawa: S.E. Dawson.

Klein, D. 1982. "The Dark Side of Marriage: Battered Wives and the Domination of Women." In N. Rafter and E. Stanko (eds.), *Judge, Lawyer, Victim, Thief: Women, Gender Roles and Criminal Justice*. Boston: Northeastern University Press.

_____. 1973. "The Etiology of Female Crime: A Review of the Literature." *Issues in Criminology* 8, 3.

Klein, S., and A. Long. 2003. *A Bad Time to Be Poor: An Analysis of British Columbia's New Welfare Policies*. Vancouver: Canadian Centre for Policy Alternatives-B.C. Office.

Kline, M. 1997. "Blue Meanies in Alberta: Tory Tactics and the Privatization of Child Welfare." In S.B. Boyd (ed.), *Challenging the Public Private Divide: Feminism, Law and Public Policy*. Toronto: University of Toronto Press.

Knelman, J. 1998. *Twisting in the Wind: The Murderess and the English Press*. Toronto: University of Toronto Press.

Konopka, G. 1966. *The Adolescent Girl in Conflict.* Englewood Cliffs, NJ: Prentice Hall.

Koyama E. 2002. *Instigations from the Whore Revolution.* Portland: Confluere Publications

Kramer, R., and T. Mitchell. 2002. *Walk Toward the Gallows: The Tragedy of Hilda Blake, Hanged 1899.* Don Mills, ON: Oxford University Press.

Kruttschnitt, C. 1982. "Women, Crime and Dependency." *Criminology* 195.

_____. 1980–81. "Social Status and Sentences of Female Offenders." *Law and Society Review* 15, 2.

Laberge, D. 1991. "Women's Criminality, Criminal Women, Criminalized Women?: Questions in and for a Feminist Perspective." *Journal of Human Justice* 2, 2.

Labrum, B. 2005. "The Boundaries of Femininity: Madness and Gender in New Zealand, 1870–1910." In W. Chan, D. Chunn and R. Menzies (eds.), *Women, Madness and the Law: A Feminist Reader.* London: Glasshouse Press.

Lacombe, D. 1994. *Blue Politics: Pornography and the Law in the Age of Feminism.* Toronto: University of Toronto Press.

Laframboise, D. 1999. "Men and Women are Equals in Violence." *National Post* July 10.

_____. 1997. "Sugar and Spice Not So Nice." *Globe and Mail* October 11.

_____. 1996. *The Princess at the Window.* Toronto: Penguin.

Laishes, J. 2002. *The 2002 Mental Health Strategy for Women Offenders.* Ottawa: Correctional Services of Canada: Mental Health Services. Available at <http://www.csc-scc.gc.ca/text/prgrm/fsw/mhealth/toc_e.shtml>. (Accessed October 13, 2005.)

_____. 1997. *Mental Health Strategy for Women Offenders.* Ottawa: Correctional Services of Canada, Federally Sentenced Women Program.

Laishes, J., and S. Lyth. 1996. *Intensive Healing (Mental Health) Project.* Ottawa: Correctional Services of Canada, Federally Sentenced Women Program.

Lalonde, L. 1997. "Tory Welfare Policies: A View from the Inside." In D. Ralph, et al. (eds.), *Open for Business, Closed for People: Mike Harris's Ontario.* Halifax: Fernwood.

Landsberg, M. 2001. "Plight of 'incorrigible' women demands justice." *Toronto Star* May 6.

Laner, M. 1974. "Prostitution as an Illegal Vocation." In C. Bryant (ed.), *Deviant Behaviour.* Chicago: Rand McNally.

LaPrairie, C. 1996. *Examining Aboriginal Corrections in Canada.* Ottawa: Supply and Services Canada.

_____. 1994 *Seen But Not Heard: Native People in the Inner City.* Ottawa: Aboriginal Justice Directorate, Minister of Justice and Attorney General of Canada.

_____. 1993. "Aboriginal Women and Crime in Canada: Identifying the Issues." In E. Adelberg and C. Currie (eds.).

LaRocque, E. 2000. "Violence in Aboriginal Communities." In K. McKenna and J. Larkin (eds.), *Violence Against Women: New Canadian Perspectives.* Toronto: Inanna.

Lawrence, S., and T. Williams. Forthcoming. "Swallowed Up: Drug Couriers at the Borders of Canadian Sentencing." *University of Toronto Law Journal.*

Lee, T. 2004. "In and Out: A Survivor's Memoir of Stripping." In C. Stark and R. Whisnant (eds.), *Not for Sale: Feminists Resisting Prostitution and Pornography.* North Melbourne: Spinifex.

Leonard, E.D. 2003. "Stages of Gendered Disadvantage in the Lives of Convicted Battered Women." In B. Bloom (ed.).

_____. 1982. *Women, Crime and Society: A Critique of Theoretical Criminology.* New York: Longman.

Levi, L., M. Frankenhauser, and B. Gardell. 1986. "The Characteristics of the Workplace and the Nature of Its Social Demands." In S. Wolf and A. Finestone (eds.), *Occupational Stress: Health and Performance at Work.* Littleton, MA: PSG.

Lewis, J. 2000. "Controlling Morality: Law, Morality and Sex Work." In R. Weitzer (ed.), *Sex for Sale: Prostitution, Pornography and the Sex Industry.* New York: Routledge.

Lewis, J., and E. Maticka-Tyndale. 2000. "Licensing Sex Work: Public Policy and Women's Lives." *Canadian Public Policy* XXVI, 4.

Lezubski, D., J. Silver, and E. Black. 2000. "High and Rising: The Growth of Poverty in Winnipeg." In J. Silver (ed.), *Solutions that Work: Fighting Poverty in Winnipeg.* Winnipeg, MB: Canadian Centre for Policy Alternatives (Manitoba) and Fernwood Publishing.

Linehan, M. 1993. *Cognitive-Behavioral Treatment of Borderline Personality Disorder.* New York: The Guilford Press.

Little, M. 2003. "The Leaner, Meaner Welfare Machine: The Ontario Conservative Government's Ideological and Material Attack on Single Mothers." In D. Brock, (ed.), *Making Normal: Social Regulation in Canada.* Scarborough, ON: Nelson Thompson Learning.

_____. 2001. "A Litmus Test for Democracy: The Impact of Ontario Welfare Changes on Single Mothers." *Studies in Political Economy* 66.

_____. 1998. *No Car, No Radio, No Liquor Permit: The Moral Regulation of Single Mothers in Ontario, 1920–1997.* Toronto: Oxford University Press.

Lloyd, A. 2005. "The Treatment of Women Patients in Secure Hospitals." In W. Chan, D. Chunn and R. Menzies (eds.), *Women, Madness and the Law: A Feminist Reader.* London: Glasshouse Press.

Lobel, S. 1993. "Sexuality at Work." *Journal of Vocational Behavior* 42.

Lombroso, C., and E. Ferrero. 1890 [1985]. *The Female Offender.* New York: Appleton.

Los, M. 1990. "Feminism and Rape Law Reform." In L. Gelsthorpe and A. Morris (eds.).

Lowman, J. 2001. *Identifying Research Gaps in the Prostitution Literature.* Research Note. Department of Justice Canada, Research and Statistics Division.

_____. 2000. "Violence and the Outlaw Status of (Street) Prostitution in Canada." *Violence Against Women* 6, 9.

_____. 1992. "Against Street Prostitution." *British Journal of Criminology* 32, 1.

_____. 1991 "Street Prostitutes in Canada: An Evaluation of the Brannigan-Fleischman Opportunity Model." *Canadian Journal of Law and Society* 6.

_____. 1986. "You Can Do It, but Don't Do It Here: Some Comments on Proposals for the Reform of Canadian Prostitution Law." In J. Lowman, M. Jackson, T. Palys, and S. Gavigan (eds.).

Lowman, J., and L. Fraser. 1996. *Violence Against Persons Who Prostitutes: The Experience in British Columbia.* Ottawa: Department of Justice Canada.

Lowman, J, M. Jackson, T. Palys, and S. Gavigan (eds.). 1986. *Regulating Sex: An Anthology of Commentaries on the Findings and Recommendations of the Badgley and Fraser Reports* Burnaby: School of Criminology, Simon Fraser University.

Lowman, J., R.J. Menzies, and T.S. Palys. 1987. "Introduction: Transcarceration and the Modern State of Penality." In J. Lowman et al. (eds.), *Transcarceration: Essays in the Sociology of Social Control*. Aldershot: Gower.

Lugtig, S., and D. Parkes. 2002. "The Charter of Rights and Freedoms Twenty Years Later: Where Do We Stand?" *Herizons* 2002.

Luther, D. 2003. *Report of Inquiries into the Sudden Deaths of Norman Edward Reid and Darryl Brandon Power*. St. John's, NL: Queen's Printer.

Luxton, M., and J. Corman. 2001. *Getting By in Hard Times: Gendered Labour at Home and on the Job*. Toronto: University of Toronto Press.

MacDonald, I., and B. O'Keefe. 2000. *Canadian Holy War: A Story of Clans, Tongs, Murder, and Bigotry*. Surrey: Heritage House.

MacDonald, K. 2003. *Federally Sentenced Women: Canada's Breach of Fiduciary Duty and Failure to Adhere to International Obligations*. Submission of the National Association of Women and the Law to the Canadian Human Rights Commission. Available at <www.elizabethfry.ca/caefs_e.htm>. (Accessed January 14, 2006.)

MacDonald, M., and M.P. Connelly. 1989. "Class and Gender in Fishing Communities in Nova Scotia." *Studies in Political Economy* 30.

MacGuigan Report. 1977. *Report to Parliament: Subcommittee on the Penitentiary System in Canada*. Ottawa: Ministry of Supply and Services.

MacKay, R.D. 1995. "Insanity and Unfitness to Stand Trial in Canada and England: A Comparative Study of Recent Developments." *Journal of Forensic Psychiatry* 6.

MacKinnon C. 1979. *Sexual Harassment of Working Women: A Case of Sex Discrimination*. New Haven: Yale University Press.

MacKinnon, M., and K. Lacey. 2001. "Bleak House." *Globe and Mail*, August 18: F1, F8.

Macklin, A. 2002. "Public Entrance/Private Member." In B. Cossman and J. Fudge (eds.).

MacLeod, L. 1980. *Wife Battering in Canada: The Vicious Circle*. Ottawa: CACSW.

MacPherson, D. 2001. *A Framework for Action: A Four-Pillar Approach to Drug Problems in Vancouver*. Vancouver: City of Vancouver.

Maher, L. 1995. "Dope Girls: Gender, Race and Class in the Drug Economy." Unpublished doctoral dissertation. Rutgers, The State University of New Jersey.

Mahoney, J. 1999. "Woman Freed of Dangerous Offender Label." *Globe and Mail*. June 30: A3.

Mahood, L. 1990. *The Magdalenes: Prostitution in the Nineteenth Century*. London, Routledge.

Maidment, M. Forthcoming. *Doing Time on the Outside: Deconstructing the Benevolent Community*. Toronto: University of Toronto Press.

_____. 2005. "Doing Time on the Outside: Transcarceration and the Social Control of Criminalized Women in the Community." Unpublished PhD Dissertation. Department of Sociology and Anthropology, Carleton University, Ottawa.

Maier, I. 1992. "Forced Cesarean Section as Reproductive Control and Violence: A Feminist Social Work Perspective on the 'Baby R' Case." Unpublished Master's thesis, Simon Fraser University, Burnaby, BC.

Manitoba Child and Youth Secretariat. 1996. *Report of the Working Group on Juvenile Prostitution*. Winnipeg: Manitoba Child and Youth Secretariat.

Mann, R. 2003. "Violence Against Women or Family Violence? The 'Problem' of Female Perpetration in Domestic Violence." In L. Samuelson and W. Antony (eds.), *Power and Resistance: Critical Thinking About Canadian Social Issues*. Halifax: Fernwood.

_____. 2000. *Who Owns Domestic Abuse? The Local Politics of a Social Problem*.

Toronto: University of Toronto Press.

Maracle, B. 1993. *Crazywater: Native Voices on Addiction and Recovery*. Toronto: Penguin.

Maroney, H., and M. Luxton. 1997. "Gender at Work: Canadian Feminist Political Economy since 1988." In W. Clement (ed.), *Understanding Canada: Building the New Canadian Political Economy*. Montreal: McGill-Queen's University Press.

Marsh J., A. Geist, and N. Caplan. 1982. *Rape and the Limits of Law*. Boston: Auburn House.

Martin, D. 2002. "Both Pitied and Scorned: Child Prostitution in an Era of Privatization." In B. Cossman and J. Fudge (eds.).

_____.1993. "Casualties of the Criminal Justice System: Women and Justice Under the War on Drugs." *Canadian Journal of Women and the Law* 6.2.

_____.1992. "Passing the Buck: Prosecution of Welfare Fraud; Preservation of Stereotypes." *Windsor Yearbook of Access to Justice* 12.

Martinson, D., M. MacCrimmon, I. Grant, and C. Boyle. 1991. "A Forum on *Lavallee* v. *R*: Women and Self-Defence." *University of British Columbia Law Review* 25, 1.

Marx, K. 1974 [1859]. *Capital*. Volume 1. New York: International.

Masuch, C. 2004. "Man-Haters, Militants and Aggressive Women: Young Women, Media Representations and Feminist Identity." Unpublished MA Thesis, Queen's University, Kingston.

Matthews, D. 2004. *Review of Employment Assistance Programs in Ontario Works and Ontario Disability Support Program*. Report to The Honourable Sandra Pupatello, Minister of Community and Social Services. Available at <http://www.incomesecurity.org/index.html>. (Accessed July 5, 2005.)

Matthews, N. 1994. *Confronting Rape*. London: Routledge.

Mauer, M., and M. Chesney-Lind (eds.). 2002. *Invisible Punishment: The Collateral Consequences of Mass Imprisonment*. New York: The New Press.

Mawani, R. 2002a. "In Between and Out of Place: Mixed-race Identity, Liquor, and the Law in British Columbia, 1850–1913." In S. Razack (ed.), *Race, Space, and the Law: Unmapping a White Settler Society*. Toronto: Between the Lines.

_____. 2002b. "Regulating the 'Respectable' Classes: Venereal Disease, Gender, and Public Health Initiatives in Canada, 1914–35." In J. McLaren, R. Menzies and D. Chunn (eds.), *Regulating Lives: Historical Essays on the State, Society, the Individual, and the Law*. Vancouver: University of British Columbia Press.

McClintock, A. 1993. "Maid to Order: Commercial Fetishism and Gender Power." *Social Text* 37.

McCorkel, J. 2004. "Criminally Dependent? Gender, Punishment, and the Rhetoric of Welfare Reform." *Social Politics* 11, 3.

_____. 2003. "Embodied Surveillance and the Gendering of Punishment." *Journal of Contemporary Ethnography* 32, 1.

McDonagh, D., K. Taylor, and K. Blanchette. 2002. "Correctional Adaptation of Dialectical Behaviour Therapy (DBT) for Federally Sentenced Women." *Forum on Corrections Research* 14, 2.

McDonald, L., B. Moore, and N. Timoshkina. 2000. *Migrant Sex Trade Workers from Eastern Europe and the Former Soviet Union: The Canadian Case*. Ottawa: Status of Women Canada.

McEvoy, M., and J. Daniluk. 1995. "Wounds to the Soul: The Experiences of Aboriginal Women as Survivors of Sexual Abuse." *Canadian Psychology* 36.

McGillivray, A. 1998. "'A moral vacuity in her which is difficult if not impossible to explain': Law, Psychiatry and the Remaking of Karla Homolka." *International Journal of the Legal Profession* 5, 2/3.

McGovern, C. 1998. "Sugar and Spice and Cold as Ice: Teenage Girls are Closing the Gender Gap in Violent Crime with Astonishing Speed." *Alberta Report* 25.

McGrath, A. 1992. "Mental Health Services for Women." *Healthsharing* Spring/Summer.

McIntyre, M. 2005. "Court Eyes Native Women's Plight: Rare Ruling Allows Groups to Seek Dismissal of Manslaughter Charge." *Winnipeg Free Press*, March 3.

McIvor, S., and E. Johnson. 2003. *Detailed Position of the Native Women's Association of Canada on the Complaint Regarding the Discriminatory Treatment of Federally Sentenced Women*. Submission of the Native Women's Association of Canada to the Canadian Human Rights Commission. Available at <www.elizabethfry. ca/caefs_e.htm>. (Accessed January 14, 2006.)

McIvor, S., and T. Nahanee. 1998. "Aboriginal Women: Invisible Victims of Violence." In K. Bonnycastle and G. Rigakos (eds.), *Unsettling Truths: Battered Women, Policy, Politics, and Contemporary Research in Canada*. Vancouver: Collective Press.

McKeever, G. 1999. "Detecting, Prosecuting, and Punishing Benefit Fraud: The Social Security Administration (Fraud) Act 1997." *Modern Law Review* 62, 2.

McLaren, A. 1993. "Illegal Abortions: Women, Doctors, and Abortion, 1886–1939." *Journal of Social History* 26, 4 (Summer).

_____. 1990. *Our Own Master Race: Eugenics in Canada, 1885–1945*. Toronto: McClelland and Stewart.

McLaren, A., and Arlene T. McLaren. 1997. *The Bedroom and the State: The Changing Practices and Politics of Contraception and Abortion in Canada, 1880–1997*. Second edition. Toronto: Oxford University Press.

McLaren, J. 1987. "White Slavers: The Reform of Canada's Prostitution Laws and Patterns of Enforcement, 1900–1920." *Criminal Justice History* 8.

_____. 1986. "Chasing the Social Evil: Moral Fervour and the Evolution of Canada's Prostitution Laws, 1867–1917." *Canadian Journal of Law and Society* 1.

McLeod, H. 2004. "A Glimpse at Aboriginal-Based Street Gangs." A Report for the Royal Canadian Mounted Police "D" Division, Winnipeg, Manitoba for the National Aboriginal Policing Forum held in Ottawa, ON. Hosted by Pacific Business and Law Institute, September 22nd and 23rd.

McMullin, J., Davies, L., and G. Cassidy. 2002 "Welfare Reform in Ontario: Tough Times in Mothers' Lives." *Canadian Public Policy* 28, 2.

McQuaig, L. 1993. *The Wealthy Banker's Wife: The Assault on Equality in Canada*. Toronto: Penguin.

Medrano, M. 1996. "Does a Discrete Fetal Solvent Syndrome Exist?" *Alcoholism Treatment Quarterly* 14, 3.

Menzies, R. Forthcoming. "Virtual Backlash: Representations of Men's 'Rights' and Feminist 'Wrongs' in Cyberspace." In D. Chunn, S. Boyd, and H. Lessard (eds.), *Reaction and Resistance: Feminism, Law and Social Change*. Vancouver: University of British Columbia Press.

_____. 2001. "Contesting Criminal Lunacy: Narratives of Law and Madness in West Coast Canada, 1874–1950." *History of Psychiatry* 7.

_____. 1989. *Survival of the Sanest: Order and Disorder in a Pre-Trial Psychiatric Clinic*. Toronto: University of Toronto Press.

Menzies, R., and D.E. Chunn. 2005. "Charlotte's Web: Historical Regulation of 'Insane' Women Murderers." In W. Chan, D. Chunn, and R. Menzies (eds.), *Women, Madness and the Law: A Feminist Reader.* London: Glasshouse Press.

_____. 1999. "The Gender Politics of Criminal Insanity: 'Order-in-Council' Women in British Columbia, 1888–1950." *Histoire sociale/Social History* 31, 62.

Menzies, R., D.E. Chunn, and C.D. Webster. 1992. "Female Follies: The Forensic Psychiatric Assessment of Women Defendants." *International Journal of Law and Psychiatry* 15, 1 (January).

Merton, R. 1938. "Social Structure and Anomie." *American Sociological Review* 3 (October).

Miller, E. 1986. *Street Woman.* Philadelphia: Temple University Press.

Miller, J.B. 1986. *What Do We Mean by Relationships?* Work in Progress No. 22. Wellesley, MA: Stone Center

Miller, J.B., J. Jordan, A. Kaplan, I. Stiver, and J. Surrey. 1997. "Some Misconceptions and Reconceptions of a Relational Approach." In J. Jordan (ed.), *Women's Growth in Diversity: More Writings from the Stone Center.* New York: Guilford Press.

Miller-Young, M. 2005. "Black Tale: Women of Colour in the American Porn Industry." *Spread* 1,1.

Millett, K. 1971. *The Prostitution Papers: A Candid Dialogue.* New York: Avon.

Minaker, J. 2003. "Censuring the Erring Female: Governing Female Sexuality at the Toronto Industrial Refuge, 1853–1939." Unpublished PhD thesis. Queen's University, Kingston, ON.

Misra, J., S. Moller, and M. Karides. 2003. "Envisioning Dependency: Changing Media Depictions of Welfare in the 20th Century." *Social Problems* 50, 4.

Mitchinson, W. 2002. *Giving Birth in Canada 1990–1950.* Toronto: University of Toronto Press.

Mohr, R., and J. Roberts. 1994. "Sexual Assault in Canada: Recent Developments." In J. Roberts and R. Mohr (eds.), *Confronting Sexual Assault: A Decade of Legal Change.* Toronto: University of Toronto Press.

Monture-Angus, P. 2002. *The Lived Experience of Aboriginal Women Who Are Federally Sentenced.* Submission of the Canadian Association of Elizabeth Fry Societies to the Canadian Human Rights Commission. Available at <www.elizabethfry. ca/caefs_e.htm>. (Accessed January 14, 2006.)

_____. 1999. "Women and Risk: Aboriginal Women, Colonialism, and Correctional Practice." *Canadian Women's Studies* 19, 1 (Spring/Summer).

_____. 1995. *Thunder in My Soul: A Mohawk Woman Speaks.* Halifax: Fernwood.

Moore-Gilbert, B. 1997. *Postcolonial Theory: Contexts, Practices, Politics.* London and New York: Verso.

Moran, R. 1981. *Knowing Right From Wrong: The Insanity Defense of Daniel McNaughtan.* New York: Free Press.

Morgan, J., and L. Zimmer. 1997. "The Social Pharmacology of Smokeable Cocaine: Not All It's Cracked Up to Be." In C. Reinarman and H. Levine (eds.), *Crack in America: Demon Drugs and Social Justice.* Berkeley: University of California Press

Morgan, P., and K. Joe. 1997. "Uncharted Terrain: Contexts of Experience Among Women in the Illicit Drug Economy. *Women and Criminal Justice* 8, 3.

Morris, A. 1987. *Women, Crime and Criminal Justice.* London: Blackwell.

Morrisey, B. 2003. *When Women Kill: Questions of Agency and Subjectivity.* London: Routledge.

Morrison, I. 1998. "Ontario Works: A Preliminary Assessment." *Journal of Law and Social Policy* 13.

_____. 1995. "Facts About the Administration of Social Assistance/UI that Criminal Lawyers Need to Know." In *Charged with Fraud on Social Assistance: What Criminal Lawyers Need to Know*. Department of Continuing Legal Education, Law Society of Upper Canada, March 25 [unpublished].

Morrison, I., and G. Pearce. 1995. "Under the Axe: Social Assistance in Ontario in 1995." *Journal of Law and Social Policy* 11.

Mortenson, M. 1999. *B.C. Benefits Whom? Motherhood, Poverty, and Social Assistance Legislation in British Columbia*. M.A. Thesis, Simon Fraser University, Burnaby, BC.

Moscovitch, A. 1997. "Social Assistance in the New Ontario." In D. Ralph, A.Régimbald, and N. St-Amand (eds.), *Mike Harris's Ontario: Open for Business, Closed to People*. Halifax: Fernwood.

Mosher, C. 1998. *Discrimination and Denial: Systemic Racism in Ontario's Legal and Criminal Justice Systems, 1892–1961*. Toronto: University of Toronto Press.

Mosher, J. 2000. "Managing the Disentitlement of Women: Glorified Markets, the Idealized Family, and the Undeserving Other." In S.M. Neysmith (ed.), *Restructuring Caring Labour*. Toronto: Oxford University Press.

Mosher, J., P. Evans, M. Little, E. Morrow, J. Boulding, and N. Vanderplaats. 2004. *Walking on Eggshells; Abused Women's Experiences of Ontario's Welfare System: Final Report on the Research Findings on the Woman and Abuse Welfare Research Project*. Available at <http://www.yorku.ca/yorkweb/special/Welfare_Report_walking_on_eggshells_final_report.pdf>. (Accessed October 23, 2005.)

Mosher, J., and J. Hermer. 2005. *Welfare Fraud: The Constitution of Social Assistance as Crime*. A Report Prepared for the Law Commission of Canada (July). Ottawa.

Motiuk, L., and B. Vuong. 2001. "Profiling the Drug Offender Population in Canadian Federal Corrections. *Forum on Corrections Research* 13, 3.

Moyer, S. 1992. "Race, Gender and Homicide: Comparisons between Aboriginals and Other Canadians." *Canadian Journal of Criminology* 34.

Murphy, E. 1973. *The Black Candle*. Toronto: Coles. (Originally published in 1922).

Murphy, S., and M. Rosenbaum. 1999. *Pregnant Women on Drugs: Combating Stereotypes and Stigma*. New Brunswick, NJ: Rutgers University Press.

Murray, C., 1990. *The Emerging Underclass*. London: Institute of Economic Affairs.

Myers, A., and S. Wight (eds.). 1996. *No Angels: Women Who Commit Violence*. London: Pandora.

Myers, T. 1999. "The Voluntary Delinquent: Parents, Daughters and the Montreal Juvenile Delinquents' Court in 1918." *Canadian Historical Review* 80, 1.

_____. 1998. "Qui t'à debauchee?: Female Adolescent Sexuality and the Juvenile Delinquent's Court in Early Twentieth-Century Montreal." In L. Chambers and E.-A. Montigny (eds.), *Family Matters: Papers in Post-Confederation Canadian Family History*. Toronto: Canadian Scholars Press.

Naffine, N. 1997. *Feminism and Criminology*. Sydney: Allen and Unwin.

_____. 1987. *Female Crime: The Construction of Women in Criminology*. Sydney: Allen and Unwin.

National Council of Welfare. 2005. *Welfare Incomes 2004*. Ottawa: Minister of Public Works and Government Services Canada. (NCW Reports #123)

National Parole Board (NPB). 2002. *Report of the Stakeholders' Meeting on the Development of a National Parole Board Corporate Strategy for Federally Sentenced Women*. Ottawa: Aboriginal and Diversity Issues, National Parole Board.

_____. 2001. *Policy Manual*. Ottawa: National Parole Board.

Native Women's Association of Canada (NWAC). 2005. *Sisters in Spirit Campaign*. Available at <http://www.sistersinspirit.ca>. (Accessed October 19, 2005.)

Needham Report. 1978. *Report of the National Planning Committee on the Female Offender.* Ottawa: Ministry of Solicitor General.

Nelson, J. 2002. "'A Strange Revolution in the Manners of the Country': Aboriginal-Settler Intermarriage in Nineteenth-Century British Columbia." In J. McLaren, R. Menzies, and D. Chunn (eds.), *Regulating Lives: Historical Essays on the State, Society, the Individual and the Law.* Vancouver: University of British Columbia Press.

Neve, L., and K. Pate. 2005. "Challenging the Criminalization of Women Who Resist." In J. Sudbury (ed.).

Nixon, K., L. Tutty, P. Downe, K. Gorkoff, and J. Ursel. 2002. "The Everyday Occurrence: Violence in the Lives of Girls Exploited Through Prostitution." *Violence Against Women* 8, 9 (September).

Nolan, P. 2003. *Cannabis: Report of the Senate Special Committee on Illegal Drugs.* Toronto: University of Toronto Press.

Noonan, S. 1993. "Moving Beyond the Battered Woman Syndrome." In E. Adelberg and C. Currie (eds.).

O'Hara, M. 1985. "Prostitution Towards a Feminist Analysis and Strategy." In D. Rhodes and S. McNeil (eds.), *Women Against Violence Against Women.* London: Onlywomen Press.

O' Malley, P. 2004. *Risk, Uncertainty and Government.* London: Glasshouse Press.

_____. 2000. "Criminologies of Catastrophe? Understanding Criminal Justice on the Edge of the New Millennium." *The Australian and New Zealand Journal of Criminology* 33, 2 (August).

_____. 1996. "Risk and Responsibility." In A. Barry, T. Osborne and N. Rose (eds.), *Foucault and Political Reason: Liberalism, Neo-liberalism and Rationalities of Government.* Chicago: University of Chicago Press.

_____. 1992. "Risk, Power and Crime Prevention." *Economy and Society* 21, 3.

O'Marra, A.J.C. 1994. "Hadfield to Swain: The Criminal Code Amendments Dealing with the Mentally Disordered Accused." *Criminal Law Quarterly* 36.

O'Neill, M. 2001. *Prostitution and Feminism: Towards and Politics of Feeling.* Cambridge: Polity Press.

Odem, M. 1995. *Delinquent Daughters: Protecting and Policing Adolescent Female Sexuality in the United States, 1885–1920.* Chapel Hill: University of North Carolina Press.

Oliver, P. 1994. "'To Govern by Kindness': The First Two Decades of the Mercer Reformatory for Women." In J. Phillips, T. Loo, and S. Lewthwaite (eds.), *Essays in the History of Canadian Law Volume V.* Toronto: Osgoode Society.

Ontario. 2003. Ministry of Community, Family and Children's Services. *Welfare Fraud Control Report 2001–2002,* Table 1.

_____. 2002. Office of the Chief Coroner. Verdict of the Coroner's Jury into the Death of Kimberly Ann Rogers, held at Sudbury, Ontario.

_____. 2000a. Ministry of Community and Social Services. *Welfare Fraud Control Report, 1998–99.* Toronto: Queen's Printer.

_____. 2000b. Ministry of Community and Social Services. *Making Welfare Work: Report to Taxpayers on Welfare Reform.* Toronto: Queen's Printer.

_____. 1999. Ministry of Community and Social Services. *Welfare Fraud Control Report, 1997–98.* Toronto: Queen's Printer.

_____. 1995. *Report of the Commission on Systemic Racism in the Ontario Criminal Justice System.* (M. Gitten and D. Cole, Co-Chairs). Toronto: Queen's Printer.

_____. 1988. *Transitions: Report of the Social Assistance Review Committee* (SARC Report). Toronto: Queen's Printer.

Ontario Native Women's Association. 1989. "Breaking Free: A Proposal for Change to Aboriginal Family Violence." Thunder Bay, Ontario.

Osborne, J. 1989. "Perspectives on Premenstrual Syndrome: Women, Law and Medicine." *Canadian Journal of Family Law* 8.

Osborne, R. 1995. "Crime and the Media: From Media Studies to Post-Modernism." In D. Kidd-Hewitt and R. Osborne (eds.), *Crime and the Media: The Postmodern Spectacle.* East Haven, CT: Pluto Press.

Owen, B. 1998. *"In the Mix": Struggle and Survival in a Women's Prison.* Albany: State University of New York Press.

Paltrow, L. 2001. "The War on Drugs and Abortion: Some Initial Thought on the Connections, Intersections and the Effects." *Southern University Law Review* 28, 3.

Parent, C. 1994. "La prostitution ou le commerce des services sexuels." In L. Langlois, Y. Martin, et F. Dumont (eds.), *Traité de problèmes sociaux.* Québec: Institut québécois de recherche sur la culture.

_____. 2001. "Les identités sexuelles et les travailleuses de l'industrie du sexe à l'aube du nouveau millénaire." *Sociologie et Sociétés*, 33, 1.

Parent, C., and C. Bruckert. Forthcoming. "Comment Répondre Aux Besoins des Travailleuses Du Sexe De Rue ans La Région De L'outaouais." *Reflets* 2

_____. 2005. "Le travail du Sexe dans les Établissement de Service Érotiques: Une forme de travail Marginalisé." *Déviance et Société* 29, 1.

Pate, K. 2005. "Prisons: Canada's Default Response to Homelessness, Poverty, and Mental Illness — Especially for Women." Conference presentation at the 11th United Nations Congress on Criminal Justice and Crime Prevention. Bangkok, April. Available at <http://www.elizabethfry.ca/pubs/bangkok/1.htm>. (Accessed January 14, 2006.)

_____. 2003. "Prisons: The Latest Solution to Homelessness, Poverty and Mental Illness." Women Speak Series, Calgary, September 18.

_____. 2002. "Labelling Young Women as Violent: Vilification of the Most Vulnerable." In K. McKenna and J. Larkin (eds.), *Violence Against Women: New Canadian Perspectives.* Toronto: Inanna.

_____. 1999a. "CSC and the 2 Per Cent Solution." *Canadian Women's Studies* 19, 1 and 2.

_____. 1999b. "Young Women and Violent Offences." *Canadian Women's Studies* 19.

Paules, G. 1991. *Dishing It Out.* Philadelphia: Temple University Press.

Pearce, F. and S. Tombs. 1998. *Toxic Capitalism: Corporate Crime and the Chemical Industry.* Aldershot: Ashgate and Dartmouth.

Pearson, P. 1998. "Death Becomes Her." *Saturday Night* 113 (December).

_____. 1997. *When She Was Bad: Women's Violence and the Myth of Innocence.* Toronto: Random House.

_____. 1995. "Behind Every Successful Psychopath." *Saturday Night* 110 (October).

_____. 1993. "How Women Can Get Away With Murder." *Globe and Mail* August 18.

Penney, J. 1983. *Hard Earned Wages: Women Fighting for Better Work.* Toronto: Women's Press

Peters, Y. 2003. *Federally Sentenced Women with Mental Disabilities: A Dark Corner of Canadian Human Rights.* Submission of the DisAbled Women's Network to the Canadian Human Rights Commission. Available at <www.elizabethfry.ca/caefs_e.htm>. (Accessed January 14, 2006.)

Pheterson, G. 1989. *A Vindication of the Rights of Whores.* Seattle: Seal Press.

Philips, L. 2002. "Tax Law and Social Reproduction: The Gender of Fiscal Policy in an Age of Privatization." In B. Cossman and J. Fudge (eds.).

Phillips, J. 1986. "Poverty, Unemployment and the Administration of Criminal Law: Vagrancy in Halifax, Nova Scotia, 1864–1890." In P. Girard and J. Phillips (eds.), *Essays in the History of Canadian Law.* Toronto: University of Toronto Press.

Phillips, P. 1997. "Labour in the New Canadian Political Economy." In W. Clement (ed.), *Understanding Canada: Building the New Canadian Political Economy.* Montreal: McGill-Queen's University Press.

Phoenix, J. 2002a. "Youth Prostitution Police Reform: New Discourse, Same Old Story." In P. Carlen (ed.), *Women and Punishment: The Struggle for Social Justice.* Portland, Oregon: Willan.

_____. 2002b. "In the Name of Protection: Youth Prostitution Policy Reforms in England and Wales." *Critical Social Policy* 22, 2.

_____. 2000. "Prostitute Identities: Men, Money and Violence." *British Journal of Criminology* 40.

_____. 1999. *Making Sense of Prostitution.* New York: Palgrave.

Pizzey, E. 1974. *Scream Quietly or the Neighbours Will Hear You.* London: Penguin.

Pollack, S. 2004. "Anti-oppressive Practice with Women in Prison: Discursive Reconstructions and Alternative Practices." *British Journal of Social Work* 34 (5).

_____. 2000a. "Dependency Discourse as Social Control." In K. Hannah-Moffat and M. Shaw (eds.).

_____. 2000b. "Reconceptualizing Women's Agency and Empowerment: Challenges to Self-Esteem Discourse and Women's Lawbreaking. *Women and Criminal Justice* 12, 1.

Pollack, S., M. Battaglia, and A. Allspach. 2005. "Women Charged in Domestic Violence Situations in Toronto: The Unintended Consequences of Mandatory Charge Policies." Woman Abuse Council of Toronto.

Pollack. S., and K. Kendall. 2005. "'Taming the Shrew': Regulating Prisoners through 'Women-Centred' Mental Health Programming." *Critical Criminology: An International Journal* 13, 1.

Pollak, O. 1950. *The Criminality of Women.* Philadelphia: University of Philadelphia Press.

Price, K. 2000. "Stripping Women: Workers Control in Strip Clubs." *Unusual Occupations* 11.

Pringle, R. 1988. *Secretaries Talk.* London: Verso.

Rachert, J. 1990. *Welfare Fraud and the State: British Columbia 1970–1977.* M.A. Thesis, Simon Fraser University, Burnaby, BC.

Rafter, N.H. 1985a. *Partial Justice: Women in State Prisons, 1900–1935.* Boston: Northeastern University Press.

_____. 1985b. "Gender, Prisons, and Prison History." *Social Science History* 9, 3.

Rafter, N.H., and F. Heidenson (eds.). 1995. *International Feminist Perspectives in Criminology.* Buckingham: Open University.

Raftner, N.H., and E.M. Natalazia. 1981. "Marxist Feminism: Implications for Criminal Justice." *Crime and Delinquency* 27 (January).

Raitt, F., and S. Zeedyk. 2000. *The Implicit Relation of Psychology and Law: Women and Syndrome Evidence.* London: Routledge.

Ratushny, L. 1997. *Self-Defence Review: Final Report.* Ottawa: Minister of Justice and Solicitor General Canada. Available at <http://www.justice.gc.ca/en/dept/pub/sdr/

rtush-ch3.html>. (Accessed October 15, 2005.)

Razack, S. 2002. *Race, Space and the Law: Unmapping a White Settler Society.* Toronto: Between the Lines.

_____. 1998. "Race, Space and Prostitution: The Making of the Bourgeois Subject." *Canadian Journal of Women and the Law* 10.

Reaume, G. 2000. *Remembrance of Patients Past: Patient Life at the Toronto Hospital for the Insane, 1870–1940.* Don Mills, ON: Oxford University Press.

Rebick, J. 2005. *Ten Thousand Roses: The Making of a Feminist Revolution.* Toronto: Penguin.

Reiter, E. 1991. *Making Fast Food.* Kingston: McGill-Queen's University Press.

Reitsma-Street, M. 1999. "Justice for Canadian Girls: A 1990s Update." *Canadian Journal of Criminology* 41, 3.

Richie, B. 1996. *Compelled to Crime: The Gender Entrapment of Battered Black Women.* New York: Routledge.

Ripa, Y. 1990. *Women and Madness: The Incarceration of Women in Nineteenth-Century France.* Minneapolis: University of Minnesota Press.

Ritzer, G. 2004. *The McDonaldization of Society.* Thousand Oaks, CA: Pine Forge.

Rivera, M. 2002. "The Chrysalis Program: Feminist Treatment Community for Individuals Diagnosed as Personality Disordered." In M. Ballow and L.S. Brown (eds.), *Rethinking Mental Health and Disorder: Feminist Perspectives.* New York: Guilford.

Roach Pierson, R. 1990. *'They're Still Women After All': The Second World War and Canadian Womanhood.* Toronto: McClelland and Stewart.

Roberts, D. 1997. *Killing the Black Body: Race, Reproduction, and the Meaning of Liberty.* New York: Pantheon.

Roberts, J. 1991. *Sexual Assault Legislation in Canada: An Evaluation Report.* Vols. 1–9. Ottawa: Department of Justice, Ministry of Supply and Services.

Roberts, M. 2005. *Using Women.* London: DrugScope.

Robinson, M. 2004. "Cam Girls are the New 'It' Girls of the Sex Industry." *Fulcrum* 65, 13.

Rolph, C. 1955. *Women of the Streets: A Sociological Study of the Common Prostitute.* London: Secker and Warburg.

Ronai, C., and R. Cross. 1998. "Dancing with Identity: Narrative Resistance Strategies of Male and Female Stripteasers." *Deviant Behaviour* 19.

Rose, N. 2000. "Government and Control." *The British Journal of Criminology* 40, 2 (Spring).

_____. 1996a. "The Death of the Social? Re-figuring the Territory of Government." *Economy and Society* (August).

_____. 1996b. "Governing 'Advanced' Liberal Democracies." In A. Barry, T. Osborne, and N. Rose (eds.).

_____. 1993. "Government, Authority and Expertise in Advanced Liberalism." *Economy and Society* 22, 3.

Rose, N., and P. Miller. 1992. "Political Power Beyond the State: Problematics of Government." *British Journal of Sociology* 43, 2.

Rose, N., and M. Valverde. 1998. "Governed by Law?" *Social and Legal Studies* 7, 4.

Rosen, R. 1982. *The Lost Sisterhood.* Baltimore: Johns Hopkins University Press.

Rosenbaum, M. 1981. *Women on Heroin.* New Brunswick, NJ: Rutgers University Press.

Ross, B. 2000. "Bumping and Grinding on the Line." *Labour/Le Travail* 46.

Ross, L. 1998. *Inventing the Savage: The Social Construction of Native American Crimi-*

nality. Austin: University of Texas Press.

Ross, R., and E. Fabiano. 1985. *Correctional Alternatives: Programmes for Female Offenders*: Ottawa: Ministry of Solicitor General Programmes Branch.

Roth, R. 2004. "Searching for the State: Who Governs Prisoners' Reproductive Rights?" *Social Politics* 11, 3.

_____. 2000. *Making Women Pay: The Hidden Costs of Fetal Rights*. Ithaca, NY: Cornell University Press.

Rothman, D. 1983. "Social Control: The Uses and Abuses of the Concept in the History of Incarceration." In S. Cohen and A. Scull (eds.), *Social Control and the State*. New York: Basil Blackwell.

Royal Commission on Aboriginal Peoples. 1996. *Report of the Royal Commission on Aboriginal Peoples*. Ottawa: Department of Indian and Northern Affairs. Available at <http://www.ainc-inac.gc.ca/ch/rcap/sg/sgmm_e.html>. (Accessed January 14, 2006.)

Ruebsaat, G. 1985. *The New Sexual Assault Offences: Emerging Legal Issues*. Ottawa: Ministry of Supply and Services.

Safe Care for British Columbia's Children: A Discussion Paper. 2004. Available at <www.mcf.gov.bc.ca/safe_care>. (Accessed April 28, 2005.)

Salzinger, L. 1991. "A Maid by Any Other Name." In M. Burnaway (ed.), *Ethnography Unbound*. Berkeley: University of California Press.

Sangster, J. 2002a. "Defining Sexual Promiscuity: 'Race,' Gender and Class in the Operation of Ontario's Female Refuges Act, 1930–1960." In W. Chan and K. Mirchandani (eds.).

_____. 2002b. *Girl Trouble: Female Delinquency in English Canada*. Toronto: Between the Lines.

_____. 2001. *Regulating Girls and Women: Sexuality, Family, and the Law in Ontario, 1920–1960*. Toronto: Oxford University Press.

_____. 2000. "Girls in Conflict with the Law: Exploring the Construction of 'Female Delinquency' in Ontario, 1940–60." *Canadian Journal of Women and the Law* 12.

_____. 1999. "Criminalizing the Colonized: Ontario Native Women Confront the Criminal Justice System, 1920–1960." *The Canadian Historical Review* 80, 1 (March).

_____. 1996. "Incarcerating 'Bad Girls': The Regulation of Sexuality through the Female Refuges Act in Ontario, 1920–1945." *History of Sexuality* 7.

Saunders, R. 2003. "Defining Vulnerability in the Labour Market." Paper presented at CPRN/LCC Roundtable on Vulnerable Workers. June 17, Ottawa.

Savaraese, J., and B. Morton. 2005. *Women and Social Assistance Policy in Saskatchewan and Manitoba*. Winnipeg: The Prairie Women's Health Centre of Excellence.

Save the Children–Canada. 2000. *Sacred Lives: Canadian Aboriginal Children and Youth Speak Out About Sexual Exploitation*. National Aboriginal Consultation Project. Ottawa: Save the Children Canada.

Schissel, B. 2001. "Youth Crime, Moral Panics and the News: The Conspiracy Against the Marginalized in Canada." In R. Smandych (ed.), *Youth Crime: History, Legislation, and Reform*. Toronto: Harcourt Canada Ltd.

_____. 1997. *Blaming Children: Youth Crime, Moral Panics and the Politics of Hate*. Halifax: Fernwood.

Schramm, H. 1998. "Young Women who Use Violence — Myths and Facts." Calgary: Elizabeth Fry Society of Alberta.

Schrecker, T. 2001. "From the Welfare State to the No-Second-Chances State." In S. Boyd, D. Chunn, and R. Menzies (eds.), *(Ab)Using Power: The Canadian Experi-*

ence. Halifax: Fernwood.

Schur, E. 1984. *Labeling Women Deviant: Gender, Stigma, and Social Control*. New York: Random House.

Scull, A. 1977. *Decarceration: Community Treatment and the Deviant: A Radical View*. New Jersey: Prentice Hall.

Scutt, J. 1979. "The Myth of the 'Chivalry Factor' in Female Crime." *Australian Journal of Social Issues* 14, 1.

Secure Care Working Group. 1998. *Report of the Secure Care Working Group*. Commissioned by the Minister of Children and Families, Province of British Columbia.

Segal, L. 1999. *Why Feminism? Gender, Psychology, Politics*. New York: Columbia University Press.

Serin, R., and D. Mailloux. 2001. *Development of a Reliable Self-report Instrument for the Assessment of Criminogenic Need*. Ottawa: Research Branch of the Correctional Service of Canada.

Shadd, A. 1991. "Institutionalized Racism and Canadian History: Notes of a Black Canadian." In O. McKague (ed.), *Racism in Canada*. Saskatoon: Fifth House

Sharma, U., and P. Black. 2001. "Look Good, Feel Better: Beauty Therapy as Emotional Labour." *Sociology* 35, 4.

Sharpe, A. 1998. "Income Distribution in Canada in the 1990s: The Offsetting Impact of Government on Growing Market Inequality." *Canada Watch* 6, June.

Shaver, F. 1996. "Prostitution: The Dark Side of the Service Industry." In T. Fleming (ed.), *Post-Critical Criminology*. Toronto: Oxford University Press.

_____. 1993. "Prostitution: A Female Crime?" In E. Adelberg and C. Currie (eds.).

Shaw, M. 2000. "Women, Violence, and Disorder in Prisons." In K. Hannah- Moffat and M. Shaw (eds.), *An Ideal Prison? Critical Essays on Women's Imprisonment in Canada*. Halifax: Fernwood.

_____. 1995. "Conceptualizing Violence by Women." In R.E. Dobash, R.P. Dobash, and L. Noaks (eds.), *Gender and Crime*. Cardiff: University of Chicago Press.

_____. 1994a. *Ontario Women in Conflict with the Law: Community Prevention Programmes and Regional Issues*. Toronto: Ministry of the Solicitor General and Correctional Services.

_____. 1994b. "Women in Prison: Literature Review." *Forum* (Special Issue on Women in Prison) 6(1). Available at <http://www.csc-scc.gc.ca/text/pblct/forum/e06/e061ind_e.shtml>. (Accessed January 14, 2006.)

_____. 1993. "Reforming Federal Women's Imprisonment." In E. Adelberg and C. Currie (eds.).

_____. 1991. *The Female Offender: Report on a Preliminary Study*. User Report 1991–3. Ottawa: Solicitor General, Ministry Secretariat.

Shaw, M., K. Rodgers, J. Blanchette, T. Hattem, L.S. Thomas, and L.Tamarack. 1991. *Survey of Federally Sentenced Women: Report of the Task Force on Federally Sentenced Women*. User Report 1991–4. Ottawa: Corrections Branch, Ministry of Solicitor General of Canada.

Shipley, S.L., and B.A. Arrigo. 2004. *The Female Homicide Offender: Serial Murder and the Case of Aileen Wuornos*. Upper Saddle River, NJ: Pearson Education/Prentice Hall.

Shostak, A. 1980. *Blue Collar Stress*. Menlo Park: Addison-Welsley.

Simon, J., and T. Baker. 2002. *Embracing Risk: The Changing Culture of Insurance and Responsibility*. Chicago: University of Chicago Press.

Simon, R. 1975. *Women and Crime*. Lexington, MA: D.C. Heath.

Single, E., M. Van Truong, E. Adlaf, and A. Ialomiteanu. 1999. *Canadian Profile: Alcohol, Tobacco and Other Drugs*. Toronto: Canadian Centre on Substance Abuse and Centre for Addiction and Mental Health.

Sjostrom, S. 1997. *Party or Patient: Discursive Practices Relating to Coercion in Psychiatric and Legal Settings*. Umea, Sweden: Borea Bokforlag.

Skrapec, C. 1994. "The Female Serial Killer: An Evolving Criminality." In H. Birch (ed.), *Moving Targets: Women, Murder and Representation*. Berkeley: University of California Press.

Sly, A, and K. Taylor. 2003. "Preliminary Evaluation of Dialectical Behavior Therapy within a Women's Structured Living Environment." Ottawa: Research Branch, Correctional Service of Canada.

Small, S.J. 1978. "Canadian Narcotics Legislation, 1908–1923: A Conflict Model Interpretation." In Wm. Greenway and S. Brickey (eds.), *Law and Social Control in Canada*. Scarborough: Prentice-Hall.

Smart, C. 1995. *Law, Crime and Sexuality*. London: Sage.

_____. 1990. "Feminist Approaches to Criminology or Postmodern Woman Meets Atavistic Man." In L. Gelsthorpe and A. Morris (eds.).

_____. 1989. *Feminism and the Power of the Law: Essays in Feminism*. London: Routledge.

_____. 1977. "Criminological Theory: Its Ideology and Implications Concerning Women." *British Journal of Sociology* 28, 1.

_____. 1976. *Women, Crime and Criminology: A Feminist Critique*. London: Routledge and Kegan Paul.

Smyth, S. 2003. "A Comparative Analysis of the Standard of Tolerance in Relation to the Labour of Exotic Dancers in Licensed Adult Entertainment Parlours." Unpublished Honours Thesis, Carleton University, Ottawa.

Snider, L. 2004. "Female Punishment: From Patriarchy to Backlash?" In C. Sumner (ed.), *The Blackwell Companion to Criminology*. Oxford: Blackwell.

_____. 2003. "Constituting the Punishable Woman: Atavistic Man Incarcerates Postmodern Woman." *British Journal of Criminology* 43, 2.

_____. 2002. "The Sociology of Corporate Crime: An Obituary (or, Whose Knowledge Claims Have Legs?)" *Theoretical Criminology* 4.

_____. 1999. "Relocating Law: Making Corporate Crime Disappear." In Elizabeth Comack (ed.), *Locating Law: Race/Class/Gender Connections*. Halifax: Fernwood.

_____. 1998. "Towards Safer Societies: Punishment, Masculinities and Violence Against Women." *British Journal of Criminology* 38, 1.

_____. 1994. "Feminism, Punishment and the Potential of Empowerment." *Canadian Journal of Law and Society* 9, 1.

_____. 1991. "The Potential of the Criminal Justice System to Promote Feminist Concerns." In E. Comack and S. Brickey (eds.), *The Social Bias of Law: Critical Readings in the Sociology of Law*. Second edition. Halifax: Fernwood.

_____. 1985. "Legal Reform and Social Control: The Dangers of Abolishing Rape." *International Journal of the Sociology of Law* 13, 4.

Solomon, R., and M. Green. 1988. "The First Century: The History of Nonmedical Opiate Use and Control Policies in Canada, 1870–1970." In J. Blackwell and P. Erickson (eds.), *Illicit Drugs in Canada*. Toronto: Methuen.

Solomon, R., and T. Madison. 1976–77. "The Evolution of Non-Medical Opiate Use in Canada, Part I, 1870–1929." *Drug Forum* 5.

Special Committee on Pornography and Prostitution. 1985. *Pornography and Prostitution in Canada*. Ottawa: Department of Supply and Services.

Spivak, G. Chakravorty. 1987. *In Other Worlds: Essays in Cultural Politics*. London: Routledge.

Stanko, E. 1997. "Conceptualizing Women's Risk: Assessment as a Technology of the Soul." *Theoretical Criminology* 1, 4.

_____. 1990. *Everyday Violence*. London: Pandora.

_____. 1985. *Intimate Intrusions: Women's Experience of Male Violence*. London: Routledge and Kegan Paul.

Stanley, L. (ed.). 1990. *Feminist Praxis: Research, Theory, and Epistemology in Feminist Sociology*. London: Routledge.

Statistics Canada. 2005a. "Family Violence in Canada." *The Daily* (July 14) Available at <http://www.statcan.ca/Daily/English/050714/d050714a.htm>. (Accessed January 14, 2006.)

_____. 2005b. *The Daily, Crime Statistics, Thursday, July 21, 2005*. Ottawa: Canadian Centre for Justice Statistics. Available at <http://www.statcan.ca/Daily/English/050721/d0507721a.htm>. (Accessed October 13, 2005).

_____. 2004. *Canadian Crime Statistics 2003*. Ottawa: Canadian Centre for Justice Statistics. Catalogue no. 85-205.

_____. 2001a. *Women in Canada*. Ottawa: Canadian Centre for Justice Statistics Profile Series. Catalogue no. 85F00033MIE.

_____. 2001b. *Aboriginal Peoples in Canada*. Ottawa: Canadian Centre for Justice Statistics Profile Series. Catalogue no. 85F0033MIE.

_____. 2000. *Adult Correctional Services in Canada*. 21, 5. Ottawa: Canadian Centre for Justice Statistics.

_____. 1993. "The Violence Against Women Survey." *The Daily* (18 November).

Steffensmeier, D. 1980. "Sex Differences in Patterns of Adult Crime, 1965–1977." *Social Forces* 58, 4 (June).

Steffensmeier, D., and E. Allan. 1998. "The Nature of Female Offending: Patterns and Explanations." In R.T. Zaplan (ed.), *Female Offenders: Critical Perspectives and Effective Interventions*. Gaithersburg, MD: Aspen.

Steffensmeier, D., and J. Kramer. 1982. "Sex-based Differences in the Sentencing of Adult Criminal Defendants." *Sociology and Social Research* 663.

Steinmetz, S. 1981. "A Cross-cultural Comparison of Marital Abuse." *Journal of Sociology and Social Welfare* 8.

Stella. 2003. *The Art of Striptease*. Ottawa: Health Canada.

Stenson, K., and P. Watt. 1999. "Governmentality and 'the Death of the Social'?: A Discourse Analysis of Local Government Texts in South-East England." *Urban Studies* 36, 1.

Stephen, J. 1995. "The 'Incorrigible,' the 'Bad,' and the 'Immoral': Toronto's 'Factory Girls' and the Work of the Toronto Psychiatric Clinic." In L. Knafla and S. Binnie (eds.), *Law, Society and the State: Essays in Modern Legal History*. Toronto: University of Toronto Press.

Strange, C. 1996. "The Lottery of Death: Capital Punishment, 1867–1976." *Manitoba Law Journal* 23.

_____. 1995. *Toronto's Girl Problem: The Perils and Pleasures of the City, 1880–1930*. Toronto: University of Toronto Press.

Strange, C., and T. Loo. 1997. *Making Good: Law and Moral Regulation in Canada*. Toronto: University of Toronto Press.

Straus, M. 1979. "Measuring Intrafamily Conflict and Violence: The Conflict Tactics

(CT) Scales." *Journal of Marriage and the Family* 41, 1.

Straus, M., and R. Gelles. 1986. "Societal Changes and Change in Family Violence from 1975 to 1985 as Revealed by Two National Surveys." *Journal of Marriage and the Family* 48.

Straus, M., R. Gelles, and S. Steinmetz. 1980. *Behind Closed Doors: Violence in the American Family*. New York: Doubleday.

Stubbs, J., and J. Tolmie. 1999. "Falling Short of the Challenge? A Comparative Assessment of the Australian Use of Expert Evidence on the Battered Woman Syndrome." *Melbourne University Law Review* 23, 3.

Sudbury, J. (ed.) 2005a. *Global Lockdown: Race, Gender, and the Prison-Industrial Complex*. London: Routledge.

_____. 2005b. "Introduction: Feminist Critiques, Transnational Landscapes, Abolitionist Visions." In J. Sudbury (ed.), *Global Lockdown: Race, Gender, and the Prison-Industrial Complex*. New York: Routledge.

_____. 2005c "'Mules,' 'Yardies,' and Other Folk Devils: Mapping Cross-Border Imprisonment in Britain." In J. Sudbury (ed.), *Global Lockdown: Race, Gender and the Prison-Industrial Complex*. London: Routledge.

_____. 2004. "Women of Color, Globalization, and the Politics of Incarceration." In B.R. Price and N.J. Sokoloff (eds.), *The Criminal Justice System and Women: Offenders, Prisoners, Victims, and Workers*. Third edition. New York: McGraw-Hill.

Sugar, F., and L. Fox. 1989. "Nistem Peyako Seht'wawin Iskwewak: Breaking the Chains." *Canadian Journal of Women and the Law* 3, 2.

Sullivan, T. 1986. "The Politics of Juvenile Prostitution." In J. Lowman, M. Jackson, T. Palys and S. Gavigan (eds.).

Sumner, C. 1990. "Foucault, Gender and the Censure of Deviance." In L. Gelsthorpe and A. Morris (eds.).

Sutherland, E. 1949. *Principles of Criminology*. Fourth edition. Philadelphia: J.B. Lippincott.

Swainger, J. 1995. "A Distant Edge of Authority: Capital Punishment and the Prerogative of Mercy in British Columbia, 1872–1880." In H. Foster and J. McLaren (eds.), *Essays in the History of Canadian Law. Vol. VI: British Columbia and the Yukon*. Toronto: Osgoode Society and University of Toronto Press.

Swift, K. 1995. *Manufacturing "Bad Mothers": A Critical Perspective on Child Neglect*. Toronto: University of Toronto Press.

Swift, K., and M. Birmingham. 2000. "Location, Location, Location: Restructuring and the Everyday Lives of "Welfare Moms." In S.M. Neysmith (ed.), *Restructuring Caring Labour*. Toronto: Oxford University Press.

Task Force on Federally Sentenced Women. 1990. *Report of the Task Force on Federally Sentenced Women — Creating Choices*. Ottawa: Ministry of the Solicitor General.

Taylor, I., P. Walton, and J. Young. 1973. *The New Criminology*. London: Routledge and Kegan Paul.

Thigpen, M., L. Solomon, S. Hunter, and M. Buell. 2004. *Developing Gender Specific Classification Systems for Women Offenders*. Washington: National Institute of Corrections.

Thomas, W.I. 1923/1967. *The Unadjusted Girl*. New York: Harper and Row.

Tom, W. 1994. *Fallen Women in the Nineteenth Century Novel*. New York: St. Martin's Press.

Tombs, S. 2002. "Understanding Regulation?" *Social and Legal Studies* 11.

Tomes, N. 1990. "Historical Perspectives on Women and Mental Illness." In R. Apple (ed.), *Women, Health, and Medicine in America*. New York: Garland.

Tong, R. 1996. "Maternal-Fetal Conflict: The Misguided Case for Punishing Cocaine-Using Pregnant and/or Postpartum Women." In C. Sistare (ed.), *Punishment: Social Control and Coercion*. New York: Peter Lang.

_____. 1984. *Women, Sex and Law*. New Jersey: Rowman and Allenfield.

Townson, M. 2003. *Women in Non-Standard Jobs: The Public Policy Challenge*. Ottawa: Status of Women Canada.

Turnbull, L. 2001. *Double Jeopardy: Motherwork and the Law*. Toronto: Sumach Press.

Ursel, J. 2002. "'His Sentence is My Freedom': Processing Domestic Violence Cases in the Winnipeg Family Violence Court." In L. Tutty and C. Goard (eds.), *Reclaiming Self: Issues and Resources for Women Abused by Intimate Partners*. Halifax: Fernwood.

_____. 1991. "Considering the Impact of the Battered Women's Movement on the State: The Example of Manitoba." In E. Comack and S. Brickey (eds.), *The Social Basis of Law: Critical Readings in the Sociology of Law*. Second edition. Halifax: Fernwood.

Valenstein, E. 1986. *Great and Desperate Cures: The Rise and Decline of Psychosurgery and Other Radical Treatments for Mental Illness*. New York: Basic.

Valverde, M. 1998. *Diseases of the Will: Alcohol and the Dilemmas of Freedom*. Cambridge: Cambridge University Press.

_____. 1995. "The Mixed Social Economy as a Canadian Tradition." *Studies in Political Economy* 47.

_____. 1994. "Moral Capital." *Canadian Journal of Law and Society* 9.

_____. 1991. *The Age of Light, Soap, and Water: Moral Reform in English Canada 1885–1925*. Toronto: McClelland and Stewart/Oxford.

Valverde, M., and L. Weir. 1988. "The Struggles of the Immoral: Preliminary Remarks on Moral Regulation." *Resources for Feminist Research* 17.

Velarde, A. 1975. "Becoming Prostituted." *British Journal of Criminology* 15, 3.

Wagner, D. 1997. *The New Temperance: The American Obsession with Sin and Vice*. Boulder, CO: Westview Press.

Waldorf, D., C. Reinarman, and S. Murphy. 1991. *Cocaine Changes*. Philadelphia: Temple University Press.

Walker, L. 1987. *Terrifying Love: Why Battered Women Kill and How Society Responds*. New York: Harper Collins.

_____. 1979. *The Battered Woman*. New York: Harper and Row.

Walker, N. 1968. *Crime and Insanity in England, Vol 1*. Edinburgh: Edinburgh University Press.

Walklate, S. 1997. "Risk and Criminal Victimization." *British Journal of Criminology* 37, 1.

Walkowitz, J. 1980. "The Politics of Prostitution." *Signs* 6, 1.

Wallace, M. 2004. "Crime Statistics in Canada, 2003." *Juristat* 24, 6. Ottawa: Statistics Canada, Canadian Centre for Justice Statistics.

Ward, T. 1999. "The Sad Subject of Infanticide: Law, Medicine and Child Murder, 1860–1938." *Social and Legal Studies* 8, 2.

Warner, S. 1996. "Visibly Special? Women, Child Sexual Abuse and Special Hospitals." In C. Hemingway (ed.), *Special Women? The Experience of Women in the Special Hospital System*. Aldershot: Avebury.

Warren, C. 1981. "New Forms of Social Control: The Myth of Deinstitutionalization." *American Behavioural Scientist.* 24 (6).

Webber, M. 1991. *Street Kids: The Tragedy of Canada's Runaways.* Toronto: University of Toronto Press.

Weber, M. 1976. *The Protestant Ethic and the Spirit of Capitalism.* London: George Allen and Unwin.

Wedderburn, D. 2000. *Justice for Women: The Need for Reform.* London: Prison Reform Trust.

Weibe, R., and Y. Johnson. 1998. *Stolen Life: Journey of a Cree Woman.* Toronto: Alfred Knopf.

Weich, R. and C. Angula. 2000. *Justice on Trial: Racial Disparities in the American Criminal Justice System.* Washington, DC: Leadership Conference on Civil Rights and Leadership Conference on Education Fund.

Weir, L. 1986. "Studies in the Medicalization of Sexual Danger: Sexual Rule, Sexual Politics, 1830–1930." Ph.D. Dissertation, York University, Toronto.

Weiss, J. 1976. "Liberation and Crime: The Invention of the New Female Criminal." *Crime and Social Justice* 6 (Fall-Winter).

Welch, M. 1997. "Regulating the Reproduction and Morality of Women: The Social Control of Body and Soul." *Women and Criminal Justice* 9, 1.

Westwood, S. 1984. *All Day Every Day.* London: Pluto Press.

White-Mair, K. 2000. "Experts and Ordinary Men: Locating *R.* v. *Lavallee,* Battered Woman Syndrome, and the 'New' Psychiatric Expertise on Women Within Canadian History." *Canadian Journal of Law and Society* 12, 2.

Wilson, E. 1983. *What is To Be Done About Violence Against Women.* Harmondsworth: Penguin.

Wirth-Cauchon, J. 2001. *Women and Borderline Personality Disorder.* New Brunswick, NJ: Rutgers University Press.

Wong, J. 2002. "Prisoner of love, sixty years ago, Velma Demerson was a teenager caught up in a great romance, then she discovered how harsh Canadian law can be." *Globe and Mail*, October 26.

Wood, E. 2002. "Working in the Fantasy Factory." *Journal of Contemporary Ethnograpy* 29, 1.

Wood, L. 2001. "Caught in the Net of Zero-Tolerance: The Effect of the Criminal Justice Response to Partner Violence." Unpublished M.A. thesis, University of Manitoba, Winnipeg.

Wood, T. 2001. "The Case Against Karla." *Elm Street* (April).

Worrall A. 2002. "Rendering Women Punishable: The Making of a Penal Crisis." In P. Carlen (ed.), *Women and Punishment: The Struggle for Justice.* Cullompton, UK: Willan.

_____. 1997. *Punishment in the Community: The Future of Criminal Justice.* Longman: London.

_____. 1990. *Offending Women: Female Lawbreakers and the Criminal Justice System.* New York: Rutledge and Keagan Paul.

Wright, M.-E. 1987. "Unnatural Mothers: Infanticide in Halifax, 1850–1875." *Nova Scotia Historical Review* 7.

Wynter, S. 1987. "Whisper." In F. Delacoste and P. Alexander (eds.), *Sex Work: Writings by Women in the Sex Industry.* Pittsburgh: Cleis Press.

Young, C. 2000. *Women, Tax and The Gendered Impact of Funding Social Programs Through the Tax System.* Ottawa: Status of Women Canada.

Zedner, L. 1998. "Wayward Sisters." In N. Morris and D. Rothman (eds.), *The Oxford History of Prison*. New York: Oxford University Press.

Zingraff, M., and R. Thomson. 1984. "Differential Sentencing of Women and Men in the U.S.A." *International Journal of the Sociology of Law* 12.

Cases Cited

Broomer v. *Ontario (Attorney General)*. 2002. *O.J.* No. 2196 ((Ont. Sup. Ct. J.), online QL (OJ).

Falkiner v. *Ontario (Ministry of Community and Social Services, Income Maintenance Branch)*. 2002. 59 *O.R. (3d)* 481; *[2002] O.J.* No. 1771 (Ont. C.A.), online QL (OJ).

Masse v. *Ontario (Ministry of Community and Social Services, Income Maintenance Branch)*. 1996. *O.J.* No. 363 (Ont. Ct. J. – Div. Ct.), online QL (OJ), leave to appeal denied, [1996] *O.J.* No. 1526 (Ont. C.A.), online (QL (OJ).

R. v. *Bedford.* 2000. S.C.C.A. No. 328.

R. v. *Bond.* 1994. *O.J.* No. 2185. (Ont. Ct. Gen. Div.), *online QL (OJ)*.

R. v. *Brandes.* 1997. O.J. No. 5443.

R. v. *Caringi.* 2002. O.J. No. 2367.

R. v. *Gladue.* 1999. 1 S.C.R. No. 699.

R. v. *Hamilton.* 2003. 172, C.C.C. (3d) 114, 8 C.R. (6th) 215 (S.C.J.).

R. v. *Hamilton.* 2004. 186 C.C.C. (3d) 129, 241 D.L.R. (4th) 490,22 C.R. (6th) 1, 72 O.R. (3d) 1 (C.A.).

R. v. *Jantunen.* 1994. *O.J.* No. 889 (Ont. Ct. Gen. Div.), *online QL (OJ)*.

R. v. *Lalonde.* 1995. 22 *O.R. (3d)* 275; *[1995] O.J.* (Ont. Ct. Gen. Div.).

R. v. *Lavallee.* 1990. Supreme Court Reports 852.

R. v. *Plemel.* 1995. *O.J.* No. 4155 (Ont. Ct. Gen. Div.), online QL (OJ).

R. v. *Sim.* 1980. *63 C.C.C. (2d)* 376 (Ont. Co. Ct. J. Cr. Ct.).

R. v. *Slaght.* 1995. *O.J.* No. 4192 (Ont. Ct. Gen. Div.), (online QL (OJ).

R. v. *Thurrott.* 1971. 5 *C.C.C. (2d)* 129 (Ont. C.A.).

Rogers v. *Sudbury.* 2001. 57 *O.R. (3d)* 460(Ont. Sup. Ct.J.).

Sauvé v. *Canada (Chief Electoral Officer)*. 2002. 3 S.C.R. 519.

State of South Carolina v. *Regina D. McKnight.* 2001. No. 00-GS-26-0432,00-GS-26-3330, S.C. Court of General Session.

Winnipeg Child and Family Services (Northwest Area) v. *G.*, (D.F.). 1997. 3 S.C.R. 925. Available at <http://www.lexum.umontreal.ca/csc-scc/en/pub/1997/vol3/html/1997scr3_0925.html>. (Accessed July 2, 2003.)

Legislation Cited

Canadian Criminal Code, L.R. 1985, ch. C-46.

City of Toronto, By-Law No. 574-2000, A by-law respecting the licensing, regulating and governing of trades, business and occupations in the City of Toronto (3 August 2000), schedule 1.

Massage Therapy Act, S.O. 1991. C-27, amended to O. Reg. 474/99.

Occupational Health and Safety Act, R.S.O. 1990. ch. C-0.1.

Ontario Municipal Act, S.O. 2001. c. 25.

Ontario Works Act. 1997. S.O. 1997, c. 25.